The Fighting Fifteenth
Alabama Infantry

The Fighting Fifteenth Alabama Infantry

A Civil War History and Roster

JAMES P. FAUST

McFarland & Company, Inc., Publishers
Jefferson, North Carolina

LIBRARY OF CONGRESS CATALOGUING-IN-PUBLICATION DATA

Faust, James P., 1953–
The fighting Fifteenth Alabama Infantry : a Civil War
history and roster / James P. Faust.
p.   cm.
Includes bibliographical references and index.

ISBN 978-0-7864-9612-9 (softcover : acid free paper) ∞
ISBN 978-1-4766-1856-2 (ebook)

1. Confederate States of America. Army. Alabama
Infantry Regiment, 15th.   2. Alabama—History—Civil
War, 1861–1865—Regimental histories.   3. United States—
History—Civil War, 1861–1865—Regimental histories.
4. United States—History—Civil War, 1861–1865—Campaigns.
I. Title.
E551.515th .F38 2014   973.7'461—dc23   2014038172

BRITISH LIBRARY CATALOGUING DATA ARE AVAILABLE

On the cover: *20th Maine & 15th Alabama*. Gettysburg,
July 2, 1863, Col. Chamberlain and the 20th Maine on
Little Round Top against Col. Oates and the 15th Alabama
(original by Dale Gallon, oil on canvas, 16" × 32", 2001.
Image courtesy Gallon Historical Art, www.gallon.com).

Printed in the United States of America

*McFarland & Company, Inc., Publishers
Box 611, Jefferson, North Carolina 28640
www.mcfarlandpub.com*

To the memory of my mother, Paula Willis,
for her lifetime of love, support and encouragement.
Without her this work would not have been possible.

Table of Contents

With cherub smile, the prattling boy,
Who on the veteran's breast reclines,

Has thrown aside his favorite toy,
And round his tender fingers twines

Those scattered locks, that, with the flight
Of *ninety* years are snowy white;

And, as a scar arrests his view,
He cries, "Grandpa, what wounded you?"

By
PVT Samuel D. Lary
Company B, 15th Alabama Infantry
(courtesy Alabama Department
of Archives and History,
Montgomery, Alabama)

Preface

I have loved reading about and studying the Civil War for as long as I can remember. I was always interested in historic battles, generals, weaponry, etc., but particularly those of the Civil War. I was indeed fortunate enough to be raised by a mother who encouraged reading and scholarship. My mother indulged me by buying any history book or magazine I wanted though today, I know the money was probably needed elsewhere.

In my mid-teenage years, someone in my family told me that I had relatives in the Civil War and to see my Aunt Bert if I wanted more information. Well, I visited my aunt and she confirmed that I had several relatives who participated in the Civil War. In one of the most pleasant afternoons I can remember, I visited Aunt Bert on Eufaula Avenue in Ozark, Alabama. She pulled out the family Bible and showed me the names and dates of births, marriages, and deaths which had been carefully recorded for several years. Then she showed me an actual photograph of my great-grandfather, William Lemuel Faust, in his Confederate uniform. She showed me a picture of his wife, Missouri Ellen Stubbs Faust, sitting and holding the same Bible I had just looked at. I was in awe.

Seeing that I was thirsting for more, my aunt told me that my great-grandfather had been captured in the war and showed me an Oath of Allegiance he had signed on June 14, 1865, prior to being released. The signed document described him as "Fair complexion, Auburn hair, and Gray eyes; and 5 feet, 10 inches high." I remember reading this and almost seeing this sixteen-year-old man appearing before my eyes. I remember thinking about how he must have been feeling at the time this photograph was taken. What had he seen, felt, touched, and smelled before, during and after this time in his life?

At that moment the focus of my interest in history was altered forever. While still interested in the battles, generals, etc., I was more interested in the individual soldier. I could read about why politicians and generals made certain decisions, but my thoughts would drift to what impact this had on the private soldier. While the major decision-makers of the day contemplated and decided strategies and tactics, what was William thinking and doing? What was he eating when in camp or on the march? What were the sights, sounds and smells during battle? How did he feel about the enemy he was fighting—or the men he was fighting with, for that matter?

I have tried to do with this book something that I've seldom read before, with the possible exception of *The Red Badge of Courage*. With this book, I have tried to give the reader an indication about what may have been going on in the mind of the major decision-makers and then quickly "zoom in" on the individual soldier and show how the decision affected him. Whether I have accomplished this dream of mine, I will let the reader decide.

This great strife has awakened in the people the highest emotions and qualities of the human soul. It is cultivating feelings of patriotism, virtue, and courage. Instances of self-sacrifice and of generous devotion to the noble cause for which we are contending are rife throughout the land. Never have a people evinced a more determined spirit than that now animating men, women, and children in every part of our country. Upon the first call, the men fly to arms; and wives and mothers send their husbands and sons to battle without a murmur of regret.

—President Jefferson Davis (Inaugural Address)

ONE

Raising a Regiment

Ozark, Alabama

"[T]he petition was a request that the name be changed from 'Woodshop' to 'Ozark.' The name occurred to Mr. E.T. Matthews from reading the history of the Ozark tribe of Indians."[1]

The Faust family was a recent addition to Dale County in a little settlement known as Ozark, in a largely unsettled area in southeast Alabama. They had packed up most of their belongings and sold the rest before moving from Sumter County, Georgia, during the winter and spring of 1861.[2]

The Faust family consisted of William (51), Henry (19), William (16), Green (14), and Milly Ann (20),[3] who was married to Henry. William, Sr. decided at the age of fifty-one that it was time for a fresh start. He had tired of the hard life of farming and had never been very successful at it, at least when compared to his father's accomplishments in the Carolinas. Eleven years earlier he had lost his wife Louisa, and within the last year had buried his mother, Ann, in Sumter County.[4] Earlier the government had given him 250 acres in Dale County, Alabama, for his service in the Creek War of 1835–36. He had finally decided it was time to move the family west and start anew.

Soon after his oldest son, Henry, married Milly Ann Barrow on December 15, 1860,[5] the expanded family headed for Dale County, Alabama. With the influx of new settlers, William could make a fair living in Ozark if he opened a store, tavern, inn, or maybe all three. He could leave the hard work of the plow and the mule far behind him in the land of his wife's and mother's graves. New settlers would be coming into the area with only the bare-bones essentials because it was cheaper to sell or give away household goods and farming equipment than to buy a wagon and a team of mules or oxen to carry them. Newly arrived settlers would need to buy items necessary for housing and making a living, so why not buy them from William? They would also be in need of food until they could plant and raise their first crops. They would need materials to build shelter, barns, and storehouses. William further reckoned the cotton wagons going to the markets in Eufaula and Greenville could bring back the dry goods and supplies that he could sell in his store. William surmised that it should be cheap to transport those goods back to Ozark because the only other option for the teamsters would be to return with empty wagons.

Ozark wasn't much of a town in 1861; only a tan yard, a log schoolhouse, a cotton gin run by Moses Matthews, and a brick store building built by Henry Z. Parker. There was also the Union Baptist Church.[6] William, Sr. hoped his fortunes would grow with the town.

The trip from Sumter County, Georgia, had infected his middle son, William Lemuel, with ambitions of his own. The whole countryside had erupted with excitement at the prospect of establishing a new country. That was the only topic of conversation in every hamlet, settlement, and town during the trip. Since South Carolina had seceded on December 20, 1860, the Southern populace had been whipped into a frenzy. Along the trip from Sumter County to Dale County, the family had heard of how Mississippi, Florida, Alabama, Georgia, Louisiana, and Texas had followed South Carolina's lead. On April 14, 1861, Fort Sumter surrendered, and U.S. President Lincoln called for 75,000 volunteers to put down the rebellion. Virginia, Arkansas, North Carolina, and Tennessee soon followed their Southern brethren. Eleven states would make up the new Confederate States of America, and the four other slave states of Kentucky, Missouri, Maryland, and Delaware might very well follow. In addition, if "Old Abe" was raising an army, the Confederacy would need an army to defend itself. Young William had decided he would become a soldier.[7]

William Lemuel probably knew that under ordinary circumstances his father would never allow him to join the militia at such a young age, but William, Sr. knew the move to Ozark was only the latest of disruptions in his son's young life. William Lemuel had lost his mother ten years earlier when he was only five. His grandmother had moved in to take care of him and his brothers, and she had recently died. Now he had to leave his friends and cousins in Sumter County and move to this new land where he didn't know a soul. Newly married Henry would be moving out shortly to begin raising a family of his own. Besides, his father had related stories of when he was in the militia, and it seemed only a little more dangerous than a joining a social club. During the militia assembly there was a lot of camaraderie and hilarities of all sorts. It would be a good break for Lemuel and a good way to meet new friends.

All of this was likely going through the mind of William, Sr. as he was trying to conceal his concerns from his sixteen-year-old son. Most fathers would be excited to have a son who was about to take a big step toward becoming a man, knowing that he would meet and bond with new friends in this frontier by way of his militia associations. This bonding was important in building lifelong friendships and business associates in rural areas. Everyone on the frontier depended on friends and neighbors a great deal. Mixed with this feeling would be a deeply felt concern that possible danger loomed for his young son. Would the North really contest the departure of the South from the Union? Would there be one Austerlitz-type battle and the war be quickly over? Would his son just be asked to guard a local bridge or crossroads somewhere, or would he actually go into battle? Some local militia had already been sent 170 miles southwest to lay siege to Fort Pickens, Florida, which the Federal garrison had yet to evacuate.[8] The future was very uncertain indeed.

During the westward journey to the militia assembly point that July morning, the prospect of seeing new lands and cities Lemuel had only heard of would likely have excited him very much. And he would be getting paid for this adventure to boot. As he left Ozark, he was leaving the drudgery of helping his father run his store. Furthermore, his father was talking about building a tavern and an inn.[9] Life in a town, even a town as small as Ozark, wouldn't seem very exciting for a boy who had been running trails in the woods and hunting and fishing all of his young life.

William stood close to five feet, ten inches tall, and with his fair complexion, black hair, and gray eyes he looked older than sixteen.[10] Although as yet he hadn't filled out like a man, he was taller than many full-grown men and could pass for an older boy. Just to be safe, he told the recruiting officer he was eighteen.

Westville, Alabama

> *"I did not understand or realize the horrors of war at the time."*[11]—Mary Love Edwards Fleming

The assembly point for the militia was a small settlement about nine miles west of Ozark called Westville. As Leroy Edwards' wagon full of children pulled into Westville, they would have found the small town with a grocery store, wood shop, blacksmith's shop, doctor's office, and a tan yard[12] buzzing with activity greatly exaggerating the size of the small village. Men and boys were milling around in small groups and more were arriving by every mode of transportation imaginable. It seemed that everyone in western Dale County was in Westville on July 2, 1861. The women were preparing long picnic tables with every kind of food a hungry Alabamian could want.

Thirty-one-year-old Leroy and his wife, Martha, had brought all seven children with them to take part in the festivities. Besides, Leroy had three brothers and a first cousin enlisting today and he wanted his children to visit all of his nieces and nephews. Nine-year-old Mary Love Edwards would probably be running, playing, chasing and teasing like there was no tomorrow.

Mary would have learned in school and from overhearing adults that the states in the South were forming their own country and raising an army in case the Northern states wanted to fight. Esau Brooks from Daleville was organizing a militia company to go fight the Yankees if they had to. Her uncle William Edwards was going to be second in command. He had recently quit his job as

Private William L. Faust, Company E. Great-grandfather of the author (author's collection).

a mechanic in Russell County and moved to Westville just to join up with his two brothers and cousin.

All little Mary would have known about the cause of the war was that many locals were concerned that the new president would abolish slavery in the South if given the chance. Mary was from a slaveholding family because her father was given a 27-year-old slave woman also named Mary, and two girls, aged nine and six.[13] Mary had heard the old men debating whether it was a good idea for the South to leave the United States or not. She would have heard her grandfather, Ambrose Edwards, arguing with Mordecai White that the South should work out their differences and remain in the United States but Mr. Mordecai thought it was a better idea to create a new country. Other men chose sides and there seemed to be no middle ground.[14]

While Mary was making her rounds of Westville, fifty-one-year-old Esau Brooks was seated behind the table in the Darien church signing the men into the militia company. Captain Brooks had already raised a militia company in Daleville in 1860 under the Military Act of the State of Alabama 1859 and 1860[15] and was familiar with the governor's procedures for doing so. Following proper protocol with the governor's blessings, Captain Brooks wasted no time in recruiting the new company.

There were 84 men and boys who signed up that day. Practically all were farmers or farm laborers and only 16 were married; of those, 15 had children. Some were related; in fact, Captain Brooks had three sons with him, one father had two sons, and there were ten sets of brothers. Mary's extended family alone contributed three brothers and a first cousin. Although most made their living from agriculture, there was also a carpenter, a painter, two lawyers, two teachers, two mechanics, a clerk, and a merchant. Eight simply listed their occupation as students; however, a total of 21 of the teenagers had attended school in the last year. Five of the farmers were slaveholders. An average soldier mustering in Westville that day could be characterized as a 22-year-old, unmarried farm laborer.[16] These men came from towns and settlements all over western Dale and eastern Coffee County, Alabama. Men talked of coming from Newton, Barnes Cross Roads, Clintonville, Daleville, Clayhatchee, Haw Ridge, and Rocky Head.[17]

The recruits were anxious to get uniforms, and Captain Brooks informed them that the women in the area were busily making uniforms for the militia company. He expressed hope that the company would be outfitted before being ordered to leave. Captain Brooks relayed to the men that he thought he would hear from Governor A.B. Moore of a departure date and destination to join other companies where they would be formed into a regiment within the next couple of days. He added that weapons and other accouterments would be supplied by the state at this regimental assembly point.

The next order of business for the 84-man company was to come up with a name for the company and elect officers. The men decided to call themselves the Dale Beauregards in honor of General P.G.T. Beauregard, the hero of the recent bombardment of Fort Sumter. The men then set about nominating and electing the officers and non-commissioned officers for the company. Since Captain Brooks had organized the company and had already commanded a militia company in Daleville, electing him as the commander was a given. Their new commander explained to them that according to regulation they should also elect 1st, 2nd, and 3rd lieutenants who would be the officers. Next they should elect a 1st, 2nd, 3rd, and 4th sergeant and then a 1st, 2nd, 3rd, and 4th corporal as the noncommissioned officers. He explained that 1st was higher in rank than 2nd, 2nd higher than 3rd and so on.

In addition to Captain Brooks, the Dale County Beauregards elected the following (age in parentheses, occupation and hometown):

1LT	William A. Edwards	(25)	mechanic	Russell County
2LT	Daniel Bryan	(27)	farmer	Daleville
3LT	John E. Jones	(20)	farmer	Geneva
1SGT	Thomas Allen Bryan[18]	(27)	farmer	Daleville
2SGT	Samuel Hogg	(28)	farmer	Westville
3SGT	John W. Mizell	(25)	farmer	Westville
4SGT	William H. Scroggins	(20)	farm laborer	Daleville
1CPL	Wesley Barryan Mills	(27)	farmer	Daleville
2CPL	Richard A. Neal	(21)	farm laborer	Westville
3CPL	Andrew J. Brooks	(20)	mechanic	Daleville
4CPL	James P. Martin	(17)	farm laborer	Newton[19]

Why these young men throughout Dale County enlisted with such zeal can only be speculated upon. A recruit might have been motivated by fervent nationalism, dreams of glory, peer pressure, a desire to impress a young woman, yearnings to escape from home, a hankering for adventure, or a youthful curiosity about the world that existed beyond the borders of Dale County. A strong Southern sense of duty and honor no doubt played a large part.[20]

The men spent the next two weeks drilling and trying to learn the rudimentary requirements of military life. The ladies of the area did finish the much-anticipated uniforms before the company left. Mary remembered long after the war that the "uniforms were made of white osnaberg, a heavy cotton cloth, with blue stripes on the trousers and jackets." She remembered how she "thrilled with pride and pleasure as she watched the soldiers marching to the drum and fife, carrying their flag so proudly, and dressed in their white uniforms."[21]

The Beauregards finally got orders to march to Fort Mitchell, Alabama, and join other militia companies from southeast Alabama for the purpose of forming a regiment. As second in command, 1st Lieutenant William Edwards[22] was very busy trying to get everything organized for the move. A route of march had to be planned for, coordination had to be made for overnight bivouacs, the men had to be fed during the trip, and their massive baggage transported. William Archibald Edwards had remained in Russell County, Alabama (near Columbus, Georgia), when his family moved to Dale County in the 1850s. He married a widow, Eliza Jones Mizell, on January 5, 1858, and decided to remain in Russell County and work as a mechanic when his family moved. When the Civil War started, William moved to Dale County to join his two brothers Ambrose Newton and Young Mansfield, and their first cousin James Russell Edwards, in enlisting together.

The Beauregards departed Westville on Thursday July 18, 1861. First Lieutenant Edwards recalled 54 years later:

No better [company] of citizen soldiers ever left any community than left Westville on the 18th day of July 1861. No more sumptuous feast was ever spread for departing patriots than was spread under the shade of the beautiful oaks that stood around old Darian [sic] church. The loving hands that prepared it have long since been wafted beyond the curse of war and rage of battles by the angels of God. In all my life I have never seen deeper and purer emotions or heard so tender farewells as followed that sumptuous feast. Husbands and wives embraced in tender love and with many it was the last embrace—fathers kissed their only babes—mothers threw a mother's arm around her son and with a mother's deep prayer sent her soldier boy to the conflict of battle and perils of war. And some of the boys felt the tender touch of the bride-to-be as they clasped hands that day. It thrilled their souls and nerved their arm for deeds of daring until they either perished in the campaign or returned home under the furled banner of the stars and bars. I have often been anxious to know if any of them that got back are left.[23]

The 87-man company (three more had joined the company since July 2) camped their first night at Frazier's Mill on Pea River, where most bathed, swam, and generally frolicked much of the night. First Lieutenant Edwards recalls, "If there were either snakes, alligators or varmints for miles around they took to the hills and swamps never to return. Such a [babble] of voices and splashing of water I have never heard."[24] Brother Ambrose recalled, "I remember the first night we camped on the banks of Pea River and bathed in its waters and spent this our first night in joyous hilarity."[25] On Friday, the company camped in the streets of Perote, Alabama, where they were again treated to a feast prepared by some of the wealthier families. On Saturday, the company arrived in Union Springs and spent Sunday there. That day, July 21, 1861, the Beauregards got word by telegraph from Virginia that the Confederates had won the Battle of Manassas. Many feared that the war would end before they might even see a Yankee. The next day the Beauregards marched to Fort Mitchell, a railroad and river station about nine miles south of Columbus, Georgia, on the Alabama side of the Chattahoochee River.

Newton, Alabama

"The prayers and unceasing solicitude of his friends in Newton will accompany him wherever he goes."[26]—From the *Newton Standard*, July 5, 1861 (speaking of M.B. Houghton)

In July 1861, Newton, Alabama, was a flourishing village, the county seat of Dale County with a courthouse, churches, schools, lawyers, physicians and other citizens. Sixteen-year-old Mitchell B. Houghton was not only attending school but working as "compositor, assistant pressman, and assistant editor"[27] of the only newspaper in town, the *Newton Standard*. Mitchell was still living at home with his 53-year-old lawyer father, his mother, and two younger sisters. Mitchell's only brother was teaching school in Russell County.[28]

Mitchell took notice of 30-year-old Captain John F. Treutlan,[29] who had traveled the 74 miles from Barbour County to Newton to supplement his militia company he was raising in Glenville, Alabama. Captain Treutlan succeeded in recruiting 16 volunteers during his trip to Newton. Mitchell describes the meeting assembled in the courthouse:

> [P]atriotic speeches were made, military ardor was intensified by the beating of drums and the shrill notes of the fife, while the women and girls sang patriotic songs amid shouts and waving of flags. A banquet was given at night and those of us who had enlisted felt that we were great heroes and were going forth to participate in a kind of holiday excursion, soon to return crowned with victorious laurels. The oratory of the occasion was very fervid and the people were wild with excitement. I had but a limited education and knew very little of the ways of the world, but felt my importance as a prospective soldier of the Confederacy. Even a theatrical troupe from Virginia was performing in Newton and two of the members got caught in the fervor [and enlisted].[30]

The 16 recruits were transported by wagon to Glenville, Alabama, where they joined a militia company calling themselves the Glenville Guards. The Glenville Guards elected the following officers and noncommissioned officers:

CPT William N. Richardson	1LT William D. Wood
2LT James H. Metcalf	3LT S.D. Stanton, Jr.
1SGT William L. Wilson	2SGT John F. McLeod
3SGT Alexander Tew	4SGT Daniel H. Thomas
1CPL J.D.L. Henley	2CPL Harlem J. Gary
3CPL Arch Carmichael	4CPL Michael McGuire[31]

After assembly the company marched off smartly to Fort Mitchell.

Abbeville, Alabama

> *"Aged fathers and mothers, brothers and sisters, and some of the boys' sweethearts were there to say good-bye."*[32]—Private William "Gus" Augustus McClendon, Company G, Henry Pioneers, 15th Alabama Infantry Regiment

Sixteen-year-old Gus[33] had already tried to join the first two companies, the "Henry Grays" and the "Henry Blues," raised in Henry County, Alabama, but was turned down because of his youth. During the late spring and early summer of 1861, Gus had been voraciously reading about the raising and organizing of armies and the early engagements between the forces of North and South. Early Confederate victories in seizing federal forts and arsenals and the relatively bloodless affairs such as the Battle of Big Bethel led Gus to fear that the war would be over before he could "get to smell gunpowder much less burn any," or before he would get to see a "wild yank."[34] After being recently told by his best girl that her sweetheart was off with the Henry Grays, Gus was all the more determined to become a Confederate soldier in the hopes of "changing her mind and her affections would be concentrated upon me."[35] With the victory of Manassas on July 21, 1861, Gus was certain he was going to miss out on this war.

Gus heard some "glorious news" when he learned an Abbeville attorney, William Calvin Oates, was organizing another company of men in northern Henry County and eastern Dale County.[36] Gus quickly signed up and the men agreed the company would be named the Henry Pioneers.[37] Captain Oates succeeded in enlisting 121 men in a short period of time. To the ladies of Abbeville, who had made a special flag for the company, "Oates delivered an eloquent and patriotic speech assuring them that the men of the company would live up to the trust that had been placed in them."[38] On July 25, Captain Oates received word to move his company to Fort Mitchell.

Early on the morning of Saturday, July 27, Gus rose early, had breakfast and bade farewell to his mother Mary ("Polly") and his sisters, Lucy Ann, Louisa, Sarah Jane, and Mary Elizabeth.[39] He departed for Abbeville with his father, Joel Tyson McClendon, and arrived to discover that the citizens had provided wagons and buggies to carry the company and their baggage to Franklin, Alabama, on the Chattahoochee River. The wealthy citizens of Abbeville had provided "large contributions of clothing, tents, mess-chests and other camp equipage,"[40] enough to have supplied a regiment in the last year of the war, according to Captain Oates. In addition, the citizens provided the commander with a check for about $2,000 to cover any incidentals. About 10:00 a.m., Gus said goodbye to his father, who told him, "My son, take care of yourself." The elder McClendon then turned to his son's commander and said, "Captain Oates, take care of my boy."[41] The company, with a large number of friends and relatives in tow, marched off to Franklin.

Lt. Colonel William C. Oates, Company G (courtesy John Grier).

When the men reached the small village they were marched to a house where they found a long table with "everything that would satisfy the hunger of man."[42] During the afternoon, friends and relatives continued to stream into Franklin. At about 5:00 p.m. Captain Oates formed the company to allow them one last goodbye with the Henry County civilians. Gus recalled that the people passed through the lines of soldiers "shaking hands with every one, with moistened eyes, and briney cheeks, speaking words of cheer, bidding us God-speed, and good-bye. It was an affecting scene. Fathers and mothers, brothers and sisters, and some of the boys' sweethearts were there to say good-bye."[43]

That night the steamboat *Jackson* arrived and the men were filed aboard to the tune of "Dixie," played by the company's small three-man band. The men followed the song with the "rebel yell" as they loaded onto the steamboat. The *Jackson* headed north and landed at

Eufaula for a short break early Sunday morning. In Eufaula, the boys mingled with members of the Eufaula City Guards, sometimes referred to as Eufaula Zouaves, who said they would be catching the next steamboat for Fort Mitchell.[44] During this short stay in Eufaula, Captain Oates purchased some very distinctive uniforms for the company consisting of bright red shirts and gray pants, giving the company the nickname of "the Red Shirted boys from Henry."[45]

Shortly after reloading the *Jackson*, Captain Oates told the men they had to vote for officers and noncommissioned officers. Oates became captain almost by default. Others elected were:

Private Joseph M. Crenshaw, Company F. Pictured after the war with his grandson, Herman Claude Crenshaw, born 1921 (courtesy Skip Shervington).

1LT Isaac T. Culver	2LT Cornelius V. Morris
3LT Henry C. Brainard	
1SGT Josiah Balkom	2SGT John T. McLeod
3SGT Josiah J. Wofford	4SGT James W. Pound
1CPL Daniel McClellan	2CPL Lott W. McMath
3CPL Frank M. Merritt[46]	

Late in the afternoon of July 28, 1861, Private Archibald N. Jackson's company of Brundidge Guards was assembled to march down to the riverbank to welcome the Henry Pioneers arriving at Fort Mitchell. Archibald[47] was a teacher in Troy who was leaving Eliza F., his seventeen-year-old wife, and new baby to fend for themselves.[48] The Brundidge boys formed up as best they could as Captain Fry's steamboat arrived with the 121[49] Henry Pioneers from Abbeville.[50] The boys from Henry County arrived at 5:00 p.m. and debarked while J.E. Harrell, A.A. Kirkland and Steven Merritt struck up "Dixie" again on their fife, bass and kettle drums, marching smartly behind their red, white, and blue flag donated by the ladies of Abbeville. Private Jackson and the other Pike County boys responded with the rebel yell. The two companies then marched a mile and a half to their new camp. The Henry Pioneers were glad to stretch their legs after experiencing the cramped quarters while aboard the *Jackson*.

Fort Mitchell, Alabama

> *"Ge-whillkins, I never in all my life saw so many soldiers and tents."*[51]—
> Private William A. McClendon, Company G, Henry Pioneers, 15th Alabama Infantry Regiment

The encampment for the ten companies from southeast Alabama was on James Cantey's plantation in Fort Mitchell, Alabama. Mr. Cantey had already raised a company (Cantey's Rifles) from Russell County on these grounds. Colonel Cantey was a Mexican War veteran serving as an officer in the celebrated Palmetto regiment of South Carolina. He won distinction in the battles of that regiment in Mexico, and was wounded in one of them. The young officer was left among the dead after a battle but was rescued by his body servant, whose plans were to bear him home for burial. The slave's detection of a faint sign of life caused him to successfully revive his master. For this deed the servant was offered his freedom, which the devoted servant refused.

Even before all the companies were assembled, elections had been held for the regimental officers. The prospective officers had even visited companies in their militia assembly areas or on their journey to Fort Mitchell to "politic" for positions. Cantey was elected colonel, the rank commanding the regiment. John F. Treutlen was elected lieutenant colonel and John Wilhite Lewis Daniel was elected major; both were from Barbour County. One private from Newton soon discovered that Colonel Cantey was a "rigid disciplinarian."[52]

Other officers and men of the regimental staff were:

James Vernoy, of Columbus, Georgia	Assistant Commissary
T.J. Woolfork, of Russell County	Assistant Quartermaster

Dr. Frank A. Stanford, of Columbus, Georgia	Surgeon
Dr. W.G. Drake, of Barbour County	Surgeon
Lock Weems, of Macon County	Adjutant

The noncommissioned officers of the staff were:

Van Marcus, of Columbus, Georgia	Sergeant-Major
Joseph R. Breare, of Dale County	Commissary-Sergeant
H.D. Doney, of Columbus, Georgia	Quartermaster-Sergeant
Charles Smith, of Columbus, Georgia	Color-Sergeant
T.J. Bass, of Barbour County	Ordnance Sergeant[53]

With the regimental staff organized, it was time for Colonel Cantey to summon the company commanders for the designation of letters to the companies as required by army regulations. The company commanders, unfamiliar with any organization above that of a militia company, were easily influenced (or misled, some in the regiment would later infer) by their new commander. Colonel Cantey was only able to procure enough Mississippi rifles to arm two companies, and he issued these weapons to his company, the Cantey Rifles, and the Midway Southern Guards. The rest of the regiment would have to be armed with "old altered smooth-bore George Law muskets."[54] Colonel Cantey convinced the company commanders that the two companies supplied with rifles should be designated Company A and B, respectively, because they would be performing the special task as skirmishers and would also be serving on the right and left flanks of the regiment because of their advanced weaponry. Eight of the ten company commanders agreed with the colonel's recommendation.

Next, Colonel Cantey told the remaining eight company commanders that they should cast lots for the remaining designations of C, D, E, F, G, H, I, and K companies.[55] ("J" would not be used because of the nineteenth-century tendency of writing "I" and "J" almost exactly alike.) It wasn't explained to the naïve company commanders that the captains' seniority of rank would follow these designations; i.e., the captain of Company A would outrank the captain of Company B, B over C, and so on. This would prove to be a source of serious contention for the regiment for the remainder of the war.

The ten companies with their colorful nicknames and county of origin were organized as follows:

Company	Nickname	County of Origin
A	Cantey Rifles	Russell County
B	Midway Southern Guards	Barbour County
C	Macon Commissioners	Macon County
D	Ft. Browder Roughs	Barbour County
E	Dale Beauregards	Dale County
F	Brundidge Guards	Pike County
G	Henry Pioneers	Henry and Dale Counties
H	Glenville Guards	Barbour and Dale Counties
I	Quitman Guards	Pike County
K	Eufaula City Guards	Barbour County
L	Pike Sharpshooters	Pike (now Bullock) County; was later added to the regiment in the spring of 1862.[56]

When the men enlisted into their militia companies, most had enlisted for one year. To be accepted by the Confederate Army, however, the men had to extend their enlistment to "three years or the duration of the war," which every man did at Fort Mitchell without exception.

In addition to their weapons, the 1,000 or so men of the 15th Alabama Infantry Regiment were also issued bayonets, cartridge boxes, cap pouches, and knapsacks.[57] Feeling more like real soldiers, these tough frontier men of the 15th Alabama found military life relatively easy to adapt to. However, for men who depend on individual mettle to survive on the frontier, military discipline was by far the hardest adjustment to make. These hardheaded men were unaccustomed to taking orders from anyone who was not an elder in their family; now they found themselves required to obey orders from men they didn't even know, regardless of the age or social status of the man giving the order.

The men, most of whom had probably never seen a community the size of their regiment, were amazed at the sight of 1,000 soldiers gathered in one place. The orderly rows of white tents seemed to go on forever. One soldier from Henry County wrote, "Ge-whllikens, I never in all my life saw so many soldiers and tents."[58] The men got their first taste of military life as they were awakened every morning at 4:00 a.m. to the sound of bugles and drums beating out reveille.

After answering roll call and eating breakfast the boys would conduct squad drill, which most had already learned the basics of at their respective militia sites. When it came time for company drill, however, confusion reigned with their first introduction to the company manual of arms. One company commander wrote, "The inexperience of the men was to have been expected. Volunteers, who scarcely knew right face from left face and had never seen a company drilled through a single evolution, could not have been otherwise; but when the officers were found to be nearly, if not quite, as ignorant as the men they were attempting to instruct ... the whole thing presented a ludicrous scene."[59] One private describes the military training at Fort Mitchell as "novel and somewhat humiliating."[60] Another private said of company drill, "We would become so tangled up" at times that the situation was "laughable."[61]

Nights were the most pleasant time for the soldiers as they would sit around the campfires teasing each other and making fun of their drilling mistakes. They found telling old tales, singing songs and dancing to fiddle and harmonica music to be most pleasurable experiences. The new soldiers also participated in sports like boxing, wrestling, and racing each other. When news of minor Southern victories or new recruits arrived, the boys would erupt into the rebel yell. This bonding would prove indispensable in the coming years as men would go to every extreme to save a brother in arms on the battlefield, comfort him while sick or wounded, or share meager rations with him. Homesickness had not yet set in as the boys were not far from home and hadn't been gone that long. Fourth Corporal Barnett Hardeman Cody of G Company wrote on August 20, 1861, that the men at Fort Mitchell "faired [sic] very well, [and] had plenty to eat and drink."[62]

An exciting adventure was on the horizon to break the monotony and hard work back home, and the men could hardly wait to participate in it. War was a distant and unknown thought; fun and frolic was the order of the day. The men almost hated to hear "tattoo" every night signaling them to prepare for bed.

The day after First Manassas, Governor Andrew B. Moore of Alabama was corresponding with the Confederate Secretary of War Leroy P. Walker. As was custom, the governor was responsible for raising and equipping regiments and then turning them over to the control of the Confederate government. On July 22, 1861, he wrote that the 15th Alabama Infantry Regiment "will be organized, armed, and ready to be mustered into service in a very few days. Shall I give them marching orders, and to what point?"[63] Secretary Walker answered on July 25 and told the Governor to send the regiment to Richmond, Virginia, as soon as they were armed. He further stated that tents would be furnished in Richmond. For the first time the men of the 15th Alabama heard the order to cook "three days' rations and be ready to move at a moment's notice," a command they would hear often for the remainder of the war.

Messing

The root of the word "mess" is the Old French word mes meaning a "portion of food."[64]

"Mess" is a universal term in the military which refers to groups of soldiers. The boys broke themselves into "messes," groups of four to eight men, with neighbors and family. These messes served as unofficial squads of men who would be housed together. Individual members of the mess would divide routine duties such as cooking, foraging, and fetching firewood and water. During winter quarters they would build their own huts and live together. Men lived together in this unofficial organization and would literally give up their lives for each other. Even after the war, as survivors of the Fighting Fifteenth moved to Texas, Arkansas, or Florida, the messes would regularly write letters to each other until death and never missed an opportunity to visit an old "messmate."

Private Mitchell B. Houghton of Company H gives a valuable insight into this practice of bonding:

Private Timothy C. Lee, Company H. Shown here in a post-war photograph. He died in 1918. His wife was Sarah "Sallie" A.E. Dowling (courtesy Mary Louis Reynolds).

> The men divided into messes of three, four or even six taking turns at cooking, but the best cook usually had most of it to do, the others building fires, cutting wood or bringing water. I did not like large messes and never had more than three to divide duties with, and believe I got along better for it.... Men divided into messes, according to their likes and dislikes, but soon one found that his best friend was not inclined to cut wood, fetch water, make a fire or do his share of washing the tin plates. Others, who had been foppish in dress at home, became careless and dirty, and

others used much profanity and vulgarity. So these messes in four years became greatly changed, sometimes by death, sometimes by weeding out objectionable fellows. I remember one man, whose ill-temper, profanity and obscenity was such that he could not find a messmate who would stay with him. Another one who knew more Shakespeare than any man I ever saw was so lazy and dirty that he messed alone. Another in the next company, an old bachelor of means was so objectionable that a detail of men cut off his hair and scrubbed him, not very lightly, in the effort to get him less offensive. But long campaigning, dangers shared together, hungers and the brotherhood of comrades, finally made many of those who messed together, regard each other with a love like Jonathan and David.[65]

Second Lieutenant James R. Edwards, Company E. Pictured here in 1925 (courtesy Jean C. [last name unknown]).

Fourth Corporal Barnett Hardeman Cody gives an indication of the fluidity of mess membership while writing to relatives, "I am in a very wild mess of boys, but I will remove my washing [apparently a term signifying a change of mess] in a few days. I will go in a mess with Mr. J.R. Morris and the Whatley Boys which I think is a more civil Mess." Promotion into the officer ranks apparently required a mess of men of like rank because 2nd Lieutenant Cody wrote his sister of a new mess, "I have a very nice Mess" made up of John A. Oates, Orderly Josiah Balkom, and James R. Woodham.[66]

Even Mary Love Edwards Fleming wrote of a rather large Company E mess of some of her relatives, "a mess of eight men was formed; William A. Edwards, Billy Mizell, Billy Mobley, J.P. Martin, Ben Martin, Young M. Edwards, Ambrose Edwards, and James R. Edwards. None of these eight lost a limb, but all were wounded in some way. Young and Ambrose Edwards were in prison at Ft. Delaware."[67]

TWO

Settling in Virginia

Movement to Virginia

"We were all anxious to get to the seat of war and were delighted when orders came to break camp and [board] the cars for Virginia."[1]—Private Michael B. Houghton, Company I, Quitman Guards, 15th Alabama Infantry Regiment

On August 21, 1861, the entire regiment was ordered to strike tents and pack their cooking utensils because they were going to the capital of the new Confederate nation, Richmond. "On to Richmond," screamed the boys as they marched to the depot and boarded the trains at Fort Mitchell bound for Columbus. While waiting for the train in Columbus the boys feasted on all the watermelons their stomachs could hold—a meal many would regret later when the train lurched and bucked, causing motion sickness for many during their long trip.

Private Houghton wrote to his relatives that the men were consumed with excitement about finally breaking camp and heading to Virginia. On that "fair and fragrant" Sunday morning, "melted with sunbeams, as ever was born of night,"[2] most of the boys were about to embark on their first train ride, and it would prove to be an exciting one. The boys soon learned that the war enthusiasm in southeast Alabama was mirrored throughout other parts of the South they passed through. As the train passed the countryside, men would stop plowing to wave their hats; girls would wave white handkerchiefs from doors and windows; and in the cities groups would gather to cheer the boys on. Many of the young boys must have thought they were going to save Virginia singlehandedly. It must be true that one Confederate could whip ten Yankees.

The trains chugged on all night passing through Macon and stopped at Augusta at sunrise, where

> the patriotic ladies of that beautiful city had in waiting for us a most excellent breakfast, spread upon long board tables ... with barrels of ice water and lemonade distributed at convenient intervals; while the rough-looking soldier boys swarmed about the tables and enjoyed the luxuries prepared for them, the ladies were all among them, like so many good angels, ministering to the wants of all.... Nothing

wins men's hearts like kindness and attention, especially a good square meal when they are hungry.[3]

At every station, no matter how big or small, they were met by crowds of people eager to present bouquets and presents to the Alabamians.[4]

The boys loaded the trains again, which were moving much faster now, and passed through South Carolina, arriving at Wilmington, North Carolina, at about daybreak. It was at Wilmington where they had to cross the Cape Fear River by boat and loaded up again for Petersburg, Virginia. On the way, the regiment was allowed to stretch their legs and walk around the community of Weldon. They departed about 10:00 p.m. and traveled all night without interruption to Petersburg. Here they had to change trains again for Richmond at about 3:00 a.m. After crossing the James River, the men of the 15th Alabama saw Richmond for the first time and disembarked there. The 15th Alabama was formed in line and marched past Libby Prison, which was already being filled with Union prisoners. As the dejected "tamed Yankees" watched the 1,000 men of the 15th Alabama march by, the boys from Alabama showed little sympathy for these Yankee invaders.

Early Camp Life

> "The squeaking fifes, the beating of drums, the music of cornet bands, the marching of well dressed, well drilled, and well armed soldiers with gorgeously attired officers on their prancing chargers, dashing hither, and thither ... all had a tendency to drive away 'dull care.'"[5]—Private William A. McClendon, Company G, Henry Pioneers, 15th Alabama Infantry Regiment

Fourteen-year-old James Patrick "Pat" Brannon[6] was the drummer for the Eufaula City Guards but lived in Columbus, Georgia, before the war. Not wanting to miss out on the war because of his age, he caught a steamboat to Eufaula just for the purpose of joining as a musician. Maybe now that the 15th was settled in, he wouldn't have to carry the drum on and off the trains and play every time the Eufaula Guards entrained and detrained. Pat had left his father and mother, Alberry and Lucy, and his three sisters and baby brother back in Columbus.[7] Although only fourteen, Pat quickly became infatuated with gambling and became a constant presence when any game of chance was going on in camp, to the extent that he was, later in the war, reprimanded by the regimental commander.[8]

The regiment went into camp about one mile from the city environs by the Richmond and Yorktown Railroad. The 15th Alabama situated their camp about one mile below the "Rockets" on the north side of the James River, within sight of the grave "of old Powhatan, the great Indian prince, the father of Pocahontas."[9] A small creek flowed past the camp on a sort of island. Private Lary of Company B called this place Griffin Springs and eloquently describes it as "truly a delightful location. Springs large and plentiful are gushing rapidly out of rocks or quietly oozing from the sides of the hill. The purity of the waters, their murmuring flow, and the green enamel of moss and flowering plants to which the refreshing virtues of their streams give birth, combine to make it an enviable place."[10]

In this early stage of the war, boys were furnished anything they wanted to eat except the southeast Alabama staples of "corn bread and greens."[11] It was here that the regiment was issued ammunition for the first time, receiving 40 rounds per man. The men quickly found themselves once again in the routine of camp life, drilling two hours every morning by company and battalion drill for two hours every afternoon. Sharing the parade field was a unit from Louisiana made up of Polish immigrants commanded by a "Colonel Sooli Koski, a Polish officer of distinction," called the Polish Legion. As the rough-looking Alabama boys evacuated the field every afternoon, "the Polish Legion, with its numerous drum corps would occupy the ground." The Alabama boys entertained themselves watching the Polish soldiers drilling with not a word of English being spoken.[12]

Although the Union Army was no threat at this point, the boys were attacked every night by hosts of mosquitoes as a result of heavy rains which arrived before they had. One private from Company B compared them to the plagues of Egypt:

> To repulse this army of invasion we made fires and hovered around them in the smoke until our eyes were literally "fountains of tears"; but though whole battalions of the enemy were suffocated and perished in the flames, millions rushed in to fill their places and renew the fight. Finding it impossible to remain by the camp fires, we would roll ourselves in a blanket covering our head so completely as to exclude not only the mosquitoes, but the air, and thus remained in a state of partial suffocation, listening to the shrill war song of our assailants until the cooler winds of midnight forced them to leave the field and take refuge in their oozy entrenchments.[13]

On some occasions the men would be surprised by the long beating of drums for a regimental assembly for Colonel Cantey. Regimental drill was the most difficult drill the boys had to learn because it required the precise execution and synchronized movements of a thousand men. Later in the war, the men could conduct regimental drill under fire, unable to hear or see commanders; however, that was not the case at this early period of the war. Regimental drill was confusing for the men as they bumped into one another, stepped on each other's feet, dropped their weapons — almost everything that could go wrong did. Mistakes during regimental drill were not amusing like those in company drill because now they were under the stern, watchful eye and profane mouth of Colonel Cantey, who knew that precision during the confusion of battle would save lives. As one private characterized Colonel Cantey, he was a rigid disciplinarian. He would react to drill mistakes with anger and cursing so the men would not forget. The following years would demonstrate the men didn't forget.

On August 20, Special Orders Number 129 ordered Colonel Cantey's regiment to proceed to Manassas, Virginia, on the 22nd and report for duty to General Joseph Johnston, commanding the Army of Virginia. The regiments' numbers had probably swelled to 1200 by this time. While marching through Richmond on August 18, 1861, the regiment halted in front of the President's Mansion and was addressed by President Jefferson Davis. At the Central Railroad Depot they were addressed by John Gill

Shorter, who had just been elected governor of Alabama. Afterwards, the regiment was loaded onto boxcars, "like cattle" according to one private, and again were greeted all along their route to northern Virginia by young girls cheering the Alabamians for aiding in the defense of their state. The men of the 15th were the first Alabama troops to pass by this route and the "patriotic ladies and beautiful Virginia girls"[14] were particularly thankful for the reinforcements from so far away. The boys detrained at Manassas Junction, marched about five miles north, and went into camp in an old field called "Pageland," a short distance north of the Gainesville and Warrenton Turnpike, and about one mile west of the field where the Battle of Manassas had taken place a month earlier.

Colonel Cantey, his staff and company commanders soon got the men in the routine of camp life again. Setting up tents, getting water and firewood, and establishing guard posts and rosters became the order of the day. Near the 15th Alabama were encamped the 21st North Carolina, the 21st Georgia, and the 16th Mississippi Infantry regiments.[15] The same men who were awed at the sight of a thousand men encamped at Fort Mitchell now had a view of nearly five thousand men camped in close proximity to each other. These four regiments were soon placed into the same brigade (or "brigaded" together) under Brigadier General Crittenden. His brigade was placed in the division of Major General G.W. Smith. Crittenden was soon promoted and sent to the Western Theater, and Brigadier General Isaac Trimble of Maryland was assigned to command the brigade. Soon afterward, the brigade was transferred to Major General Richard S. Ewell's Division.

Tour of the First Manassas Battlefield

> "I am quite certain that every officer and man in the regiment availed himself of the opportunity of inspecting this first battle-field of the war."[16]—Captain William C. Oates, Company G, Henry Pioneers, 15th Alabama Infantry Regiment

Toward the end of August the company commanders were given the opportunity to tour the Manassas Battlefield with their men on a field trip. The men were struck by the horrors of war for the first time. Eight hundred forty-seven men died at the Battle of Manassas and most were buried in shallow graves on the battlefield. The dead horses and mules simply lay where they had been killed. The men's romantic notions of war were washed away just as the rain had washed away the dirt of many of the shallow graves. Hands and feet protruded from of the earth. The smell of rotten, decaying flesh was mixed with the aroma of fennel and pennyroyal trampled by the tens of thousands of men who participated in the battle. Many of the men mused this distinctive smell arose because Yankee bodies gave off a smell different from that of Rebel bodies. Buzzards circled overhead waiting for the intruders to leave so they could continue their feeding. Wild hogs rooting around for human grub were less shy and continued their feeding undisturbed.

The impact on the soldiers can best be described by them. Samuel D. Lary of

Left: **Major General Richard S. Ewell, Commander, Ewell's Division (Library of Congress).** *Right:* **Brigadier General Isaac R. Trimble, Commander, Trimble's Brigade (Library of Congress).**

Company B wrote home, "The field is covered with the half decaying and partially devoured carcasses of man and beast—all of which speak in dumb eloquence of 'man's inhumanity.'"[17] A soldier from Company G spoke for all the 15th Alabama when he wrote that the sight put them on the road toward the deadly realties of war and soldiering.[18] Another private from the same company wrote, "These were sad scenes and furnished food for reflection."[19] The men were free to wander around the battle-field littered with paper torn from cartridges while they picked up minie balls and pieces of shell to send home as souvenirs, all the while being careful not to step on the bloodstained grass. The men who could read shared with those who could not the inscriptions on the signboards posted which marked what regiment stood where and what general might have died there. The pockmarked Henry House and the trees cut in half by minie balls gave the boys a harsh lesson about the power of 19th century ballistics. The boys returned to camp a "wiser set of boys than we were when we started out in the morning."[20]

Disease

> *"'Tis here the reaper commenced the harvest of death which had already gathered and still continues to reap the choicest heads in the regiment."*[21]—Private Samuel D. Lary, Company B, Midway Southern Guards, 15th Alabama Infantry Regiment

It was at Pageland that the 15th Alabama first encountered their deadliest foe of the war when measles, mumps, and typhoid descended on the Fighting Fifteenth like a Biblical plague. Few of these rural Alabama farmboys had ever been exposed to or inoculated against common campground diseases. Contagious diseases decimated the Confederate ranks. "Not less than 150 men of the regiment died that fall ... from the effects of measles and the want of proper treatment and attention."[22] The Adjutant Report for the regiment for the month of November alone shows that 60 died of disease. A private from Newton described this winter as the "most trying period of the war. I say this because it was a period of enforced idleness with little to break the monotony of camp life but with drills and parades."[23]

The men had not even fired their weapons or been fired upon, but death was all around them. Their naive, romantic illusions of war were also dead. The thought of dying so far away from home probably terrified these boys from Alabama. The boys in the hospital likely yearned for a tender mother, wife or sister to care for them while in the last throes of death. Their dying wish was to "be buried with their fathers and in the companies of their youth."[24] Unfortunately the "Dead March" (military funeral procession) simply became another routine camp duty, albeit a more solemn one.

Not even the surgeons of the day understood that these diseases were contagious. Soldiers would often not be evacuated to the hospital at Haymarket when symptoms first appeared, but only when they couldn't perform camp duties anymore. About 100 of the regiment died over a span of six weeks.[25] This number represented 10 percent of the regiment's strength!

In the latter part of October the regiment marched to another campsite in an old oak grove located between Manassas Junction and Bull Run Creek near Centreville. The men were instructed to build huts using logs, mud, and canvas. About 300 of the regiment were hospitalized and had to be moved to St. Paul's Episcopal Church in Haymarket, a little village about fifteen miles west of the camp. About 200 men from the 15th Alabama were soon buried in the yard of the improvised hospital.[26] Men filled up the pews within in a short time, and many more were housed in tents surrounding the church grounds. The sick were attended to by two surgeons from the 15th Alabama, Dr. Francis A. Stanford, and Dr. Shepherd of Eufaula, who was nearly 75 years old. Stanford had carefully selected Haymarket as the site for the regimental hospital; one soldier remarked that Dr. Stanford missed "no opportunity to provide for the well-being of the invalids."[27]

As winter progressed, the infectious diseases continued to cut through the ranks of the 15th Alabama. The initial symptoms of high fever, rash, runny noses, watery eyes, and coughing would be followed by pneumonia and encephalitis (brain inflammation) as a result of the measles. Others would suffer middle-ear infections, severe diarrhea, and convulsions. "The worst cases, and there were hundreds of them among the troops of the 15th Alabama, resulted in death."[28]

Disease was particularly devastating to Company L from Perote, Alabama, which arrived to join the 15th Alabama in late March or early April. Few, if any, of these men had been exposed to the diseases that afflicted the armies in the field. On May 12, 1862, Private Martin Monroe Stough of Company L wrote his wife, "Our company is now reduced to about twenty, and those who have gone to the hospitals are dying very fast. We have some ten or twelve men already, and it is thought that a number of others will die."[29] Assuming Company L arrived with 100 men this is a disease rate of 80 percent!

Though the winter was miserable and homesickness ever-present, the 15th Alabama had plenty of food, clothing, and even luxuries which relatives and friends had sent from home. One wrote of the bounty he had received: "Fine dinners, at which roast turkey and good Virginia beef were in abundance."[30] Another private writes, "Our currency [Confederate money] was good for a few months of our camp life and we could purchase fine Norfolk oysters at fifty cents a quart and the vegetables and fruits with which Virginia abounded, at reasonable prices."[31] But with the inflation of the Confederate dollar, "the peddlers and their wares soon disappeared."[32]

The unsanitary conditions of stationary camp life certainly contributed to the enormous amount of sickness and death among the men. The abundance of meat also proved to have its downside. At a time in our history of a very distinct division of labor, when men and boys worked in the fields and women and girls worked in the house, few of these

Private William G. Banks, Company L. Pictured here possibly before the war. He married Mary Jane Copeland in 1859, and he died in 1900 (courtesy Cynthia Tomblin).

farmers would have known how to properly prepare food. One private wrote, "This was the time that the frying pan and the raw flour and fresh beef got in their deadly work. The men, fresh from their homes with no experience in cooking, did not know how to prepare the food furnished and the flap jack and half cooked roast produced dysentery and the men died by the scores."[33] A private from Newton remembered, "I have seen many excellent quarters of Virginia clover-fed beef lying in our camp on the snow, the men at liberty to help themselves, but untouched for the very sight got to be nauseating."[34]

Winter Quarters at Manassas

> *"During that long and disagreeable winter the men had no cause to complain."*[35]—Captain William C. Oates, Company G, Henry Pioneers, 15th Alabama Infantry Regiment

It was in winter quarters that the 15th was assembled and marched to witness their first execution. Two Irishmen from the famous Wheat's Battalion from New Orleans of Taylor's Brigade were court-martialed for insubordination and surrounding units were assembled to witness the serious consequences of breaching military orders. The 15th watched as a squad from the battalion marched in front of the two insubordinates and heard the command of "Ready, aim, fire." They heard the shots

Winter quarters at Manassas (Library of Congress).

and saw the two lifeless bodies fall to the ground. One can never know what thoughts Private Alpheus Brooks of Company E, son of Captain Essau Brooks, was thinking at this time, but he would find himself on the wrong end of a firing squad three years later.[36]

In December 1861, the men were issued their long-promised gray uniforms. As they had been fitted in September, some of the youngsters had outgrown their designated uniform, but there were plenty of others to try on due to the large number of deaths and discharges. The men strutted around in their new clothes proud as peacocks. The caps even had their company designations on them. The soldiers also drew good woolen overcoats to help deal with the cold Virginia winter.[37]

The boys drew their first pay, two months' worth, which would be $22 for privates. Soldiers finally had money to "buy writing paper, postage stamps, apples, cakes, candy, ground peas and chestnuts."[38] Writing and receiving letters from home is a very uplifting activity for any soldier in any war. One soldier wrote his family on May 3, "It dose me a heep of good to get letters from you all."[39] Sutlers, merchants who followed the troops around selling their wares, were still plentiful at this time of the war when Confederate money was still worth something.

On the strategic side, the Confederate Army of Virginia under General Joseph Johnston was facing the Union Army of the Potomac under General George McClellan. Both commanders were extremely cautious men, so both armies spent the winter of 1861-62 maneuvering and sparring or shadow-boxing, but neither side was serious about bringing on a large battle. Both were content in training and organizing their forces to avoid another debacle like First Manassas, where two untrained mobs were thrown at each other. General Johnston ordered a withdrawal for the 15th Alabama on March 1, 1862. While marching south and destroying railroads and bridges, the regiment reached the vicinity of the Rappahannock River. There, Ewell's Division was left as rear guard for the army. The 15th Alabama was sent about two miles on the east side of the river to tear up a railroad. Here they came under cannon fire for the first time, but no record of casualties can be found. A Private Casper W. Boyd from Company

General Joseph Johnston, Commander, Army of Virginia (Library of Congress).

I wrote: "Thay began to fier bums and cannons ball at us about twelve o'cloc on the 28th Mar ceased firing about sunset did not any of us get hurt some of bum and balls fell pretty clost to us."[40]

The rest of the winter passed with little more enemy activity. During the winter, an officer and two or three men from each company were sent home on recruiting duty. Using the carrot and stick, the Confederate Congress had encouraged recruitment by offering a $50 bounty for those new recruits enlisting. In addition, the 1st Conscript Act would take effect on April 16, 1862, requiring enlistment for those white males between the ages of 18 and 35. Over 300 new recruits arrived in March to replenish the badly depleted ranks of the ten companies. In addition, a full new company, the Pike Sharpshooters, from Perote, Alabama, was added to the regiment. This new company would be designated Company L.

Camp Life

"There is almost any kind of amusement here, and many appear to enjoy themselves as well as heart could wish."[41]—Private Martin Monroe Stough, Company L, Pike Sharpshooters, 15th Alabama Infantry Regiment

Although we read of movements, battles, sieges, and so forth when we read of war, any soldier from any war will tell you that the vast majority of a soldier's time is spent in camp. Training, refitting, and guard duty is the order of the day. The only fighting is against the boredom of camp life which consumes most of a soldier's actual wartime experience. This was no exception for the men of the 15th Alabama during the Civil War.

The only real wartime duty of a soldier in camp during the Civil War was "picket duty." If one can imagine an army as a house with a "picket" fence guarding its access and egress, the soldiers on picket duty would be the vertical boards in the picket fence protecting the army. Picket duty would rotate so that a small squad of men with an officer or noncommissioned officer would have the duty for two or three days every two to three weeks. This would involve relieving a squad four to five miles away from the main body of the army. Sometimes the men would be lucky enough to have a house, barn, or some other structure to protect them from the elements, but more often than not they would only have a makeshift lean-to. Their duty was simply to watch for enemy encroachments and act as a 19th century Early Warning System. If they could escape the watchful eye of their superiors, pickets of both sides would use this time to fraternize with the enemy and exchange newspapers, Southern tobacco for Northern coffee, and other hard-to-get items. Southerners were particularly willing to bargain after the Union blockade increasingly tightened its stranglehold on the South as the war progressed.

While in camp, company and regimental drill consumed much of the day, usually at two-hour intervals for six to eight hours per day. The messes would spend much of the rest of the day in maintenance of their quarters, acquiring water and firewood, and gathering and cooking food.

Like soldiers throughout time, the Alabama boys found ways to entertain themselves. Private Houghton of Company I wrote:

> Several of the company had their musical instruments until forced marches caused them to disappear, and thus we had music, and a glee club gave excellent oral entertainments around the camp fires or under the tree, but these too, disappeared in the severe campaigns. At first we had chess, checkers, cards and games, but after the first year all games except cards were abandoned.[42]

Considering card playing, especially gambling, as sinful, Private Houghton reported, "I have seen men playing poker on a knapsack within ten steps of a preacher discoursing to men sitting on the ground around him." Apparently many agreed that card playing was sinful, as he noticed that most would refuse to take cards into battle with them. He states that when the men "pressed forward to form in line of battle, one could walk a long distance on cards strewn by the way, and I have never seen a pack of cards on one of the thousands of dead, either friend or foe, I saw on battlefields." He estimated, "Perhaps nine-tenths of the soldiers played some game of cards and about three-fourths indulged in gambling."[43] Private Barnett Cody from Company G agreed with this assessment as he wrote home, "I am sorry to say that we have a great deal of card playing going on in our Regiment and Company."[44]

Receiving word from home was and remains a favorite among soldiers throughout the ages; the men of the 15th Alabama were no exception. Private Casper Boyd of Company I wrote, "It dose me a heep of good to get letters from you all."[45] Private Martin Stough of Company L writes his wife, "You cannot imagine how it cheers up my drooping spirits to hear from you."[46]

Many of the men attended preaching and prayer meetings, which were held quite often. The Confederate Army as a whole, and the Army of Northern Virginia in particular, underwent several revivals of faith during the war that swept through the ranks and engulfed almost all of the soldiers. Living with death so much a part of daily life, this is easily understandable. Private Cody wrote to his minister father, "We go to preaching every Sunday here," and "we had a protracted meeting here in camps for 3 or 4 nights, there will be preaching tonight at candle-light.... Very large crowds attend preaching."[47] Private Boyd states that his greatest pleasure was finding a place of seclusion and simply reading his Bible.[48]

Some simply found pleasure in lying on their blankets and studying the stars. Some of the more educated men would give informal classes about "the different constellations and the mythological fables with which the ancients surrounded those groups."[49]

THREE

The Foot Cavalry

Strategic Situation of Spring 1862

"Always mystify, mislead and surprise the enemy, if possible. And when you strike and overcome him, never let up in the pursuit so long as your men have strength to follow. The other rule is, never fight against heavy odds if by any possible maneuvering you can hurl your own force on only a part, and that the weakest part, of your enemy and crush it. Such tactics will win every time, and a small army may thus destroy a large one in detail, and repeated victory will make it invincible."[1]—Lieutenant General Thomas "Stonewall" Jackson, Commander of the Valley Army

The fall and winter of 1861-62 had proved disastrous for the Confederacy. New Orleans, the South's largest city, had fallen to Union naval forces. The loss of Forts Henry and Donelson had given Union river flotillas control of central Tennessee as far south as Huntsville, Alabama. It quickly became obvious that President Jefferson Davis's idea of a defensive war was not working. General Robert E. Lee, Davis's military advisor, would finally get his way in pressing for offensive operations.

On the Federal Side during April and May in Virginia, after constant pressure from President Abraham Lincoln, Union General McClellan was reluctantly induced to move his Army of the Potomac on Richmond. His strategic maneuvers were to set the stage for the rest of the spring and summer '62 campaigns in Virginia. Not wanting to have to fight his way the 100 miles south from Washington to Richmond, McClellan embarked his 100,000-plus Army of the Potomac by ship and debarked at Fort Monroe on the lower peninsula of Virginia. Johnston countered this move by sending two divisions to the peninsula but left the 15th Alabama in Ewell's Division to keep an eye on the Union forces south of Washington.

Here is the strategic situation in Virginia:

1. McClellan's Union Army of the Potomac is cautiously moving up the peninsula towards Richmond with 128,864 men opposed by Confederate General Joseph Johnston's 53,688 Confederates.

2. McDowell's Union Corps of 30,000 men is protecting Washington and being watched by Ewell's Confederate Division of 8,500 men

about halfway between Washington and Richmond.

3. Union Generals Banks and Fremont are in the Shenandoah Valley with 21,000 and 17,000 troops, respectively, faced by "Stonewall" Jackson's Division of 6,000.[2]

As one can see, the situation for the Confederacy looked bleak indeed. Almost 200,000 Union troops were invading Virginia, which was defended by a third that number of Confederates. This dire situation demonstrates how the genius of two generals and the fighting spirit of soldiers like the men in the 15th Alabama can overcome the worst of odds.

General Robert E. Lee was not a troop commander at this time but was a military advisor to Confederate President Jefferson Davis. Lee, an engineer by training, had a genius for geography and described the Shenandoah Valley as a "shotgun leveled at the head of Washington."[3] Lee based his strategy on three factors:

First Lieutenant James M. Ellison, Company C (courtesy Alabama Department of Archives and History, Montgomery, Alabama).

1. The Shenandoah ran northeast to southwest. In other words, it ran toward Washington but away from Richmond.

2. Lee knew from serving with McClellan during the prewar period that the Union general was extremely cautious and was not going to move on Richmond with any degree of aggressiveness.

3. He didn't think Lincoln would allow McDowell to move his corps for fear Washington would be unprotected.

In the Shenandoah he saw possibilities. The two Union generals, Fremont and Banks, were political appointees and no match for the wily Stonewall Jackson, irrespective of the numbers. Lee's plan was to have Ewell's Division reinforce Jackson, drive Fremont and Banks from the Shenandoah and threaten Washington. Lee hoped this would "freeze" McDowell in place, and prevent any reinforcements from reaching McClellan. If all went well, Jackson's combined force would then be free to join General Johnston and his Army of Virginia in front of Richmond and assail the slothful McClellan. After causing

Lieutenant General Thomas J. Jackson, Commander, Valley Army (Library of Congress).

McClellan to retreat from the gates of Richmond, Johnston's Army could assault McDowell before it could be reinforced with the remnants of McClellan's army of the Potomac. It was indeed a bold plan but the only chance the South had.

In accordance with Lee's plan, Ewell's Division was attached to General "Stonewall" Jackson's Division in the middle of April 1862, making a combined force hereinafter referred to in history as the "Valley Army." The untested men of the 15th Alabama were about to become part of one of the most brilliant campaigns in military history, Jackson's Valley Campaign. The new recruits heard the command to cook three days' rations, pack their knapsacks with everything they could carry, and destroy everything else—an order they would become very accustomed to in the years to come.

Shenandoah

"It takes a person with an iron Constitution to stand his [Jackson's] marches. I have often marched day and night without a thing to eat. When we march from fifteen to twenty five miles a day. If all of our Generals was like Jackson this war would not last long."[4]—4th Corporal Barnett H. Cody, Company G, Henry Pioneers, 15th Alabama Infantry Regiment

First Lieutenant J.M. Ellison[5] of Company C drew $1,500 on February 21, 1862, in order to return to Macon County on recruiting duty. Representatives from each company returned to their recruiting base to do the same. The company recruiting officers returned with their recruits to replenish the ranks of their companies that had been so depleted by death and discharges in time for spring campaigning.

On the first of March 1862, Captain Peter V. Guerry,[6] the commander of Company C, returned from a meeting of the 15th Alabama's company commanders and staff and ordered his officers and noncommissioned officers to ensure the men cooked three days' rations and be prepared to move. First Lieutenant Ellison and the other officers started barking out orders and getting the men ready. Ewell's Division left its winter camps at Manassas Junction and marched to the Rappahannock River. The 15th came under artillery fire for the first time as the men were tearing up railroad tracks near the river. Private Casper Boyd of Company I wrote home "[T]hay began to fier bums and cannons ball at us about twelve o'cloc on the 28th Mar ceased firing about sunset did not any ... get hurt."[7]

Ewell's Division marched across the Rapidan River toward the Blue Ridge and on to Gordonsville, which was a junction for the Virginia Central and the Orange and Alexandria railroads. It was here that Company L joined the regiment. The Pike Sharpshooters, from Perote, Alabama, were mustered into service on March 15, 1862, and became the eleventh company as they joined the regiment at Brandy Station. Their commander was Dr. Robert H. Hill, who requisitioned 114 uniforms, thus adding that many muskets to the regiment's numbers.[8] The 15th rested here for a couple of weeks enduring an unusually late cold front with sleet and freezing winds blowing in. Many of the men, particularly the new arrivals, caught pneumonia and camp fever (probably typhus) and had to be evacuated to Chimborazo Hospital.

On April 30, the men were formed up four abreast and were marched towards Swift Run Gap, which crossed the Blue Ridge Mountains into the Shenandoah Valley. The 15th would be the only Alabama regiment in the Shenandoah, and the Wiregrass men found the valley a very pleasant change from their winter quarters in Virginia. One company commander remembered of the citizens: "Their hospitality was unbounded. No Confederate soldier was ever turned away hungry from one of those rude and humble homes so long as they had subsistence for themselves within."[9] Private Casper Boyd of Company I wrote his parents, "[T]his is [a very] healthy [portion] of the country we have the best of water to drink the finest spring here in the mountains that I ever saw."[10]

Captain Dekalb Williams, Company F, shown here post-war. He married Mary Magnolia Mathews in 1854. He owned DeKalb & Simeon Williams Dry Goods in Troy, Alabama (courtesy Dianne Smith).

Private Thomas H. Walden, Company H. Pictured post-war with (probably) his wife, Martha Curry Walden (courtesy Cheryl Osburne)

Ewell's Division consisted of Trimble's Brigade, Taylor's Brigade from Louisiana, and Early's Brigade of Virginians. The division marched across the Rapidan River toward the Blue Ridge and on to Gordonsville. On April 30, the division passed through Swift Run Gap and into the Shenandoah Valley. As the regiment reached the peak of the Blue Ridge and started down the other side they were met by bands playing "The Girl I Left Behind Me" and other songs which boosted the morale of the tired boys. Private Houghton of Company H wrote after the war, "I had never heard anything so beautiful and inspiring and in fact I have not since."[11]

Ewell's Division arrived at Front Royal on the morning of May 23 and prepared for battle as they piled all their baggage in the quartermaster wagons. One private said they "divested themselves of everything except a blanket and a change of under garments."[12] Ewell's Division was held in reserve during the fighting between Jackson and Banks at Front Royal on May 23, Winchester on May 25, and Strasburg on June 1. The Fighting Fifteenth chased the defeated Federals through the streets of Winchester all the way to Harpers Ferry, where the enemy found temporary refuge behind their fortifications. Outside of Harpers Ferry a sad example of the inexperience of the regiment resulted in the death of Private John Trawick of Company E, Dale Beauregards. Private Trawick was shot in the heel when a rifle accidentally discharged near Harpers Ferry. He was evacuated to the hospital in Winchester. Later the Dale County boys learned that he had died shortly after arrival on May 25.[13] They were not seasoned soldiers yet but would become so shortly.

The Alabama boys returned to Winchester and spent a couple of days tearing up the Baltimore and Ohio Railroad. They also helped themselves to Banks's massive commissary stores. Soldiers of the Valley Army would begin to refer to their adversary as "Commissary" Banks because of the generous captures. The 15th Alabama spent the next week and a half, until June 1, tearing up the railroad, paroling prisoners, and loading the captured stores for transport. First Lieutenant Ellison wrote home that the Valley Army had captured a large number of wagons, 6,000 bushels of corn and a large amount of coffee, sugar, and other stores.[14] After the "mop up" and capturing Winchester on May 25, the army came into possession of the rest of Banks's supplies of two miles of wagons, cannon, and more commissary stores, including $100,000 worth of medicine.[15] Large numbers of prisoners and small arms were also taken.

On June 6 the division reached Harrisonburg and followed the Port Republic Road to the small village of Union Church not far from Cross Keys. Several soldiers of the 15th wrote home about seeing General Jackson during these marches riding up and down the line and the men cheering and waving their hats in honor of their beloved commander. One private wrote, "He came in a gallop on his chestnut brown horse, sitting not gracefully but easily, with the visor of his cap well down over his brow and a pleased expression on his countenance.... The men were wild with enthusiasm whenever he appeared."[16] One officer from Company C wrote, "He took off his cap & galloped.... What hollering you never heard."[17]

This Federal army under command of Major General John C. Frémont and Brigadier General James Shields outnumbered Jackson two to one. They were trying to catch Jackson in a vise between them and destroy the Valley Army. Frémont approached from the west on Jackson's right and Shields marched on a parallel on the east side of the south fork of the Shenandoah.

The next morning the 15th moved in the direction of Port Republic and camped at a church called Cross Keys. On Sunday morning, June 8, about 9:00 a.m., the regiment formed in line of battle on the left of the turnpike at the end of a piece of woods that surrounded the church. Company A, with their Mississippi rifles, were thrown forward beyond the church and cemetery to act as skirmishers. Seeing a brigade of Union infantry passing the regiment's unsecured right flank, Colonel Cantey ordered a withdrawal through a wheat field and behind a fence and ordered the men to lie down behind the fence, which ran along a ridge.

The regiment suffered their first combat losses during this delaying action on June 8. As the company had crossed the wheat field they had to climb a tall rail fence as they were being pursued by the enemy.[18] 3rd Lieutenant Henry Brainard[19] of Company G had the foresight to run ahead of the soldiers and tear down as much of this fence as possible. Private Houghton saw a Yankee take deliberate aim at him as he crossed the fence and the bullet slammed in the top rail as he climbed it.

The soldiers looked across the 150 yards at some woods with an open field between them. Shortly the skirmishers rejoined the regiment with Union skirmishers in hot pursuit. One private wrote:

> All of these things created such suspense that it caused a chill to pervade my system to the extent of causing my knees and teeth to knock together as though I had an old fashioned shaking ague. The hair on my head seemed to rise and was sorter like the quills of a fretfull porcupine.... I looked around to see if anyone else was in my condition, and I soon found it to be a pretty general complaint among the boys.[20]

The nervous Alabamians were ordered to lie down behind the fence and remain quiet and not fire until ordered to do so.

Around 10:00 a.m. the Yankees emerged from the woods and advanced with great precision. The Union troops advancing on them were from the 6th Pennsylvania Bucktails. When the Bucktails were about 75 to 100 yards away, the order to "fire" was finally given. The smoke created by this volley made it impossible to see any more, but a second volley was fired anyway. Captain William Richardson[21] of Company H screamed out, "Boys, give them hell!"[22] When the smoke cleared, the boys could see that the Pennsylvania Bucktails had fallen back to the protection of the woods. The Bucktails reformed and tried to flank the 15th when they were mowed down by the 21st Georgia on the 15th Alabama's flank.

Seeing another flanking movement to their right, Colonel Cantey ordered his regiment to "move by the right flank." The purpose and importance of the confusing and hated regimental drills were finally being realized by the soldiers of the 15th now as they conducted the movement with utmost precision. General Trimble arrived to personally take control. Colonel Cantey wanted to capture a Union battery of artillery that was damaging his regiment with solid shot and canister. Forty-three-year-old Private J.M. Singleton of Company C was killed by some grapeshot hitting him below the throat. The 15th again encountered the remnants of the Bucktails protecting the battery and unleashed a fresh volley into them that sent them fleeing from the field for good.

As the Fighting Fifteenth followed up their pursuit of the Bucktails, Private Moses G. Maybin[23] of Company G saw a big Yankee appearing dead but holding the strap of his overloaded haversack in one hand. Wanting the haversack for himself, Private Maybin told his fellow soldiers, "Boys, I am going to take that haversack." As his 5'9" frame bent over to grab it in a full run, the big German tightened his grip and yelled "Nau, nau." A shaken Private Maybin dropped the sack, stepped back, looked in amazement with big blue eyes, raised his hat revealing his brown hair, and politely said, "I beg your pardon, sir, I thought you were dead."[24] Unfortunately for the regiment, the Bucktails had done their duty because they managed to give the battery time to limber and get out of harm's way.

This engagement crushed Frémont's left flank. The Confederates erupted in a rebel yell waving their hats over their heads. At about the same time, the Alabama soldiers heard a rebel yell coming from the direction of Port Republic, which meant Jackson's Division had whipped Shields's forces. At Cross Keys on June 8, the 15th Alabama had fought their first battle and performed admirably. The Valley Campaign was over. That evening the 15th Alabama buried the dead, removed the wounded, and collected the large quantity of small arms off the field. First Lieutenant DeKalb Williams[25] of Company F wrote his brother, "We were busy all night getting up the arms and accoutrements—we gathered somewhere between 5 and 600 stand[s] of arms, the most of them excellent guns; we captured any quantity of knapsacks and haversacks, blankets and clothing of every description and kind."[26] Many of the men took this opportunity to trade their muskets for the better rifled weapons used by the Union forces and replenish their knapsacks with Union goods. Of the 425 men engaged, the 15th Alabama lost nine dead and thirty-three wounded.[27]

Killed	Wounded	Missing
Company A		
PVT Wesley C. Foster	PVT John W. Teal	1LT William T. Berry
	PVT Thomas E. Turner	PVT James F. Phillips
Company B		
	PVT James Y. Boyd, severe hand	
	PVT George T. Denham, lung	
	PVT Thomas J. Ford, mortally	
Company C		
PVT J.M. Singleton, grapeshot below throat	PVT Joseph W. Baker	
	2CPL Allen Crowley	
	PVT Luther D. Johnson, hand amputated	
	PVT Thomas Singleton, mortally	
Company D		
PVT Robert Beathy	PVT Robert Biddy, mortally	
	PVT Thomas S. Moffette	
	PVT James R. Eidson	
	PVT William Garland, mortally	
	2LT Angus A. McIntosh	

Killed	Wounded	Missing
Company E		
2LT Wesley B. Mills		
Company F		
	PVT George W. Brazil	
	PVT Green L. Childs, slightly	
	PVT Matthew E. Meredith, right hand, 3 fingers	
Company G		
	PVT William N. Bullard, severely	
	PVT William Fears, severely (lost eye)	
	PVT John Melvin, foot	
	PVT Benjamin Morris	
	PVT William J. Parrish (lost 2 fingers)	
Company H		
Company I		
	PVT Casper W. Boyd, mortally	PVT S. Perry Pitts
	PVT William T. Linton, severely	PVT Bradberry Wilson
	PVT Elenda R. Thomas, thigh, right arm & shoulder	
	PVT Thomas A. Walters, severely (leg)	
Company K		
PVT Dennis P. Kenny	PVT Nelson Cummings	
	PVT James R. Towler	
	2SGT William Toney, mortally	
	PVT Randolph W. Wellborne, hand	
	PVT Charles M. Worthington	
Company L		
Captain Robert H. Hill	PVT Eli Meredith	
	PVT William E. Robertson, severely[28]	

General Trimble wrote in his After Action Report: "I accordingly in person moved the Fifteenth Alabama to the right along a ravine and, unperceived, got upon the enemy's left flank and in his rear, marching up in fine order as on drill." Colonel Cantey had prepared the Alabamians well. The 15th Alabama performed a regimental maneuver "as on drill." Colonel Cantey was proven right that military training before battle saves lives during battle, and the regiment had learned its lesson well.

Captain Oates of Company G wrote of the aftermath of this magnificent campaign:

In three months Stonewall Jackson had marched six hundred miles; fought four pitched battles, seven minor engagements, and daily skirmishes; had defeated four armies [each larger than his own]; captured seven pieces of artillery, ten thousand stands of arms, four thousand prisoners, five hundred wagons and teams, three hundred head of beef cattle, and a very great amount of stores, inflicting upon his adversaries a known loss of ten thousand men, with a loss upon his own part comparatively small.[29]

From this point on Jackson's command would be known as the "Foot Cavalry" because of their marching speed. One company commander complained, "My feet were blistered all over, on top as well as bottom. I was never so tired and sleepy."[30] Private Orsamus Moates wrote his wife, "I am well except my feet which are worn out."[31]

Shelby Foote writes of the accomplishment of Jackson's Valley Army: "[H]is troops had covered 646 miles of road in forty-eight marching days." His descriptions of the captures are slightly different from that of Oates: "3,500 prisoners, 10,000 badly needed muskets, nine rifled guns, and quartermaster stores of incalculable value."[32] The Fighting Fifteenth performed admirably in their first battle. General Ewell gave special praise to the 15th Alabama in his After Action Report by writing, "The regiment made a gallant resistance"[33] at the Battle of Cross Keys. General Trimble's report of the Battle of Cross Keys, June 8, mentioned: "To Colonel Cantey for his skillful retreat from picket, and prompt flank maneuver, I think special praise is due."[34]

The day after the battle, the regiment moved to Weyer's Cave, where they encamped and enjoyed some badly needed rest and reflection. After all of the rapid marching, particularly along the two pike roads (paved with cobblestones) in the Shenandoah, the Alabama boys suffered from what was to become their biggest logistical irritant of the war: the lack of suitable footwear. Many of the boys were without shoes and the ones they had were in such disrepair as to make them almost useless. Those not lucky enough to find a dead Yankee to requisition shoes from simply collected rawhide from local butchers and fashioned moccasins, but many just went barefooted. This would prove to be a major logistical deficiency for all Confederate soldiers throughout the entire war.

Meanwhile, on June 2, 1862, General Lee assumed command of the Confederate Army in Virginia after Johnston was wounded. Lee changed the official name of the army to the Army of Northern Virginia. No better army was ever created in the Western Hemisphere, and it was led by one of the greatest military geniuses in history. He would preserve its name in history in the coming months and the 15th Alabama would be a part of it.

Because only the first part of Lee's brilliant strategy had been achieved due to Jackson's excellent execution, it was time for Part Two. Jackson's Foot Cavalry was to join General Lee at the gates of Richmond to assist in defeating McClellan's Army of the Potomac. The Valley Army took a very badly needed rest until June 17 when they headed out for Richmond. At about 8:00 a.m. the regiment reached the foot of the Blue Ridge Mountains, and upon their ascent they were able to admire the entire Valley Army "dressed in gray marching four abreast, stepping in quick time, with their bright muskets and bayonets glittering in the sun."[35] Many veterans stated this left a lasting impression on the men of the regiment.

The 15th Alabama marched through the beautiful western and middle parts of

Virginia, helping themselves to English cherries along the way. They reached Ashland, a station on the Fredericksburg Railroad twelve miles from Richmond, on June 25. So in eight days the "Foot Cavalry" marched 135 miles. Their march through Richmond would be remembered by of the survivors in the 15th Alabama, for "people had gathered on each side of the street to welcome and cheer us on."[36] Word had reached Richmond of the success of Stonewall Jackson's Foot Cavalry, whose achievements were welcome news to the entire South after so many setbacks over the past ten months. "The ovation that we received from the old men and women, the beautiful girls and boys made each one feel himself a hero from the Shenandoah Valley."[37]

Private George Bailey, Company D (courtesy John Allbritten III).

Cold Harbor

"Jackson's arrival with his corps from the Valley to reinforce Lee, was anxiously looked for."[38]—Private William A. McClendon, Henry Pioneers, Company G, 15th Alabama Infantry Regiment

Already exhausted from the Valley Campaign and the subsequent march to the Peninsula, Jackson and his command assumed positions on the extreme left of the Confederate line (just east of Richmond) before what was to become the Seven Days Battle. Lee's intent was for Jackson to flank the Union right and attack McClellan's forces from the rear. Due to exhaustion and an uncharacteristic lethargy on the part of Jackson, this never happened, and the Confederates were reduced to very destructive frontal attacks on the prepared Union lines. The 15th arrived into this buzz saw on the evening of June 26.

The next morning, Friday, June 27, General Trimble was leading his brigade on the field, riding in front of the 15th Alabama, the lead regiment. Moving onto the battlefield, twenty-year-old Frank Champion of Company I and the rest of the 15th Alabamians caught their first glimpse of General Lee as they passed Hogan's house. As the Alabamians marched by they observed Jackson rein his horse, salute and shake hands with the new commander.[39] The Alabama boys caught sight of two of the greatest military commanders of any war shaking hands. Before the war, Frank had worked as a grocer in Joshua Ogletree's store in Troy, Alabama[40]; soldering had greatly changed his life in the last year.

As the Alabamians approached the line of battle they were met by shot and shell exploding over them, blowing out the tops of trees with limbs and branches falling all about them. The brigade halted here for a short while to allow the rest of the division to catch up. Lawton's Brigade of Georgians filed in on their right while Taylor's

Louisianans filed in on their left. Company A formed in front as skirmishers for the 15th. As the regiment resumed its movement forward Colonel Cantey could be heard yelling, "Steady, Fifteenth Alabama!"[41] As the 15th advanced through the bombardment, they passed through what used to be a Union camp with tents still erected, campfires still burning, "and a good many valuables."[42]

The Fifteenth continued walking forward in perfect alignment. Officers gave the correct orders and the men followed exactly as the line negotiated obstacles but yet maintained their formations while under fire. Suddenly, Private Frank Champion and the men heard the skirmishers of Company A in front being hotly engaged. Some Confederates from other units came running through the 15th's lines headed for the rear and could be heard yelling, "You need not go in; we are whipped." The Alabama boys could be heard replying, "Get out of our way, we will show you how to do it!"[43] The Alabama boys soon encountered fire from a "red-legged Zouaves regiment"[44] posted on a hill fortified with fallen trees.

At about 2:00 p.m., Colonel Trimble realized it was a losing battle to remain in the open and exchange fire with the fortified Zouaves. He ordered the men to fix bayonets and charge the enemy without stopping to fire a shot. Captain Peter Guerry[45] of Company C fell dead with a minie ball through his head.[46] After the battle, Colonel Trimble described this charge with adjectives such as "rapid," "resolute," and "defiant."[47] The 15th Alabama swept the Zouaves from the top of the hill and unleashed a devastating volley into the retreating enemy as they were running down the other side of the hill. The regiment remained on the hilltop, continuing their deadly fire on the enemy below them.

Private Frank D. Champion of Company I found a riderless horse, mounted it, and began to rally the men, riding up and down the line shouting encouragement.[48] Many soldiers mistook him for an officer because of his bearing and confidence. During this exchange of gunfire, Private Robert McKnight of Company G was struck in the forehead by a minie ball which flattened out on his skull but did not penetrate.[49] Eighteen-year-old Benjamin Morris of Company G fell wounded.[50] Soon smoke covered the battlefield but the Alabamians learned they could continue firing at flashes of guns, buttons, bayonets or any sight of the Yankees. The men continued firing like this for the next two to three hours. The yelling and cheering and the sounds of small arms and cannon were so loud, the only way a soldier knew if his musket had discharged was when he felt a kick against his shoulder. Muskets became so hot that the soldiers were afraid to pour powder in them; many grabbed the muskets of the wounded and dead and continued firing. This firing continued until the soldiers began to run low on ammunition. After exhausting the ammunition of the Union and Confederate dead and wounded, the soldiers held

Private James M. Whitehead, Company H. Post-war photograph. His nickname was "Bud." He died in 1920 (courtesy Susan Starrs).

their position by simply lying on the ground still under fire, awaiting resupply of ammunition.

General Ewell rode up and profanely inquired about the slackening of fire. When informed by a 15th company commander that the men were out of ammunition he ordered them to "fix bayonets" (even though bayonets were already fixed) and to hold their position, and he announced that reinforcements were on the way. Ewell left, and minutes later, the men were delighted to see an ammunition detail arrive. As the soldiers quickly refilled their cartridge boxes, they noticed the 5th Texas come up from the rear, fired one volley into the Yankee line, and they too fixed their strange-looking saber bayonets.

When the order "charge" was finally given, the Texans and Alabamians screamed out the rebel yell and charged down the hill. Although "the canopy of smoke was so thick that the sun was gloomingly red in the heavens,"[51] the combined forces charged into the direction of the Yankees. When they reached the bottom of the hill they discovered that their foe had not only been repelled but had been completely annihilated. The Texans veered off to the right and aimed their charge on a ten-gun Union battery. Upon hearing the rebel yell from that direction, the Alabamians knew the cannon had been captured.

The Alabamians joined in with the yelling and waving hats in the air in a moment of exhilaration. The 15th Alabama went into camp on the battlefield. The soldiers of the regiment searched for wounded comrades and took particular satisfaction in taking the shoes off the many dead Union soldiers and rummaging through their haversacks. They found them "rich with hard tack and bacon, a sack of ground coffee, with a string of dried apples about two feet long in each sack."[52] Soldiers continued looking for wounded with torches as night descended upon the battlefield. The boys from Alabama spent the night around campfires recalling the day's events with excited pride, drying out their sweat-drenched clothes, and enjoying the coffee, bacon, and hard tack provided by their enemy.

This was indeed a memorable day for the 15th, not only because they saw and fought under the command of Robert E. Lee for the first time, but because of the 412 entering the Battle of Gaines' Mill, 34 would be killed and 110 wounded.[53] This would not be the last time that one third of the regiment became casualties. Losses to company commanders were particularly costly. Captain Peter Guerry of Company C was killed leading his men into battle. Captain Lock Weems of Company A[54] was mortally wounded and Captain George Malone[55] of Company F was so seriously wounded that he was discharged from the service.

Killed	Wounded	Missing
Company A		
PVT Joseph A. Holt	PVT James Aaron	
PVT Wesley M. Whitley	PVT James Broughton, severely	
	PVT William C. Griffin, severely	
	PVT John B. Johnson, severely left side of body & through nose	
	PVT William A. Jones, severely	

Killed	Wounded	Missing
	PVT John H. Stringfellow, severely right arm	
	PVT John Taff, severely	
	PVT Joseph Turner, mortally	

Company B
Killed	Wounded	Missing
PVT Thomas J. Burke	PVT John D. Bowen	
PVT John Crosby	PVT William A. Edwards	
PVT Samuel J. Feagin	PVT H.L. Harper	
	PVT William D. Mosley, mortally side	
	PVT Hardy K. Norris	

Company C
Killed	Wounded	Missing
CPT Peter V. Guerry	PVT Benjamin J. Burks	
PVT Ivy McGrady	PVT James T. Etheridge, severely	
PVT James M. Skinner	PVT David J. Jackson, mortally	
	PVT Amos P. Mansel	
	PVT Benson Strickland, mortally	
	PVT John B. Turner	
	PVT Joel Wicker, mortally	
	PVT Eugene B. Woodham	

Company D
Killed	Wounded	Missing
PVT William R. Lewis	PVT George W. Bailey, thumb	
PVT Franklin Wright	PVT Jack V. Caraker	
	PVT A.W. Douglas	
	CPT Blant A. Hill, slightly	
	PVT Robert Sam Jones	
	PVT James R. Maddux	
	2LT Angus A. McIntosh	
	PVT W.H. Quattlebum	
	PVT Benjamin F. Streeter	
	PVT Dozier Thornton	
	PVT David H. Zorn, severely (arm amputated)	

Company E
Killed	Wounded	Missing
PVT Rufus A. Athon	PVT William H. Briley	
PVT Thomas Murphy	PVT Lawrence D. Brooks, severely left leg	
PVT Wiley J. Stephens	PVT Richard D. Byrd	
	2CPL Thomas S. Mills	
	PVT Billy Capers, severely leg	
	PVT Hartwell B. Nevels, mortally	
	PVT Green B. Scogin, severely	
	PVT John L. Skinner	

Company F
Killed	Wounded	Missing
PVT Green F. Carlisle	PVT Stephen E. Andrews, mortally	
PVT Walter S. Glenn	PVT John N. Bray	
PVT Willis R. Harden	PVT Zacharia Bussey	

Killed	**Wounded**	**Missing**
PVT James T. Perry	PVT Green L. Childs, slightly	
PVT F.M. Rudd	PVT William Crane	
PVT Reuben W. Anderson	PVT Acy M. Downing, hand amputated	
	PVT Isaiah Elliot	
	PVT David Farmer	
	PVT Peter J. Hough	
	PVT Edward A. Hutchinson	
	PVT William Lindsey, severely	
	PVT George Y. Malone	
	PVT C.O. Minshew	
	PVT William N. Reeves	
	PVT S. Morton Sneed, severely	
	PVT William J. Tillery	

Company G

PVT Martin V.B. Box (heat exhaustion)	PVT Henry B. Johnson	PVT Stewart Merrit (deserted)
PVT Samuel Dickinson	PVT John C. Jordan, severely	
	PVT Robert S. McKnight, severely head	
PVT Andrew Murphy (battle fatigue)	PVT James N. Shepard, severely	
	PVT Christopher C. Stone, severely	
	PVT Edward J.J. Ward	
	PVT John H. Whatley, severely	

Company H

PVT William A. McLeod	PVT Richard Coleman, mortally
PVT John Melvin	PVT Jeff B. Hendley, mortally
PVT William W. Reynolds	PVT Mark M. Holsey
PVT Benjamin J. Spivey	PVT John J. Jones, severely
PVT T. King Searcy	PVT John C. McIntire, severely
PVT Daniel S. Walker	PVT Barton S. Reneau, left thigh
	PVT Daniel A. Spurlock, mortally
	PVT William W.B. Weston, severely
	PVT James M. Whitehead, left thigh (amputated)

Company I

PVT W. Thomas Craig	PVT Isaac N. Andress, severely
PVT John W. Park	PVT John C. Evans, severely eye
PVT Richard Walker	PVT Alex T. Farmer, mortally
PVT James Whatley	PVT George W. Linton, severely
	PVT Bob Edward McMoy, loss left thumb & index finger
	PVT James T. Rushing, severely
	PVT James W. Scarbrough
	PVT John Strickland, severely

Company K

PVT Amos Bush	PVT Columbus C. Bell
PVT William W. Evans	
PVT John H. Grice	

Killed	Wounded	Missing
Company L		
PVT David J. Stough	PVT Marcus L. Brooke	
	PVT Lee M. Bryan, severely	
	PVT Howell McClendon, mortally	
	PVT James McClaney, severely	
	1SGT George W. Peach, mortally	
	PVT Enoch Renfroe, right leg	
	PVT Robert H. Wicker[56]	

The men of the 15th Alabama had fought their first large-scale battle and had again performed admirably. General Ewell wrote in glowing terms of the performance of the 15th in his After Action Report: "I cannot speak too highly of the conduct of these troops, which were immediately under my observation. They were opposed to constantly renewed forces of the enemy, and held their ground against vastly superior numbers, advantageously posted after the troops immediately to their right had fallen back, gaining ground slowly against large odds."[57]

In the battle of Seven Days, Lee's Army of Northern Virginia had captured 52 fine Union guns, 31,000 rifles and 10,000 prisoners, and had killed or wounded 15,849 Federals. However, the South paid a dear price in the 20,614 casualties during the Seven Days Battle.[58] Lee accomplished his objective, however, and succeeded in dislodging McClellan from the gates of Richmond. The Fighting Fifteenth could not yet rest for there was another Union Army looming further north. They were about to begin Phase 3 of Lee's plan.

The men of the regiment awoke on the morning of June 28 with the stiffened joints of someone thirty or forty years older. The dehydration of the day before caused fluid to desert the joints. The adrenalin-induced exertion of the previous day no longer masked the aches and pains of the quiet morning. The regiment awoke to a battlefield with Confederates stretching their aching joints and searching for water, many proudly wearing their new shoes made north of the Mason-Dixon Line. After attending roll call and listening for the names of friends and relatives who might not answer, some started collecting firewood and others started the campfires. The Alabamians made coffee and stewed dried apples. Others enjoyed the ham, crackers, condensed milk, pressed vegetables, chocolate, and green tea taken from the confiscated enemy haversacks.[59] Most had to eat in a hurry because they knew the call would come for details to bury the dead and collect weapons and supplies from the battlefield.

The 15th didn't fight that day but were ordered to secure an abandoned depot of supplies near a railroad. The 15th camped at the improvised depot and maintained guard on it all night with orders not to build fires. The men found "scores of barrels of ground coffee, sugar, rice, syrup, salt, tea, flour and meal."[60] The regiment packed as much as they could in their already full knapsacks.

Lee used the short respite after the battle to reorganize his forces into two corps and promoted Jackson and James Longstreet to command them. The 15th Alabama remained in Ewell's Division, which remained under Jackson's command, or II Corps.

Second Manassas

"Thousands of these poor fellows lay on the ground, in some places I could have walked for hundreds of yards on the dead and wounded Federal troops."[61]—Captain William A. Edwards, Company E, Dale Beauregards, 15th Alabama Infantry Regiment

By June 27, 1862, President Lincoln had become so concerned for the security of Washington that he created the Army of Virginia consisting of the remains of Frémont's and Banks's Corps, and McDowell's untested Corps. Major General John Pope was assigned to command this new army. As McClellan was loading his defeated army on barges under the protection of his gunboats, Lee knew he had to move quickly before these two armies would have time to merge.

On July 13, Captain William Edwards[62] roused his company of Dale County boys because Jackson's Corps was on the move. They were to go north to Gordonsville, where they spent the remainder of the month watching Pope's new army to monitor their intentions. Scouts reported back with the news that Pope had apparently given his men free rein to pillage and commit horrendous atrocities upon the civilian population. By the time the order was given to move on August 7, the Confederates were just aching to engage the new Union army. Jackson was to move on the right flank of Pope's Army under General Banks. Colonel Cantey, in the meantime, had returned home on sick leave and Major Alexander Lowther was given command of the regiment.[63]

The Confederates remained in camp for a few days and on July 17 Jackson's Corps took up a line of march toward Richmond. The 15th Alabama had to march through portions of the battlefield where most of the dead had not yet been buried, so the stench was almost unbearable. The next day the boys marched through Richmond, where the streets were lined on both sides with grateful Virginians cheering them on. All were again anxious to catch a glimpse of the famous "Stonewall" Jackson and his Foot Cavalry. The regiment halted about four miles north of Richmond and encamped there. On the 20th the regiment was loaded onto railroad cars at Hanover Junction for Gordonsville, where they detrained and marched some five or six miles in the direction of Orange Court House, and went into camp.

On August 7, the 15th awoke and began to slowly advance toward Culpeper Court House. They stopped on the banks of the Rapidan River and settled down to camp, not being allowed to build fires. The boys had a sleepless night, for not even two weeks had passed since their major engagement at Cold Harbor, and they knew that another battle was looming in their near future. On the morning of the 8th they again advanced and drove in some cavalry pickets. The enemy cavalry was pursued by Stuart's cavalry, closely followed by Jackson's Corps with Ewell's Division in the lead. The 15th Alabama was detached from Trimble's Brigade and ordered to move up to a ridge near the mountain's summit to protect an artillery battery.

The Battle of Cedar Run was fought on August 9 between Jackson's Corps and Banks's right wing of the Union Army of Virginia. The 15th Alabama was relegated to protecting Latimer's Battery during the battle and did little more than receive artillery fire but had an excellent view of the battlefield from their elevated position. Jackson again routed Banks, and the Union general again yielded a massive amount of stores for Jackson's commissary. "It was a general thing, when we tackled Banks we got rations," wrote one private from Company G.[64] Jackson gave pursuit to Banks's routed corps and encamped on the site of the enemy's camp. After ascertaining that McDowell's Corps was moving in support of Banks, Jackson returned to Gordonsville.

Killed	Wounded	Missing
Company A		
	PVT James D. Curenton	
Company F		
PVT James E. Grice, artillery		
Company H		
	PVT James A. McIntire	
Company K		
	PVT James H. Gray	PVT Pat Clark (deserted)
Company L		
	PVT William A. Brown, mortally	
	PVT S.T. Hardy	
	PVT W.L. Lain[65]	

The brigade left the position in the hands of General Hood's Division and continued their chase. During June 23 and 24, the forces exchanged artillery fire across Hazel River.

Killed	Wounded	Missing
Company B		
PVT Henry H. Kelly	PVT Thomas S. Beasley, head	
	1SGT Noah B. Feagin, severely	
	PVT William J. Ming, leg	
	PVT John L. Wright, severely left thigh	
Company C		
	5SGT William L. Bailey	
Company D		
	PVT H.J. Williamson	
Company E		
	PVT Charley C. Jones, severely	
Company F		
	PVT James E. Lewis, foot	
Company G		
	PVT George Jenkins	

Killed	Wounded	Missing
Company H		
	PVT Samuel H. Peacock	
	1LT William D. Wood	
	Harris C. Yelverton	
Company I		
PVT William N. Smith	PVT Green W. Davenport	
PVT George J. White		
Company K		
	PVT James L. Cade, right leg	
	2LT Fred M. Porter	
Company L		
PVT Jesse L. Gause[66]		

The impatient Jackson had to find an uncontested crossing site. Jackson's Corps again detached itself from Lee's Army and crossed at Hinson's Mill four miles above Waterloo, passing through the small village of Orleans, and camped for the night near Salem about two hours after dark. The men were exhausted and badly in need of rest.

As morning of August 26 approached, the corps was again set in motion with Ewell's Division leading with the Louisiana Brigade, which was followed closely by Trimble's. The corps crossed the Bull Run Mountains at Thoroughfare Gap. Along the march the 15th Alabama passed by the homes and farms that had been looted and defiled by Pope's troops. The homes had been robbed of anything of value, and what couldn't be carried away was destroyed. The boys had marched sixty miles in two days subsisting on green corn and half-ripe apples hastily gathered from the fields and orchards they passed during the march. A private in Company H remembered, "Tired, wet, wornout, all night long we pressed forward, wading streams, climbing hills, across farms, through forests and along country roads."[67]

After a meeting with General Lee, it was decided that Jackson was to take his corps, swing around the Union right, and strike in the Yankee rear at Manassas Junction. By August 27 the corps reached Manassas Junction remarkably undetected by Pope. Stuart's magnificent cavalry had protected the corps from any detection from the Union forces. They arrived at Bristoe Station on the Orange and Alexandria Railroad, quickly captured the guards, and cut the telegraph wires. As the corps approached the station with the Louisiana Brigade in the lead, they heard a whistle of an approaching train coming from the direction of Warrenton Junction. The Louisianans lined up along the train tracks and unleashed a broadside as the train ran into an obstruction and "leaped into the air."[68] The soldiers heard another whistle approaching, and the Alabamians lined up on the left of their Louisiana brethren and unleashed another, more powerful broadside with the aid of four artillery pieces and the rest of the entire brigade just before the train piled into the rear of the previous train. The engineer and fireman were killed and the Confederates discovered the train full of Union wounded, only a few of whom escaped. Soon a third train approached at full speed and met the same fate as the first two.

Jackson knew that the main Union depot was at Manassas Junction, only four miles away. Trimble volunteered to proceed to that location that night. Jackson approved and Trimble set out with the 21st Georgia and the 21st North Carolina. The 15th Alabama soldiers were happy for the rest and collapsed where they stood.

The men of the 15th Alabama were awakened the following morning before day-break and marched the four miles to Manassas Junction, where they arrived as the sun was coming up. The boys were treated to a sight they had never seen nor would ever see again: "Acres—a square mile, in fact—of supplies of every description were stacked in overwhelming abundance.... Newly constructed warehouses overflowed with rations, quartermaster goods, and ordnance stores...."[69] "We found trainloads of army supplies and sutler stores. The boys helped themselves and I got some coffee, canned fruit and other good things," wrote Private Houghton of Company H.[70] In anticipation of uncontrolled looting, Trimble's Brigade was assigned the duty of guarding this "mythical horn of plenty," as Shelby Foote described it. However, this would be one fight the brigade didn't win, as the Confederate horde engulfed the rich capture.

> Canteens were filled with molasses, haversacks with coffee; pockets bulged with cigars, jackknives, writing paper, handkerchiefs, and such.... Some, more abstemious, were satisfied with loaves of unfamiliar light-bread, which they ate like cake. Others, preferring a still richer diet, found pickled oysters and canned lobster more to their taste, spooning it up with grimy fingers and washing it down with bottles of Rhine wine.[71]

Some men confiscated Yankee haversacks and loaded them with captures.

While the men were stuffing their mouths and knapsacks, they noticed Jackson ride up to Trimble and congratulate him on his capture. Those who could overhear the conversation learned that Union troops were on their way. Apparently, the powers that be in Washington thought it inconceivable that 25,000 men could march thirty miles undetected around Pope's Army of Virginia and just sit in its rear as Jackson had done. President Lincoln thought this could only have been a cavalry raid and dispatched a train with a New Jersey brigade to clear the area of the enemy. The brigade had detrained at Bull Run and was on their way to Manassas Junction.

The New Jersey Brigade had no idea of what they were marching into. Ewell's entire division waited in ambush and, after a few volleys, quickly routed the New Jersey men, killing their commander. General Taylor of the Louisiana Brigade was also killed by the fragment of an exploding artillery shell. The boys of the 15th Alabama and their entire brigade gave pursuit for seven miles to Centreville but could not catch the frightened enemy, who retraced the rout after the Battle of First Manassas and didn't stop until they reached the safety of Washington. Trimble's Brigade marched back to Manassas Junction that evening, August 27.

Jackson Corps was thirty-five miles from Longstreet and sat completely alone in the rear of Pope's Army. Jackson's Foot Cavalry had done it again. The corps was sitting on Pope's supply line with Washington, and Jackson knew that he was in a precarious position until Longstreet's Corps could arrive. Any enemy commander, even one as incompetent as Pope, had to know this would be an opportunity to defeat his enemy in detail. Jackson knew this also and began searching for some terrain more suitable for defensive operations to place his corps until Longstreet and Lee could arrive. Pope bragged to his president that he would "bag Jackson and the whole crowd."[72]

After loading all the wagons with everything they could transport, the men were allowed one more opportunity to get all they could manage to carry. "There was a pile of bacon as large as a small house, cut into pieces of convenient size, with hundreds of boxes of hard bread opened and sitting near, and as each regiment marched by on leaving the Junction it was halted for two or three minutes and every man allowed to help himself to all that he could carry."[73] The next morning, August 29, Ewell marched his division to Centreville and remained there for the balance of the afternoon. The Alabamians were leaving behind the largest supply depot they would ever see. The soldiers were sick not only from gorging themselves the night before, but from seeing the smoke from the burning stores as they looked back toward Manassas Junction. Later in the war, when hunger pangs stabbed at their stomachs, they would likely think of this manna from heaven and smile.

On August 28, Ewell marched his division on the Warrenton Pike, recrossing Bull Run at Stonebridge. Off to the west, the men of the 15th Alabama could hear the distant booming of Longstreet's cannon trying to force his way through the Thoroughfare Gap. Could he arrive in time? Upon reaching the defensive line selected by Jackson, the regiment deployed in a line of battle with Ewell's Division in the center flanked by A.P. Hill's Division to the left and Jackson's old division commanded by Brigadier General Taliaferro on the right. The 15th Alabama, for the most part, had an excellent position occupying a railroad embankment except for an open area of some fifty yards off to the right. Still further to the right was a cut through a rise about six to eight feet deep.[74]

As the sun was going down, the 15th Alabama could see the Yankee horde approaching. One company commander wrote: "The road was blue with them for miles, marching four abreast, as though they were unconscious of danger."[75] To their right and rear the Alabama boys could see a massive cloud of dust, but whether this was Longstreet's Corps or Union reinforcements gathering to attack their flank and rear, only time would tell.

Jackson was riding up and down the line with his battle face on. After hearing from a courier that General Stuart had arrived in force and was on his right, Jackson could wait no longer. Ever the attacker who won battles by brilliant maneuvering, he raised his hand and pointed as he was looking at General Ewell, he yelled simply, "Ewell, advance!" Ewell advanced with Hays's, Early's, and Lawton's Brigades, leaving Trimble's Brigade in reserve. The brigade witnessed a battle unfolding of ten thousand men engaging each other on open terrain.

Shortly, a courier rode up and told Trimble to advance his brigade because the enemy had achieved a breach on the right of Ewell's line. Trimble gave the loudest command one 15th Alabama company commander had ever heard: "Forward, guide center, march."[76] The Confederates saw a brigade emerging from a clump of woods to their front; this was the breakthrough Ewell had sent the courier about. The Southern soldiers found out later this was Gibbon's Brigade of King's Division. The Union Brigade fired first as Trimble's Brigade hugged the ground and then returned fire. The enemy retreated behind the relative safety of a fence, and Trimble ordered a pursuit which drove them from the fence into a gulley about twenty yards away. At about this time Trimble was shot through the leg. The Alabamians lay behind the fence and exchanged fire with the 2nd Wisconsin. The enemy was armed with Belgian rifles with .56 caliber bullets that exploded upon impact. "They literally tore the old rotten fence into fragments," wrote one private from Company G.[77] Smoke filled the battlefield and night had fully set in. For an hour the men blindly fired into the dark. Amid the confusion and allegations that Confederates were firing on each other, the order was finally given to withdraw back to the railroad embankment. The men started building campfires for a restful cup of captured coffee, but Union artillery quickly zeroed in on these fires. The boys scrambled, dodging the shells and trying to put the fires out. General Ewell had been seriously wounded during this night fighting, and General Lawton assumed command of the division.

The divisions of Jackson's Corps formed up in the same line of battle as before the night assault. Ewell's Division was in the center, Trimble's and Lawton's Brigades were in front with Early's, and Taylor's Brigades in the rear as reserves. Pope wasted all of the morning and half of the afternoon of August 29 positioning his troops. At 3:30 p.m. Trimble's Brigade could see heavy assaults on A.P. Hill's Division off to the left, but all were repulsed with heavy losses.

The 15th Alabama looked across the field at their enemy as three lines of battle formed perfectly in front of them just out of musket range. The first line was met with a devastating volley that sent them all to the ground, some willingly, some not. The second line reached the first line and they too halted, followed by the third line, which did the same. They became "one interminable mass of humanity," wrote a private from Company G,[78] while ignoring the pleadings of their officers to advance. The Federals had to retreat.

The Federals reformed and with reinforcements charged again. This new assault reached the Confederate line and achieved a breach in the 50 yards of open space on the right of the 15th Alabama. Many of the Alabamians had run out of ammunition or simply didn't have time to reload and engaged in the worst hand-to-hand combat of the war for the 15th Alabama. Fists, rocks, rifle butts, and bayonets were employed against the Union attackers. "The maddened men, the flying stones, the clubbed muskets, the shouts, yells, smoke, dust, din, and rattle of musketry of that scene passes description." Private Houghton wrote, "Such a contest with rocks and butt ends of muskets I have never seen or read of before or since."[79] Enfilading fire from both sides of the Confederate line tore large holes into the Yankee mass. To make matters worse for the Yankees, the reserve Confederate brigades arrived in time to repair the breach in the line. "At last the Yankees gave way, and when they turned their backs and fled, the ground was blue with their dead and wounded," wrote Captain Oates.[80]

A famous incident occurred within the lines of the 15th Alabama that day which has frequently been written about and passed down in history. During the attack, a Union major on horseback led his regiment against the Confederate lines, and Captain

Shaaff[81] of Company A killed him with a well-placed shot. When the firing ceased, Captain Feagin[82] (acting regimental commander; Major Lowther was in the rear, sick, during the battle) began to rebuke Captain Shaaff for killing such a brave man, saying that he should have tried to capture him. General Jackson rode up and told Captain Feagin, "No, Captain, the men are right; kill the brave ones, they lead on the others."[83]

With the Union Army in full retreat, the 15th Alabama boys had time to notice their surroundings and saw the flags and banners of Longstreet's Corps approaching from the right. They were relieved to finally learn the dust they saw earlier in the day belonged to friendly troops. The whole line erupted with the rebel yell. The men knew they would not have to continue to fight the whole Union army alone.

As night fell, the troops tried to get to sleep amid the "piteous groans and wild despairing shrieks"[84] of the Union wounded to their front. One soldier from Company G lit a campfire for some bacon and coffee and could see at least a hundred dead Union soldiers illuminated around him.[85] Listening to the cries of the wounded, the Alabamians developed a new sense of respect for their enemy. They pictured themselves in the same predicament, in foreign territory, far from home, and no one to take care of them but the enemy. The Yankees had obeyed their officers just as the Alabama boys had done, but the Union boys just didn't have the quality of leadership that the Confederates were blessed with.

As the morning of August 30 broke, the Confederates were quietly aroused from their slumber. Many of the boys started making fires and went to making Yankee coffee and bacon to enjoy with their captured crackers. As the sun rose, the men of the 15th Alabama looked over the open field in their front and saw "the most sickening" carnage they would witness in the war.[86] The bodies of thousands of dead and wounded could be seen. The battlefield seemed to move as the wounded tried to crawl away or at least push a dead comrade off them. Fresh skirmishers were sent out to relieve the ones sent out the night before, but most of the day was taken up with artillery exchanges. Longstreet was on the field with two of his divisions and Lee had almost all of his troops prepared for another assault.

At about 3:00 p.m. the skirmishers came running in yelling, "Boys, look out, they are now coming!"[87] The bugler sounded "attention" followed quickly with "advance." As the Union lines appeared in the open field again, someone yelled, "Look out boys, they are coming, lots of 'em." Colonel S.D. Lee had arrived close by with 24 pieces of artillery and began decimating the Union lines at great distance. "They were so thick it was impossible to miss them," one private from Company G wrote.[88] In spite of the artillery shells, then the grape and canister, and then the musket fire when they got even closer, the brave Yankees again almost breached the Brigade line. The Yankees were repulsed with the arrival of the reserve and enfilading fire from the 15th Alabama and a regiment of Taylor's Brigade on the other side of breach. "It was not long before a general stampede among the Yankees took place ... but the slaughter among them had been great."[89] This attack was made by Porter's Corps, reputedly one of the best in the Union Army.

While Jackson's Corps was filling the Union troops with lead, Longstreet launched an attack on the Union left. Once Porter's Corps retreated, the 15th heard far down the line a rebel yell. The cheering came closer and men could be seen waving their hats in the air. As these sights and sounds came closer, the men saw General Jackson riding the line mounted on "Old Sorrel" in a slow gallop. The Alabama boys could clearly see he was "dressed in an old dusty, dingy, faded gray uniform with legs of his pants stuffed in the legs of a coarse pair of boots. Three faded stars and a wreath that he wore upon the collar of his coat was the only mark that distinguished his great-ness."[90] Stonewall halted and yelled "Attention," and in a sharp, shrill voice, "Forward." After a short celebration the whole corps advanced for about a mile and didn't find any Union soldiers standing upright. The Corps was halted, then ordered to stack arms and rest for the night. "Our whole front was the brilliant spectacle of a victorious army in pursuit of what might be correctly termed a demoralized and panic-stricken rabble."[91]

Darkness put an end to the pursuit, and by 10:00 p.m. the men finally got time for a badly needed rest. The boys were exhausted and slept in place with nothing to disturb them but the groans of the wounded and a pouring rain. The Battle of Second Manassas was over. A 15th Alabama company commander writes, "Saturday night of August 30, 1862, closed on one of the bloodiest fields of war. The Confederates were jubilant."[92] Private Houghton wrote, "The piteous groans and wild despairing shrieks of the scores of helpless wounded would have appalled any but a hardened, half starved and worn out soldier."[93] On Sunday, the following day, the ground in front of the 15th Alabama was described as a space of about three hundred yards long and two hundred yards wide literally covered with dead men. Union losses for the battle were 1,724 killed, 8,372 wounded, 5,958 missing. Lee reported the capture of 7,000 prisoners, exclusive of the 2,000 wounded left on the field. Confederate losses were 1,481 killed, 7,627 wounded, and 89 missing. Pope left on the field 30 guns and 20,000 small arms.[94]

The battle was over and the 15th Alabama had once again marched and fought superbly. Two major battles were won in as many months and the 15th Alabama Infantry Regiment was in the forefront of both. At Second Manassas, the 15th Alabama Regiment went into battle with 440 and suffered 21 killed and 91 wounded.[95]

Killed	Wounded	Missing
Company A		
	PVT James M. Cooper	
	PVT Edward W.P. Chapman, severely	
	2SGT Eben B. Edwards	
	PVT Ashbury Wooten, severely	
Company B		
PVT Thomas J. Hutchinson	PVT Alfred G. Denham	
PVT Elijah W. Owens	PVT William A. Edwards	
PVT M.L. Harper		
	PVT John W. Hughes	
	PVT James W. Hutchinson, severely, leg amputated	
	PVT Walter C. Jackson	
	PVT John C. Jones, mortally, arm and body	

Killed	Wounded	Missing
	PVT Watt P. Jones, severely arm amputated	
	PVT Emery A. Lane, severely right shoulder	
	PVT Jack McDonald	
	PVT Samuel B. McJunkins, shoulder and arm	
	PVT Daniel Milligan, right shoulder and left arm	
	PVT John M. Payne	
	PVT James P. Phillips	
	PVT John A. Tarver, severely, hip	
	PVT James H. Wheeler	
	3LT Richard E. Wright, severely, arm and lungs	

Company C

PVT John G. Key, severely
PVT Simeon Strickland
1CPL Elisha P. Vinson, mortally
PVT Green B. Vinson

Company D

Killed	Wounded
PVT J.W. Cooper	PVT Andrew J. Blount
PVT A.W. Douglas	PVT William A. Harrod
	PVT Thomas Pate
	PVT Soloman Patterson, mortally
	PVT Thomas J. Reaves
	PVT James Wilson

Company E

PVT Joseph J. Dean
PVT Jim R. Edwards
PVT Young Edwards
PVT Thomas W. Morrell
PVT William N. Sellers

Company F

Killed	Wounded
PVT Bartley C. Anderson	PVT Redin Baxley
PVT G.D. Glenn	PVT John N. Bray
2SGT William D. Hough	PVT Edward A. Hutchinson
PVT A.N. Jackson	3LT Pleasant W. Nicholson
PVT J.A. Paul	
PVT William J. Seay	
PVT Daniel J. Stephens	

Company G

Killed	Wounded
PVT William E. Bowen	PVT George L. Dukes, severely
PVT Augustus B. Harvey	PVT George W. Grice, severely
PVT Calvin J. Kirkland	PVT Jones Hickman, mortally
2CPL Lott W. McMath	PVT Andrew J. Huggins
PVT William A. Watson	PVT William J. McKnight, left ring finger
	PVT James H. Miller
	3SGT Charles A. Moody, severely

Killed	Wounded	Missing
	PVT Charlton L. Renfroe	
	PVT James A. Roney, head	
	PVT John H. Sauls	
	PVT John M. Stone	
	PVT George M. Wiggins, severely	

Company H

PVT Henry Manning	PVT William L. Bailey	
PVT William P. Reynolds	PVT Abner Holmes	
	PVT John Keels, severely	
	PVT Judge D. Loveless	
	3SGT Charles A. Moody, severely	
	PVT Joel Tew	

Company I

PVT S. Perry Pitts	PVT Joseph Bell, severely	
	PVT Seaborn N. Harris	
	PVT George W. McCormick	
	PVT Hugh McLeod	

Company K

PVT Henry M. Allen	PVT Joseph Bell, severely	
PVT James T. Brannon	PVT W.H. Gilmore, severely	
3SGT James E. Sylvester	PVT Seaborn F. McGee, mortally	

Company L

	2LT Francis M. Emerson, mortally	
	PVT William Owens[96]	

The Battle of Second Manassas was over but the maneuvering was not. Reveille woke the boys up on the morning of August 31. Stuart had informed Lee that Pope had retreated with his shattered and demoralized army to a fortified position at Centreville, where he had already been reinforced by Sumner's Corps and Franklin's Corps from McClellan's Army as it began to arrive. Lee had ordered Jackson to turn this position by crossing Bull Run at Sudley Ford. After muster and some issuance of newer, captured weapons, the corps headed for the ford in the pouring rain at about noon. Movement was slow along the Little River Turnpike that led in the direction of Fairfax Court House, a little town between Centreville and Washington. Due to the rain and the exhaustion of the men, they bivouacked after marching several miles.

Pope discovered Lee's intentions and began moving his army closer to the protection of Washington. The

Private Thomas Morrell, Company E. Post-war photograph. He was born in 1835 in Newton County, Georgia. He married Nancy Smith from Butler County, Alabama, about 1857 (courtesy Lynn Stidom).

next morning the march was continued along the same road until they reached the Middle River Turnpike, which formed a junction at Germantown with the Warrenton Pike leading to Washington. Jackson headed his corps down the pike in hopes of once again outflanking Pope's retreating army. At about 5:00 p.m. the 15th Alabama reached Ox Hill, better known as Chantilly Farm. This place was an intersection of the road from Centreville and the Little River Turnpike. No sooner had the Confederates arrived than their skirmishers were attacked. Trimble's Brigade was the rear brigade on the march in Ewell's Division, followed by A.P. Hill's Division. The 15th was ordered forward and found themselves in a thick body of woods with the drenching rain continuing to pelt them. Confusion reigned as orders could not be heard amid the firing, rain, and dense vegetation. The Alabama boys were reduced to firing in the direction of the enemy without any idea of the impact because of the dense smoke hanging low in the night air.

The Confederates had become engaged with the Union divisions of Major Generals Philip Kearny and Jesse L. Reno of Heintzlman's Corps. The soldiers of Taylor's Louisiana Brigade gave way and began running to the rear through the lines of Trimble's Brigade just arriving on the battlefield. As nightfall mixed with the rain and forest, the Louisianans charged headlong for the rear. Junior officers were commanding large units (for instance, a captain was commanding Trimble's Brigade) and the 15th Alabama joined the stampede. The acting brigade commander, Captain Brown, was shot in the head while trying to rally the frightened Alabamians.

When order was finally restored, the 15th moved forward as other regiments followed. As night fell, they pushed the Yankees back, killing Union generals Kearny and Major General Isaac I. Stevens, and crumbled the Union line. The 15th Alabama fell back to the turnpike and camped for the night. After a brisk engagement, the 15th lost another 4 killed and 14 wounded. Losses were light but embarrassment was high due to their flight to the rear.

Killed	Wounded	Missing
Company C		
	PVT John B. Turner	
Company E		
	PVT James P. Cowen	
Company G		
	PVT Allen W. Sholar	
Company H		
	PVT Mitchell B. Houghton, right temple[97]	

Pope was ordered to return to Washington, and on September 2 he issued orders to his corps commanders about what routes to take. Phase 3 of Lee's masterpiece had been achieved. Just two months earlier, McClellan was about to put a stranglehold on Richmond, two Union corps were in full control of the Shenandoah Valley in the western part of Virginia, and McDowell was occupying north central Virginia with 30,000 troops. Now all were gone. The Union forces were broken, demoralized, and cowering under the protection of Washington. Virginia was largely free from the Union invaders.

Robbing the Dead

"Of course there was nothing wrong about taking property on the battle field but robbing the dead was never favored by most soldiers."[98]—William Robert Houghton, Company G, Columbus Guards, 2nd Georgia Infantry Regiment

Most Confederate soldiers were initially repulsed at the thought of confiscating personal items from the Union dead. However, due to the lack of food, a viable currency, and clothing (particularly shoes) their personal distaste for this practice soon gave way to necessity.

Union knapsacks were often found full of luxuries for the Confederates that were not available to those in the South who didn't have access to the fruits of a blockade runner. The well-supplied Federal soldiers' haversacks were usually rich with hardtack, bacon, dried and canned fruits, soda and sweet crackers, condensed milk, pressed vegetables, chocolate, green tea, and the most precious commodity: coffee. Confiscated shirts, pants, overcoats, and hats were worn so much that Confederate soldiers were often mistaken for Union soldiers on the battlefield. Old muskets were always exchanged for the more modern Union rifles. But the most precious item was always shoes. Shoe manufacturing in the South was a largely ignored industry. When new Southern shoes were acquired, they seldom held up to the hard marching required of the Southern armies. They would quite literally fall apart.

It is very interesting to note that items would not be taken from wounded soldiers or even prisoners. Many times after a battle, Southern soldiers would gather around a dying Union soldier just waiting for him to take his last breath before stripping him of all clothing and personal effects.

Taking greenbacks or gold and silver off the dead was something few soldiers would do, at least in the presence of their fellow soldiers. Oates wrote of James M. Rhodes of Company K, Eufaula Guards, "After a great battle he would slip away from his place in the ranks at night to plunder dead Yankees, and next day on some occasions he would have so many watches on him that the ticking reminded those who came near him of being in a jewelry store."[99] After waking up after a battle the dead Union soldiers would have their pockets turned out. The soldiers may have figured that if they didn't rob the dead, those on burial detail would.

Private William T. Bynum, Company K (courtesy Patricia Offutt).

A lot of the men were motivated by friends and family who were imprisoned in the North. Prisoners could supplement their starvation diet by buying from sutler stores in the prison. Of course, the sutlers in the North wouldn't accept Confederate money, so one soldier starting robbing the dead in order to mail greenbacks to his brother. After the war he discovered that the money never made it through the guards.

FOUR

Sharpsburg, Fredericksburg and Winter Quarters

"Maryland, My Maryland"

> *"It is a very lamentable thing that this war can't be settled. The [enemy] has lost many brave men as well as we. I do think the like of killed and wounded was never seen as was killed in the MD [Maryland] Campaign. I [laid] down my pallet to sleep the night of the 18th after the battle on the 17th with not less than 150 yankees dead within 50 steps of me."*[1]—
> First Lieutenant James Ellison, Company C, Macon County Commissioners, 15th Alabama Infantry Regiment

With so many victories behind him, General Lee was left in something of a quandary. He couldn't attack Washington since it was the most fortified city in the world and defended by three times the number of men he had at his disposal. He couldn't remain where he was because after a constant spring and summer of campaigning and looting, northern Virginia had been stripped of grain and his wagon train was inadequate to import enough even to feed the horses, not to mention his troops.[2] A third alternative would be to move southward, but that would give up northern Virginia to the Union, which so much Confederate blood had been shed to retake. The last option was to cross the Potomac and live off Northern resources for a change.

There has been a lot written on the reasons why Lee invaded the North. Some think he was trying to win European recognition for the Confederacy. Others say it was to convince the population of Maryland to join their slaveholding brethren and add their star to the Confederate Flag. Some say Lee wanted the Northern armies pushed as far away from Richmond as possible. Some say it was because he wanted to influence the upcoming congressional elections in the North. While all of these reasons, no doubt, contributed to his decision, the most practical explanation is probably logistics. Not only could he feed his army in the North but his movement there and the consequent Union countermoves would hopefully allow farmers in northern Virginia an unmolested harvest. *If* England and France recognized the Confederacy, and *if* Maryland seceded, and *if* more Democrats could be elected in Congress, all the better; but it is unlikely any of these were the primary reasons.

The worn-out Army of Northern Virginia was certainly not prepared for an invasion. Lee wrote Davis on September 3, "The army is not properly equipped for an invasion of an enemy's territory. It lacks much of the material of war, is feeble in transportation, the animals being much reduced, and the men are poorly provided with clothes, and in thousands of instances are destitute of shoes."[3] There had been so many commanders killed and wounded their replacements had to be made a priority to avoid another debacle like the one that happened at Chantilly. Colonel James A. Walker of the 13th Virginia was given command of Trimble's Brigade. Lt. Colonel Lowther reported in sick again and was with the wagon trains in the rear. The 15th Alabama was commanded by Captain Isaac Feagin from B Company.

On September 3–4, Captain Edwards Dale Beauregards moved north to White's Ford and crossed the Potomac into Maryland on the 5th. As the 15th Alabama Infantry Regiment splashed across the Potomac, the bands played "Maryland, My Maryland." As soon as the men crossed and got dressed they erupted with the rebel yell. Watching the invasion of his homeland and accustomed to seeing the well-fed and equipped Northern soldiers, a Maryland boy described the Southern army as "vermin-infested scarecrows, hairy and sunbaked, with nothing bright about them but their weapons and their teeth."[4] The Southern soldiers made the boy think of wolves: "They were the dirtiest men I ever saw ... a most ragged, lean, and hungry set," although, he adds, "Yet there was a dash about them that the northern men lacked. They rode like circus riders. Many of them from the far South spoke a dialect I could scarcely understand. They were profane and talked incessantly."[5]

After crossing onto Northern soil for the first time, the 15th Alabama marched to the Monocacy River, near Frederick, and made camp and rested for a few days where the Baltimore and Ohio Railroad intersected with the river. During the march to Frederick the reception was mixed; as one private from the 15th Alabama wrote, "Some of the houses we were greeted with cheers and smiles, and the waving of hats and handkerchiefs by the women, girls and boys, ... but at others the doors would be closed which was a token that we were an unwelcome guest."[6] In contrast to Pope's forces in Virginia, the men had strict orders from Lee not to disturb any private property. Although the apple trees "fairly groaned under the weight of ripe apples,"[7] the Southerners were only allowed to gather those that lay on the ground. Pope's men, on the other hand, would steal money, candlesticks, silverware, and anything they could carry. They would smash furniture and china, slash portraits, slaughter livestock and burn barns.

Because of the humiliation at Second Manassas, Pope was relieved of command and the remnants of his army were incorporated into the Army of the Potomac, still commanded by McClellan. Lee knew his cautious opponent wouldn't be making any serious attacks. Fortified with this confidence, Lee wrote Special Orders 191 on September 9, 1862, and split his forces once again in the face of superior numbers. The order sent Jackson's Corps to capture Harpers Ferry and Longstreet's Corps to Frederick, Maryland. Although the two corps would be outside of supporting distance to each other, Lee knew his opponent would be loath to leave the protection of the Washington fortifications. Unfortunately this order would fall into the hands of McClellan, and he would not be acting in his usual overly cautious manner this time.

Early on the morning of September 10, the 15th Alabama was given orders to prepare to move, and Captain Edwards roused the sleepy Dale County boys of Company E. Neither the privates nor the officers knew what was brewing as they watched the corps assemble to march. A.P. Hill's Division marched by, headed towards Frederick. Ewell's Division fell in and was followed by Taylor's Division. Their first day's march found the corps on the west side of South Mountain, where they went into camp on the Hagerstown turnpike. The men were issued one ear of corn, which they roasted; after spreading bacon grease and salt on it, they enjoyed this luxury before getting a well-rested sleep with no Union troops near.

The next morning the corps proceeded toward Williamsport on the Potomac, where they camped on the 11th. The next morning the boys recrossed the Potomac and proceeded to Martinsburg. The boys were headed west and most had surmised they were headed again for Harpers Ferry, where they arrived on the 13th. Jackson invested the place and quickly occupied all of the high ground around the town. After a bombardment of the Union positions for two hours on September 15, the rebel yell was heard along the line as white flags were seen being raised throughout the town. Jackson wrote his wife that the Union losses were "12,520 prisoners, 13,000 small arms, 73 cannon, and a goodly haul of quartermaster stores."[8]

The surrender didn't take place any sooner than needed. McClellan was moving on the divided Confederate forces with uncharacteristic vigor. The Confederate forces were not only divided but outnumbered about three to one. On the morning of September 15, 1862, Lee formed Longstreet's Corps behind the strongest terrain he could find behind Antietam Creek with his headquarters in the village of Sharpsburg, Maryland, and awaited attack and reinforcement from Jackson.

Jackson left A.P. Hill's Division behind to gather up the captures and parole the thousands of Federal prisoners. He set out with Ewell's and Taylor's Divisions about midnight and marched for 12 miles. The men were ordered to cook rations for three days and be prepared to march at 5:00 a.m. the next morning. The boys got up and answered roll call but were ordered to stack arms and rest until further notice. At about 10:00 a.m. the 15th Alabama started out east on a pace set by Jackson at three miles per hour with ten-minute breaks every hour. Many of the men couldn't keep pace and straggling became a serious problem, particularly for those without adequate shoes.

Between 12:00 p.m. and 2:00 p.m. the men again crossed the Potomac at Shepherdstown about two miles from Sharpsburg; they could hear the booming of cannon from that direction. The corps, minus Hill's Division, arrived on the battlefield about 3:00 p.m. and was ordered to stack arms. At dark, the brigade was moved in the direction of the firing, passing Dunker's Church, which was being used as a hospital. The brigade relieved Hood's Brigade of Texans on the left part of Lee's line and immediately sent out pickets, who spent the rest of the night exchanging fire with Union pickets.

Having a huge numerical advantage and knowing the Confederate dispositions, McClellan had every advantage a commander could want. Once on the battlefield, however, he attacked Lee's Army with piecemeal assaults and refused to commit his reserve when needed. The resultant battle would be the bloodiest day of the American Civil War, with positions changing hands many times; however, the day would end with both sides holding the same terrain they started out with.

Colonel Lowther again reported in as sick, which meant a major battle was brewing. However, the regiment was again ably commanded by Captain Feagin of Company B. Early on the September 17, 1862, the 15th Alabama saw their skirmishers rushing in and braced themselves for an attack. Jackson's artillery opened up "a furious fire." The 15th Alabama was on the extreme right of Ewell's Division and tied into Longstreet's Corps on their right. About two hundred yards in the rear of the 15th was located "not less than twelve artillery pieces crowning a hill opposite Dunker's Church."[9] The Alabama veterans hugged the ground as shot and shell passed not more than ten feet above their heads.

Close on the heels of the skirmishers came the 15th Maine, who halted at a fence about fifty yards from the 15th Alabama. The Fighting Fifteenth loaded and fired on their knees, raising themselves just high enough to fire from their entrenchments. The 15th Maine lost heavily and made several attempts to cross the fence, but each time would retreat to the woods, from which they would return to the vicinity of the fence for what little cover it could provide. The fighting on the left was "raging with great fury," and Hood's Brigade of Texans had returned to assist in the defense. Ammunition for the Alabamians began to run low and details were ordered to the ordnance train.

Luckily, the fire had slackened from the enemy troops as they had retreated back to the woods again. The 15th Alabama was lying down, conserving their ammunition, when General D.H. Hill rode up demanding, "What regiment is lying here?" Captain Feagin replied, "The 15th Alabama.... We are out of ammunition." Hill yelled at Feagin, "Haven't you got bayonets? Take rocks and go forward."[10] Feagin ignored the rash order because D.H. Hill was not in his chain of command, plus the order was ludicrous. General Hill pressed for a court-martial of Captain Feagin after the battle for failing to obey his orders. The officers sitting on the court-martial not only exonerated Captain Feagin but complimented him for his good judgment.

D.H. Hill was in command of Colquitt's Brigade of Georgians and ordered them forward, where they ran into Hooker's Division of Sumner's Corps. A stream of wounded Georgians came pouring through the 15th Alabama lines, followed shortly by the rest of the brigade, which was hotly pursued by Hooker's Division. The 15th Alabama held the line this time; perhaps the humiliation of Chantilly Farm was still fresh in their minds. The artillery to their rear unleashed a shower of grape and canister upon the advancing Federals, stopping them in their tracks. Union batteries on the other side of Antietam Creek replied with a thunderous counterfire on the Rebel batteries, and the 15th was caught in this deadly crossfire.

To remain in position was suicide. The men of the 15th, some with orders and some not, ran a gauntlet of exploding shells coming in and friendly fire going out until they reached the safety behind the Confederate artillery. Many of the men found General Colquitt trying to reform his Georgia Brigade and joined in with them. These refugees were being formed into a "stragglers' brigade"; the men refilled their cartridge boxes and fell in line behind a fence, with a cornfield in front. General Ewell was trying to rally the men, with hat in hand screaming at the top of his voice, "Men, for God's sake, fight. You must fight, you must fight." The commander of Company E credited General Ewell's action here with saving the day for the Confederates. Captain Edwards writes, "His presence and cheering words acted like magic. His men rallied a well nigh lost battle."[11]

Battle was raging all along the line. McLaws' and Walker's Divisions had arrived from Harpers Ferry and stabilized Jackson's Corps on the left. Longstreet's Corps on the right was hanging on by a thread. Colquitt ordered his command of refugees forward through the cornfield to help the left of Longstreet's line. This composite command met some Union troops advancing through the cornfield and dispatched them with one volley. The firing continued until the smoke became so thick that neither friend nor foe could be identified.

The arrival of A.P. Hill's Division had checked the progress of the enemy and they fell back. Colquitt remained in the cornfield but allowed the troops not in his brigade to break ranks and find their units. During the night the 15th Alabama was reforming near Dunker's Church. Men attempted, many in vain, to find their brothers, cousins, and messmates. When the unit reassembled as a regiment again they were rejoined with their division and placed in line ready for a renewal of the attack in the morning. McClellan did not attack the next day but asked for a truce at about 11:00 a.m., so removing the wounded and burying the dead became the duty of the day until late afternoon. Satisfied that McClellan was not going to attack and unable to supply his army bottled up as he was, Lee had no option but to recross the Potomac and return to Virginia during the night of September 18.

Although Lee's Army had inflicted enormous casualties upon the Army of the Potomac, Lee had lost a full one-fourth of his army at Sharpsburg. Casualties for the 15th Alabama were particularly high among the commanders. The regimental commander, Major Lowther, had proved time and again that he was going to report sick before any engagement. Captain Feagin was the only captain standing with the 15th, and he was severely wounded at Boteler's Ford during the withdrawal. Captain Oates of Company G was sick during the battle but returned to take command of the regiment on September 21.

During the last two engagements the 15th Alabama had broken and fled, and the lack of leadership was no doubt a major reason. The men had proven their mettle over the summer, but like the Federals, they were suffering from a serious lack of leadership of men of appropriate rank. Although Captain Feagin had performed admirably and was cited by the acting brigade commander in his official report: "Captain Feagin, commanding the Fifteenth Alabama regiment, behaved with a gallantry consistent with his high reputation for courage and that of the regiment he commanded."[12] At Sharpsburg, in particular, the 15th Alabama had a colonel as brigade commander, a captain as a regimental commander, and lieutenants commanding companies.

The campaign ended with Lee losing 13,609 men and inflicting 27,276 losses upon his adversary (including the captures of Harpers Ferry). Although McClellan didn't resume his attacks on September 18, Lee couldn't sustain his army at Sharpsburg and retreated back into Virginia unmolested. Of the 300 engaged in the 15th Alabama, 9 were killed and 75 wounded.[13]

Killed	Wounded	Missing
Company A		
	3LT Hugh Fields	
	PVT Andrew M. McKissack, severely, arm	
	PVT Jackson J. Wade	
Company B		
PVT Issac C. Owens	PVT John W. Hughs	*PVT William M. Callaway
	PVT James P. Lee, mortally	
	PVT Jack McDonald	
	PVT Thomas P. Thompson	
Company C		
	PVT Billy H. Hurt	*PVT James A. Slaton
		*PVT John F. Snipes
Company D		
SGT William C. Newton	PVT Jack V. Caraker	*PVT A.J. Coats
	PVT William A. Harrod	
	PVT William T. Helms	
	PVT A.J. Jeffcoat, right hand	
	PVT Thomas S. Moffette	
	PVT W.J. Robertson	
	PVT S. Lewis Spence	
Company E		
PVT Thomas M. Saunders	PVT Benjamin F. Bigbie	
PVT William N. Sellers	PVT Jesse M. Carmichael, right hand amputated	
	PVT Joseph W. Cotton	
	PVT Crawford G. Dillard	
	PVT William Dooling	
	1SGT Ambrose N. Edwards	
	PVT Young Edwards	
	PVT Barry W. Fleming	
	PVT William W. Jones	
	1CPL Thomas S. Mills, head	
	PVT Abram Powell	
	PVT Benjamin V. Walding, severely	
	PVT James M. Williams	
	PVT Harmon H. Windham	
	PVT Steven M. Woodham, severely, left foot	

Killed	Wounded	Missing
Company F		
PVT James I. Galloway	PVT Joe Crenshaw	PVT Thomas A. Collier
	PVT James B. Hutchinson	PVT Hershall V. Glenn
	PVT William D. McDowell, mortally	PVT James R. Norris
	PVT J. Rodgers	
	1LT DeKalb Williams	
	PVT Eliga Young, mortally	
Company G		
1SGT Josiah Balkom	1CPL George W. Brazil	PVT Robert Parker
	PVT Joseph J. Carr, mortally	
	PVT Augustus H. Dozier	
	1CPL Lewis Hicks, mortally, face	
	PVT Charles S. Kincey	
	5SGT Moses G. Mabin, mortally	
	4SGT James W. Pound	
	PVT Tolison N. Shepard	
	PVT Jacob Whitehead, severely, right arm	
	PVT Samuel E. Woodham	
Company H		
	5SGT John G. Archibald, severely	*PVT Green S. Eason
	3CPL Arch Carmichael, mortally	
	PVT William Crews	
	PVT Samuel H. Peacock	
	1LT William D. Wood	
Company I		
PVT Jasper Devane	2LT John E. Carter	PVT J. Hanchy
PVT John J. Underwood	PVT William P. Coombs	
	2CPL Sam H. Gardner	
	PVT William McCleod, left ear	
	PVT Thomas A. Walters	
Company K		
	PVT James H. Caison, thigh	PVT William E. Skinner
	PVT Stephen R. Grice, mortally	
	PVT Burrel V. McKilcane	
	PVT James F. Tate	
Company L		
PVT Elijah Smith	PVT Henry L. Perkins, right shoulder[14]	

*wounded and captured

Supplies were so sparse in Virginia, Lee had to spread his army all across northern Virginia so they might better sustain themselves during the upcoming winter. This proved to be very difficult, as he had to keep his factions within supporting distance in case the Army of the Potomac chose to invade again. On September 22, 1862, with Captain Oates in command, the regiment marched past Falling Waters and went into camp near Bunker's Hill, five miles northeast of Winchester. There was no town here, only a large spring and fertile ground. During this respite, the men turned in their anti-quated muskets and were issued new Enfield rifles from the captures at Winchester. Appropriate am-munition (.56 caliber minie ball) was also issued.[15] After a few days they were moved to Berryville and tore up the Manassas Gap Railroad. Major Lowther rejoined the regiment here.

Private Jesse Carmichael, Com-pany E. Post-war photograph. He practiced law in Newton, Ala-bama, was a state representative and state senator, probate judge, judge of the Third Circuit and edi-tor of *Southern Star* published in Ozark, Alabama (courtesy Mari-anne Myers).

The 15th Alabama spent twenty days of Octo-ber in this camp. Before leaving, the boys were or-dered to tear up the railroads around the area. Jackson's Corps made a leisurely march crossing the Blue Ridge in the direction of Culpeper Court House and on to Port Royal south of Fredericks-burg. The men had yet to build winter quarters, and winter moved into Virginia early that year.

Fredericksburg

> "At Fredericksburg some of the boys swapped their bad shoes for good ones, they traded with the dead Yankees; many also got good overcoats. I had a good one or I should have stripped one off of a Yankee."[16]—4th Cor-poral Randolph C. Smedley, Company I, Quitman Guards, 15th Alabama Infantry Regiment

Exasperated with McClellan's reluctance to fight and Lee's unmolested retreat from Sharpsburg, Lincoln relieved McClellan of command for the last time. Ambrose Burnside (who, because of his facial hair, inspired the term "sideburns") was selected to command the Army of the Potomac. Burnside, who was not going to be fired because of inactivity, took his army of 121,402 men and 312 pieces of artillery out of their comfortable winter quarters and put them in motion, moving them south on November 15. Furthermore, he had 27,724 more men and 97 guns twenty miles to the north. With the Conscription Law in full effect, Lee's numbers had swelled to 78,511 men supported by 275 guns.[17]

Major Lowther had reported in as sick, so the chilled Alabamians knew battle was imminent. When the orders came to cook three days' rations and get ready to move on December 10, any doubt was removed.

Lee guessed correctly that Burnside was going to assault his forces in the vicinity of Fredericksburg. Burnside had stationed his powerful artillery on Stafford Heights across the Rappahannock from the city of Fredericksburg. Burnside would move his forces across a pontoon into Fredericksburg under this artillery umbrella from Stafford Heights. Lee entrenched his troops in excellent defensive terrain out of range of Burnside's artillery and awaited the impending attack. Looking at the ground the Union army must cross, Longstreet told Lee, "General, we cover that ground now so well that we comb it as with a fine-tooth comb. A chicken could not live on that field when we open on it."[18]

Jackson spent the day and night of December 12 forming his line on the right of Longstreet, who was already strongly posted on and around Marye's Heights. A.P. Hill's Division was tied in with Longstreet to Hamilton's Crossing on the railroad. General Early, who was commanding Ewell's Division and Jackson's (old) Division, composed a second line, and D.H. Hill's Division was held in reserve. Stuart's Cavalry covered Jackson's right, completing the Confederate dispositions. A heavy fog masked the forming of the Union Army on the morning of December 13, but 5th Sergeant Randolph Smedley and the rest of the men of the 15th Alabama could hear the Union officers shouting commands preparing to advance, thus creating an eerie scene for the men. One private in the 15th Alabama wrote, "All was feverish with expectation."[19]

Between 9:00 and 10:00 a.m. the sun burned off the fog and the whole Union Army was in view, densely packed together for assault. When the advance came close enough for the artillery, more than 100 pieces of Confederate cannon unleashed their shot among the packed formations. As the brave men in blue advanced closer, they were introduced to deadly grapeshot and canister. The men moved on and were subjected to the rifle fire from Longstreet's infantry. The Army of the Potomac assaulted Longstreet's line five times that day, all with the same results. While watching this butchery from Marye's Heights, Lee made his famous quote: "It is well that war is so terrible—otherwise we would grow too fond of it."[20]

After each retreat, the shoeless Confederates, many without overcoats or blankets to protect them from the northern Virginia winter, began to taunt their opponents, "Come on, blue belly! Bring them boots and blankets! Bring 'em hyar!" While these assaults were going on, Burnside tried to extend his left beyond Jackson's right for an assault on Jackson's front and right flank. Stuart's cavalry, particularly Alabamian Major John Pelham from Alabama, made excellent work with Stuart's Horse Artillery and prevented this flank maneuver. Union Generals Sumner and Hooker had failed to even reach Longstreet's lines. It was now up to Franklin's two corps to overrun Jackson's Corps.[21]

Trimble's Brigade was commanded by Colonel R.F. Hoke of North Carolina and was positioned behind General Maxey Gregg's Brigade of South Carolinians. Captain Oates was in command of the 15th Alabama for the first time in battle. The South Carolinians began to fall back and Gregg was killed trying to rally them. Hoke's

Brigade was on the right of Early's defensive line on Prospect Hill and the 15th was to the extreme left of Hoke's line. As the South Carolinians streamed through the 15th Alabama lines, the Alabama boys had to wonder if the regiment would break and run as they had at Chantilly under similar circumstances, but they didn't. As they were ordered to advance, 4th Corporal Smedley and the rest of the 15th calmly obeyed; they fixed bayonets and held their fire until the retreating Confederates had cleared their lines. When the South Carolinians had cleared their front, the 15th unleashed a volley into the packed Union lines, raised the rebel yell, and charged into the Yankees with "their bayonets lowered and murder in their eyes."[22]

The brigade "swept everything before it in handsome style," continuing the charge for about a quarter of a mile down the hill and into a railway cut where hundreds of Union soldiers were frantically waving white handkerchiefs. The charge was so inspiring that units to the right and left joined in the assault and completely routed the Union left. The 15th Alabama charge continued to a ditch where more Yankees were found cowering in fear. Suddenly, the brigade found itself within range of the powerful Union artillery on Stafford Heights, which opened a "killing fire." Hoke, realizing this, ordered the brigade back to the railway cut, but the artillery had already opened up on them. Hoke's horse was so frightened by the intense fire that the horse threw him from the saddle with his foot stuck in the stirrup, dragging him "some distance" before being stopped.

After Colonel Hoke recovered his senses he ordered the Alabamians to fall back from the protection of the railway cut to a small ditch to their rear barely ten yards in front of the six-gun Jeff Davis Battery from Alabama. The battery was pouring deadly fire into the retreating Yankees and the Union siege guns from Stafford Heights were trying to silence them. Oates said, "The position of the Fifteenth [was] as perilous and disagreeable as well could be."[23] A sergeant in Company I later wrote home, "[T]here was not even a sprig to shelter us from the ball, grape, and canister which was being poured into our ranks from the enemy's batteries."[24] Jack Champion had his foot broken by grape shot.[25] Finally, dark descended and the hellish artillery fire ceased.

Shortly after dark Jackson sent out the order to remove all accouterments, except canteens and cartridge boxes, fix bayonets, and move forward. The men's thoughts may have drifted to their only night fighting experience at Second Manassas and Hazel River, prompting dread at what lay before them. The men were halted once again at the railway cut, where they would have preferred to stay during the artillery duel. The dead and wounded Yankees lay all around them and litter details were organized to take the wounded to the rear. Skirmishers were sent forward and the rest of the men scavenged Union bodies for shoes, blankets, and overcoats to help deal with the cold December night. The skirmishers heard the horrible groans of the wounded Yankees of the 13th Pennsylvania Reserves to their front, many slowing freezing to death.

During the night of December 13, the 15th Alabama was relieved of its position and marched about two hundred yards to the rear. It was after midnight and the boys were not allowed to build fires because of the fear of the Union cannon. The men were left to simply huddle together and try to sleep in the freezing damp weather. On this night, the Alabama farm boys looked into the skies and observed their first and only "aurora borealis, seldom visible this far south and never before seen by most of the Confederates, who watched with amazement."[26] One Southerner wrote "that the heavens were hanging out banners and streamers and setting off fireworks in honor of our great victory."[27]

The 15th was awakened the next morning and put in line to await more attacks. The night of December 14 was particularly brutal: they were pelted with sleet and snow all night, but the men were at least allowed to build fires for the first time in 40 hours. December 15 also passed without a resumption of attacks. The shattered remnants of the Army of the Potomac used the cover of darkness during the night of December 16 to recross the Rappahannock.

When the slaughter was finished, the Army of Northern Virginia had won its most lopsided victory yet. The Federals had lost 12,653, the Confederates a third less with 4,201. In addition, the Confederates gleaned 11,000 stands of small arms from the field.[28] The 15th Infantry Regiment went in with about 300 men and suffered one killed and 34 wounded.[29]

Killed	Wounded	Missing
Company A		
	PVT James B. Hill	
	PVT Jackson J. Wade	
Company B		
	PVT Joseph T. Beard	
	PVT Alfred G. Denham	
	PVT Henry H. Hodges	
	PVT Walter C. Jackson	
	PVT Andrew J. Lane, left leg	
	PVT A.P. McMillan	
	PVT George W. Pope	
	PVT Whitson Pugh	
Company C		
	PVT Samuel J. Murdock, mortally	
	PVT Green B. Vinson	
Company D		
	PVT George W. Bailey, thumb	
	PVT Andrew J. Blount	
	PVT John W. Hudgins	
	PVT W.J. Robertson	
Company E		
	PVT Joseph J. Dean	
	1SGT Ambrose N. Edwards	
	PVT Young Edwards	
	PVT James Latimer	
	PVT John L. Morrell	
	PVT Frank J. Saunders, finger	

Killed	Wounded	Missing
	PVT Warren W. Vance	
	PVT James M. Williams	

Company F

	PVT William W. Carter, mortally	
	PVT David G. Ray	

Company G

	PVT Carter Askew, mortally	
	PVT James Griffin, mortally	
	PVT Henry B. Johnson, mortally	
	1CPL Daniel McClellan	
	PVT William Phillips, hand	
	PVT William Trimmer	
	PVT Samuel E. Woodham	

Company H

PVT Necy Benton	PVT Alvin Holmes	
	PVT Thomas Jefferson	
	PVT Henry J. Murphy	
	PVT Frank M. Rice	
	2LT David H. Thomas	

Company K

	PVT James M. Brown, left hand	
	PVT Zennimon Garner	
	PVT Evan G. Grice, left knee	
	PVT John Nelson	
	PVT Andrew J. Roberts	
	PVT James A. Spurlock	

Company L

	PVT Thomas R. Collins	
	PVT W.G. Morgan	
	PVT John L. Newton[30]	

Once the sun burned off the fog the next morning, Private Houghton could see "some hundreds of dead lying on the frozen ground and nearly all had been stripped of clothing taken by our men to ward off the cold." Colonel Hoke wrote, "I cannot say too much in praise of the officers and men under my command. All did their duty nobly and went into the fight with a spirit of determination."[31]

These men were certainly entitled to finally take a rest. Since April they had defeated seven different Union generals in thirteen engagements, large and small. They had inflicted upon the enemy 71,447 killed and wounded, and had captured 34,478 prisoners, 162 pieces of artillery, and 85,000 small arms.[32] The 15th Alabama Foot Cavalry had marched all over north, west, central, and east Virginia from Manassas to the Shenandoah to the Peninsula back to Manassas into Maryland to Harpers Ferry back into Maryland and then to Fredericksburg. It is of little wonder that so many lacked shoes. Few armies in the history of warfare have accomplished so much in a span of nine months.

Brigadier General Evander Law, Commander, Law's Brigade (Library of Congress).

Fredericksburg strengthened the confidence of the men of the 15th Alabama who had become tried and true veterans. When Confederates ran through their lines at Chantilly, the 15th broke and ran with them, but at Fredericksburg they held steady. When they were caught in an artillery cross-fire at Sharpsburg, they broke and ran, but they held firm at Fredericksburg. Diseases had about run their course throughout the regiment, which now had a veteran core that could be counted on for the rest of the war.

Jackson moved his corps down the river about twelve miles, within three miles of Port Royal, and finally went into winter quarters. After staking out their campsite, the men began gathering logs and planks to build their crude huts for the winter. The huts couldn't be built any sooner than needed, for January brought four to five inches of snow on the ground for most of the month. During the winter of 1863, the Confederate Congress passed a new law requiring that brigades be made up of regiments from the same states. The 15th Alabama was transferred into a brigade commanded by Brigadier General Evander M. Law, whose brigade now consisted of the 4th, 15th, 44th, 47th, and 48th Alabama regiments.

The Alabama Brigade was placed in Major General John Bell Hood's division in Longstreet's First Army Corps. The Fighting Fifteenth was saddened to leave Trimble's old Brigade, and particularly Jackson's Corps. The men had a great attachment to "Stonewall," who had led them to so many victories and no defeats.

To make matters worse the men had to leave their comfortable winter quarters they had constructed. The 15th Alabama was moved to Marye's Heights, where they were relieved to find equally comfortable quarters constructed by Longstreet's Corps.

Suffolk

> *"Captain, they have killed my old mess mate and best friend and I am now ready to fight until they kill me or I kill some of them."*[33]—Private Jesse Flowers, Company E, Dale County Beauregards, 15th Alabama Infantry Regiment

In February 1863, the powers that be in Richmond were concerned about another attempt to take Richmond, this time via the sea. Lee sent Longstreet with two of his divisions, Pickett's and Hood's, to move closer to Richmond. This move was satisfactory with Lee, as it would send about one third of his army to another supply source further south. In early February, the two divisions were ordered to prepare two days of rations and get ready to move at a moment's warning. Oates was still in command of the 15th Alabama and formed them up to march with their new brigade and division.

Snow began to fall when the order arrived to prepare to march, and temperatures plummeted during the night of February 16. The snowfall continued throughout the next day, coming down so heavily at times that it was difficult to see more than a hundred yards. To make matters worse, a cold rain fell during the third day's march, turning the road into a knee-deep combination of slush and mud. This was the most severe march the Alabamians had made to date, for the regiment, like most Confederate units, was ill-equipped for marching in such weather. They had left with two days' rations, which were gone. Another day's march in knee-deep snow and mud was to be endured before food was made available. Weary men were forced to pile up brush and logs for crude beds to keep from sleeping on the ground.[34]

The boys marched through Richmond on Saturday, February 21, and set up camp about three miles south of the city, on the Petersburg Road. General Longstreet set up his headquarters in Petersburg. The men were not in good spirits. They were forced to leave their comfortable winter quarters around Fredericksburg, force marched in the snow and rain, and found themselves south of Richmond, where they had to sleep on the cold, wet ground. The men's mood didn't get any better when they were ordered to draw and cook two days' rations and get ready to move yet again on March 18. Captain Oates said this was "the worst marching I ever saw during the war."[35] It sleeted and rained just enough to make slush of the heavy snow, and all the while the men were pelted by a powerful cold wind coming out of the north. The men were asked to retrace their steps toward Richmond, which all soldiers hate to do, even in the best weather. Oates said one soldier got so miserable as to shoot off one of his toes to get out of the march. The reason for this countermarch was never made known to the soldiers. The regiment marched 24 miles through this torrent. The 15th had to sleep in the snow that night without their tents. The exhausted boys were allowed to rest on March 19 and again passed through Richmond to encamp south of the city. Friday night was the third consecutive night they slept in the snow.[36]

During March, Hood ordered the division onto a train, and they again passed through Richmond towards Petersburg. After detraining, the boys marched ten or twelve miles and encamped near the railroad so they could retrain quickly, if need be, and reinforce Lee. The 15th Alabama spent the month of March in this camp.

On April 1, the 15th Alabama was ordered to Suffolk. The two divisions were marched through the streets of Petersburg and took the Jerusalem Plank Road. The boys spent three or four days on this march towards Suffolk. There were 17,000 Federals defending eight forts and fourteen miles of entrenchments there.[37] Longstreet's mission was to bottle up the Union garrison in their fortifications while his commissary agents scoured the countryside for supplies for Lee's Army. The Confederates drove the Yankees into their fortifications and built their own fortifications parallel to the Union lines. The two divisions spent the rest of April sharpshooting with the Suffolk garrison. "Sharpshooting was the order of the day on through the month of April,"[38] said one private. Life on this line was miserable: the men were not allowed to build fires and were subjected to Federal artillery from Suffolk, as well as gunboats on the Nansemond River. As one gunboat opened fire on April 15, Private Eugene B. Woodham of Company C threw himself to the ground when a shell landed close in front of him and exploded under him, blowing him to pieces.[39]

Captain Oates set up a skirmish line to cover his withdrawal on May 3. While serving on the skirmish line, James Willis of Company B was mortally wounded by a minie ball through the abdomen.[40] Second Corporal Henry Cameron of Company E was also killed. His best friend, Jesse Martin of Westville, carried Henry's body to the rear and carefully placed him on the ground. He screamed at his company commander, "Captain, they have killed my old mess mate and best friend and I am now ready to fight until they kill me or I kill some of them."[41]

Colonel Treutlen resigned his commission, effective April 28, 1863, citing health reasons. Lowther was entitled to be colonel by right of seniority, but he had been absent since early December of the previous year. Oates had been in command thus far during 1863. Lowther had sent several letters requesting discharge on the grounds of disability but all were ignored by the War Department. Brigadier General Law unilaterally accepted one of them and dropped Lowther from the rolls. Captain Feagin was next in seniority but elected to wave his claim in favor of Oates. Both were summoned before an examining board. Oates was for colonel and Feagin for lieutenant colonel. Both were found competent and Law submitted an application for Oates's and Feagin's appointments to the War Department.[42]

During demonstrations in front of the Union lines, the 15th Alabama suffered 4 killed and 18 wounded.[43] Lieutenant Noah B. Feagin of Company B received his second of four wounds suffered during the war.[44] However, the foraging expeditions "succeeded in sending long trains of wagons heavily loaded with hams and bacon, side meat, salted fish, and flour and cornmeal, all of which were plenteous in the region."[45]

Killed	Wounded	Missing
Company B		
PVT Frank B. Callaway	3LT Noah B. Feagin	
PVT James R. Willis	PVT Neal A. McCaskill, mortally	
Company C		
PVT Eugene B. Woodham		
Company E		
PVT Henry A. Cameron	PVT Jack Jernigan	
Company H		
	PVT Thomas J. Brooks, severely	
Company K		
		PVT Owen Cherry, deserted[46]

Seeing movement by yet another new Union commander, "Fighting Joe" Hooker, Lee ordered Longstreet to rejoin him and Jackson in the vicinity of Fredericksburg on April 30, 1863. Longstreet's commissary wagons were still in the countryside, some as far south as North Carolina, and he would need a day or two to recall them all. The Federals in Suffolk were aware of the coming battle in northern Virginia and launched demonstrations upon Longstreet's forces on May 2 to prevent his movement north. The assaults of these untried garrison troops were easily repulsed and Longstreet's Corps abandoned their positions on the night of May 2. The 15th Alabama reached Ivor Station at about 1:00 p.m. on May 3 after a tiring march through the deep sand prominent in this part of Virginia. Straggling was severe and men became sick and fainted during this march. At Ivor Station the men boarded the cars for Petersburg. William C. "Billy" Jordan was one of the stragglers but caught up to the trains as they were leaving. When he discovered the car Company B had boarded, Jordan made a dash for his comrades as the train pulled out and managed to board the car amid the cheers of his comrades.[47] The trains were on their way back to the Army of Northern Virginia. The regiment passed through Richmond on May 8 and continued by train to Culpeper, and then to camps near Raccoon Ford on the Rapidan River, arriving there May 14. The regiment remained there until June 3.[48]

The Battle of Chancellorsville was fought on May 2 and 3, 1863. May 3 proved to be the second bloodiest day of the war. Lee again defeated the Army of the Potomac, which had more than twice the soldiers he had, in probably his most magnificent victory of the war. On the march from Suffolk the regiment learned of the mortal wounding of "Stonewall" Jackson, the commander they loved so much, at Chancellorsville. They had never lost a battle under his command.

After arriving in the vicinity of Fredericksburg, the regiment encamped in a grove of chestnut trees and a clover pasture about half a mile in the rear of the Raccoon Ford on the Rapidan River. Their mission was to picket the river crossing here. The men of the 15th enjoyed this campsite very much. No Union troops were in the area, and the men enjoyed fishing in the Rapidan and the warm days and cool nights of May. While at this camp, Oates was promoted to full colonel, effective April 28, 1863, and officially given command of the 15th Alabama Infantry. However, the Confederate Congress never approved this promotion; they didn't deny it, they just didn't act on it.

Private William C. Jordan, Company B (courtesy Mark Akerman).

Foraging

"The rations given us were often insufficient to appease hunger, and consequently there was more or less foraging to supplement the deficiency."[49]— Mitchell B. Houghton, Company G, Henry Pioneers, 15th Alabama Infantry Regiment

Foraging occurred when men would leave camp, or even a march, to go into the countryside and find food on their own. Small groups of men or individuals would scour the countryside for any supplement to their meager rations. Technically, foraging was not allowed in the Army of Northern Virginia, but most officers turned a blind eye because they knew foraging was necessary to supplement the often inadequate rations issued by the Confederate Commissary. Some of most interesting stories of the 15th Alabama come from their exertions in foraging.

A favorite story occurred during the Gettysburg Campaign, as told by Captain William Edwards of Company E, Dale County Beauregards. General Lee had given orders that no private property was to be disturbed. The men had been encamped in an oak orchard with "a bunch of fine hogs browsing for acorns all day." The men had been watching this and salivating at the thought of eating some Yankee pork. Later that evening, word came down to Captain Edwards that the men could kill one hog for supper. Captain Edwards called the company together and told them they could kill one hog, so make it the largest of the bunch. Before he could stop them they had killed three hogs and had one so near death that Captain Edwards let them finish killing the fourth one. While this hog killing was going on, a little man named Silas Peters came running out of the woods with Samuel Hogg (Oates described him as a big, overgrown man) in hot pursuit. Peters was screaming, "Help me, Captain, help me, Captain!" Captain Edwards finally stopped the two and inquired what was happening. Hogg said that Peters had hit him in the leg with a rock and had almost broken it. Peters replied, "Captain, you told us to kill the biggest hog and he was the biggest one I saw."[50] The camp erupted in laughter and even Sergeant Hogg was laughing as he limped off to his tent.

Private Mitchell Houghton of Company I, Quitman Guards, wrote of two men who went to a man's house where all they wanted was to raid his beehives for honey. However, the hives were protected by a "fierce dog." Houghton wrote, "By some means they made friends" with the dog and made off with two stands full of honey. The owner of the beehives protested to the commanding officer the next day, saying that he left the dog to protect his property. The commander asked him why the dog failed to do his duty, and the man replied, "The scoundrels stole the dog too."[51]

While the troops were in Maryland, probably during the Sharpsburg Campaign, the locals had hidden their food and valuables. The men were unsupplied for days so they would take their ramrods and probe into the gardens and surrounding areas of the house and discover "cans of preserves, apple butter, and other things buried against the coming of such visitors."[52]

Edwards relates another story of when he was company commander of the Beauregards. One of his soldiers, Private James Latimer, showed up at roll call in the morning with a broken arm. After inquiring as to what happened, Captain Edwards was told that Latimer and another soldier, known only as "Uncle Dave," had left after midnight to get some water for cooking. Captain Edwards didn't pursue the matter further, although he found it strange that men would be cooking in the middle of the night. He later found out that Latimer and Uncle Dave had left camp that night to steal apples from a nearby orchard. Latimer climbed a tree to get apples but grabbed a hornets' nest instead. In his haste to get out of the tree, a limb gave way and Latimer fell to the ground, breaking his arm.[53]

Oates relates a favorite story of 2nd Sergeant William Holley of Company G, Henry Pioneers. The regiment had marched by a grocery store and camped about a half a mile from the store. Holley collected canteens from the men, returned to the store, and asked to buy some liquor. The store owner refused, saying he didn't have any liquor, although Holley saw a barrel inside the store. Holley returned later that night with an auger and a bucket he had stolen from a woodshop, crawled under the store, and bored a hole through the floor and into the barrel of whiskey. He filled the bucket and the canteens and returned to camp. Holley was "merry for two or three days," and none of the officers knew where he had gotten the whiskey.[54]

Foraging could turn out to be a hazardous experience. Private T.P. Croswell of Company L, Pike Sharpshooters, died from wounds he received from a citizen while stealing beegums.[55] His death was a little over two months after his enlistment. Oates tells of one veteran who was pelted with rocks until he fled from a woman's cherry tree.[56]

Soldiers often came up with ingenious excuses if caught with the fruits of their foraging. If a soldier was caught with a warm piece of pork he might say that the hog attacked him and he had to kill the hog for his own protection. Soldiers discovered that a piece of corn on a fishhook placed on a line could be used to lure a chicken to follow the soldier back to camp. The soldier didn't steal the chicken, but the chicken simply followed the soldier to the camp. Milk would be stolen from suffering, neglected cows that needed to be relieved of their milk for their own comfort and safety.[57]

The thirteen-year-old drummer for Company K, Patrick Brannon, was upset when he heard that the stores captured at the first investment of Harpers Ferry would be sent to Richmond. He thought it fairer that the captures be distributed among those who had done the capturing. He left his unit and proceeded to gather all the spoils he could carry. He was captured by Confederate guards, and since he was so far away from his unit, he was arrested as a deserter. After hearing of his arrest, an officer from the 15th Alabama arrived to absolve him and return him to his unit. Pat took off again to gather the just stores for his company and was again arrested. Pat bribed his captor with a full Union haversack and continued his confiscations. He was again arrested and provided his guard with another loaded haversack. After gathering all he could carry, young Pat returned to Company K to distribute the contraband to his grateful company.[58]

FIVE

Gettysburg

"My dead and wounded were nearly as great in number as those still on duty. They literally covered the ground. The blood stood in puddles in some places on the rocks; the ground was soaked with the blood of as brave men as ever fell on the red field of battle."[1]—Lt. Colonel William C. Oates, Commander, 15th Alabama Infantry Regiment

Reorganization and Movement

"The seat of war will be moved from Va. to this country at least for a while. We are here and the Yankees can't run us away I don't think. Our army is in good fighting condition, and large enough to hold its own against almost any force of Yankees."[2]—Dr. A.E. McGarity, Surgeon, 15th Alabama Infantry Regiment

With the death of Jackson, Lee reorganized his army yet again on May 30, into three corps, promoting Generals Ewell and A.P. Hill to corps command. The 15th Alabama was unaffected and remained in Law's Brigade, Hood's Division, Longstreet's I Corps.

On June 5, Hood's Division watched from atop a railroad embankment as Major General J.E.B. Stuart, forever the showman, put his horsemen, stretching out three miles, on review at Brandy Station. The men watched with amazement the 10,000 horsemen. "It was a beautiful sight,"[3] recalled Oates. A private from Newton recalled, "The [cavalry] in columns of fours marched by. The horses were in good trim and the men in high spirits. The procession seemed endless. Then came battery after battery of artillery and the gray hosts of the infantry. These men were all tried veterans inspired with a spirit of invincible determination and the bearing of heroes."[4]

Politicians and other civilians from the Richmond area arrived in droves to watch the military review. Among those in attendance was Thomas W. Watts from Alabama, the Confederate attorney general. The attorney general "held in his hand a fine pocketknife, with which he had been whittling," and a private in the 15th Alabama said: "Mr. Attorney, I wish that you would give me that knife." With those words the bighearted Alabamian stepped forward and handed it to him, which brought forth a hearty cheer from the men."[5]

Since Richmond was not being threatened, General Lee asked for and received permission to head north again and try to give northern Virginia an unmolested growing season and harvest. Union General Grant had a stranglehold on Vicksburg, Mississippi, and not wanting to lose troops for Vicksburg's defense, Lee suggested that another invasion of the North might just draw Federal troops from the siege of Vicksburg. In addition, Lee could feed his army off the resources on Union soil. There was still hope that a major victory in Union territory might reopen the possibility of European recognition, or at least influence the Northern populace to sue for peace.

Lee used the Shenandoah as his highway to the North with the Blue Ridge Mountains protecting his right flank. Lee had the strongest army he would ever command: 75,000 men, 7 brigades of cavalry, and 287 guns. The supply wagon trains alone were 17 miles long.[6] The Order of March was Ewell's II Corps followed by Hill's III Corps, and Longstreet's I Corps bringing up the rear. The 15th Alabama once again crossed the Potomac on June 23. Oates wrote, "The Fifteenth Alabama had 600 men in ranks

Lieutenant General James E.B. Stuart, Cavalry Commander, Army of Northern Virginia (Library of Congress).

and 42 officers when we started on that march, and during its progress lost four men by desertion and over fifty by heat and sickness."[7] He also added that the 15th Alabama was "the strongest and finest regiment in Hood's Division."[8]

Major Lowther returned to the 15th Alabama about the first of June 1863, and much to his surprise and displeasure, Oates was the new colonel and Isaac Feagin the lieutenant colonel. Lowther felt Law had ignored military procedure governing seniority. Lowther had not waived his right to the command and therefore, in his opinion, Law had denied him the office of colonel of the 15th Alabama. Lowther submitted a protest through Law to the War Department, and in the meantime refused to serve under Oates.[9]

On June 10, General Ewell's Corps (in the lead) stormed Winchester and at the cost of 270 men captured 4,000 prisoners, 25 cannon, 250 wagons, 400 horses, 3,000 head of cattle, and 5,000 barrels of flour.[10] The rest of the Union troops in the Shenandoah sought refuge in Maryland and continued in the direction of Washington.

On June 15, 1863, Captain Brainard, 1st Lieutenant John Oates, and 2nd Lieutenant Barnett Cody of Company G, Henry Pioneers, got their company up and formed into column to fall in line with the rest of Longstreet's Corps. They marched through the streets of Culpeper toward the Blue Ridge Mountains. The June days were hot, marching was slow, and stragglers were many. On June 17, Hood's Division only marched fifteen miles.

The following day, the 15th Alabama crossed the Shenandoah and suffered from a cold rain that night at camp near Snicker's Ferry. As Major General Hood was supervising the crossing, Private William "Pike" Youngblood[11] of Company I approached the general sitting on his horse and requested permission to take off his clothes before wading the river. Major General Hood replied in the negative, stating there was no time. William dutifully entered the river, which he said was "biting cold," but escaped to a rock projecting itself out of the water. He reentered the river only after ordered to do so.[12] On June 20, they were ordered to retrace their steps and cross the Shenandoah River yet again. That night the rain finally stopped and the men were allowed to cook rations for the first time in many days.[13]

During the early morning of June 26, rain was falling again as Law's Brigade took up the march and reached the swollen Potomac at Williamsport around 8:00 a.m. The 15th crossed the Potomac here while military bands on hand were playing "Dixie" and everyone was in high spirits. Private Mitchell Houghton wrote of the crossing as "the grandest display I ever witnessed."[14] General Hood wrote in his memoirs, "Never before, or since, have I witnessed such intense enthusiasm as that which prevailed throughout the entire Confederate Army."[15] The 15th Alabama picked up the march and crossed this little sliver of Maryland and into Pennsylvania the evening of June 26. Many of the men bragged that they had eaten breakfast in Virginia, dinner in Maryland, and supper in Pennsylvania. That night Law's Brigade encamped south of Greencastle, Pennsylvania.

Lieutenant Colonel Arthur J.L. Fremantle, a British military observer following Lee's Army, wrote of these soldiers: "The Confederate has no ambition to imitate the regular soldier at all; he looks the genuine rebel; but in spite of his bare feet, his ragged clothes, his old rug, and tooth-brush stuck like a rose in his button-hole, he has a sort of devil-may-care, reckless, self-confident look, which is decidedly taking."[16]

The Alabamians arrived at Chambersburg, Pennsylvania, around noon on June 27; Law's Brigade passed through the town and set up camp in some shady woods about two miles outside of town. For the next two days, the 15th remained in camp except when roaming the countryside looking for food, clothes, etc. Although Lee had once again given orders that no private property was to be disturbed, the men of the 15th Alabama were helping themselves to the Pennsylvania countryside. The officers of the 15th busied themselves trying to prevent the men from foraging, but the land just offered too much fresh grain, apple butter, bread, milk, and fat livestock for the men to control themselves.

On June 30, Law's Brigade received orders to march east through Fayetteville and to New Guilford. The brigade arrived there on the morning of July 1 and set up camp in an oak grove. The commanders had had enough of trying to control the men and turned a blind eye to the foraging.

This new freedom was interrupted by the distant rumble of artillery to the east. The veteran ears of the 15th knew that a battle was looming in their near future. Around nightfall, orders came for Law's Brigade to rejoin Hood's Division. Colonel Oates passed the word to Captain Brainard and his other company commanders to cook three days' rations and be ready to march at 3:00 a.m.[17]

Little Round Top

When all was ready, Law's Brigade stepped out smartly at about 4:00 a.m. on July 2, 1863. The first day of the Battle of Gettysburg had been fought the day before with elements of A.P. Hill's III Corps advancing to the little town of Gettysburg for the purpose of getting shoes for the men in the town. Hill's Corps, with the help of Ewell's II Corps, had pushed back Union cavalry and I and XII Corps through the town. However, the two Confederate corps failed to take the high ground south of town. Longstreet's I Corps was far from the battlefield and strung out in a long line of march. Lee sent word to Longstreet to close up quickly.

From New Guilford, the 15th Alabama marched through Fayetteville, over the South Mountain, and through the villages of Cashtown and McKnightsville. As the men approached the battlefield their senses became engorged with the sights, smells, and sounds of battle. The rising sun exposed the Confederate field hospitals where the wounded were being treated. The moans of wounded and screams of amputees likely pierced the hearts of the men of the 15th Alabama as they were about to enter battle. The smell of gunpowder hung low with the morning mist.

Between noon and 2:00 p.m., Law's Brigade reached Herr's Ridge, about a mile west of Gettysburg. Longstreet later credited the brigade commander, "Law completed his march of twenty-eight miles in eleven hours, the best marching done in either army, to reach the field of Gettysburg."[18] This had been a forced march and the canteens had long been emptied. The men of the 15th Alabama were already tired, hungry, and thirsty and had yet to fire a shot. Water in this part of the battlefield was in short supply; however, the men were given a short rest on Herr's Ridge, while Lee and Longstreet conferred on where to place Hood's Division.

Confusion within Longstreet's staff caused needless marching and counter-marching for the already tired soldiers. The July sun was hot when the men finally arrived on Seminary Ridge sometime before 4:00 p.m. Law's Brigade was formed in line along Warfield Ridge with the 15th Alabama in the center, the 44th and 48th Alabama Regiments on their right, and the 47th and 4th Alabama Regiments on their left. Benning's Georgia Brigade was on the left of Law's, and Robertson's Texan Brigade was to the left of Benning. The Alabamians got another short rest as Longstreet and Hood argued over deployment of Hood's Division. Hood wanted to swing south around the two Round Tops into the Union rear, where he had received reports the Union supply trains were parked. Longstreet finally ended the argument and ordered Hood to send his division forward in compliance with Lee's directive.

As the soldiers of the 15th Alabama were hunkered down awaiting orders, Union artillery opened up on them. One soldier wrote: "The heart is heavy; the blood feels as if it was congealed; the breath comes short and quick."[19] The men began shedding their blankets and other excess baggage.

Officers screamed out the order to advance over the sounds of the incoming artillery. The Alabama Brigade had to cross a wheat field as the Union artillery from Devil's Den changed from artillery shot to canister and grape shot. As this artillery fire was tearing into the ranks of the Confederates, the men had to cross creeks, extricate themselves from mud, and still maintain alignment with the rest of the brigade. Lt. Colonel Isaac Feagin went down with a leg wound which led to amputation. Privates Alsop Kennedy, Company B, and William Trimble, Company G, fell dead. Private G.E. Spencer of Company D took a severe wound from a shell fragment. He would later be declared permanently disabled and discharged.[20]

Under orders from Law, the 44th and 48th Alabama Regiments crossed the 15th Alabama's rear and became intermingled with Robertson's Texas Brigade. This left the 15th Alabama as the far right regiment on the entire Confederate army line. To make matters worse, the 15th Alabama started to receive fire from their front from the green-uniformed 2nd U.S. Sharpshooters, or Berdan's Sharpshooters. Brigade skirmishers had failed to clear them and now Oates had another mission. He sent Captain Shaaff and Company A to scatter the Sharpshooters and remove this nuisance. These men would miss most of the upcoming fight.

No student on the Battle of Gettysburg can truly understand what happened that day without reading Lt. Colonel Oates's account of the battle on Little Round Top. The 15th Alabama contested the most valuable piece of terrain in the largest battle ever fought in the Western Hemisphere.

The men had passed a well several hundred yards to the rear. Oates ordered that two men from each company were to gather up the canteens to find this well and refill them with water. Unable to find the regiment upon their return, the 22 men stumbled into the Sharpshooters and were captured along with the much-needed water.[21]

After suffering many casualties, the remaining 500 members of the regiment "continued their uphill charge, scrambling hand over hand around and across huge boulders and through heavy underbrush, to call a halt at last on the lofty summit [of Round Top], panting for breath and wishing fervently that they had not sent their canteens off to be filled just before they received orders to advance."[22] At this point the 15th Alabama found themselves standing on the most prominent piece of terrain on the entire battlefield. From this location, the Alabamians could look out over the entire Union line and even the town of Gettysburg.

While the men of the 15th Alabama were catching their breath, Oates received orders to descend this prominence and occupy Little Round Top. "Oates protested briefly, to no avail, then got his parched and weary men to their feet; feet that had already covered no less than thirty miles of road and mountainside since 3 o'clock that morning."[23] While ascending to his new objective, the regiment was joined by two more Alabama and two Texas regiments, all from Hood's Division. Unfortunately for the Confederates, eight Union regiments had started ascending the other side of Little Round Top fifteen minutes earlier and got to the top first.

On the far right of this line, the 15th Alabama was opposed by the 20th Maine. Shelby Foote writes of the intense battle that followed:

> The conflict was particularly desperate on the far left [from the Union point of view], where the 20th Maine, made up of lumberjacks and fishermen under Colonel Joshua Chamberlain, a former minister and Bowdoin professor, opposed the 15th Alabama, Oates' own regiment, composed for the most part of farmers. Equally far from home—Presque Isle and Talladega were each 650 crowflight miles from Little Round Top, which lay practically on the line connecting them—the men of these two outfits fought as if the outcome of the battle, and with it the war, depended on their valor; as indeed, perhaps it did, since whoever had possession of this craggy height on the Union left would dominate the whole fishhook position.[24]

The 20th Maine was hunkered down behind a hastily constructed barricade of rocks and trees. Two-thirds the way up Little Round Top, the 20th Maine delivered a devastating volley into the ranks of the 15th Alabama. The fire was the most destruc-

Little Round Top (Library of Congress).

tive, Oates wrote later, that he had ever encountered. Two artillery pieces were spraying canister into his ranks. The 15th managed to force back a portion of the 20th Maine's line. The lines charged and countercharged each other four times, engaging in intense hand-to-hand combat. A Maine man reached for the regimental colors held by Private John G. Archibald of Company H when 1st Sergeant Patrick "Pat" O'Connor drove his bayonet through the man's head.[25]

The fighting was the most intense the 15th Alabama would encounter during the entire war. Captain Brainard, commanding Company G, ordered his company forward and was killed. As he fell he exclaimed, "O God, that I could see my mother!" and died. First Lieutenant John A. Oates then became commander and fell mortally wounded with eight bullets passing through him.[26] Second Lieutenant Barnett Cody was next in command and shot through the left groin, mortally wounded.[27] When Oates gave one of his commands "forward," Captain Joseph Ellison of Company C echoed the command, "Forward, my men, forward!" and was shot through the head, killing him instantly.[28] Private John Keels of Company H was shot through the throat and ran across the mountain breathing "at his neck."[29] Oates mounted a boulder and discharged his pistol at the enemy while Private Holloway of Company G knelt next to him, aimed his rifle and was shot in the left temple.[30] Captain William Bethune of Company K was shot in the face.[31]

The remnants of the 2nd Sharpshooters and a company of the 20th Maine had occupied a stone wall to the right of the Alabamians, where they laid an enfilading fire into the Confederates. "While one man was shot in the face, his right-hand or left-hand comrade was shot in the side or back. Some were struck simultaneously with two or three balls from different directions."[32] Captain DeBernie B. Waddell, serving as adjutant, approached Oates requesting permission to take 40 or 50 men and advance to the cover of rocks on the 15th Alabama's right for the purpose of delivering an enfilade fire into the 20th Maine. Oates consented and soon this detachment was doing "splendid work"[33] firing into the flank of the 20th Maine.

Oates could see that the struggle could have but one end if it continued at this rate. Five regiments fighting uphill against eight who were supported by artillery in defense of a position judged to be nearly impregnable proved to be impossible, but so long as there was a hope of reinforcements, Oates would fight. "Return to your companies; we will sell out as dearly as possible,"[34] he told his captains—but shortly, a courier arrived with nothing more substantial than Law's compliments (Law was now performing as division commander as Hood had been seriously wounded). Oates ordered a withdrawal at about 5:45 p.m. Just as the word was passed, the Maine men, who had exhausted their ammunition, launched a downhill bayonet attack. 'When the signal was given we ran like a herd of wild cattle,"[35] Oates later admitted. Whether a "signal" was given or not is still open to debate. Colonel Chamberlain wrote in his report, "An officer fired his pistol at my head with one hand, while he handed me his sword with the other."[36] This officer was twenty-two-year-old 2nd Lieutenant Robert Wicker from Perote, Alabama, of Company L. Colonel Chamberlain was so impressed with his bravery that he protected him from harm during the counterattack.[37] Waddell's men were almost all captured. Waddell escaped and took command of Company A.

During the 20th Maine's charge, an officer and two enlisted men became separated from the main line. As the men tried to find their regiment they encountered Lieutenant Joseph R. Breare from Company E with 15 men. The Federals surprised the Confederates and demanded their surrender, which Breare consented to. First Lieutenant Breare was surprised to discover that he allowed his men to be captured by just three men and was so impressed with the Federal officer's accomplishment that he retrieved a silver cup from his haversack and presented it to the officer.[38]

Company A finally rejoined the regiment and unleashed a volley into the pursuing Federals. The survivors who eluded the charging 20th Maine finally rested on the summit of Big Round Top. Oates collapsed from exhaustion and command was turned over to Captain Blanton Hill. The men bivouacked near the Snyder house for the night. Oates ordered a roll call and only 242 men answered,[39] less than half of those marching that morning. The 20th Maine suffered 136 killed and wounded while inflicting 172 casualties on the 15th Alabama.[40]

"It was a very solemn and lonely night,"[41] wrote one of the enlisted men. The monotonous pleas of the wounded broke through the stillness of the night and created a chorus of sounds that could not be ignored. Some of the men tried to slip into the Union lines hoping to retrieve a wounded comrade but were taken under fire and sadly had to retreat to their bivouac site. A picket from the 44th New York remembered that the night "was terrible, some [of the wounded] were crying, some praying and some swearing. All wanted help."[42]

Fifth Sergeant William Johns from Midway, Alabama, of Company B was left on the battlefield shot through the left thigh and hip and unable to move. He nearly drowned when it started raining that night and only survived by placing his hat over his face. The Yankees evacuated him on the night of July 3, his second anniversary as a Confederate soldier.[43]

On July 3, the remnants of the 15th Alabama spent the day reorganizing their line and fortifying their position on Big Round Top. Shortly after 1:00 p.m. they felt the earth shake as the artillery preparation for Pickett's Charge begin. At around 5:00 p.m. Union cavalry proceeded to push in the 15th's skirmishers, then launched a full-scale mounted charge. The entire brigade fired into the charging cavalry, emptying many saddles, even killing Union General Farnsworth. This was to end the 15th Alabama's fight in the Battle of Gettysburg.

For the first time in its history the 15th Alabama was soundly defeated and thoroughly routed. They were asked to accomplish a superhuman feat and fell short. The 15th suffered terribly in this engagement; of the 644 engaged, 18 were killed, 67 wounded, and 84 missing.[44] Among the casualties as reported by the first sergeants (many of those listed as wounded later died and/or were captured by the enemy) were:

Killed	Wounded	Missing
Company A		
	P.H. Smith	J.C. Horn
	Jas. Robinson	Jas. M. Berden
	J. Eason	

Killed	Wounded	Missing
Company B		
A. Kennedy	1SGT F. Hitchcock[45]	SGT J.D. Calaway
A.G. Denham	SGT C.A. Parker	SGT W.M. Johns
W.A. Edwards	CPL T.J. Coleman	
John McDowell	E.B. Swinney	
	E. Lane	C.O. Newman
	H.R. Morris	G.J. Owens
	B.E. Kindrick	O. Bell
	B.S. Kendrick	W. Pugh
	A.P. McMilan	T.J. Bledsoe
	D. Stone	
	F. Gresham	
Company C		
Captain Ellison	W.H. Mansil	SGT W.H. Hurt
SGT B. Bibby	C. Pugh	SGT J.E. Segar
A.P. Mansil	R.W. McDonald	T.J. Coleman
		J.A. Slaten
		J.A. Wicker
Company D		
	G.E. Spencer	SGT Johnson
	Danl Hardyog	CPL D. Stewart
	A.J. Jefcoat	CPL Eidson
		A. McGilvery
		C.J. Jackson
		J.R. Eidson
Company E		
Jasper Curenton	SGT C.L. Mezell	LT J.R. Breare
C.B. Smith	SGT J.R. Johnson	SGT A.W. Edwards
	W.F. Jones	Wm. Dulling
	F. Willis	R.R. Painter
	Jas Latimore	A.R. Roundtree
	Wm. Pouncey	C.V. Atkinson
	W.C. Fleming[46]	W. Faust
	Jas. Welch	B.F. Bigby
		John Mullins
Company F		
N.W. Lindsey	SGT D.W. Miles	J.B. Hutchinson
	W.E. Meridy	G.B. Lecroy
	David Farmer	G.E. Rivers
		W.E. Rudd
		J.P. Moore
		J.M.F. Mills
Company G		
W. Trimmer	H.C. Branard	J.N. Pounds
J.J. Bzawell	John A. Oates	M.E. Byrd
W.R. Holloway	B.G. Cody	W.L. Balkum
		L. Dukes

Killed	Wounded	Missing
		W. Emfinger
		R.J. Galaway
		J.C. Jordan
		G. Jenkins
		A.S. Kerkland
		Aaron Kirkland
		John Melvin
		Jas. Melvin
		Robert Parker
		Danl Riley
		A. Roney
		T.O. Kelley
		R. Short
		J.W. Shepherd
		C.C. Stone
		J.R. Woodham
		L.E. Woodham

Company H

Killed	Wounded	Missing
John Reels	SGT T.B. Gray	SGT J.W. Cowart
	J.R. Woodham	CPL J.D. Loveless
	Calvin Pope	J. Henley
	George Gill	J. McIntire
	M.A. Melvin	Abner Holmes
	J.D.L. Smith	W.B. Weston
	F.M. Rice	M. Mcguire
		J.W. Crawford
		W.E. McNeil
		J.F. McLeod

Company I

Killed	Wounded	Missing
CPL S.H. Garner	J.C. McCormick	C.N. Carpenter
	Neal McLeod	John Strickland
	C.N. Mallet	A.J. Ogletree
	T. Martin	C.S. Smedley
		N.J. Peters
		CPL S.A. Stewart

Company K

Killed	Wounded	Missing
J.W. Brown	W.J. Bethune	SGT C. Madden
W.H. Hall	J.W. Murdock	CPL P. Lynch
John Nelson	Jeff Allbritt	R.J. Croft
	W. Bingham	B. McKlevane
	W.H. Harold	M. Anderson
	J. Ritledge	G.W. Dudley

Company L

Killed	Wounded	Missing
SGT S. Vinson	SGT R. Barner	D. Kelley
	CPL Henderson	J.H. Stough
	J.L. Newton	E.A. Sellers
	D.M. Henderson	W.P. Sellers[47]
		P. McMorris[48]

Four of the 15th Alabama's officers lay dead on the field, one was wounded, and three were missing. Seventy-two of its men were killed, 190 wounded and 81 were missing.[49]

Returning to Virginia

The Confederate Army braced itself for a counterattack during the next couple of days but none came. Dripping wet by the rain, the beaten and battered men of the Fighting Fifteenth departed the Gettysburg battlefield about 2:00 a.m. on July 5, 1863. The regiment moved over South Mountain at a leisurely pace and reached Hagerstown, Maryland, by midnight on July 6. Rations were distributed and cooked on the next day. On July 10, the regiment resumed its march at 7 a.m. The Potomac was swollen by the heavy rain and Lee couldn't cross his army for a week. General Meade could possibly have destroyed

Private William P. Sellers, Company L (courtesy Boyd Smith).

the weakened Army of Northern Virginia here but made no movements to do so. The Confederates weren't able to cross the swollen river until July 13 and 14. The disastrous Gettysburg Campaign was finally over.

On July 23, 1863, the remnants of the 15th were asked to guard the flank of the retreating Confederate Army near Battle Mountain, Virginia. The regiment was formed in a line of battle along a fence upon a hill where they easily repulsed a regiment of Union cavalry biting at the heels of the retreating Confederates. On the morning of July 24, the 15th was relieved by Munford's Cavalry, and Colonel Oates set the regiment in motion to rejoin the retreating Confederate column. As the men passed a field of ripe blackberries, they were allowed to breakfast on the delicious berries since they had no rations left. The march was resumed and at about 11:00 a.m. they encountered some more Union cavalry under General Kilpatrick reinforced by a battery of artillery. Colonel Oates ordered the men into battle line again near Big Battle Mountain and cleared the cavalry from the road. Unfortunately, 1st Lieutenant Edmond P. Head of Company D was killed in the assault.[50] Privates William Crane, C.O. Minshew, and Daniel J. Stephens from Company H were wounded.

By August 1863, Law's Brigade was encamped along the Rappahannock River, near Fredericksburg, where the regiment "got back to the routine of military life."[51]

Captivity

"The sentinel must enforce his orders by bayonet or ball."[52]—Major General Albin Schoepf, Commandant of Fort Delaware, Delaware

Confederate prisoners captured at Gettysburg (Library of Congress).

The eighty or so prisoners from the 15th Alabama were marched south to Frederick, Maryland. From there they were transported by rail to Baltimore and on to Fort Monroe, Virginia, for processing. The captured Confederates were processed there by General Schenck on July 9. On July 12, the Alabama men boarded a steamer for the journey into Chesapeake Bay to the Chesapeake and Delaware Canal, then through the canal to Delaware City, Delaware, and finally to Fort Delaware, Delaware, where most were interned for the remainder of the war. According to one prisoner, the conditions aboard the transport steamer were intolerable. Evidently the boat had been used to haul animals, the "hold being foul with animal refuse." The prisoners were packed into the hold so closely spaced that it was impossible to sit down.[53]

The members of the Fighting Fifteenth captured at Gettysburg were:

Captured	Wounded/Captured
Company A	
PVT George J. Eason	
Company B	
PVT Ocus Bell	PVT J.D. Callaway
PVT James T. Bledsoe	4SGT William N. Jones

Captured

PVT Thomas J. Coleman
PVT Alfred G. Denham
PVT Charles O. Newman
PVT George J. Owens
PVT George W. Pope
PVT J.D. Westbrook

Company C

PVT Thomas C. Coleman
PVT Billy H. Hurt
PVT James A. Slaton
PVT Julius A. Wicker

Company D

PVT J.W. Eidson
4CPL James R. Eidson
PVT A.B. Gilver
PVT Charles J. Jackson
3SGT Felder Johnson
PVT Angus McGilvary
PVT Benjamin F. Stevens

Company E

PVT Cornelius V. Atkinson
PVT Albert W. Austin
PVT Benjamin F. Bigbie
2LT Joseph R. Breare
PVT William Dooling
1SGT Ambrose N. Edwards
PVT William L. Faust
PVT Doss C.D. Fleming
PVT John H. Landingham
PVT John L. Morrell
PVT William R. Painter
PVT William T. Pouncey
PVT Arthur R. Roundtree
PVT Christopher C. Stone
PVT James M. Welch

Company F

PVT J. Hutchinson
PVT James B. Hutchinson
PVT G.B. Lacroy
PVT Frank M. Metts
PVT James P. Moore
PVT George B. Reeves
PVT William E. Rudd

Company G

PVT William C. Alexander
PVT Madson L. Balcom
PVT George L. Dukes
PVT William Enfinger

Wounded/Captured

PVT Benjamin E. Kendrick, mortally
PVT Robert S. Kendrick, left foot

PVT William H. Mansel, severely left
  side, arm, and thigh
PVT Richard M. McDonald
2SGT J.E. Seegar

PVT William F. Johnson, mortally

2LT Barnett H. Cody, mortally groin
PVT Aaron S. Kirkland, right leg
PVT Robert Parker, left lung and
  left thigh

Captured

PVT Ransom J. Galloway
PVT George Jenkins
PVT Samuel O. Kelley
1SGT James W. Pound
PVT Charles W. Raleigh
PVT Allen W. Sholar
PVT Richard Short
PVT Christopher C. Stone
PVT J.E. Woodham
PVT Samuel E. Woodham

Company H

2SGT John W. Cowart
PVT James W. Crawford
PVT J.D. Hendley
PVT Abner Holmes
PVT Augustus Holmes
PVT Judge D. Loveless
4CPL Michael McGuire
PVT James A. McIntire
PVT John F. McLeod
PVT Neely E. McNeil
PVT William W. Weston

Company I

PVT Coleman N. Carpenter
PVT Absalom J. Ogletree
PVT N.J. Peters
PVT Capel S. Smedley
PVT Sidney A. Stewart
PVT John Strickland

Company K

PVT Scott M. Anderson
PVT John C. Beasley
PVT G.W. Dudley
PVT Pat Lynch
3SGT Cicero Madden
PVT Burrel V. McKilcane
PVT James L. Murdock
PVT E.A. Sellars
PVT James F. Tate
PVT Elijah Woodward, deserted
  and captured

Company L

PVT Joseph Anderson
PVT George W. Garrett
PVT George R. Henderson
PVT David A. Kelley
PVT Phil McMorris
PVT W.G. Morgan

Wounded/Captured

PVT Alfred A. Roney, left thigh
PVT James N. Shepard, mortally left
  thigh

PVT Calvin Pope, right thigh
PVT John D. Smith, left foot

PVT Thomas Martin, right shoulder
PVT John C. McCormick, right
  shoulder amputated

PVT Thomas J. Albritton
PVT Reuben J. Craft
PVT William H. Harrell
PVT John I. Ingram, thigh and left
  arm amputated
PVT G.E. Spencer, head

PVT George R. Henderson, knee
  and right shoulder
PVT John L. Newton, left leg

Captured   **Wounded/Captured**

PVT William P. Sellers
PVT J.H. Stough
2LT Robert H. Wicker[54]

Fort Delaware is on Pea Patch Island in the Delaware River. Although the U.S. Commissary-General of Prisoners pronounced the island "a very suitable place for the confinement of prisoners of war," medical inspectors thought otherwise. One of the latter wrote, "[T]his post is utterly unfit location for a prison much more for a hospital. Lying so low, its level being some six feet below high tide, it is impossible to properly drain it or to prevent its surface being constantly marshy and wet."[55] By the end of July 1863, the POW population at Fort Delaware had swelled to 12,595, the highest concentration of prisoners the island had experienced up to that time. With additional prisoners the entire population on Pea Patch Island grew to more than 16,000; the island had become the largest city in the state of Delaware, even eclipsing the population of Delaware's capital, Wilmington, by a few hundred.

The commandant of Fort Delaware was Major General Albin Francisco Schoepf, a Polish-born immigrant. General Schoepf was a veteran of the armies of both Austria and the Ottoman Empire. He became commandant on April 13, 1863, and remained so until the end of the war.

According to historian Thomas Flagel, Fort Delaware was one of the deadliest prisons during the Civil War. With a capacity of 10,000 prisoners, it held up to 16,000 at its peak, claiming 2,460 lives. Worsening the camp conditions of dismal rations and exposure was the occurrence of torture. With the permission of Schoepf, camp guards employed gagging, hanging by thumbs, clubbing, random shootings, and other transgressions.[56] He was known by some of the prisoners as "General Terror."

The marshy location, inclement weather, brutal treatment, and overcrowded conditions at Fort Delaware prisoner of war camp on Pea Patch Island in the middle of the Delaware River all combined to make the Confederate inmates miserable. It was the starvation diet, however, that imposed the greatest hardship and led to the most deaths. In retaliation for suffering endured by Union prisoners in Southern camps, the U.S. government reduced the rations of the Rebel prisoners. The men stared out across the river to fertile fields of grain and corn, yet they sat starving.[57]

Needless to say, the typical day for the prisoners revolved around the scheduled two meals a day. One prisoner wrote, "We get two meals per day, the first about 11 a.m. and the second about 4 p.m. The following is bill of fare: forenoon, three crackers (sometimes a piece of light bread), a small ration of beef or pork, and half cup of coffee. Afternoon, three crackers (sometimes a ration of beef or pork) and a cup of soup."[58]

Confederate Captain John S. Swann described these rations: "The bread was made of rye and wheat flour, well cooked, but the piece very small, about half enough for a well man. The meat [was] a small chunk of beef. Occasionally all sinew or mostly bone. It was cut up very carelessly, and very small, not half a ration."[59] Another prisoner described his daily ration as "six, sometimes four, hard crackers and ¹⁄₁₀ of a pound of rusty bacon (a piece the size of a hen's egg) for 24 hours. But for the past five days we have not had a morsel of meat of any kind." He further described the rations as "so full of worms, and stank so that one had to hold his nose while eating it."[60] Another prisoner described the morning meal as a "3 inch long, 1 inch thick piece of cornbread, yellow in color, a small piece of bacon or beef, and a cup of decoction of logwood and beans called coffee."[61] Another described the afternoon meal as "bread again, and two to three ounces of "loud-smelling pickled beef—'red horse' as it was called—and a tin cup of miserable stuff, called soup, so mean that I could not swallow it."[62] Another prisoner recalled, "[T]he meat was fat and had the potential of being good, but it was killed the day before and brought in about 9:00 a.m. It was covered with green flies and usually so bad that it could not be eaten."[63]

The mess hall in the prison barracks held about 1,000 prisoners at one time. Each group filed into the mess hall where the individual ration was set up on mess tables, with a Union sergeant stationed at each table. The prisoners took their places, each man in front of a ration, and at the signal, the men took their rations and filed out of the mess. The process was then repeated, sometimes taking up to six hours.[64]

Needless to say, the prisoners consumed most of their time trying to supplement their starvation diet. This was done in one of two ways: Randolph Shottwell stated, "[T]he catching and eating of huge rats has become a common thing."[65] Captain Swann related how they prepared the rats: "The rats were cleaned, put in salt water a while and fried," and further stated, "Their flesh was tender and not unpleasant to the taste."[66]

The only other supplement to the prison diet was the sutler, who, in addition to selling paper, pencils, coffee, pots and pans, wood, molasses, tea, tobacco, fruits and vegetables, would sell to those lucky enough to have money. The prisoners could acquire money by receiving packages from the outside from friends and family, and then only if the guards didn't intercept the money. For those able-bodied enough to work, the need for laborers was constant for engineering projects, general maintenance of the barracks, and the ongoing battle with the tides of the Delaware River, all of which offered employment. For a day's work, the pay scale was 75 cents a day to dig ditches, carpenters earned 25 cents, and carrying lumber was done for a small piece of tobacco.[67]

Prisoners also made money by working as craftsmen. Prisoners made rings, pins, buttons, chains, charms, and puzzles out of any piece of bone, horn, brass tack, tin, wire, or copper that they might find. Gutta-percha was another material that was put to good use. Gutta-percha was first discovered as a by-product of the rubber-making process. It was a light and imperishable material used to make jewelry in the early Victorian era. Buttons made out of gutta-percha were used at the fort for material to make items such as rings, watch seals, and chains. These elaborate and beautiful pieces, along with miniature machines, toys, violins, banjos, and wall ornaments, were sold to the richer prisoners or to the guards, who would buy large quantities and sell them to visitors to the island. In particular, fans made out of white pine and trimmed with silk of different colors were in great demand with Northern ladies; some of these fans sold for $2.50 each. Shoemakers were able to repair shoes once again. Watchmakers were repairing watches, barbers were cutting hair, and gamblers were all able to make extra money.

On the upside of captivity, these young Southern men were able to build a society which reflected their civilian life rather than of their military. A chess club, a debating society, a theatrical club, and a poetry society all flourished within the prison.[68] Religious services were held every Sunday, in addition to a divinity class, a Bible class, and a daily prayer meeting. Sports were very popular, with boxing being the favorite.[69] Prisoners could also pass their time by continuing their education. A prisoner could study law, medicine, or theology. Prisoners could attend lectures or learn a foreign language.

The starvation diet, putrid water, and unsanitary conditions left the prisoners susceptible to diseases which killed them in droves. A report from the Medical Inspector's Office focused on November 1863 through January 1864. There was an average of 22.2 percent sick or hospitalized daily. Mortality was recorded as 311 in three months. The diseases that killed these men were smallpox, which claimed 112 in three months; diarrhea, 60; pneumonia, 45; scurvy, 15; typhoid fever, 12; erysipelas, 11; dysentery, 10; and typho-malarial fever, 9.

Approximately 2700 Confederate soldiers died while being held captive at Fort Delaware. About 2400 are buried at Finn's Point National Cemetery located across the Delaware River. The marker reads:

ERECTED BY THE UNITED STATES TO MARK THE BURIAL PLACE OF 2436 CONFEDERATE SOLDIERS WHO DIED AT FORT DELAWARE WHILE PRISONERS OF WAR AND WHOSE GRAVES CANNOT NOW BE INDIVIDUALLY IDENTIFIED

The surviving members of the 15th Alabama remained in confinement until July 14, 1865, when they signed an Oath of Allegiance and were transported home.

General Orders No. 109 from the War Department required that transportation

Oath of Allegiance (author's collection).

be provided to these returning POWs by water and/or by rail to a point nearest their homes. A record at Fort Delaware was made by a federal quartermaster officer who delivered 3,000 returning Confederate POWs collected at Fort Delaware and Point Lookout to Mobile, Alabama, sometime in June 1865. Unfortunately, the date of delivery was not given.

Private Henry Robinson Berkeley of Virginia kept a detailed prison diary while at Fort Delaware during the last four months of the war. He noted on June 14 that the "Alabama boys were called out but did not get off." The next day, June 15, he wrote, "Taliaferro and Mercer left this morning for their homes, also all the Alabama boys." Between Henry Robinson and the federal QM officer, one could conclude that all of the Alabama enlisted prisoners, and perhaps the officers as well, were shipped together by water and eventually delivered at Mobile. One would assume that from Mobile, the 15th Alabama boys detrained in Greenville or Eufaula and walked the rest of the way home.

SIX

The 15th Moves West

Chickamauga

> *"I know Mr. Davis thinks he can do a great many things other men would hesitate to attempt. For instance, he tried to do what God failed to do. He tried to make a soldier of Braxton Bragg...."*—General Joseph E. Johnston

In early September of 1863, young Thomas Wright of Company B, Midway Southern Guards, was hearing rumors that Longstreet's Corps was going to be sent west to help stop Union advances in Tennessee and Georgia since the fall of Vicksburg, Mississippi. Seventeen-year-old Thomas had recently been promoted fifth sergeant for his gallantry on Little Round Top. Fifth Sergeant Wright was hoping that a trip west would give him an opportunity to visit his home in Spring Hill, Alabama, and look in on his parents John and Sarah.[1] All of Thomas's older brothers had already sacrificed greatly for the Southern cause. The eldest, William, had died of measles two years earlier on September 22, 1861. The next oldest, 3rd Corporal John Wright, had his left leg amputated as a result of a wound at Hazel River on August 22, 1862. Third oldest, Richard, was initially elected third lieutenant and later promoted to second lieutenant, and lost his right arm from a Union minie ball at Second Manassas.[2] He returned to service after Gettysburg but couldn't perform his duties and had recently resigned on August 15. Henry was wounded in the hip at Sharpsburg in 1862 and discharged in January 1863 for an "aneurism of the ascending aorta." Thomas was the youngest of the five brothers who enlisted, and he may have been wondering who would take care of his fifty-seven-year-old father and fifty-one-year-old mother if something should happen to him.

About September 6, 1863, General Longstreet was ordered to take two divisions of his corps to the west to join Braxton Bragg's Army of Tennessee. This would be the only time during the war that the South really took advantage of their interior lines and transferred a large number of troops between their two main armies. General Bragg, probably the most hated and incompetent general in the Southern Army, was largely responsible for the failure of the South to hold onto Tennessee and north Alabama. The Union Army under General Rosecrans was in Chattanooga and poised for

93

a strike into the Deep South, carrying the war into Georgia. Due to the transfer of Longstreet's Corps, the elite and battle-hardened 15th Alabama Regiment would participate in two of the largest battles of the Civil War, Gettysburg and Chickamauga, in a little over three months.

The regiment was thus able to retrace in reverse its 1861 train ride to Atlanta. The men were again met by a still patriotic populace as the train made frequent stops so the soldiers might enjoy "abundant and excellent lunches."[3] Law's Brigade (Sheffield was in command as Law still commanded Hood's Division) arrived in Atlanta on September 15, where they were issued new clothing, including hats and shoes.[4] Longstreet's Corps, minus Pickett's Division, arrived in Ringgold, Georgia, on September 16, 1863, and encamped for the night without their camp equipment, which had been left behind. Incompetent leadership from the Army of Tennessee affected the corps immediately. The regiment was instructed to prepare rations for two days, but as they left Ringgold they were given the wrong road to march. They spent the night and the next day retracing their steps, thereby exhausting their rations as well as their legs. On September 19 they would again go into battle without breakfast, just as had happened at Gettysburg, so they would fight exhausted from marching and hungry once more.[5]

On September 18, Bragg ordered his Army of Tennessee to occupy the crossings at Chickamauga Creek ("River of Death" in Cherokee) about ten miles south of Chattanooga. Longstreet's Corps was placed on the left of the Confederate battle line. On the morning of September 19, the brigade to the left of the 15th Alabama fell back without orders with a Union brigade in hot pursuit. The 15th fell back a short distance, advanced into the flank of the pursuing enemy, and forced them to fall back. The men continued their charge for about a mile, capturing a battery of Union artillery and many prisoners. Oates was injured in the hip by a piece of shrapnel but did not evacuate from the field. This was all of the action the 15th engaged in on September 19. They encamped on the battlefield, still without provisions. Rations arrived after midnight and the men awoke to eat "most ravenously," as Oates puts it.

The morning of Sunday, September 20, the Battle of Chickamauga began in earnest. The Confederate battle plan was that the right flank of the army would attack, and if that succeeded the center and left would join the assault. In anticipation of the attack, Union General Rosecrans moved troops from his center and right to reinforce his left. General Longstreet's keen eye noticed that Union troops were moving from his front, leaving a large gap in the Union line. At around 11:00 a.m. he ordered his entire corps forward, which smashed through the Union lines and caused a rout of the entire Union Army. Due to the dust and smoke, the 15th Alabama found themselves lost after the advance. Ever the warrior, Oates headed the men to their left, where fighting was observed. Oates ordered the 15th forward into the flank of the Union troops defending some high ground with two pieces of artillery. The Federal troops turned their attention and artillery on the regiment. The 15th Alabama drove the Union troops from the hilltop, captured the two artillery pieces, and found more on the other side of the hill. The 15th Alabama continued their pursuit of the enemy for "nearly a mile."[6]

As the pursuit continued, the 15th was unsupported and unable to find friendly units on their right or left. Furthermore, informed that other Union troops were approaching the hilltop the 15th Alabama had just vacated, the men knew this move would leave themselves surrounded. The 15th had to stop their pursuit and retake the hilltop, which they did in quick order. Unconnected with friendly units and unaware of the battle lines, they fortified this hilltop with logs and fired on any enemy troops they saw. This was a very confused battlefield for the boys from southeast Alabama. Confederate and Union units were lost and intermixed with each other, but the 15th was in a strong position. Today there is an iron tablet set up at this location on Snodgrass Hill marking the location of the 15th Alabama.

While on Snodgrass Hill the soldiers of the Fighting Fifteenth could fire in almost any direction and hit the enemy. Even though they had a strong position, the Union soldiers were all around them. The soldiers were loading and firing as rapidly as possible. Oates noticed young Thomas Wright's powder-stained face and said he was the "busiest chap I ever saw, down on his knees loading and firing, but taking aim at every shot."[7] Seventeen-year-old Thomas had been promoted to fifth sergeant ten days earlier for his gallantry. Oates slapped him on the shoulder and said, "Tommie, my boy, give it to them," to which the young cross-eyed boy replied, "That is what I am doing, colonel." Oates was limping along the line shouting encouragement, correcting gaps, monitoring ammunition consumption, and seeing to the wounded. As he returned to Company B's sector he noticed young Thomas's lifeless body. He had been shot through the head.[8]

Enfilading fire caused the 15th to retreat off of Snodgrass Hill, but the commander managed to rally the men. The boys counterattacked, catching the Federals on the hill off guard, and managed to retake the hill. The Union forces had had enough. The battle for the Fighting Fifteenth was finally over.

The regiment had fought gallantly and contributed greatly to the Confederate victory at Chickamauga. Noticing the hole in the Union line and sending his Corps through it was largely responsible for Longstreet's winning the most decisive Confederate victory in the Western Theater during the war. The regiment lost "eleven killed and one hundred and twenty-one wounded" out of about 450 engaged.[9]

The Union Army had been thoroughly beaten and began retreating toward Chattanooga, Tennessee. In spite of the urgings of his officers, and in defiance of common sense, General Bragg refused to order a pursuit of the Union Army and possibly cause its destruction. General Bragg was satisfied with encircling the Federal Army in the city of Chattanooga and trying to starve them out. The killed and wounded were:

Killed	Wounded	Missing
Field and Staff		
	COL William C. Oates, slight in hip	
Company A		
J.J. Broughton	SGT W.L. Blackmon, slight, in hand	
	PVT C.M. Broadwaters, slight, in knee	
	PVT A.M. McKissack, severe, in hips	
	PVT Calvin Sulevant, slight, in hip	

Killed	Wounded	Missing

Company B

PVT Jacob Pruitt

SGT T.D. Wright

CPL G.T. Denham, leg amputated
PVT H.H. Hodge, leg amputated
PVT J.W. Hughs, severe, in shoulder
PVT W.J. Ming, slight, in head

Company C

CPL W.T. Acrey

PVT E.C. Talbot

PVT Alfred Crowley

SGT Allen Crowley, severe, in thigh
PVT H.W. Cooper, slight, in wrist
PVT J.H. Head, slight, in thigh
PVT B.R. Wilkerson, slight, in hip
PVT J.M. Conway, slight, in elbow
PVT J.L. Chatham, slight, in foot

Company D

PVT James Wilson

SGT J.H. Long, slight, in leg
PVT G.W. Bailey, severe, in shoulder
PVT J.V. Cariker, slight, in leg
PVT F.L. Gregory, slight, in hand
PVT J.B. Matthews, slight, in head
PVT J.A. Norton, severe, in leg
PVT W.H. Quattlebum, severe, in leg
PVT Godwin Streeter, slight, in arm

Company E

PVT W.R. Harris

1LT J.E. Jones, slight, in leg
PVT Elvin Jones, severe, in foot
PVT W.W. Mobley, slight, in hip
PVT R.L. Kenon, mortal, in head
PVT John Alexander, thigh broken
PVT B.F. Dean, leg amputated
PVT J.W. Cotton, severe, in arm
PVT John Munn, severe, in hand
PVT C.C. Barnes, severe, in back
PVT John Murphy, thigh broken
PVT Henry Faust, slight, in leg
PVT William Mizell, severe, in leg
PVT Thomas Mullins, slight, in arm
PVT F. Curreton, mortal, in side
PVT J.J. Dean, severe, in ankle
PVT J.R. Johnson, slight (?)

Company F

Captain D. Williams, slight, in hip
SGT W.J. Smith, severe, in side
PVT G.C. Bray, slight, in side
PVT William Crane, slight, in hand
PVT G.W. Grice, severe, in thigh
PVT Joseph Garner, leg amputated
PVT William Hursey, severe, in side
PVT Y.H. Holloway, slight, in breast
PVT J.A. Langford, slight, in thigh

Killed	Wounded	Missing

PVT J.T. Prior, slight, in breast
PVT D.G. Ray, slight, in hand

Company G

Killed	Wounded
PVT J.M. Smith	2LT T.M. Renfroe, severe, in arm
PVT W.G. Moore	SGT J.C. Whatley, severe, in face
PVT J.T. Lane	PVT L.R. Bagwell, severe, in leg
	PVT A.A. Cockroft, in head
	PVT D.C. Cannon, slight, in leg
	PVT Cornelius Enfinger, severe, in face
	PVT W.T. Defnall, through thigh
	PVT T.J. Miller, slight, in shoulder
	PVT R.L. Medlock, slight, in hand
	PVT Henry Ott, arm amputated
	PVT W.J. Parish, thigh broken
	PVT W. Phillips, 2 fingers amputated
	PVT T.N. Shepherd, slight, in arm
	PVT Uriah Woodham, severe, in foot

Company H

Killed	Wounded
PVT W.L. Holley	1LT F.L. Boothby, severe, in side
	SGT D.H. Thomas, slight, in foot
	CPL J.M. Semms, severe, in hand
	PVT Henry Murphree, slight, in hand
	PVT W.S. Brown, severe, through shoulder and face
	PVT W.B. Houghton, slight, in hand
	PVT J.C. McIntire, severe, in shoulder
	PVT T.J. McIntire, thumb amputated
	PVT C.A. Moody, slight, in thigh
	PVT Uriah Smith, leg amputated
	PVT J.T. Williams, leg amputated
	PVT J.W. Williams, slight, in foot
	PVT H.C. Yelverton, severe, in thigh

Company I

Killed	Wounded
PVT T.J. Holland	PVT K.P. Powell, in head
	PVT G.E. Powell, slight, in arm
	PVT D.B. Murphree, severe, in foot
	PVT Wilson Powell, slight, in arm
	PVT S.N. Harris, severe, in lungs
	PVT C.W. Foster, slight, in shoulder
	CPL Byrant Wilson, slight, in arm
	SGT H.A. Thompson, slight, on shoulder
	PVT A.B. Graham, finger amputated
	PVT I.M. Owens, slight, in side
	PVT T.B. Raley, slight, in shoulder
	PVT J. Redmon, slight, in ankle
	PVT B.W. Peters, slight, in neck

Killed	Wounded	Missing
Company K		
SGT R.W. Welborn	1LT F.M. Porter, left arm amputated	
	CPL J.R. Watts, slight, in leg	
	PVT N. Cummings, slight, in shoulder	
	PVT R.W. Brannon	Pat McIntire
Company L		
	SGT C.H. Bonner, mortal wound	
	SGT J.L. Osburne, slight, in foot	
	PVT N. Baker, severe, in thigh	
	PVT O.W. Hicks, slight, in thigh	
	PVT R.W. Powell, slight, in back	
	PVT W.L. Lewis, slight, in hip[10]	

Oates claimed every soldier in his command expected to be on the road behind the fleeing Federal army the night of September 20 or at least the morning of September 21. Oates figured it was only common sense to follow up the victory achieved on Sunday. "The victory of Chickamauga, won at a fearful cost," Oates later wrote, "was rendered barren by the inaction and lack of enterprise of the commanding general."[11]

Private John Prior, Company F. Post-war photograph. He died in Pike, Alabama. He never married. The child pictured is unidentified (courtesy Richard Ferguson).

Lookout Valley

"On the night of the 27th of October, [we] landed on the south side of the river at Brown's Ferry, surprised the enemy's pickets stationed there...."— From Grant's After Action Report

Sometime in early October a little red-haired boy by the name of "Billy" Bethune approached Lt. Colonel Oates and wanted to join the 15th. Oates looked at the young boy and declined. When the boy threatened to find another unit to accept him, Oates gave him a rifle and sent him forward. Billy was from Columbus, Georgia, and wanted to make a name for himself. He had lost his father in the 1850s and was living with his paternal grandparents, John and Cherry.

The 15th Alabama was positioned with the rest of Law's Brigade by Lookout Mountain. In the middle of October 1863, the 15th Alabama was ordered to pass over the mountain into Lookout Valley and position themselves along Lookout Creek to harass Union supply wagons. While there, the regimental commander succeeded in buying a "small herd of beef cattle and ninety sheep." The regiment also was able to requisition a field of corn and a corn mill. The men of the 15th "had fresh corn-bread and an abundance of the finest fat beef and mutton for the next two weeks."[12] The men had a pleasant place to camp, and had no duty to perform except picketing along the river where the Yankees might be expected to cross.[13] After four months of hard fighting and marching on empty stomachs, the men were enjoying a badly needed rest and excellent fresh food. Duty was so relaxed that the Alabamians like Private Mitchell B. Houghton of Company H traded newspapers and tobacco with the Federal pickets.[14]

On October 24, 1863, General Grant replaced General Rosecrans and assumed command of the Union Army in Chattanooga. Grant began at once to reopen his supply lines. Unfortunately for the South, General Bragg, a personal friend of the Confederate president, would remain in command of the Army of Tennessee. Grant was not a man to sit idly by with the enemy tightening its grip on his supply lines. Grant set about immediately to open his communications and the 15th Alabama was astride one of his most important supply lines.

The 15th was guarding the southern bank of Lookout Creek at Brown's Ferry. Grant personally sent his chief of engineer to this location to survey the land and prepare for an attack to push the 15th Alabama from the ferry and all Southern forces out of Lookout Valley and off Lookout Mountain. As soon as October 27, Oates reported to General Jenkins (who replaced Law as commander of Hood's Division) of suspicious movements across the river. Oates had placed five companies on picket duty along the river with his remaining six companies as a mobile reserve. Sergeant Billy Jordan recalled that the men along the river were thinly stretched with "three to five men at a post at intervals from two hundred to four hundred yards apart."[15]

Oates got word on the night of October 27, 1863, that Union forces were crossing the river at other points. Before light on the morning of the 28th, he got word that they were crossing at Brown's Ferry. Captain Feagin, commanding Company B, was using a small cabin as his headquarters. The captain and Sergeant Billy Jordan were awakened at daylight by the shouts of "Yankees are coming." Before he knew it, Feagin's company was in full retreat. Jordan was ordered to take a cavalryman's mount and warn Oates's headquarters so that the reserve could be mobilized.[16]

The reserve was awakened and started for the ferry in the darkness where they heard the enemy cutting trees and constructing breastworks. Oates ordered his company commanders to order the men to walk up on the Yankees in the darkness and each man to "place the muzzle of his rifle against the body of a Yankee when he fired."[17] As daylight was coming, the 15th Alabama ambushed some of these Yankees and captured eleven of them. Many Alabamians occupied the breastworks but soon discovered they were surrounded by the enemy, who began firing at them from every side. Oates had no more reserves to send into the battle.

Some of the men broke and ran for the rear and some rallied and returned to their breastworks. Matters were very confusing in the dark, with some positions abandoned and overrun by an enemy of unknown strength and some positions continuing to be manned. The Union soldiers quickly encircled those manned positions and captured many Alabamians. Private Houghton gives us a rather typical account. Having lost a brother-in-law, Caleb Olive, at Gettysburg, Private Houghton was still nursing a wounded hand from Chickamauga. When the men in his breastworks broke for the rear, he called to his companions, "Let's go back, I do not see anything to run from." He succeeded in rallying "twelve or fifteen" and they returned. A short time later the men heard the rustling of leaves and the "tramp of men" in their rear and could tell in the dim moonlight that the men appeared better uniformed and armed, as well as bigger in size. Houghton asked what regiment they were from and was told the 74th Ohio. Private Houghton surrendered and discovered his commander, Captain Richardson, and fifteen other men had done the same.[18]

The 15th Alabama suffered severely. Oates himself was shot through the hip and was evacuated to a house nearby. He soon noticed his men "scattered over the yard, bleeding and begging for water, with no one to help them. The litter-bearers were busy bringing back wounded."[19] Among them was young Billy Bethune being carried by Jimmie Rutledge. When inquired what had happened, Jimmie said, "He is shot in the back." Billie spoke up in indignation with a child's voice, "Major, he is a damned liar; I was shot *across* the back."[20]

About this time General Law arrived with the other three regiments of his brigade, as well as the Texas Brigade. Law surveyed the situation and saw that a large force of the Union army had already crossed the creek and a pontoon bridge was already in place. Law withdrew his brigade, leaving many of the wounded, the dead, their camp and baggage, with all of the men's blankets and clothing, to the enemy.[21] Grant had deployed 4,000 men against the 240 men[22] of the 15th Alabama and soundly defeated them. After the battle was over, Major Lowther appeared and took command of the 15th as Oates was severely wounded. Supplies were soon flowing into Chattanooga; the siege had been broken.

Although a skirmish in terms of Civil War battles, the 15th Alabama lost severely at Brown's Ferry; out of about 240 engaged, fifteen had been killed, 40 wounded,[23] and at least thirteen captured. One could assume the large number of dead compared to the wounded is due to occupation of the breastworks, where their bodies were protected but their heads were not; therefore, most of the mortal wounds were probably head wounds. To make matters worse, the 15th had to abandon their cooking utensils, tents, blankets, and clothes to the enemy.[24] By the time that Brigadier General Law had arrived he estimated the enemy at 6,000.

Bragg's siege of Chattanooga was ended if he could not retake Lookout Valley. Longstreet was ordered to accomplish the nearly impossible feat. Longstreet chose to launch a night attack. Law was ordered to block the Federal forces at Brown's Ferry from reinforcing the Federals to be attacked. The Federals at Brown's Ferry, under Schurz and Steinwehr, were awakened at midnight on the morning of October 29. The generals immediately set their commands on the move to the direction of the firing. The 15th Alabama was deployed along the crest of Smith's Hill on the far right of Law's Brigade with Company G on the far right of the 15th's line.

The 33rd Massachusetts burst from some trees only twenty yards from the 15th's breastworks. The first volley felled sixty members of the Massachusetts regiment.[25] As the Alabamians reloaded, they fixed bayonets. The 33rd launched another attack which dislodged the 44th Alabama to the left of the 15th Alabama, thus leaving an exposed left flank. Waddell, commanding the company on the left, began receiving fire from the rear. Waddell attacked the Federals within his lines, but then he started receiving fire from the position he had just moved from. Waddell ordered a retreat and the whole regiment quickly followed suit. Lowther had left to rally the 44th Alabama and arrived just in time to see his regiment in a headlong movement to the rear. Law ordered the 4th Alabama and with the rallied 44th plugged the gap in the Confederate lines.[26]

The panic in the dark was contagious. The 15th Alabama "retreated in great confusion, some of the officers lost their swords, some lost their hats, etc."[27] Private Houghton recalled that part of the regiment "stampeded to the rear." He and about a dozen men returned to Smith's Hill and were captured.[28] One of the captured was Captain William A. Richardson, who yelled to a group of soldiers, "Well, boys, that was a devil of a fright we got a while ago." The soldiers he was talking to were from the 73rd Ohio, who quickly informed him that he was a prisoner of war. Captain Richardson exclaimed, "Look here, gentlemen, I am most egregiously mistaken. I thought this was the 15th Alabama. By heavens, this ought not to count."[29]

Killed	Wounded	Missing
Company A		
PVT Joseph Potee	PVT James L. Culiver, severely	PVT Henry H. Brown
Company B		
PVT John M. Payne		PVT Joseph T. Beard
		PVT William A. Edwards
		PVT Walter C. Jackson
Company C		
	PVT William A. Baker, hand	
Company D		
	1SGT James H. Long	PVT William Eidson
		PVT S. Lewis Spence
Company E		
PVT Eason Flowers	PVT Benjamin A. Daughtry, severely	
PVT William W. Jones	3SGT Benjamin A. Lanier	
PVT Jackson E. Keahey		
PVT Jesse R. Martin		
PVT David Snell		
Company F		
PVT Redin Baxley,		

Killed	Wounded	Missing
	PVT Eli Cox, wounded left arm and lung	
	PVT Anderson Mobley,	
	PVT J. Wilson Greenway, severely wounded	
	PVT Edward A. Hutchinson, severely	
	PVT Philip L. Minshew	

Company G

| | PVT William M. Galloway | PVT Edward R. Brantley |

Company H

| | | PVT Mitchell B. Houghton |
| | | CPT William N. Richardson |

Company K

| | PVT James H. Gray, mortally | PVT James H. Caison |
| | PVT Rob M. Espy | |

Company L
PVT W.H. Gilmore[30]

Left: **Private Anderson Mobley, Company F (courtesy Robert W. Hastings).** *Right:* **3rd Sergeant Benjamin A. Lanier, Company E (courtesy Joyce White).**

East Tennessee

> *"This was the hardest winter that we had ever experienced. It rained, sleeted and snowed so much that the earth became so full of water until a little stomping around our camp-fires would cause water to rise."*[31]—Private William McClendon, Company G, Henry Pioneers, 15th Alabama Infantry Regiment

Seeing Union reinforcements pouring into Chattanooga, Tennessee, General Bragg inexplicably weakened his army further by ordering General Longstreet to take his corps with additions of cavalry and another infantry division and retake Knoxville,

Tennessee, in early November 1863. Longstreet did so under protest, as he was against abandoning the high ground of Lookout Mountain, and he didn't think the 15,000 men provided were enough to besiege the 25,000 Union troops entrenched at Knoxville under Burnside.

The only way this campaign could have succeeded was to catch the Union forces by surprise with rapid movements before they could consolidate behind their fortifications in Knoxville. This proved impossible because of the many creeks and rivers which had to be crossed. The only pontoons Longstreet possessed had to be transported by rail, and railway cars were scarce in this part of the South. To make matters worse, during this winter campaign in the Appalachian Mountains was the lack of rations that Bragg had promised. The lack of shoes was so severe that the men improvised a shoe shop that tried to produce shoes for the soldiers with a small supply of leather. Moccasins were made out of the leather turning the hairy side next to the foot. Although these shoes were inadequate, the practice saved many men from having frostbitten feet.

The Alabama Brigade was marched to Cleveland, Tennessee, on November 9, where the brigade commander learned that no railway cars were available, arriving at their destination on November 13.[32] By November 15 the men from southeast Alabama were anxious to meet the enemy so they could replenish their supply of food and equipment, especially blankets.[33] The weather was already cold and a two-day rain made conditions more miserable. The night of November 15, both armies were too close together to allow fires. The Confederates attempted a flanking maneuver, which failed, and the Federals were allowed to withdraw within the warm confines of Knoxville unmolested.

Longstreet arrived before Knoxville on November 17, 1863. The Fighting Fifteenth found the Federals before them "skillfully disposed and well dug in."[34] Longstreet had no choice but to lay siege to the enemy forces that were probably better supplied than his own troops. General Grant had placed troops to occupy the rail line feeding Longstreet's troops and predicted that Longstreet would have to "take to the mountain passes." But Longstreet disappointed his adversaries by tightening his grip on the superior forces within Knoxville. Longstreet was reading dispatches that Bragg's depleted army had been thrown back from Chattanooga by Grant and correctly assumed that more attention would soon be placed on him. As time was running out, Longstreet ordered an assault on the Knoxville fortifications to commence on November 29.

The assault was a disaster almost from the start. The Union forces had placed telegraph wire about ankle- to knee-high to slow the Confederate assault. The Confederates had to fight the wire, frozen ground, and a sleeting rain while attacking an entrenched enemy. The men finally reached the trench, but then had a nine-foot-high parapet to assault while slipping in half-frozen mud. Without scaling ladders, the men tried climbing on each other's shoulders, but just weren't able to do so due to the nature of the ground, not to mention the blasts of musketry and improvised hand grenades from the enemy above.[35]

Longstreet got official dispatches informing him that Bragg had fallen back on

Dalton, Georgia, after his defeat. Furthermore, he was ordered to dispatch all units not in his two-division corps to reinforce Bragg. On December 3, Longstreet put his troops on trains and headed toward Virginia, not Georgia; unfortunately most of the wounded and sick would be left behind. His western campaign was over. Longstreet's Knoxville Campaign cost his corps 129 killed, 458 wounded, and 226 captured.[36] The 15th Alabama suffered six killed and 21 wounded.[37]

Killed	Wounded	Captured
Company A		
	PVT James R. Chambers	PVT Robert P. Chambers
	1LT Hugh Fields	
	4SGT Arthur Fields	
Company B		
PVT Thomas P. Thompson	PVT James M. Conaway	
Company C		
	3CPL William S.P. Singleton	PVT N.G. Chandler
	PVT Green B. Vinson,	PVT David S. Cooper
	severely	PVT Thomas J. Guerry
		PVT Lewis Springs, deserted
Company E		
PVT Agerton Farmer	PVT Joe Crenshaw, right	
PVT David Farmer	shoulder	
PVT Dennis W. Miles	PVT John W. Gibson	PVT William H. Flowers,
	PVT Archibald Jackson	deserted
		PVT Noah D. Peacock
		PVT Thomas J. Seay
		PVT John W. Sheffield
Company G		
2SGT John T. McLeod	PVT John J. McCoy	PVT James O. Deel
PVT James O'Dell	PVT Tolison N. Shepard	PVT John T. Melvin
		PVT James A. Trawick
Company H		
PVT Henry Andrews	1LT David H. Thomas	PVT Alfred M. Jones
		PVT Alex Lynn
		PVT John N. Smith
		PVT John Tew
		2LT William L. Wilson
Company I		
CPT Frank Parks	PVT Green McClendon	PVT Jeff Hazellwood
	PVT O.J. Moates	PVT William T. Linton
		PVT Roderick Morrison
		PVT James W. Satcher
Company K		
PVT James A. Spurlock	PVT William M. Lloyd,	PVT John A. Seegars
	left leg amputated	

Killed	Wounded	Captured
Company L		
PVT Wesley Smith	PVT Jefferson F. Bean[38]	

The retreat did not ease the suffering of the 15th Alabama as the weather was bitterly cold and many of the men were shoeless. Trails of blood from bare feet that could be seen in the ice and snow marked the route of Longstreet's Corps. A member of Longstreet's staff recalled, "It was bitter winter weather, the ground hard and sharp with ice.... Their bleeding feet left marks at every step."[39] For the rest of the campaign, rations, clothing, and camp equipment were sorely needed. The loss of their clothes and equipment at Brown's Ferry was on the mind of every man.

While the 15th was in winter quarters in East Tennessee, desertions became almost epidemic. After almost three years of hard campaigning and fighting, living in horrid conditions on little better than a starvation diet, poor leadership from Lowther (as claimed by Oates), and ever-present homesickness, it appears that the 15th Alabama Infantry Regiment might be coming apart. A private from Company I wrote, "The winter of '63–4 at Morristown, Tenn., was peculiarly hard. We had no huts, rations were scant and poor, as were blankets, clothing and shoes. We did not get a mail for three months. Plug tobacco could not be had...."[40] At a time when replacements became a trickle of conscripts; battle losses, disease, and desertions continued to reduce the 15th to a mere skeleton of a once powerful regiment.

Killed	Wounded	Deserted
Company A		
	PVT John R. Gardner	PVT Thomas Bell
		PVT Thomas J. Hatcher*
	PVT Henry Quentin*	
		PVT Franks Samuels*
		PVT William H. Briley
Company B		
		PVT Miles Bell*
		PVT John D. Bowen (did not desert but captured)
		PVT James P. Phillips (did not desert but captured)
		PVT Jack Willis
Company D		
	Thomas S. Moffette, mortally	PVT John W. Hudgins*
Company E		
		PVT Jack Jernigan (did not desert but captured)
		PVT Matthew Knight
		PVT Thomas W. Morrell*
		PVT William H. Windham*
		PVT Pleasant W. Nicholson (did not desert but captured)

Killed	Wounded	Deserted
Company G		
		PVT Robert L. Medlock
		PVT John S. Parrish
		PVT William Smith
		PVT James R. Woodham
Company I		
1SGT J. Hanchy	PVT James D. Jones	
Company L		
		PVT Ewen A. Rich (did not desert but captured)[41]
*Captured		

Cooking and Eating

"Rations were often insufficient to appease hunger."[42]—Private Mitchell Houghton, Company I, Quitman Guards, 15th Alabama Infantry Regiment

The gathering and cooking of rations consumed most of the time for Confederate soldiers whether in camp or on the march. The rations provided by the Confederate Commissary were often sporadic and insufficient.

The men missed coffee the most. In the early part of the war the men could depend on captures from Union knapsacks and supply wagons. As the war digressed into trench warfare, coffee became nonexistent unless a blockade runner happened to run the gauntlet and return with some. Sassafras tea was tried, but as a steady diet, it was unsatisfactory. Parched corn meal, potatoes and other substitutes were tried as replacements for coffee during the last year of the war.

Salt was always scarce after the first year. Each man treasured a little in a box tied up in a rag in his haversack, but in damp weather it frequently lost its savor, as well as its substance. The men became so desperate even gunpowder was used as a substitute.[43]

Cooking utensils were plentiful at first. After a time the men were reduced to an oven and frying pan for each mess, and later to a skillet for each company. When the pot and spider wagon drove up, each company had a man to claim its skillet, some being marked with a file, but frequently disputes as to ownership occurred. A soldier would occasionally tie a frying pan or skillet to his knapsack, hence the famous expression "tote his own skillet," so well known to the Alabama veterans. Halted for the night in a rain in the wet woods, one would wonder how he could light a fire. Soon a little glimmer appeared, when some man had obtained a little dried inner bark of a dead tree, cedar twigs or dry leaves, or a piece of newspaper, the little flame was carefully fed with pieces of dead twigs until it became a fire, then a hundred hands bore away little torches of twigs to become the parents of other campfires. Some would gather wood for the night; some take the canteens and get water, and with the cheerful blaze would arise the shouts of laughter and the hum of conversation. The meal, if they had any, being over, the old campaigner would bathe his feet in cold water, rub the bottoms with tallow (hog fat, from a hog that had been fed corn), if he could get it, and toast them before the fire in order to harden them for the next day's march.[44]

Cornmeal was often so coarse as to not stick together when baked, and in a haversack in rainy weather it would crumble. The men cooked biscuits with the aid of soda and grease fried out of bacon. When ovens or skillets were scarce, the men often had to wait turns. Later they got only poor beef and flour, and the bread was of very poor quality. In the spring the men would strip the bark off a hickory or poplar and make a beautiful tray in which to knead the flour into dough. But these luxuries were not always accessible, and many a commissary wagon would drive up in dark wet woods, after a hard day's march, and the flour for a whole company would be dumped on an oil cloth or a blanket. Then with cold water the men would mix the flour, often without salt, on an oil cloth, and bake in ovens, skillets or frying pans; or if these were not available, then a string of dough would be wrapped around a ramrod and held to the fire, then turned often until it was baked, or partially baked.[45]

In a newly built fire on the damp earth, the men could not bake an ash cake, nor could they cook cornbread on ramrods, so they had to take turns waiting for the skillet. The Confederate soldiers preferred bacon to beef, because they could eat the former raw and had little trouble in preparing it; the men felt the bacon afforded more strength and fortified them better against the cold. Sometimes the beef was so wretchedly poor that it was hard for even a hungry man to eat it. More often than not the men would chop it up, bones and all, and set it by the fire to simmer all night, and then parch some flour in the frying pan to make gravy and get a good meal out of very poor material. If the men got enough to eat there was always merriment, shouts and laughter, but if rations failed, the men were sullen and gloomy.[46]

SEVEN

Back in Virginia

Wilderness

> "Fast preparations are [in the] making to meet the hero of Yankeedom
> [Grant], we care not who meet us when Gen. Lee is our leader."[1]—3rd Ser-
> geant James Greenway, Company F, Brundidge Guards, 15th Alabama
> Infantry Regiment

After his substantial victories at Forts Henry and Donelson, Vicksburg, and Chattanooga, Lincoln felt he finally found in Grant the man he needed to bring the war
to a final conclusion. Lincoln made Grant commander of all Union forces. While
keeping General Meade in command of the Army of the Potomac, Grant was going
to physically place himself with that army to take Lee's Army of Northern Virginia
head-on. Union armies would no longer head south and retreat after Lee defeated
them, giving the Southern Commander time to rest and refit his great army. Grant's
strategy was to engage the enemy throughout the undermanned South and hammer
them into submission by a war of attrition. The Fighting Fifteenth would suffer heavily
during the last year of the war, and recruits had declined to a dribble of conscripts.
The first encounter of these two great commanders would be the Battle of the Wilderness on May 5–7, 1864.

The Fighting Fifteenth was anxious to get back under the control of Lee again.
They boarded the trains for Charlottesville, Virginia. After arriving there the brigade
marched the morning of April 26 to Gordonsville. While there they were issued new
uniforms and Enfield rifles. Food was also available with each mess, including a pound
of bacon, sugar, coffee, rice, salted vegetables and beans.[2]

Word had arrived that General Lee would be reviewing the I Corps on April 29.
"Guns were burnished and rubbed down while cartridge boxes and belts received a
good buff. Brass buttons and buckles were polished until they looked like new, and
shoes and boots were greased to perfection."[3] With every member standing erect with
shoulders back and chest out, each presented arms as the reviewing party passed.
Each company gave a proud salute. The men would never forget how majestic their
beloved commander appeared astride Traveler.

On the morning of May 2, Perry moved the brigade to a new campsite near Gordonsville. The men passed by Brigadier General Law's tent, where Law was under arrest, and Oates stopped to chat. On May 4 the men were given that familiar order to cook three days' rations and be prepared to move within the hour. The men were on the move by 4 p.m.[4]

Grant had assembled 122,000 men to oppose Lee's 60,000. The Wilderness was the same location of the great victory of Chancellorsville which the 15th Alabama had missed a year earlier while they were salvaging coastal Virginia for subsistence for the Army of Northern Virginia. The Wilderness was aptly named, for it was an area of very dense woods. As the 15th was being placed in the line of battle, the men caught a glimpse of their beloved Army Commander:

> To reach our position we had to pass within a few feet of General Lee. He sat on his fine gray horse "Traveler," with the cape of his black cloak around his shoulders, his face flushed and full of animation. The balls were flying around him from two directions.... A group of General Lee's staff were on their horses just in rear of him. He turned in his saddle and called to his chief of staff in a most vigorous tone, while pointing with his finger across the road, and said: "Send an active young officer down there." I thought him at that moment the grandest specimen of manhood I ever beheld. He looked as though he ought to have been and was the monarch of the world. He glanced his eye down on the "ragged rebels" as they filed around him in quick time to their place in line, and inquired, "What troops are these?" And was answered by some private in the Fifteenth, "Law's brigade." He exclaimed in a strong voice, "God bless the Alabamians!" The men cheered and went into line with a whoop.[5]

Fifth Sergeant Randolph Smedley of Troy, Alabama, Company I, Quitman Guards, was one of the more faithful writers in the regiment in the latter part of the war. His letters to his father are very detailed. Fifth Sergeant Smedley had been captured at Gettysburg but was exchanged shortly thereafter. He, like all of the men of the 15th, was delighted to rejoin the Army of Northern Virginia with which they had won so much glory. The eight months of being mismanaged in Georgia and Tennessee was a frustrating time. Their new brigade commander wrote of his troops: "They saw that their reunion had occurred at a crisis when lofty qualities were in demand and great things were to be done; and they rose with the emergency. The stronger the pressure upon them, the greater the rebound and the firmer their resolution seemed to become."[6]

The 15th passed the familiar scene of an intense, large-scale engagement up ahead as they marched passed the III Corps field hospital. The shrieks, screams, and the moaning of the wounded reminded all of what could soon happen to them. The smell of blood and the sight of amputated legs and arms piled up outside the makeshift field surgery tents undoubtedly added to their fears. Once past the gruesome sights and sounds, the Alabamians met a seemingly endless stream of wounded being carried to the hospital or stumbling along as best they could.

The hardened veterans of the Fighting Fifteenth surged forward toward the enemy and encouraged those Confederates of other units running from the enemy to turn around and join them because they were "Longstreet's boys." They had come to save the day. Lee noticed the obese Captain James J. Hatcher of Company L, struggling to keep up with his company, and shouted encouragement: "Go on, my brave Alabama captain, and drive them back."[7]

General Perry, commanding Law's Brigade, heard one retreating soldier yell, "Courage boys; Longstreet's men are driving them like sheep!"[8] General Perry claims that these 4,000 men routed 30,000 Union veterans with their furious attack.[9] While advancing with such speed the brigade began to receive an enfilading fire from a patch of woods to its extreme left. General Perry ordered the 15th Alabama to attack that area, unaware of the number of enemy troops in the woods. General Perry said he witnessed the successful execution of his orders of "one of the most brilliant movements I have ever seen on a battlefield."[10] Perry later recalled that the 15th "had wheeled through an arc of at least sixty degrees, had traversed the intervening open ground, had entered the woods at a charge and were driving its occupants—more than twice their number—in the wildest confusion before them; and but more than five minutes had elapsed since the giving of the order!" General Perry ended his account of the battle with, "The Fifteenth Regiment had arrived on the left at the crisis of the engagement and delivered its decisive blow."[11]

The hardened veterans had faced off against the 6th and 15th Heavy Artillery, fighting as infantry, who had spent the war thus far with easy duty manning the Washington defenses. Neither regiment had fired a shot in combat.[12] Oates ordered a charge and every Alabamian sprang forward in the attack. The 15th routed the Federals and chased them for about half a mile. Afterwards, the seasoned veterans knew without receiving orders to construct breastworks in anticipation for a counterattack. The 15th repulsed four separate and determined attacks. Finding themselves unsupported, the 15th Alabama retreated about 300 to 400 yards, and fell in line with the Confederates. This ended the fighting of May 5, 1864. Discipline had been restored under Lt. Colonel Oates; not one man retreated without being ordered. The battlefield yielded the most booty that Private Billy Jordan of Company B had "ever beheld."[13] The Fighting Fifteenth was finally able to replenish themselves with all the camp equipment lost at Lookout Valley. Rations and extra clothes quickly filled their haversacks.

The 6th was simply taken up with skirmishing, but about 10:00 a.m. on May 7, the regiment was ordered to attack an enemy that was strongly posted in heavy timber. The attack succeeded in dislodging the Yankees and the regiment set up a new battle line on the hill it had just captured.

Longstreet had once again succeeded in flanking the Federals and was preparing for a final blow into the rear of the Union army when he was shot by his own confused men in the dense undergrowth. The same thing happened at almost the exact spot a year

Private David F. Averett, Company A. Post-war photograph. He died in 1927 at Winnfield, Winn Parish, Louisiana (courtesy Robert Luke).

earlier to "Stonewall" Jackson. Although he was severely but not mortally wounded, Longstreet's wounding would halt the advance of the Confederates. Grant lost 17,666 killed, wounded, and captured, while Lee lost 7,800.[14] Grant had been soundly defeated in his first battle with Lee. So much so, in fact, that Grant went into his tent, threw himself on his cot and started sobbing uncontrollably. From May 5 to May 7 of 1864, the 15th Alabama suffered 4 killed and 27 wounded, with 11 captured.[15]

Killed	Wounded	Captured
Company A		
PVT John A. Smith	PVT David F. Averett, severely, head	PVT William S. Broughton
	PVT Isaac Basset	
	PVT Isaac H. Tate, severely, groin	
Company B		
	1SGT James G. Hitchcock, severly, leg	PVT D.H. Sweeney
	PVT Emery A. Lane	
	PVT Thomas L. White, mortally, leg amputated	
Company C		
	PVT John A. Burt, severely, thigh	
Company D		
	4SGT D.D. Burkhalter, severely, left arm	
Company E		
	2SGT Samuel Hogg, severely, cheek	PVT Miles L. Keahey
	PVT William W. Mobley, slightly, foot	
	PVT Silas B. Peters, severely, arm	
Company F		
	3SGT John N. Bray, slightly, neck	PVT Thomas A. Collier*
		PVT Rufus King
	PVT James A. Langford	
	PVT James W. Langford, severely, right forearm	
	PVT M.V. Rudd, slightly, face	
	PVT William J. Seay, severely, leg	
Company G		
4CPL John M. Stone	PVT Young J. Vicker, severely, legs	PVT J.H. Lester
	1SGT John C. Whatley, mortally	PVT John A. Woodham
Company H		
	5SGT John G. Archibald	PVT John T. Berry
	3SGT James M. Sims, slightly, wrist	

Killed	Wounded	Captured
	2LT David H. Thomas, severely, hip and back	
Company I		
PVT Green W. Davenport	PVT N.D. Pugh, slightly, leg	
PVT William P. Powell	3SGT Alsey F. Sanders, slightly, left arm	
	2SGT Hiram A. Thompson, slightly	
Company K		
	PVT Benjamin F. Culpeper, slightly, hand	PVT James Rutledge
	PVT James M. Rhodes, slightly, hand[16]	

*wounded and captured

Grant did emerge from his nervous breakdown and declared, "Whatever happens, there will be no turning back."[17] Even though he had just suffered the first serious defeat of his military career, his determination meant that the Fighting Fifteenth would be involved in constant fighting until the end of the war. The North could replace 17,666 casualties more easily than the South could replace 7,800. Making matters worse, Bragg's defeat at Chattanooga would allow Union forces access to the Confederate interior, where they would destroy foodstuffs, transportation and communication facilities, and any industries needed by the Confederacy for the prosecution of the war.

Spotsylvania

> "On the 8th the enemy made 3 attempts to take our works but were paid dearly for their trouble every time, for each attempt was a failure and their loss was heavy."[18]—1st Sergeant Randolph Smedley, Company I, Quitman Guards, 15th Alabama Infantry Regiment

It soon became apparent that Grant's strategy was to continue to move to Lee's right, forcing Lee to keep his army between the Army of the Potomac and Richmond. Grant's next objective was Spotsylvania Court House. First Sergeant Smedley and the 15th Alabama conducted a night march on May 7 to reach Spotsylvania before the Union troops. In the early morning hours of May 8, they were allowed thirty minutes of rest and to partake in their "cold, scanty rations,"[19] as described by Oates. At around 10:00 a.m. they heard firing to their front and were ordered to repel a Union attempt to "get possession of our road."[20] The 15th succeeded in driving the Union forces back and were ordered to take up defensive positions on a ridgeline to their rear. The 15th Alabama boys tore down a fence and piled up the wood for their protection; this was the "beginning of ten miles of defensive works subsequently constructed by the Confederates upon the field of Spotsylvania Court House."[21]

In between skirmishes the 15th continued to improve their fortifications until only their heads were exposed. Although fighting was heavy during the battle, the 15th Alabama spent May 9 and 10 simply skirmishing with the enemy. On May 10, an assault was easily repulsed by the 15th Alabama. Details were sent forward to collect discarded weapons until each man had four or five rifles ready to fire.[22]

The skirmishing continued day and night, and the 15th hadn't had a night's sleep for the last six days. Firing would inexplicably erupt each night for no apparent reason, and each side would remain awake fearing a night attack. Oates discovered the reason as he saw Private James "Jim" Rhodes from Company K running into the lines after one such eruption of fire. Oates inquired why he was out in front of the lines since he was not on picket duty. Oates found out that this practical joker was going out each night to the Union lines and yelling out commands while firing two pistols. The Yankees would wake up and start firing, fearing a surprise night attack. Private Rhodes proudly told Oates that he wasn't allowing the Union troops to sleep at night. Oates admonished him that the Confederates weren't getting any sleep either.[23]

Grant spent the next eight days probing and assaulting the Confederate breastworks to no serious effect. Any breaches in the Confederate defenses were successfully counterattacked by Lee's mastery of the battlefield and the determination of the battle-hardened Confederate soldier. Much of the fighting was bloody and hand-to-hand. The battle ended on May 18. Again Grant had been soundly defeated, losing around 6,820 men with Lee losing barely one third that number.[24] The casualties of the 15th during the battle were:

Killed	Wounded	Captured
Company A		
PVT Jep Brown	2SGT Eben B. Edwards, left arm	PVT Washington P. Bass
PVT John Taft	amputated	
	PVT Thomas A. Miller, mortally, hip	
Company B		
	PVT Thomas S. Beasley, severely, arm	
	PVT John M. Payne, slightly, hand	
Company C		
	PVT Alfred M. Burdett	
	PVT H. Halton	
Company E		
1CPL Robert E.	PVT Billy C. Mizell, slightly	
Patterson		
Company F		
PVT William R.	1CPL George W. Brazil, slightly, thigh	
Beasley	PVT James J. Ferror, slightly, foot	
	PVT Bartley W. Ketcham, severely, leg	
	1LT Thomas J. Prior, slightly, shoulder	
	2LT John N. Wadsworth, slightly, head	
Company G		
	PVT Augustus H. Dozier	
	PVT Irvin Hicks, severely, thigh	
	PVT John D. Shepard, slightly, thigh	

Killed	Wounded	Captured
Company H		
	PVT Frank L. Boothby, slightly, shoulder	PVT T.J. Herring
Company I		
PVT George E. Powell 1SGT John J. White	PVT John M. Catrett, severely, side	
Company K		
	PVT Marion W. Green, severely, head	
Company L		
	1SGT Dixon D. Bonner, severely, thigh PVT E.T. Matthews, mortally[25]	

During the night of May 19, Grant started his army in motion again to his left. Most of the Army of Northern Virginia was engaged in skirmishing daily, but the 15th Alabama was not so engaged until May 31. The regiment was ordered into some abandoned trenches and easily repulsed some enemy assaults. The next couple of days were spent improving the regiment's defenses.

Second Cold Harbor

> "I never in all the bloody conflicts that I had been in, saw such a destruction of human lives. They literally piled on top of one another."[26]—2nd Lieutenant William McClendon, Company G, Henry Pioneers, 15th Alabama Infantry Regiment

The fighting that took place June 1–12 would become known as the Battle of Second Cold Harbor. On June 2, the regiment was ordered to Cold Harbor and arrived that afternoon. The men spent the entire night preparing breastworks and completed them as the sun was coming up in the rear of abandoned breastworks. General Law (in charge of his brigade again) had set a trap for the Union forces. His plan was for the enemy to assault the first (unoccupied) line and then be surprised at the second (occupied) line, where he had the entire brigade entrenched. Grant was bearing down with 110,000 men. Reinforcements had replenished Lee's ranks to 60,000. Richmond was barely ten miles to their rear. As stated, the trenchworks were completed in time for a major assault the next morning. Oates had requested and received a twelve-pounder artillery piece to complement his defenses. The enemy charged in column formation, ten men deep from Smith's Corps, and after capturing the abandoned line were "receiving a perfect storm of lead from both sides."[27] The artillery piece, with canister, added to the hail of lead. The Yankees were so densely packed that "it was hardly possible for a ball to pass through without hitting someone."[28] The enemy endured the fire of the 15th Alabama and their brigade for 30 minutes and, it was said, lost about 5,000 men. "They literally piled on top of one another,"[29] wrote a private. The 15th suffered three dead and five wounded.[30]

By the time a second assault by the 23rd and 25th Massachusetts regiments happened twenty minutes later, some Georgia troops had arrived and began loading the rifles for the Alabamians. Oates said this was the most destructive fire he had ever seen. A Federal said, "It seemed more like a volcanic blast than a battle and was just as destructive." Within two minutes not a Massachusetts man was standing. Those not killed or wounded were lying in front of the Confederate line and not moving. A company was sent forward and captured about one hundred prisoners, including the colonel who had led the charge. The enemy could be heard preparing their own fortifications during the night. The next morning, firing between the lines was intermittent. One said the stench from the Union dead was "so nauseating that it was almost unendurable.... The dead covered more than five acres of ground about as thickly as they could be laid."[31] A six-hour armistice was finally granted for the burying of the Union dead.

After the armistice the sharpshooting resumed and continued incessantly. Grant's forces achieved no breakthrough anywhere along the Confederate lines. Grant suffered 7,000 casualties at Cold Harbor, most in the course of eight minutes, while Lee suffered under 1,500.[32] The 15th Alabama suffered 5 killed and 12 wounded.[33] In the last thirty days of campaigning, Grant had lost 54,929 men while Lee had lost 27,000.[34]

Killed	Wounded	Captured
Company B		
4CPL John F. Cain		
Company C		
PVT Joseph W. Baker		
Company D		
	PVT Thomas Varnadore, severely, shoulder	
Company E		
PVT Green Keahey		
Company F		
	PVT William W. Ketcham, severely, head	
Company G		
	PVT John J. McCoy, severely, head	
	PVT Robert Parker, right arm amputated	
Company H		
PVT William Gillenwater	PVT John J. Jones, severely, wrist	
	4CPL Henry Murphy, severely, arm	
Company K		
3LT Pat O'Connor	2LT Pulaski H. Brown, both hands	
	PVT John R. Boone, severely, forearm	
	PVT Benjamin F. Culpeper[35]	

Fussell's Mill

*"Our boys moved with the spirit and alacrity, and, upon reaching the
front, showed Grant's chargers how to charge."*[36]—Captain Francis Shaaff,
Company A, Cantey's Rifles, 15th Alabama Infantry Regiment

Grant again moved his army with a wide left swing around Lee's right flank heading toward Petersburg, the indispensable rail hub supplying Richmond and Lee's Army. Major Lowther arrived from Richmond with a colonel's commission and orders to command the 15th Alabama. Oates refused to serve under him and was given command of the 48th Alabama. Oates went to Richmond himself and met with President Jefferson Davis, but Davis explained he could not undo an act of Congress. On July 1, 1864, Oates terminated his long association with the 15th Alabama and assumed command of the 48th Alabama.

The 15th Alabama moved out of their entrenchments at about 1 a.m. on July 29 and marched through the quiet streets of Petersburg during the early morning hours.[37] They boarded the cars of the Richmond and Petersburg Railroad at 8 a.m. for the short ride to Rice Station. By sundown the Alabamians were in place on New Market Heights. "For two weeks, duty north of the James was easy. The sniper's bullet, the relentless sun, the dust and the stench of Petersburg trenches were left behind."[38]

"During the hot night of August 13, the steady rumble of artillery wagons and the tramp of hundreds of horses alerted Field (commanding Hood's Division) that the Federals were mounting an offensive against him. The signaling of dozens of boat whistles of Hancock's fleet of troop transports gave additional notice that it would be a major undertaking."[39] Union General Hancock's Corps was to assault the rear of the Confederates to prevent their evacuation to Petersburg. The 15th Alabama was about to participate in one of its bloodiest battles in its storied history at Fussell's Mill. The two main armies were both in a race for Petersburg, so little attention has been given to this bloody affair in the history of the Civil War.

On Tuesday, August 16, 1864, Hood's Division had been split in two by Hancock's forces. The 15th and 48th regiments were the first to arrive of Law's Brigade, covering the last mile at double time. The 15th had to form their battle line under bombardment from the Union batteries.[40] The 15th Alabama marched into some woods to attack Hancock's left flank. Because of the woods, the regiment found itself barely fifty yards from the enemy when both sides opened a terrific fire at each other. The 15th and the 48th Alabama attacked with their characteristic ferocity into the Union flank and rear and took over 250 prisoners.

Lowther was struck in the side and command was passed to Captain Shaaff. Captain Strickland of Company I was struck in the hand, wrist, and left ear by the same minie ball.[41] Private William Defnall had his right arm shot off by a cannonball while carrying the regimental colors and died of hemorrhage.[42] Sergeant Billy Jordan took up the colors and continued the charge. Sixteen-year-old Henry Dorris was killed after serving in the Confederate Army for only 46 days.[43] Lieutenant Dozier Thornton, leading Companies D and L, took gunshot wounds to the right ankle, right buttock and left leg.[44] 4th Sergeant Thomas S. Mills of Company E was severely wounded in the shoulder (his fourth wound of the war).[45] The two Confederate regiments succeeded in regaining some old Confederate trenches and drove the Union forces from the field; Oates, in command of the 48th Alabama, was shot through the arm, requiring amputation.

Captain Shaaff, commanding the Fighting Fifteenth wrote, "Our boys moved with the spirit and alacrity, and, upon reaching the front, showed Grant's chargers how to charge." Shaaff's opinion was that Richmond was saved by the desperate attack at Fussell's Mill.[46] General Hancock agreed with him when four years later he met with Oates in 1868. Hancock told him that if he had known the attackers were only made up of two small regiments he would have captured all and pushed on to Richmond.

Through careful examination of individual military records, it becomes apparent that the regiment suffered terribly in this little-known battle. The 15th Alabama lost fully one third of their number, suffering 13 killed and 90 wounded.[47] Oates writes that the dead and wounded of the 15th and 48th Alabama covered an entire acre. This would be their last battle in open terrain and was arguably their best effort of the war.

Killed	Wounded	Captured
Company A		
PVT James M. Cooper	1LT Hugh Fields, severely, arm	
	LTC Alexander A. Lowther, severely, body	
	PVT A.M. McMillard, severely, arm	
	5SGT John W. Screws, severely, thigh	
	1CPL John P. Tillery, severely, lung	
Company B		
	PVT John W. Hughs, severely, shoulder	
Company C		
	PVT Joshua L. Chatham, severely	
Company D		
	PVT Thomas J. Reaves, severely, foot	
	1LT Dozier Thornton, severely, right heel, right buttock, left leg	
Company E		
	PVT Joseph H. Bell, mortally, leg	PVT Alpheus W. Brooks, deserted
	PVT Joseph W. Cotton, severely, arm	
	PVT Joseph J. Dean, severely, head	
	PVT Thomas G. Dillard	
	PVT Jesse Flowers, mortally, right shoulder	
	PVT Joseph G. Jones, slightly, thigh	
	3SGT Benjamin A. Lanier, severely, side	
	4SGT Thomas S. Mills, severely, shoulder	
	PVT John W. Price, slightly, leg	
	PVT Samuel Wade, mortally, leg	
	PVT John B. Yelverton, severely, thigh	

Killed	Wounded	Captured
Company F		
	PVT Peter J. Hough, slightly, leg	
	PVT William Holmes, severely	
Company G		
	PVT William Fears, slightly, chest	
	PVT John J. McCoy, severely, leg	
	PVT Bryant Melton, severely, leg	
	LTC William C. Oates, severely, arm amputated	
	PVT Gillum Riley, severely, chest	
	5SGT John H. Whatley, severely, thigh	
Company H		
	PVT John C. Cunningham, severely, forearm	
Company I		
PVT Henry Dorris	CPT William H. Strickland, severely, left hand	
PVT William R. Duck		
Company K		
	PVT Daniel Beasley, severely, body	
Company L		
	PVT R.W. Allen, mortally, shoulder	
	3SGT Jefferson F. Bean, slightly, side	
	1SGT Dixon D. Bonner, seriously, arms and side[48]	

Siege of Petersburg and Richmond

"Men can stand a hungry spell for a short while, but long starvation will sap the strength of any army. Our men grew gaunt, lean and haggard."[49]—Private Mitchell B. Houghton, Company H, Glenville Guards, 15th Alabama Infantry Regiment

Grant realized he couldn't defeat Lee in open battle; however, through his dogged determination he had succeeded in forcing the Army of Northern Virginia to protect the Confederate capital and its logistical lifeline, Petersburg. The entire Army of Northern Virginia settled into thirty-five miles of earthworks protecting Richmond and Petersburg. Petersburg was the indispensable railroad junction supplying the army and the capital. The dwindling Confederate Army would spend the next eight months in these trenches. Grant may not have been the tactician Lee was, but he was going take Richmond the way he took Vicksburg: by using his vast resources in men, transportation, and ordnance to choke the life out of his enemy.

The Army of Northern Virginia, on the other hand, was finally bottled up. They no longer had the luxury of foraging off the land or occupying victorious battlefields and supplying themselves off the corpses and supply depots of their enemy. All supplies had to come from Southern resources that were increasingly being destroyed in Georgia, the Carolinas and the Shenandoah Valley. To make matters worse, these dwindling supplies had to be transported along dilapidated rail lines that were also being destroyed.

As Napoleon famously stated, "An army marches on its stomach," and there would be a lot of empty stomachs for the next eight months. Even if reinforcements were available, which they were not, Lee could not have fed them. The men saw their daily ration reduced "to a pint of cornmeal, baked into pones when there was time, and an ounce or two of bacon."[50] One veteran would say, "I thanked God I had a backbone for my stomach to lean up against."[51] The Southerners were losing weight and strength at an alarming rate and would "pant and grow faint" at the slightest exertion.[52]

Shoes had always been a scarce requisition item in the Southern army, but now the problem would get much more acute. Getting shoes from well-shod Union corpses was always a dividend of a successful battle on the open field. There would be no more such field battles, only constant bombardment and sharpshooting from opposing trenches.

Possibly, the worst shortage was that of metals, particularly copper, indispensable in the manufacture of percussion caps. "Riflemen in the critical outer pits were limited to eighteen caps a day, while their Union counterparts across the way complained of bruised shoulders from being required to expend no less than a hundred rounds in the same span."[53] Other metals had to be scavenged from incoming projectiles. Furloughs were even offered for soldiers to collect so many pounds of fragments.

As terrible as conditions were in the Richmond-Petersburg trenches, losses were

"The Dictator," a 13-inch mortar, used at Petersburg (Library of Congress).

low among the 15th Alabama. During the siege, Lee used Field's Division (formally Hood's) as his mobile reserve.[54] This new mission was a positive one since they would receive occasional breaks from the filth, stench, and boredom of trench life. However, it was a dangerous mission in that they would be used as the "plug" for Union break-throughs of the Confederate lines.

The first such mission occurred on September 29, 1864, when the enemy occu-pied Fort Harrison. The division commander headed out with only Law's Brigade because of the lack of transportation on the rickety Confederate rail system. The men had to run the final five miles when they reached the Confederate breastworks near Fort Gilmer shortly after 2 p.m.[55] The 15th Alabama had barely gotten in place when the Texas Brigade on their right was assaulted by the First United States Colored Troops (USCT) of the X Corps. This would be the first time the Alabamians had wit-nessed Negro troops in battle. The men of the 15th Alabama cheered the Texans on "as if they were on a charge." The boys from the Wiregrass had heard of atrocities committed by the black troops and watched their demise with a mixture of anger and fear.[56]

As night fell on September 29, the Alabamians could hear the Federals strength-ening the fortifications of Fort Harrison. The Confederates were being positioned for a dreaded night assault. The Fighting Fifteenth wouldn't be issued rations until the next day. To the delight of the men, the planned night assault did not take place but was postponed until the morning of September 30.

The Alabamians were not in the main assault but were given the mission of cap-turing a redoubt northwest of Fort Harrison. For the second time in as many days, the 15th encountered Negro troops. They easily drove in the USCT skirmishers and captured the redoubt. As the main assault failed, the 22nd USCT counterattacked the Confederate columns and came under fire of the 15th Alabama and the other reg-iments of Law's Brigade. With the failure of the main assault, Law's Brigade had to retreat under the cover of darkness.

Killed	Wounded	Captured
Company B		
2CPL M.L. Harper		
Company C		
	PVT John R. Draghn, severely, breast	
Company D		
PVT Thomas Pate		
Company F		
PVT David G. Ray		
Company G		
PVT Joshua C. Creech		
Company H		
	PVT Thomas J. Brooks, leg	
	PVT George W. Gill, severely	

Killed	Wounded	Captured
Company I		
PVT B. Wright Mosley	PVT John Q. Deese, severely, foot	
	PVT Thomas A. Grey, slightly, chest	
	PVT Hugh McLeod, slightly, hand	
Company L		
	PVT George W. Garrett, severely, shoulder[57]	

The next such hole that needed "plugging up" occurred in a couple of battles along Darbytown Road. The first battle occurred on October 7, 1864, when Lee attempted to retake the exterior line above Fort Harrison. The mission for the 15th Alabama was to drive in the skirmishers of Union cavalry and drive the cavalry from their position. With Company G deployed as skirmishers, the men erupted with the rebel yell and quickly routed the surprised cavalry before easily capturing their camp, a cannon, and most of the enemy. Near the cannon an "oversized" Yankee demanded the surrender of Lieutenant McClendon of Company G when Private Jim Rhodes of Company K ordered the Yankee to "Surrender yourself, G—d d—n you." McClendon liberated the enemy's sword belt and wore it for the rest of the war, taking it home afterward.[58]

The Fighting Fifteenth continued their assault, driving the 100th New York from their breastworks, but were halted when the 10th Connecticut stood their ground. The attack was stalled. The brigade netted nine pieces of artillery, ten caissons, two battle flags, 100 horses, and over 100 prisoners.[59]

The second Battle of Darbytown occurred on October 13. After losing Fort Harrison, Lee had to rebuild his fortifications closer to Richmond. Grant ordered an advance to drive the Confederates from their construction work. The Union line advanced on the 15th Alabama skirmishers, Company K, firing steadily as they advanced. The commander, 1st Lieutenant Henry W. Glover (of Company B but commanding Company K), was mortally wounded in the head.[60] This reconnaissance in force led Grant to draw the conclusion: "To attack now we would lose more than the enemy and only gain ground which we are not prepared to hold."[61] Unfortunately for the Union, an assault had already been ordered due to a miscommunication.

The men of the Fighting Fifteenth knew an assault was coming as soon as they heard the commands of the Union officers of the 1st Brigade, Ames' Division, X Corps. According to 2nd Lieutenant McClendon, the men had "resolved to stand to the last and give them the bayonet in the event they came near enough." He remembered later that "there was no thought of surrendering or retreating."[62] As soon as the Federals entered a clearing, the 15th poured a devastating fire into them, disrupting their formations. The attacking Federals numbered about 570 men, and about half were lost within minutes.[63] The commander of one of the Union regiments wrote, "I have not seen a more hopeless task undertaken since I entered the service than that attempted by the assaulting column today."[64] The 15th Alabama built their winter quarters directly behind these fortifications and would remain there until the early days of April 1865.[65]

Killed	Wounded	Captured
Company A		
	PVT Alias E. Averett, slightly, hand	*PVT James F. Phillips
	PVT John B. King, mortally, left shoulder	PVT S.M. Ragland
	CPT Francis K. Shaaff	
Company B		
PVT W.S. Wesley	CPT Noah B. Feagin	
	2SGT John M. Payne, severely, thigh	
Company C		
	PVT John A. Burt, severely, arm	
	PVT William H. Cooper, slightly, thigh	
Company D		
	PVT Jack V. Caraker, mortally	
Company E		
	PVT Frank Hartzog	
	PVT John Munn, severely, leg amputated	
	PVT W.J. Robertson, slightly, thigh	
	PVT James Lammons, severely, head	
	PVT H.J. Williamson, slightly, leg	
Company F		
	PVT Joseph Wilson, severely, shoulder	
Company G		
	PVT David C. Cannon, severely	
	PVT Charles H. Harris	
	PVT Andrew J. Huggins, slightly, side	
	PVT D.C. Kinnon, slightly, chest	
	PVT Pugh Kirkland, slightly, back	
	PVT Elija W. Lingo, severely, right ankle	
	PVT Henry W. McLeod, slightly, heel	
	PVT James H. Miller, severely, right thigh	
	PVT Thomas J. Miller, mortally	
	4SGT John D. Shepard, slightly	
	PVT Edward J. Ward, mortally, abdomen	
	PVT John Woodham	
Company H		
	PVT Thomas B. Gray	
	PVT Matthew W. Lynn	
	3SGT James M. Sims, severely, arm	
	PVT Lemuel C. Smith, slightly, arm	
Company I		
PVT John Redman	PVT John Helms, slightly, chest	
	PVT James D. Jones, slightly, leg	
	PVT Benton W. Peters, severely, leg	
	PVT H.C. Powell, severely, shoulder	

Killed	Wounded	Captured
	PVT James T. Rushing	
	PVT S.B. Smith, severely, leg amputated	
Company K		
	PVT Clark J. Faulk, foot	
	PVT Evan G. Grice, slightly, head	
	1CPL Woodruff F. Hill, severely, left leg	
Company L		
	PVT Charles K. Dean, slightly, leg	
	PVT P.R. Eddins, slightly, chest	
	PVT John L. Newton, severely, foot[66]	

*wounded and captured

The 15th Infantry Regiment had been paid once in the last eight months. The men couldn't even afford to buy a sweet potato when a wagon full of them arrived in camp one day.[67] The scarcity of money and rations caused some good men to become despondent and lose all hope of success. Consequently, through the months of January, February and March, desertions became frequent. The men may have figured that if the war could be won and a Confederate government firmly established, their families would be taken care of by pensions in the event of their death. The men didn't mind facing death, but if their government was defeated, their families would not be taken care of if they died. These were not cowardly men who chose to desert; many had been wounded two, three, or four times.

It must have deeply hurt General Lee to watch his finely honed Army of Northern Virginia deteriorate under these conditions. Grant had already lost 35,000 men in frontal assaults since June and would not make that mistake again. He didn't need to; he simply continued to lengthen his lines, forcing Lee to counter with his line, thus stretching the thinly occupied Confederate trenches even further to 37 miles by February 1865. Meanwhile, Sherman, with 60,000 men, was moving almost unopposed through Savannah, Georgia, and both capitals of the Carolinas. After capturing Raleigh, North Carolina, he was headed to join Grant. The 15th Alabama's losses during the siege were:

Killed	Wounded	Captured
Company A		
		*PVT John L. Broughton
		*PVT E.L. Davidson
		*PVT Thomas R. Johnson
Company B		
4CPL John F. Cain		
Company C		
	PVT John M. Head	*PVT Thomas A. Coghill
	1LT William B. Lloyd, slightly, thigh	PVT Thomas R. Watts
		*PVT Bascom K. Wilkerson

Killed	Wounded	Captured
Company D		
PVT Angus McGilvary		
Company E		
	5SGT Barry W. Fleming, severely, left forearm	*PVT Benjamin A. Daughtry
	3SGT Benjamin A. Lanier	**PVT Andrew Murphy
		**PVT John Murphy
		*PVT Samuel J. Preston
		*PVT Warren W. Vance
Company F		
	PVT John Jackson, slightly, thigh	PVT Owens W. Graham
	PVT Stephen J. Rodgers	**PVT Jeff E. Hussey
	PVT Archibald Jackson, slightly, thigh	1SGT L. Scott Knowles
Company G		
		*4CPL William N. Bullard
		PVT R.M. Campbell
		*PVT Irvin Hicks
		*PVT Andrew J. Huggins
		*PVT David W. Merrit
		**PVT Charles W. Raleigh
		*PVT John Riley
		*PVT James A. Roney
		*PVT Lewis M. Sasser
		*PVT John D. Shepard
		*PVT John Woodham
Company H		
	PVT Charles A. Moody, mortally	*O.J. Moates
Company I		
PVT James L. Norris	PVT Simon D. Wilson, severely right arm amputated	
PVT Bradberry Wilson		
Company K		
	PVT Columbus Bell, right thigh	*PVT Edmond Batchelor
		*PVT John J. Carter
Company L		
	PVT Benagay Bass	*PVT Levi Blair
		PVT Rich W. Rowell[68]

*deserted and captured by the Union
**deserted but not captured by the Union

By April 1865, Lee knew he had to do something; staying in the trenches of Richmond and Petersburg was no longer an option. Lee attempted his breakout in early April and made it to Appomattox Court House, where he was left with no alternative but to surrender his once magnificent army. Lee was surrounded, out of food and ammunition, and surrendered on April 9, 1865. It is unknown how many men General Lee surrendered, but he accepted 25,000 rations for his soldiers from Grant.

"Lowther led the 15th Alabama to its final formation. Once the largest regiment in the brigade, the 15th Alabama brought an aggregate strength of 219 to the field of surrender."[69] The 15th Alabama Infantry Regiment ended the war as one of the most accomplished regiments from either side. Those soldiers who could be confirmed by service records to be present during the surrender of April 9, 1865, were:

Company A

PVT Eli F. Broughton
PVT George J. Eason
PVT John R. Gardner
PVT Asa M. Keeling
PVT Michael Murry
PVT James P. Newberry
PVT Robert S. Warlick

Company B

PVT Thomas S. Beasley
PVT J.D. Callaway
PVT William M. Callaway
PVT Robert J. Eubanks
PVT Daniel L. Kendrick
3CPL Eugene P. Lane
PVT Samuel J. Ming
PVT William J. Ming

Company C

3SGT Douglas D. Guerry
PVT Green B. Vinson
PVT Silas Walker

Company D

PVT Henry J. Day
PVT J.W. Day
PVT F.L. Hatcher
3SGT William W. Johnson
PVT Robert S. Jones
PVT William T. Dillard
PVT W.H. Quattlebaum

Company E

PVT James Andrews
PVT B. Newton Curenton
PVT William B. Davis
PVT James E. Dillard
PVT Thomas G. Dillard
3CPL John W. Glenn
2LT Jim R. Edwards
PVT George F. Hogg
3SGT Samuel Hogg
PVT William H. Jolly
PVT Charley C. Jones
PVT Elvin Jones
PVT Joseph G. Jones
PVT Benjamin J. Martin
PVT Daniel McSwain
PVT William W. Mobley
PVT Samuel Q Mullins
PVT Anderson Peek
PVT Abram Powell
PVT Augustus B. Tommie
PVT William R. Trawick

Company F

PVT A.N. Anderson
3SGT John N. Bray
4SGT George W. Brazil
PVT Benjamin H. Galloway
1SGT James H. Long
PVT Hershall V. Glenn
PVT Thomas H. Holloway
PVT John B. Hough
PVT Frank M. Logan
PVT Philip L. Minshew
PVT J.A. Paul
PVT William T. Paulk
PVT John T. Prior
2CPL William N. Reeves
PVT Frank M. Roundtree
PVT James E. Rudd
PVT M.V. Rudd
PVT Francis M. Smith
PVT Samuel W. Warrick

Company G

PVT Thomas H. Acree
PVT William Y. Carr
PVT Augustus H. Dozier
PVT Charles H. Harris
PVT Bebe S. Hughes
PVT Allen A. Kirkland
PVT Pugh Kirkland
3SGT Elijah W. Lingo
2LT Augustus McClendon
PVT Robert S. McKnight
PVT William J. McKnight

Company H

PVT Thomas J. Brooks
2SGT John W. Cowart
Ord SGT Willliam Crews
1CPL Cader A. Lee
PVT Alexander Pope
PVT Barton S. Reneau
PVT Joshua L. Smith
PVT John D. Smith
PVT Lemuel C. Smith
PVT Joel Tew
PVT Harris C. Yelverton

Company I

PVT Isaac N. Andress
PVT James P. Ballard
4SGT Brantley G. Barnett
PVT Joseph Bell
PVT George Bennett
PVT Squire H. Burgess
SGT Frank D. Champion
PVT Isaac P. Folmar
4CPL Bailey T. Freeman
PVT Alfred B. Graham
PVT Thomas A. Grey

Company G	Company H	Company I
PVT Henry W. McLeod		PVT Joshua W. Harris
PVT James M. Melvin		PVT Richard A. Harris
PVT James R. Morris		PVT James T. Hightower
SMJ Green C. Renfroe		PVT James Hill
PVT John D. Shepard		PVT James D. Jones
PVT John D. Sowell		PVT George W. Linton
		2CPL William J. McAllister
		PVT Williamson McCarra
		PVT John McClendon
		PVT William McCleod
		PVT J. Henry Osburn
		PVT Isaac H. Parks
		PVT Thomas B. Railey
		PVT M.J. Segars
		PVT Capel S. Smedley
		1SGT Randolph C. Smedley

Above left: **Private John W. Allen, Company L. Pictured here after the war with his wife, Susan Ann Arrington. He died in 1912 in Dallas, Texas (courtesy Jim Rogers).** *Above right:* **Private Henry J. Day, Company D. Post-war photograph. He died October 22, 1927 (courtesy Jim Dark).** *Bottom right:* **Private Isaac P. Folmar, Company I. Married Rachel Virginia Stringer on January 27, 1859. He served as a sharpshooter until the surrender. Pictured here post-war (courtesy Jerome Folmar).**

Company G

Company H

Company I

PVT Blackman Strickland
PVT David Stroud
2SGT Hiram A. Thompson
PVT Thomas Wilson
PVT Hayne L. Wolfe
PVT Jacob H. Wolfe

Company K

CPT William J. Bethune
PVT Pat Brannon
PVT James L. Cade
PVT Nelson Cummings
COMSGT Jeptha Hill
PVT James M. Loflin
PVT Andrew J. Roberts
PVT John A. Seegars
2CPL James R. Watts
PVT Julius C. Wicker

Company L

PVT John W. Allen
PVT Benagay Bass
4SGT Thomas R. Collins
PVT P.R. Eddins
PVT George W. Garrett
PVT Allen F. Hart
PVT W.A. Haynes
PVT George R. Henderson
2SGT W.L. Lain
PVT J. Lloyd
PVT Lee Lloyd
PVT Benjamin F. Long
PVT W.G. Morgan
PVT Hugh Norris
5SGT J.L. Osburne
PVT William Owens
1CPL Noah Post[70]

Southern Cross of Honor

The Confederacy awarded the Southern Cross of Honor (the Confederate equivalent of the U.S. Medal of Honor) to twenty-two members of the 15th Alabama during the Civil War. Those men, with a short biography, are:

Company A

Charles E. Averett

Private Averett's correct name was Alvis Early Averett. The 1860 Census shows him living with his parents John (51) and May (45) in Reeltown, Alabama. Alvis followed his brother David, who had enlisted in Company A, 15th Alabama. Alvis enlisted February 5, 1864, at the age of 17 at Tallassee, Alabama. He was awarded the Southern Cross of Honor on December 10, 1864, by General Order No. 87 after serving only eight months. Oates describes him as a "faithful, young soldier." Military records show that he was admitted to Howard's Grove Hospital on August 27, 1864, probably from a wound at the Battle of Fussell's Mill. He received a slight hand wound on October 7, 1864. Private Averett served until Lee's surrender on April 9, 1865.

According the 1870 Census, Alvis moved to California and is living with Alexander and Mary Lewis in Watsonville, Santa Cruz County, working as a store clerk in

Mr. Lewis's general store. Voter registration records have him living there as early as 1869. Between 1871 and 1875 he had moved to Soledad, Monterey, California, and in the 1880 Census he is married to A.L., who was born in Iowa. They have a son and a daughter. Alvis is working as a general merchant. No other census records exist, but voter registration records for 1888 and 1892 have him living in Santa Clara County, California, still working as a merchant. The 1892 record describes him as 6'0" tall, light complexion, gray hair, and gray eyes.

Company B

M.L. Harper

M.L. Harper is not available in any census records prior to the war. He enlisted in the Confederate Army at Fort Mitchell on July 3, 1861, at the age of 21 as a private. He is listed as a single farmer. Oates writes that he "was a good soldier" and that he was wounded at Cold Harbor, although military records don't substantiate this. He was wounded at Second Manassas on August 28, 1862, and admitted to the Charlottesville Hospital on September 18. Records indicate that he deserted from that hospital on September 29. Sometime during May and June of 1863 he was on furlough. He received a clothing issue on July 1, 1863. Private Harper was promoted to second corporal on September 22, 1863, and was again on furlough during November and December 1863. On December 24, 1863, he again received a clothing issue. On May 2, 1864, he was again at the Charlottesville Hospital for "Lurunculus," which is simply a boil. Second Corporal Harper was killed in action on September 30, 1864, yet received the Southern Cross of Honor posthumously on December 10, 1864, by order of General Order No. 87.

Company C

William H. Cooper

Prior to the Civil War, William was a single farmer living with family members Joseph W. (73), Julia (52) and Mary L. (16) at Creek Stand, Alabama.

William enlisted in Company C, 15th Alabama on February 2, 1862, at Creek Stand. Private Cooper was wounded at the Battle of Chickamauga on September 20, 1863, and hospitalized at Floyd House and Ocmulgee Hospital in Macon, Georgia, on September 23. He was available for muster at the end of October 1863. He received a clothing issue on October 3, 1864. On October 13 he received a slight wound to the thigh. Private Cooper received additional clothing issues on October 18 and December 5 of 1864. On December 10, 1864, he was awarded the Southern Cross of Honor by General Order No. 87. On December 16, he received another clothing issue. On January 7, 1865, he was given a furlough to Creek Stand, Alabama. He was described as 5'7", light complexion, gray eyes, light hair, and a farmer. He surrendered with Lee's Army on April 9, 1865.

In the 1870 Census he is living alone at Silver Run in Russell County and working as a farmhand. In 1880 he is living at Warrior Stand, Alabama, with his 20-year-old wife Dasie and 6-month-old daughter, Mary. William is working as a laborer.

COMPANY D

William Washington Johnson

According to the 1860 Census, William is single and working as a farm laborer for the Sampson D. and Missouri C. Helms family; he is also living with them.

On July 3, 1861, he enlists in Company D, 15th Alabama Infantry at Fort Browder, Alabama. The May-June 1863 muster roll lists him as a 3rd sergeant, and the September-October 1863 muster roll lists him as a second sergeant. He received clothing issues on September 10, November 22 and 30, 1864. On December 10, 1864, he was awarded the Southern Cross of Honor according to General Order No. 87. He received another clothing issue on December 16, 1864. On April 9, 1865, he surrendered with the Army of Northern Virginia.

William Johnson is only found on the 1880 Census, where he is married to Mahala Johnson and living in Tanyard, Pike County, Alabama. They had five children.

Robert Samuel "Sam" Jones

Sam was born on September 7, 1839, in Hawkinsville, Barbour County, Alabama. In the 1860 Census he is listed as a student and still living with his parents, Samuel and Selina. Samuel Sr. is a very wealthy farmer.

Sam joined Company D, 15th Alabama Infantry on July 3, 1861. Oates wrote in his book on page 627 that Private Jones was wounded at Cold Harbor on June 27, 1862, although I couldn't verify this in his military records. He was elected CPL on October 1, 1862, while at the 3rd Alabama Hospital. He was transferred to the 3rd Alabama Hospital from Chimborazo Hospital on April 12, 1863, with something wrong with his right foot. The May through October 1863 muster rolls list him as "absent on furlough." The January-February 1864 muster roll lists him as a private. He received clothing issues on October 3, November 17 and 22, 1864. On December 10, 1864, he received the Southern Cross of Honor by General Order No. 87. Sam surrendered with the Army of Northern Virginia on April 9, 1865.

W.H. Quattlebaum

Wilkes Horry Quattlebaum was born September 18, 1844. At the age of 17 he enlisted in Company D, 15th Alabama Infantry at Fort Browder, Alabama, on March 8, 1862. Oates writes on page 629 that Private Quattlebaum was wounded at Cold Harbor, which would have been June 27, 1862. On December 31, 1862, he was in a hospital because he was paid there. For the muster roll of September-October 1863, he was again in the hospital, and for the November-December 1863 muster roll he is listed as on furlough. He received clothing issues on October 21 and November 17 of 1864. On December 10, 1864, he was awarded the Southern Cross of Honor by order of General Order No. 87. Private Quattlebaum served on until the surrender on April 9, 1865.

After the war Wilkes married Jane Anna Maria Stanford in 1867 at Georgetown, Stewart County, Georgia. They are still living there in the 1870 Census. In the 1900 Census they are living in Rochelle, Wilcox County, Georgia, and in the 1920 Census they are in Jones Creek, Clinch County, Georgia. They had eleven children over the years. Wilkes died on October 14, 1927.

COMPANY E

James Russell Edwards

James was born February 29, 1840. At the time of his enlistment James was a single farmer.

He was entered into the Dale County Beauregards by Captain Brooks on July 3, 1861, as a private. Private Edwards was honored with the privilege of carrying the regimental colors. He was wounded on August 30, 1862, at the Battle of Second Manassas. Private Edwards received the following promotions: on New Year's Eve of 1863 he was promoted to fifth sergeant; in June of 1864 to second sergeant; and November 1, 1864, to second lieutenant. On December 10, 1864, 2nd Lieutenant Edwards received the Southern Cross of Honor, which was the Confederate equivalent of the Medal of Honor. Oates writes that he was a "hard fighter and always conspicuous in action" and "universally respected by all who knew him." He was the commander of Company E at the time of surrender.

After the war James married Sarah E., and in 1880 they had settled in Westville, Alabama, where they were farming. The family is James (40), Sarah E. (30), Thomas (11), Ada (8), Willow (7), May (3), and Mary (1). Oates wrote that he was a "Respected citizen of Dale [County]." James died on May 4, 1890, and is buried at the Newton City Cemetery on Killebrew Street in Newton, Alabama.

Benjamin J. Martin

In the 1860 Census of Newton, Alabama, the Martin brothers are attending school and working as farm laborers with their large family. Their farming parents are Haywood (47) and Emily (38). The rest of the family are: Benjamin (18), James P. (16), William D. (14), Simon S. (12), Haywood (10), Franklin P. (8), Sarah E. (7), Eldridge (4), and Lilly (9 months). All of the children, age 7 and above, had attended school within the year. Franklin is the first child born in Alabama, which leads us to believe the family moved to Alabama between 1850 and 1852. All family members before Franklin were born in North Carolina. Also living on the farm are two female slaves, 27 and 2 years of age.

Benjamin joined the Dale County Beauregards on July 3, 1861, by Captain Brooks. Private Martin was promoted to second corporal on July 10, 1864. He received clothing issues on October 4 and December 16 of 1864. Second Corporal Martin surrendered with the Army of Northern Virginia on April 9, 1865. It is unfortunate that we do not know more of his service because we do know that he was awarded the Southern Cross of Honor on December 10, 1864.

Benjamin moved to Montgomery County, Texas, and died there on June 6, 1910. He is buried at Old China Grove Baptist Church Cemetery in that county.

Abraham Powell

Abraham was the child of Abraham (1806) and Lilia (1812), who settled in Dale County, Alabama. Other children were: L.B. (1839), Rachel E. (1844), Emiline (1845), William A. (1849), Perry (1852), Caroline (1854), Mary J. (1856), and Rhoda (1860–1883).

Abraham was born in Georgia. Abraham (21) was a farmer in High Bluff, Alabama, in the 1860 Census. He was married to Emily J. (19), also born in Georgia.

Abraham joined the Dale County Beauregards on March 3, 1862. Private Powell was wounded at Sharpsburg, Maryland, on September 17, 1862. He was admitted to Chimborazo Hospital for unknown reasons on May 4, 1863. He was on furlough during the July-August 1864 muster roll. In 1864, Private Powell received clothing issues on October 4 and 21, November 17 and 30, and December 8. He must have been well dressed when he received the Southern Cross of Honor on December 10, 1864. He was one of only three Dale County Beauregards to receive this prestigious award. On January 19, 1865, Private Powell was discharged and described as "25 years, 5'8", fair complexion, blue eyes, light hair, farmer." At this point of the war, he probably couldn't get through the Union lines and get home, because he surrendered with the Army of Northern Virginia on April 9, 1865.

Company F

Hershall V. Glenn

In the 1860 Census, Hershall is living with parents John and Elizabeth Glenn and his three sisters.

On March 4, 1862, Hershall joined Company F, 15th Alabama Infantry in Brundidge, Alabama. Oates mentions that Private Glenn was "a good soldier." Private Glenn was captured at Sharpsburg on September 17, 1862, but exchanged at Aiken's Landing on November 10, 1862. Military records show that he was at the Winder Hospital from October 31 to December 31, 1862. He again was admitted to an Eastern District Hospital on January 7, 1863. Private Glenn received clothing issues on October 23, November 18 and 22, 1864. He was awarded the Southern Cross of Honor by order of General Order No. 87 on December 10, 1864. Private Glenn surrendered with the Army of Northern Virginia on April 9, 1865.

All that is known of Hershall's postwar life is that he married Manerva L. Bizzell on July 30, 1868.

Archibald N. Jackson

Archibald was living alone and farming in the 1860 Census. He enlisted into Company F, 15th Alabama on July 3, 1861, at the age of 26. According to page 663 in Oates's book, Private Jackson was wounded at Knoxville on November 25, 1863. The muster roll of November-December 1863 lists him as "sick at hospital." In the muster roll of January-February 1864, Private Jackson is listed as absent without leave. Private Jackson received clothing issues on October 21 and November 10 and 30 of 1864. Oates writes that he died in a skirmish on December 1, 1864. He was posthumously awarded the Southern Cross of Honor on December 10, 1864, according to General Order No. 87.

John Jackson

According to the 1860 Census, John is farming with wife Martha M. They have three children and are living in Bibb, Pike County, Alabama.

John joined Company F, 15th Alabama Infantry on March 1, 1862, at the age of 39. Oates writes on page 663 that he was wounded at Suffolk, Virginia, on May 3, 1863. Muster rolls show Private Jackson "sick at hospital" from May to August 1863. From January 1 through May 21, 1864, he was on "extra duty as shoemaker." On October 4, 1864, Private Jackson received a clothing issue, and on October 10 he received a slight thigh wound. He received more clothing issues on October 23, November 1 and 22, and December 8 of 1864. On December 10 he received the Southern Cross of Honor by order of General Order No. 87. On December 16 he received another clothing issue. Private Jackson served on to Lee's surrender on April 9, 1865.

In the 1870 Census he has added two more children and is farming in Brundidge, Alabama. In 1880 he and his wife have two daughters and a grandson living with them in Grimes, Pike County, Alabama.

Company G

David Crockett Cannon

Nothing is known about David prior to the war. David enlisted in Company G, 15th Alabama in Abbeville, Alabama, on July 3, 1861, at the age of 15. Oates describes him as "an excellent and brave soldier" on page 681 of his book. Private Cannon was in the Chimborazo Hospital for debility from April 12 to April 20, 1862. He was severely wounded at the Battle of Chickamauga on September 20, 1863, and hospitalized at Floyd House and Ocmulgee Hospitals in Macon, Georgia, on September 23. After hospitalization, records show that he was placed on furlough. Private Cannon was still at the hospital for the November-December 1863 muster roll and the January-February 1864 muster roll. For the September-October 1864 muster roll he is listed as "sick in camp." He received a clothing issue on October 23. On December 10, 1864, he received the Southern Cross of Honor by order of General Order No. 87. On December 30 he received another clothing issue. On January 21, he deserted to the Federal lines and was captured. He took the Oath of Allegiance at Bermuda Hundred, Virginia, and sent to Washington, D.C. He was transported to Jacksonville, Florida, and released from Union custody.

In the 1870 Census David is living with Elizabeth Cannon in Tyler, Texas, working as a farm laborer. In 1880, he and Elizabeth are living in Houston, Texas, with two adopted children and a boarder. David is working as a farmer.

Herrin F. Satcher

In 1860, Herrin is working as a farm laborer and living with his farming parents, H.M. and Dicey, at Curenton's Bridge, Henry County, Alabama.

At the age of 23, Herrin enlisted with Company G, 15th Alabama Infantry at Abbeville on July 3, 1861. Oates describes Private Herrin as "an intelligent man and one of the best soldiers in the company, and none better in the regiment," on page 701 of his book. He was placed in the General Hospital in Charlottesville, Virginia, between June 22 and July 29 of 1862 for "acute pneumonia." Private Herrin was promoted to second corporal on May 12, 1863. The January-February 1864 muster roll listed him as "deserted," and the remaining records show him as a private, so he might have been reduced in rank. He received clothing issues on October 23 and December 16 of 1864. While it is not in his official records, it is believed he received the Southern Cross of Honor on December 10, 1864. Oates writes that he was "killed near Petersburg, Virginia, April 2, 1865."

COMPANY H

No recipients.

COMPANY I

Brantley G. Barnett
The 1850 Census shows Brantley being raised by his single, farming father, Landa. He has an older brother and two younger sisters. The family is living in Pike County.

Brantley enlisted in Company I, 15th Alabama Infantry in Troy, Alabama, on July 3, 1861. On page 729, Oates writes that Private Barnett "was a good soldier." From July 19 through August 26, 1862, he was in Howards Grove Hospital for fever. He was promoted to third corporal on August 3, 1862, and fourth sergeant on June 1, 1864. He received clothing issues on November 1 and 17, 1864. On December 10, 1864, 4th Sergeant Barnett received the Southern Cross of Honor by order of General Order No. 87. He received another clothing issue on December 16. Fourth Sergeant Brantley surrendered with the Army of Northern Virginia on April 9, 1865, and there is no record of his ever being wounded during the war.

Brantley married Eveline in 1867. In 1879 they had one daughter and were living in Crenshaw County, Alabama. Brantley was working as a farmer.

Solomon James Rushing
In the 1860 Census Solomon is living with his parents William C. and Mary Rushing and six younger siblings. William is a farmer.

Solomon joined Company I, 15th Alabama in Troy, Alabama. Oates describes Private Rushing as "a splendid young soldier" on page 739 of his book. Lt. Colonel Oates thought so highly of Private Rushing that he made him his orderly for the duration of the time Colonel Oates was commander of the 15th Alabama. Private Rushing was severely wounded at Cold Harbor and hospitalized at the General Hospital #21 in Richmond from July 12 to July 26. He was given 30 days' furlough to go home and recover. He received clothing issues on October 4 and November 1 of 1864. On December 10, 1864, he was awarded the Southern Cross of Honor by order of General Order No. 87. Private Rushing continued his service until the surrender on April 9, 1865.

In the 1870 Census, Solomon is married to E.R., and they have two children living in DeSoto Parish, Louisiana. In the 1880 Census the family is farming in Hopkins County, Texas, with four children.

COMPANY K

Clark J. Faulk

Clark married Martha Stanford on February 28, 1854. He worked as a mechanic.

Clark enlisted in Company K, 15th Alabama on July 3, 1861, in Eufaula, Alabama, at 35 years old. He was elected third corporal. Oates writes in his book on page 746 that 3rd Corporal Faulk "was a fine soldier ... one of the best soldiers in the company." He was reduced in rank to private for unknown reasons. On October 3, 1864, Private Faulk received a clothing issue. Oates also writes that he was severely wounded on the Darbytown Road, Virginia, on October 7, 1864. Military records show that this was a severe wound to his foot. He was admitted to Howards Grove Hospital. On December 10, 1864, he received the Southern Cross of Honor by order of General Order No. 87. Private Faulk served on until Lee's surrender on April 9, 1865.

Nothing further is known of Clark.

Evans Grice

According to the 1860 Census, Evans is living with his parents, John and Nancy, and three brothers and two sisters in Eufaula. John is a blacksmith.

On July 3, 1861, Evans enlisted into Company K, 15th Alabama Infantry Regiment. Oates writes on page 751 that Private Grice made "an excellent soldier." From March 9 to April 11, 1863, he was in General Hospital #18 for pneumonia and transferred to Amelia Court House. Private Grice was wounded at Fredericksburg on December 13, 1862; his brother Steven was mortally wounded here. The surgeon describes Private Grice's wound as "near the left knee, ball making slight abrasion of skin but producing considerable swelling from the contusion." He lost his other brother William to disease in April 1863. Private Grice received clothing issues on October 10 and November 11, 1864. He surrendered with the Army of Northern Virginia on April 9, 1865.

The 1880 Census shows Evans married to Mary in Hillardsville, Henry County, Alabama. They have 4 children, ages 3–11. Evans died on February 23, 1920, in Dothan, Alabama.

Woodruff F. Hill

Woodruff was born on March 19, 1845, in Barbour County, Alabama. In the 1860 Census he is living with his father E.P. Hill in Columbus, Georgia, who is working as a clerk.

On July 3, 1861, Woodruff joined Company K, 15th Alabama in Eufaula, Alabama. Oates writes that he was a "good soldier" on page 753 of his book. Private Hill was promoted to 3rd Corporal on April 1, 1862, and later was promoted to 1st corporal (date unknown). He spent from September 25, 1862, to February 19, 1863, in the 8th Division Hospital in Danville, Virginia, for chronic rheumatism. While there he received a clothing issue on January 17, 1863. On October 4, 1864, he received a clothing issue. He was severely wounded in the left leg on October 7 at Darbytown Road, Virginia. First Corporal Hill was hospitalized at Howards Grove Hospital and transferred at some point to Jackson's Hospital in Richmond. On December 10, 1864, he received the Southern Cross of Honor. First Corporal Hill was captured by the Union forces occupying Richmond on April 10, 1865, and transported to the General Hospital at Point Lookout, Maryland, by the hospital transport *Thomas Powell.* He took the Oath of Allegiance on June 26, 1865. His oath describes him as "dark complexion, black hair, hazel eyes, 5'6"."

Woodruff married Elendor Harden on December 28, 1874, in Marianna, Florida. They had four children. Woodruff died on December 18, 1931, in Graceville, Florida.

COMPANY L

James F. Bean

According to the 1860 Census, James is living with his parents, Levi and Emily, and eight brothers and sisters in Farriorville, Pike County, Alabama. Levi is a farmer.

James joined Company L, 15th Alabama Infantry in Perote, Alabama. Oates describes him as a "good soldier" on page 762 of his book. Shortly after his arrival in Virginia he was admitted to the Chimborazo Hospital on April 12, 1862, for measles. He was transported to Danville Hospital on May 28 and remained there until July 9. Private Bean was wounded at Knoxville on November 25, 1863, and again on August 16, 1864, at Fussell's Mill, where he received a slight wound to the side. He received clothing issues on October 4 and November 17, 1864. On December 10 he was awarded the Southern Cross of Honor by order of General Order No. 87. On December 15 he was promoted to third sergeant and received another clothing issue the next day. Oates writes that he was reduced in rank due to disobedience, although he was still a third sergeant when he surrendered with Lee on April 9, 1865.

James is found in the 1870 Census living alone in China Grove, Bullock County, Alabama.

Thomas R. Collins

In the 1860 Census, Thomas is living with his widowed mother, Adna, and four younger brothers and sisters in Indian Creek, Alabama. Thomas is working as a farmer.

On March 11, 1862, Thomas joined Company L, 15th Alabama in Perote, Alabama. Oates describes him as "a fine, young soldier" on page 763 of his book. Private Collins was in the hospital at Charlottesville for debility from June 20, 1862, until July 2, 1862. He was wounded at the Battle of Fredericksburg on December 19, 1862. Private Collins was promoted to second corporal on January 1, 1863. He was given a clothing issue on October 21, 1864, and promoted to fourth sergeant on December 1, 1864. He was awarded the Southern Cross of Honor on December 10, 1864, by order of General Order No. 87. Fourth Sergeant Collins surrendered with the Army of Northern Virginia on April 9, 1865.

In 1870 Thomas is married to Lutarzee with a nine-month-old daughter in Hopkins, Texas. Thomas is living next door to his brother William and working as a farmer.

Leroy Lloyd

Oates gives Leroy's first name as "Levi," military records refer to him as "Lee," and the census reports have him as "Leroy." Knowing the inaccuracies in Oates's book and the military records, I will refer to him as the name given in the census. The 1860 Census has Leroy farming in Perote, Alabama, with his mother Catherine and five brothers and one sister.

Leroy joined Company L, 15th Alabama Infantry in Perote on March 11, 1862. According to military records he was never wounded; however, he was in Chimborazo Hospital from October 29 to November 29, 1862. Oates describes him as "a fine soldier" on page 766 of his book. Private Lloyd received clothing issues on October 10 and November 17, 1864. He received the Southern Cross of Honor on December 10, 1864, by order of General Order No. 87. Private Lloyd surrendered on April 9, 1865, with the Army of Northern Virginia.

In the 1880 Census, Leroy is living with his wife Sarah and three children in Perote. Leroy is still a farmer.

Appendix A: Service Records

Company A

Aaron, James: 19, enlisted 7/03/61, single, farmer. Severely wounded at Cold Harbor 6/27/62. Deserted 7/18/63 at Bunker Hill, VA, captured 7/23/63 and sent to Camp Chase, OH. Took oath on 6/10/64 and joined U.S. Navy on 7/21/64; assigned to Wheeling, VA (now WV). 5'8", sallow complexion, blue eyes, auburn hair. Hometown: Dover, AL.

Alford, William: 35, enlisted 7/03/61, married, farmer. Died 3/02/62 of typhoid. Hometown: Oswichee, AL.

Averett, Alias E.: 17, enlisted 2/05/64, single, farmer. Slightly wounded hand at Darbytown Road 10/07/64. Awarded Southern Cross of Honor 12/10/64. Served to Lee's surrender 4/09/65. "A brave boy and a good soldier." Hometown: Tallassee, AL.

Averett, David F.: 23, enlisted 7/03/61, single, farmer. Severely wounded head at Wilderness 5/06/64. Promoted to 1CPL and 1SGT (early '65). "[O]ne of the best soldiers in his company." Hometown: Tallassee, AL.

Bass, Washington P.: 21, enlisted 7/03/61, single, teacher. Captured Spotsylvania 5/10/64 and sent to Ft. Delaware. Signed oath and released 6/16/65. Promoted 1SGT 8/14/62, 3LT 2/16/63, and 2LT 9/01/63. 5'6", dark complexion, black eyes, black hair. Hometown: Dover, AL.

Basset, Isaac: 17, enlisted 7/03/61, single, farmer. Wounded Manassas 8/28/62, Sharpsburg 9/17/62, and Wilderness 5/06/64. Served through the surrender 4/09/65. Hometown: Mechanicsville, AL.

Bell, Thomas: 30, enlisted 9/14/63, single, tailor. Deserted 12/05/63 Morristown, TN. Hometown: Augusta, GA.

Berry, William T.: 32, enlisted 7/03/61, single,

farmer. Elected 1LT. Captured Cross Keys 6/08/62 and paroled 6/15/62. Resigned 1/21/63 due to rheumatism and neuralgia. Hometown: Columbus, GA.

Blackburn, W.L.: 18, enlisted 7/03/61, single, farmer. Severely wounded Chickamauga 9/19/63, slightly wounded hip Wilderness 5/06/64, and Chester Station 6/17/64. "A true and brave soldier—among the best." Hometown: Beulah, AL.

Boswell, John J.: 18, enlisted 7/03/61, single, student. Detailed as colonel's orderly much of the time. Transferred to Company C, 17th Georgia 8/14/62. Hometown: Columbus, GA.

Broadwater, Charles M.: 27, enlisted 12/06/62, married, farmer. Severely wounded Chickamauga 9/19/63, leg amputated. NOK: B.B. Broadwater, wife. "A good and brave soldier." Hometown: Sandfort, AL.

Brock, E.C.: 18, enlisted 7/03/61, single, farmer. Discharged 11/27/61. Hometown: Glenville, AL.

Broughton, Eli F.: 20, enlisted 7/03/61, single, farmer. Wounded Sharpsburg 9/17/62. Served to Lee's surrender. Court-martialed for "slipping out of fight at Darbytown" 10/07/64. Hometown: Seale Station, AL.

Broughton, James.: 21, enlisted 7/03/61, married, farmer. Severely wounded Cold Harbor 6/27/62. Killed Chickamauga 9/20/63. "A good and brave soldier." Hometown: Seale Station, AL.

Broughton, Jonathan "John" J.: 25, enlisted 7/03/61, married, farmer. Wounded Manassas 8/28/62 and Knoxville 11/25/63. Deserted and captured 1/30/65, sent to Elmira. "A good soldier and fighter." Hometown: Seale Station, AL.

Broughton, William S.: 18, enlisted 7/03/61, single, farmer. Wounded Gettysburg 7/02/63. Captured Wilderness 5/06/64, sent to Elmira. Took oath and released 6/23/65. 5'5", fair complexion, blue eyes, light hair. "A fine soldier." Hometown: Seale Station, AL.

Brown, Henry H.: 19, enlisted 3/01/63, single, farmer. Captured Lookout Valley 10/28/63, sent to Camp Morton, IN. "True as steel, and one of the bravest of the brave." Hometown: Seale Station, AL.

Brown, J.W.: Died 11/25/61 of typhoid.

Brown, Jeptha "Jep": 22, enlisted 7/03/61, married, farmer. Killed 6/08/64 Spotsylvania. "Faithful Soldier." Hometown: Seale Station, AL.

Chambers, James R: 24, enlisted 3/25/62, married, farmer. Wounded Sharpsburg 9/17/62 and Knoxville 11/25/63. "True as steel, and one of the bravest of the brave." Hometown: Russell County, AL.

Chambers, Robert P.: 17, enlisted 7/03/61, single, farmer. Detailed as nurse. Captured Knoxville 12/05/63, sent to Camp Chase, OH, and Ft. Delaware, DE. Took oath and released 6/14/65. "Behaved very cowardly at Raccoon Mountain 1863/10/27. Very much disposed to shirking duty. A first rate hospital rat." 6'0", fair complexion, dark eyes, dark hair. Hometown: Dover, AL.

Chapman, Edward W.P.: 28, enlisted 7/03/61, married, farmer. Severely wounded Manassas 8/30/62. NOK: M.E. Chapman, wife. Hometown: Oswichee, AL.

Cooper, James M.: 23, enlisted 7/03/61, single, farmer. Wounded Manassas 8/28/62. Killed Fussell's Mill 8/16/64. "One of the bravest and best; a severe loss." Hometown: Creek Stand, AL.

Culifer, James L.: 30, enlisted 1/17/63, married, farmer. Severely wounded Lookout Valley 10/27/63. Discharged and assigned to Invalid Corps 12/10/64. Hometown: Haw Ridge, AL.

Curenton, James D.: 28, enlisted 7/03/61, married, carpenter. Double hernia and detailed as teamster. Wounded Cedar Run 8/09/62. Hometown: Pleasant Hill, GA.

Davidson, E.L.: 30, enlisted 7/03/61, married, farmer. Detailed to the arsenal in Columbus, GA, and returned to the front in the summer of '64. Deserted and was captured 1/24/65. "Not much of a soldier, rather poor." Hometown: Seale Station, AL.

Dorsey, M.D.: 42, enlisted 7/03/61, married, merchant. He was appointed Quartermaster SGT. Died at home. Hometown: Columbus, GA.

Eason, George Jeff: 18, enlisted 7/03/61, single, farmer. Severely wounded in leg and cap-

tured Gettysburg 07/02/63. Exchanged 3/?/64, served to Lee's surrender. "A good and brave soldier."

Edwards, Eben B.: 25, enlisted 7/03/61, single, farmer. Promoted 1CPL and 2SGT 3/01/62. Wounded Manassas 8/28/62 and Spotsylvania 5/12/64; left arm amputated. Discharged to Invalid Corps 9/25/64. "A true brave soldier, one of the best." Hometown: Seale Station, AL.

Edwards, Rigdon E.: 21, enlisted 7/03/61, single, farmer. Died 12/04/61. Hometown: Seale Station, AL.

Ellington, Josiah: 21, enlisted 7/03/61, single, farmer. Died 10/28/61. Hometown: Dover, AL.

Fields, Hugh: 19, enlisted 7/03/61, single, student, elected 2SGT. Promoted 1SGT 8/14/62, 3LT 8/14/62, 2LT 1/02/63, and 1LT 1/31/63. Wounded Sharpsburg 9/17/62, Knoxville 11/25/63, and severely in the arm Fussell's Mill 8/16/64. Served to Lee's surrender. Hometown: Villula, AL.

Flowers, Jacob: 27, enlisted 1/17/63, married, farmer. Died 2/19/63 measles. NOK: Sarah Flowers, wife. Hometown: Westville, AL.

Foster, Wesley C.: 21, enlisted 7/03/61, single, farmer. Killed Cross Keys 6/08/62. NOK: Elizabeth Foster, mother. Hometown: Crawford, AL.

Frazier, Arthur: 18, enlisted 7/03/61, single, farmer. Wounded Knoxville 11/25/63. Promoted CPL 8/14/62, 5SGT 3/01/63, and 4SGT. 5'9", dark complexion, blue eyes, dark hair. "A good and brave soldier, one of the best." Hometown: in AL.

Fuller, George R.: 22, enlisted 7/03/61, married, farmer. Discharged 4/16/62. Hometown: Sanford, AL.

Gardner, John Robert.: 17, enlisted 7/03/61, single, farmer. Wounded: Dandridge 01/16/1864. Served to Lee's surrender. Hometown: New Harmony, AL.

Garner, Robert L.: 19, enlisted 7/03/61, single, farmer. Discharged 7/__/62 for disability. Took oath from Provost Marshal Montgomery, AL. 6'2", sallow complexion, blue eyes, dark hair. Hometown: Wetumpka, AL.

Garner, Vincent B.: 21, enlisted 7/03/61, single, farmer. Died 1/11/63. "A good and brave soldier, one of the best." NOK: James Garner, father. Hometown: New Harmony, AL.

Gillenwaters, Nathan H.: 22, enlisted 7/03/61, single, farmer. Discharged 7/12/62. Hometown: Glennville, AL.

Goins, T. Jeff: 18, enlisted 3/29/62, single, farmer. Died 6/14/62 pneumonia. Hometown: Columbus, GA.

Goolsby, Richard: 32, enlisted 7/03/61, married,

farmer. Discharged 6/14/62. Hometown: Huntsville, AL.

Graves, Samuel: 25, enlisted 7/03/61, married, farmer. Died at home 1/09/62. NOK: Nancy Graves, wife. Hometown: Columbus, GA.

Griffin, William C.: 18, enlisted 7/03/61, single, butcher. Severely wounded Cold Harbor 6/27/62. Discharged 2/06/63 "inflammation of right ankle." 5'8", dark complexion, brown eyes, dark hair. Hometown: Augusta, GA.

Hancock, G.H.: In hospital 6/19/62, left arm amputated.

Harris, Lewis: 18, enlisted 9/14/63, single. Joined the regiment as it passed through Augusta, GA. Deserted 9/20/63. Hometown: Augusta, GA.

Hatcher, Thomas J.: 18, enlisted 7/03/61, single, shoemaker. Detailed as ambulance driver. Deserted and captured 12/29/63. Hometown: Columbus, GA.

Haws, Irvin: 18, enlisted 7/03/61, single, farmer. Discharged 12/04/61 due to disability. Hometown: Oswichee, AL.

Haynes, George W.: 24, enlisted 7/03/61, single, policeman. Discharged 06/14/62. 6'0", dark complexion, gray eyes, dark hair. Hometown: Columbus, GA.

Hendry, Frank C.: 28, enlisted 4/16/62, married, farmer. Wounded Deep Bottom 8/16/64. Hometown: White Sulphur Springs, GA.

Hill, James B.: 16, enlisted 7/03/61, single, farmer. Wounded Fredericksburg 12/13/62. Deserted Bunker Hill, VA, 7/18/63 and captured 7/23/63. Sent to Fort Delaware, DE. Took oath and released 6/14/65. 5'8", ruddy complexion, brown eyes, black hair. Hometown: Glenville, AL.

Holt, Joseph H.: 25, enlisted 7/03/61, single, farmer. Killed Cold Harbor 6/27/62. "A good and brave soldier." Hometown: Crawford, AL.

Hooper, M.W.: 22, enlisted 7/03/61, single, farmer. Died 12/28/61, pneumonia/typhoid. Hometown: Crawford, AL.

Horn, James Columbus: 17, enlisted 3/01/63, single, miller. Wounded Gettysburg 7/02/63 and severely wounded Deep Bottom in the knees 8/16/64. Accidently shot himself Dandridge, TN. Captured Macon, GA, 5/20/65. Hometown: Seale Station, AL.

Jewell, James Otis: 41, enlisted 7/03/61, married, farmer. Discharged 9/25/62 for heart hypertrophy. 6'1", light complexion, blue eyes, light hair. Hometown: Seale Station, AL.

John, S.: 45, enlisted 7/03/61, married, farmer. Discharged 11/16/61 for hernia. 5'9", dark complexion, gray eyes, black hair. Hometown: Seale Station, AL.

Johnson, John B.: 32, enlisted 7/03/61, married, blacksmith. Severely wounded Cold Harbor 6/27/62 in left side of the body and through the nose. Detailed as blacksmith. Accidently shot himself in the foot 6/18/64. Hometown: Seale Station, AL.

Johnson, Moses G.: 24, enlisted 7/03/61, married, farmer. Discharged 12/11/61 for tuberculosis. Hometown: Seale Station, AL.

Johnson, Thomas R.: 24, enlisted 7/03/61, married, gunsmith. Deserted and captured 1/24/65. "Poor soldier and much disposed to shirk." Hometown: Seale Station, AL.

Jones, William A.: Enlisted 7/03/61, farmer. Severely wounded Cold Harbor 6/27/62 and Hanover Junction in left forearm 5/24/64. Reduced from CPL. Hometown: Oswichee, AL.

Keeling, Asa M.: Enlisted 7/03/61, single, farmer. Served to Lee's surrender.

King, John B.: 18, enlisted 7/03/61, single, farmer. Promoted 4CPL 3/01/63. Reduced in rank "at his own request." Mortally wounded left shoulder Darbytown 10/07/64. Died 10/11/64. "A good and brave soldier." Hometown: Locust Grove, AL.

Kurey, Julian C.: 16, enlisted 10/16/62, single, apprentice. Served as regimental drummer. Transferred to Co. F, 56th Va.

Lavender E.C.: Hospital 4/13/63.

Lowther, Alexander A.: 35, enlisted 7/03/61, married, farmer. Elected CPT, promoted MAJ 1/25/62, and COL 4/28/63. Severely wounded body Fussell's Mill 8/16/64. Hometown: Columbus, GA.

McGehee, Thomas J.: 21, enlisted 7/03/61, single, farmer. Detailed to arsenal Columbus 3/15/64. Hometown: Columbus, GA.

McKissack, Andrew Martin: 18, enlisted 7/03/61, single, farmer. Severely wounded Sharpsburg right thigh 9/17/62, wounded Chickamauga 9/19/63, and left forearm 8/06/64. 6'1", dark complexion, blue eyes, dark hair. Hometown: Wacoochee Valley, GA.

McMillan, P.M.: Was in hospital 4/12/62, "left without permission."

McMillard, A.M.: Was severely wounded arm Fussell's Mill 8/16/64.

Marcus, Van: 28, enlisted 4/13/61, married, merchant. Elected SMG. Transferred from 2nd GA. 5'6", light complexion, blue eyes. Hometown: Columbus, GA.

Miller, Thomas A.: 16, enlisted 7/03/61, single, farmer. Mortally wounded Spotsylvania hip 5/11/64, died 5/13/64. "For a long time in bad health, but at the last in better, and made a good and brave soldier." Hometown: Seale Station, AL.

Murey, Michael: Enlisted 5/02/62. Served to Lee's surrender.

Newberry, James P.: 14, enlisted 7/03/61, single, farmer. Regimental drummer. Served to Lee's surrender. Hometown: Columbus, GA.

Nuckolls, Thomas J.: 30, enlisted 7/03/61, single, lawyer. Elected 3LT and promoted 2LT 11/04/61. Resigned 12/30/62 after Schaaf was promoted over him. Hometown: Columbus, GA.

Nuckolls, William T.: 21, enlisted 7/03/61, single, farmer. Elected 2LT. Died 11/04/61.

Perdue, James M.: 32, enlisted 12/25/61, single, farmer. Killed Gettysburg 7/02/63. Hometown: Columbus, GA.

Peters, B.: Hospital 10/08/64.

Phillips, James F.: 18, enlisted 7/03/61, single, farmer. Captured Cross Keys 6/08/62 and paroled. Severely wounded left thigh Wilderness 5/06/64 and wounded both thighs and captured Darbytown Road 10/07/64. Took oath and released 6/16/65. 5'8½", dark complexion, hazel eyes, dark brown hair. Hometown: Columbus, GA.

Potee, Joseph: 37, enlisted 7/03/61, single, farmer. Detailed as teamster. Killed Lookout Valley 10/27/63. Hometown: Wacoochee Valley, AL.

Ragland, L.M.: 17, enlisted 9/03/64. Court-martialed for "slipping out of a fight." Hometown: Wacoochee Valley, AL.

Ragland, S.M.: farmer. Captured Darbytown Road 12/10/64, sent to Point Lookout, MD. Released 5/14/65.

Ramsey, Daniel J.: 21, enlisted 7/03/61, married, farmer. Died 10/06/61 measles. Hometown: Oswichee, AL.

Quentin, Henry: 30, enlisted 6/09/61, single, shoemaker. Transferred from 5th AL. Wounded Cold Harbor 6/27/62. AWOL several times. Deserted and captured 12/29/63. Born in Canada. Hometown: Hamden, AL.

Roberson, James: 20, enlisted 7/03/61, single, farmer. Detailed as nurse, launderer. Wounded Gettysburg 7/03/63. Hometown: Oswichee, AL.

Roberson, R.: 18, enlisted 7/03/61, single, farmer. Died 10/28/61. Hometown: Glenville, AL.

Rucker, F. Pope: 30, enlisted 7/03/61, married, stage driver. Detailed as a teamster. Hometown: Columbus, GA.

Ryan, Benjamin L.: 29, enlisted 7/03/61, single, stage driver. Reduced in ranks and detailed as a teamster. Deserted Bunker Hill 7/15/63 and captured 7/23/63. "Released by order of the President 12/01/64" to remain north of the Ohio River. 6'0", florid complexion, dark eyes, dark hair. Hometown: Columbus, GA.

Samuels, Frank: 18, enlisted 7/03/61, single, farmer. Detailed as teamster. Deserted 2/

13/64 Morristown, TN. Hometown: Hurtsboro, AL.

Screws, John W.: 18, enlisted 7/03/61, single, farmer. Promoted 1CPL 1/01/63 and 5SGT 6/16/64. Severely wounded thigh Fussell's Mill 8/16/64. "A good, brave soldier." Hometown: Mechanicsville, AL.

Shaaff, Francis Key: 28, enlisted 5/20/61, single, soldier (U.S. Cavalry). Transferred from 1st KY. Appointed 1 SGT, promoted 3LT 8/14/62, and CPT 8/14/62(?). Wounded Darbytown Road 10/07/64. Served to Lee's surrender. "One of the best officers in the regiment." Hometown: Columbus, GA.

Smith, Charles V.: 38, enlisted 7/03/61, single, worked in livery stables. Promoted 3SGT and 2LT 1/06/64. Assigned as regimental forage master and Color SGT. Captured 5/04/65 Holly Grove, NC. Hometown: Columbus, GA.

Smith, John A.: Enlisted 7/03/61, single. Killed Wilderness 5/06/64. "A good and brave soldier." NOK: Samuel W. Smith, father.

Smith, Pinckney "Pink" H.: 20, enlisted 7/03/61, single, farmer. Wounded Gettysburg 7/03/63. "A good and brave soldier."

Stratford, John B.: 28, enlisted 7/03/61, single, teacher. Died 2/27/62 typhoid. Hometown: Villula, AL.

Stringfellow, John H.: 25, enlisted 7/03/61, married, farmer. Severely wounded Cold Harbor right arm 6/27/62 and disabled. Discharged 7/09/64, assigned to Invalid Corps with duty at Columbus, GA. Hometown: Seale Station, AL.

Sullivan, Calvin: 35, enlisted 1/17/63, married. Mortally wounded Chickamauga 9/20/63, died 3/15/64. NOK: Mary Sullivan, wife.

Taff, John: 26, enlisted 4/11/61, single, farmer. Transferred from 5th AL 1/14/62. Severely wounded Cold Harbor 6/27/62. Killed by a sharpshooter Spotsylvania 5/10/64. Hometown: Tuscaloosa, AL.

Tate, Isaac H.: 17, enlisted 4/01/63, single, farmer. Severely wounded scrotum Wilderness 5/06/64. "A good and brave soldier." Hometown: Wacoochee Valley, AL.

Tate, James M.: 19, enlisted 7/03/61, single, farmer. "Would be a good soldier if he had health." 5'10", dark complexion, blue eyes, dark hair. Hometown: Wacoochee Valley, AL.

Teal, Burrell K.: 25, enlisted 7/03/61, married, farmer. Discharged 12/28/61 disability. Hometown: Mechanicsville, AL.

Teal, John Wesley: 18, enlisted 7/03/61, single, farmer. Wounded Cross Keys 6/08/62, disability and discharged 5/??/63. Hometown: Mechanicsville, AL.

Thompson, Matthew D.: 18, enlisted 12/17/62,

single, farmer. Discharged 2/26/63 "fluid of lung." "Played off sick at Fredericksburg and sent to hospital, and procured a discharge. No account." Hometown: Sandfort, AL.

Thornton, John T.: 42, enlisted 7/03/61, married, blacksmith. Discharged 11/19/62 "stricture of urethra." 5'9", light complexion, blue eyes, dark hair. Hometown: Wacoochee Valley, AL.

Tillery, John P.: 18, enlisted 7/03/61, single, farmer. Promoted to 2CPL and 1CPL. Seriously wounded lung Fussell's Mill 8/16/64. "A good and brave soldier." Hometown: Dover, AL.

Turner, George: 62, enlisted 7/03/61, single, farmer. Discharged 11/24/61 "infirmity from age." 5'8", light complexion, blue eyes, light hair. Hometown: Glenville, AL.

Turner, Joseph: 22, enlisted 7/03/61, single, farmer. Mortally wounded Cold Harbor 6/27/62, died 11/09/62. "A good and brave soldier." Hometown: Dover, AL.

Turner, Thomas E.: 18, enlisted 7/03/61, single, farmer. Wounded arm Cross Keys 6/18/62. Captured while guarding forage wagons 1/25/64 Knoxville, sent to Rock Island, IL. "A good and brave soldier. For a long time in wretched health."

Vann, James M.: 19, enlisted 7/03/61, single, farmer. Elected 1SGT. Died 11/06/61 pneumonia. NOK. Henry M. Vann, father. Hometown: Villula, AL.

Wade, Jackson J.: 17, enlisted 7/03/61, single, farmer. Wounded Sharpsburg 9/17/62 and mortally wounded Fredericksburg 12/19/62, died 11/06/62. NOK: Eliza Avant, mother.

Wade, Thomas: 21, enlisted 7/03/61, single, farmer. Discharged 12/14/61. Hometown: Dover, AL.

Walston, Lafayette: 22, enlisted 7/03/61, single, farmer. Died 11/15/61 pneumonia. Hometown: Mechanicsville, AL.

Warlick, Monroe: 20, enlisted 7/03/61, single, carpenter. Died 11/09/61 diarrhea. Hometown: Glennville, AL.

Warlick, Robert S.: 30, enlisted 7/03/61, single, carpenter. Regimental fifer. Served to Lee's surrender. Hometown: Seale Station, AL.

West, Andrew J.: 40, enlisted 7/03/61, married, farmer. Discharged 11/16/61 "infirmity from age." Hometown: Columbus, GA.

Whitley, Wesley M.: 18, enlisted 7/03/61, single, farmer. Killed Cold Harbor 6/27/62. Hometown: Dover, AL.

Williams, James H.: 17, enlisted 3/01/63, single, farmer. "Shot himself in hand; it is believed purposely and got off home.... A coward and shirker. Very bad egg."

Williams, William G.: 18, enlisted 7/03/61, single, farmer. Severely wounded shoulder 5/31/64 Ashland. Deserted and captured. "A good and brave soldier." 6'0", fair complexion, hazel eyes, dark hair. Hometown: Mechanicsville, AL.

Wooten, Ashbury: 21, enlisted 7/03/61, single, farmer. Severely wounded Manassas thigh and left hip 8/28/62 disabled. "A good and brave soldier." Hometown: Columbus, GA.

Wooten, Benjamin: 40, enlisted 7/03/61, single, carpenter. Died 11/14/61 pneumonia. Hometown: Columbus, GA.

Company B

Bass, Thomas J.: 19, enlisted 7/03/61, single, student. Appointed Ordnance SGT. Died 10/19/63. Hometown: Midway, AL.

Beard, Joseph T.: 19, enlisted 7/03/61, single, farmer. Captured Front Royal and exchanged. Wounded Fredericksburg 12/19/62. Captured Lookout Valley 10/29/63, sent to Camp Morton, IN. Hometown: Midway, AL.

Beasley, Joseph T.: 26, enlisted 7/03/61, single, farmer. Captured Falling Waters 7/14/63, sent to Fort Delaware, DE. Died 3/05/64 "inflammation of the bowels." Hometown: Midway, AL.

Beasley, Thomas S.: 33, enlisted 7/03/61, single, farmer. Wounded head Hazel River 8/22/62 and severely wounded lower arm Spotsylvania 5/26/64. Served to Lee's surrender. Hometown: Midway, AL.

Bell, Miles: 20, enlisted 8/15/62, single, farmer. Deserted New Market, TN, and captured. Given oath and released 2/06/64. Hometown: Haw Ridge, AL.

Bell, Ocus: 18, enlisted 8/15/62, single, farmer. Captured Gettysburg 7/02/63 sent to Fort Delaware. Died 2/07/64 pneumonia. Hometown: Haw Ridge, AL.

Bevel, Alexander: 20, enlisted 7/03/61, single, farmer. Discharged 12/17/61 spinal irritation. Dark complexion, dark eyes, dark hair. Hometown: Indian Creek, AL.

Blakley, Columbus C.: 24, enlisted 7/03/61, single, carpenter. Died 3/11/62. Hometown: Midway, AL.

Bledsoe, James T.: 25, enlisted 7/03/61, single, carpenter. Wounded Manassas 8/30/62. Captured Gettysburg 7/02/63, sent to Fort Delaware. Took oath and released 6/14/65. 5'10", ruddy complexion, hazel eyes, dark hair. Hometown: Pine Grove, AL.

Bowen, John D.: 23, enlisted 7/03/61, single,

farmer. Detailed as teamster. Wounded Cold Harbor 6/27/62. Captured Mossy Creek, TN 1/25/64. Took oath and released 6/22/65. 5'4½", florid complexion, gray eyes, brown hair. Hometown: Midway, AL.

Boyd, James Y.: 30, enlisted 7/03/61, married, dentist. Severely wounded hand Cross Keys 6/08/62. Discharged 11/20/64, assigned to Invalid Corps with duty at hospital in Columbus, GA. Hometown: Midway, AL.

Bradberry, James T.: 20, enlisted 7/03/61, single, farmer. Died 11/25/61 measles. Hometown: Spring Hill, AL.

Brooks, John Harry: 17, enlisted 7/03/61, single, farmer. Died 11/09/61 measles. Hometown: Spring Hill, AL.

Burke, Thomas J.: 18, enlisted 7/03/61, single, student. Killed Cold Harbor 6/27/62. Hometown: Spring Hill, AL.

Cain, John Frank: 17, enlisted 7/03/61, single, farmer. Promoted 4CPL 1/01/64. Killed 6/21/64 by sharpshooter. Hometown: Spring Hill, AL.

Callaway, B. Frank: 19, enlisted 3/18/62, single, farmer. Killed Suffolk 5/03/63. Hometown: Midway, AL.

Callaway, J.D.: 21, enlisted 7/03/61, single, student. Wounded and captured Gettysburg 7/03/63, sent to Fort Delaware, DE. Exchanged 10/31/64. Served to Lee's surrender. Hometown: Midway, AL.

Callaway, William M.: 19, enlisted 7/03/61, single, farmer. Wounded and captured Sharpsburg 9/17/62, exchanged. Served to Lee's surrender. Hometown: Midway, AL.

Cargill, Jason: 25, enlisted 3/15/62, single, farmer. Died 6/01/62. Hometown: Indian Creek, AL.

Chatham, John: 17, enlisted 7/03/61, single, farmer. Died 10/13/61 measles. Hometown: Midway, AL.

Coleman, Benjamin Franklin: 21, enlisted 7/03/61, single, student. Elected 2LT, resigned 5/24/62. Hometown: Midway, AL.

Coleman, Thomas J.: 24, enlisted 7/03/61, married, farmer. Captured Gettysburg 7/02/63, sent to Fort Delaware, DE. 5'11", ruddy complexion, hazel eyes, dark hair. Hometown: Indian Creek, AL.

Colwell, Joseph: 28, enlisted 7/03/61, single, farmer. Discharged 12/11/61 "organic stricture urethra." Hometown: Enon, AL.

Conaway, James Madison: 28, enlisted 7/03/61, married, farmer. Wounded Knoxville 11/25/63. Hometown: in AL.

Cope, Wilburn: 22, enlisted 7/03/61, single, farmer. Died 10/10/61 measles. NOK: John Wilburn, father. Hometown: Arbivitus, AL.

Cosby, John: 26, enlisted 3/18/62, single, farmer. Killed Cold Harbor 6/27/62. Hometown: Midway, AL.

Crew, T.J.: Enlisted 7/03/61. Died 10/04/61. NOK Caroline Crew, mother. Hometown: in AL.

Crews, John S.: 19, enlisted 7/03/61, married, farmer. Died 11/12/61. Hometown: Indian Creek, AL.

Denham, Alfred George: 28, enlisted 7/03/61, married, farmer. Wounded Manassas 8/28/62 and Fredericksburg 12/19/62. Captured Gettysburg 7/02/63, sent to Fort Delaware, DE. 5'7", sallow complexion, hazel eyes, brown hair. Took oath and released 6/14/65. Hometown: Pine Grove, AL.

Denham, George T.: 22, enlisted 7/03/61, single, painter. Wounded Cross Keys lung 6/08/62 and severely wounded Chickamauga left foot amputated 9/20/63. Hometown: Indian Creek, AL.

Edwards, Robert: 18, enlisted 3/16/62, single, farmer. Died measles 5/09/62. Hometown: Chambers County, AL.

Edwards, William A.: 22, enlisted 7/03/61, single, farmer. Wounded Cold Harbor 6/27/62 and Manassas 8/28/62. Captured Lookout Valley 10/29/63, sent to Camp Morton, IN. Took oath and released 6/12/65. 5'3¾", florid complexion, gray eyes, light hair. Hometown: Chambers County, AL.

Eubanks, Robert J.: 17, enlisted 7/03/61. Served to Lee's surrender. Hometown: Indian Creek, AL.

Feagin, Isaac B.: 27, enlisted 7/03/61, single, merchant. Elected CPT and promoted LTC 4/28/63. Commanded regiment Manassas, Chantilly, Sharpsburg, and Shepherdstown. Wounded by shell Shepherdstown 9/19/62. Severely wounded right leg amputated at the thigh and captured Gettysburg 7/02/63. Exchanged 3/10/64, assigned to Invalid Corps. "He was courageous and faithful." Hometown: Midway, AL.

Feagin, Noah B.: 17, enlisted 7/03/61, single, student. Promoted 1SGT, 3LT 9/25/62, 2LT 2/05/63, 1LT 4/25/63, and CPT 8/08/63. Severely wounded Hazel River 8/22/62, Suffolk 5/03/63, and leg Darbytown Road 10/07/64. Hometown: Midway, AL.

Feagin, Samuel J.: 20, enlisted 7/03/61, single, farmer. Killed Cold Harbor 6/27/62. NOK: James M. Feagin, father. Hometown: Midway, AL.

Fennel, W. Henry: 20, enlisted 7/03/61, single, farmer. Died 12/03/61 typhoid. NOK: Absolom Fennel, father. Hometown: Pine Grove, AL.

Ford, Thomas J.: 22, enlisted 7/03/61, single, farmer. Mortally wounded Cross Keys 6/08/62, died 7/07/62. Hometown: Indian Creek, AL.

Gary, William Patrick: 22, enlisted 7/03/61, single, farmer. Promoted 2SGT, 3LT 5/12/63, and 2LT 8/15/63. Wounded Manassas 8/29/62. Served to Lee's surrender. Hometown: Spring Hill, AL.

Grisham, Ferdinand: 18, enlisted 7/03/61, single, farmer. Killed Gettysburg 7/02/63. Hometown: Pine Grove, AL.

Hall, Wiley M.: 26, enlisted 7/03/61, single, farmer. Died 11/24/61 fever. Hometown: Midway, AL.

Hancock, James L.: 25, enlisted 3/14/62, single, farmer. Died 5/10/62. Hometown: Midway, AL.

Harper, Cincinnattus: 17, enlisted 11/15/63, single, farmer. Furlough at time of Lee's surrender. Hometown: Fort Browder, AL.

Harper, M.L.: 21, enlisted 7/03/61, single, farmer. Promoted 2CPL 9/22/63. Wounded Cold Harbor 6/27/62 and Manassas 8/28/62. Killed Fort Harrison 9/30/64. Awarded Southern Cross of Honor 12/10/64. Hometown: Fort Browder, AL.

Harper, Thaddeus C.: 20, enlisted 7/03/61, single, farmer. Died 11/27/61 typhoid/pneumonia. NOK: William Harper, father. Hometown: Fort Browder, AL.

Hendrick, W.J.: Died 10/30/62. Hometown: in AL.

Hicks, Andrew Jackson: 26, enlisted 7/03/61, single, farmer. Died 11/28/61 typhoid. NOK: Nancy Hicks, mother. Hometown: Indian Creek, AL.

Hill, Egbert: 24, enlisted 7/03/61, single, farmer. Elected 3SGT. Died 9/25/61. Hometown: Midway, AL.

Hitchcock, James Gibbs: 20, enlisted 7/03/61, single, merchant. Promoted 2CPL 4/??/62 and 1SGT 9/22/62. Slightly wounded left shoulder Gettysburg 7/02/63, severely wounded leg Wilderness 5/06/64, and severely wounded arm Deep Bottom 8/16/64. Hometown: Midway, AL.

Hodges, Henry H.: 21, enlisted 7/03/61, single, farmer. Wounded Fredericksburg 12/19/62 and mortally wounded Chickamauga 9/19/63, died 10/01/63. "Deserves much credit for gallantry on field of battle." Hometown: Spring Hill, AL.

Howard, T.J.: Died 10/30/62 typhoid.

Huffman, Jonathan: 17, enlisted 7/03/61, single, farmer. Died 1/25/62 double pneumonia. NOK: Margaret Huffman, mother. Hometown: Indian Creek, AL.

Hughs, Berry A.: 23, enlisted 7/03/61, single, farmer. Hired his brother John as a substitute. Hometown: Tuskegee, AL.

Hughs, John W.: 20, enlisted 2/15/62, single, farmer. Substituted for brother Berry. Wounded Manassas 8/28/62, Sharpsburg 9/17/62, and severely wounded shoulder Fussell's Mill. Home on furlough when Lee surrendered. Paroled Montgomery, AL. 5'8", dark complexion, blue eyes, dark hair. Hometown: Tuskegee, AL.

Hutchinson, James W.: 21, enlisted 7/03/61, single, student. Severely wounded Manassas, leg amputated, 8/30/62. Discharged 11/21/62. 6'0", dark complexion, hazel eyes, dark hair. Hometown: Chambers County, AL.

Hutchinson, Thomas J.: 21, enlisted 7/03/61, single, student. Killed Manassas 8/30/62. "Killed ... while nobly performing his duty as a soldier." Hometown: Midway, AL.

Jackson, Walter C.: 20, enlisted 7/03/61, single, farmer. Wounded Manassas 8/28/62 and Fredericksburg 12/19/62. Captured Lookout Valley, sent to Camp Morton, IN, and Fort Delaware, DE. Took oath and released 6/14/65. 5'7", ruddy complexion, gray eyes, red hair. "One of the best soldiers in the regiment." Hometown: Pine Grove, AL.

Jackson, William P.: 23, enlisted 7/03/61, single, farmer. Died 10/13/61 measles. Hometown: Pine Grove, AL.

Johns, Lewis J.: 25, enlisted 3/08/62, married, farmer. Died 5/06/62 typhoid. Hometown: Pine Grove, AL.

Johns, William N.: 18, enlisted 7/03/61, single, teacher. Promoted 3CPL 9/22/62, 5SGT 6/01/63, and 4SGT 9/01/63. Severely wounded left thigh and captured Gettysburg 7/02/63. "[Doctors] wanted to operate and join broken femur together but Johns wouldn't allow." Exchanged 5/??/64. Discharged 7/09/64 to Invalid Corps and assigned to Columbus, GA. Hometown: Pine Grove, AL.

Johnson, William H.: 20, enlisted 7/03/61, single, farmer. Died 10/03/61 typhoid. NOK: A. Padgett, mother. Hometown: Mt. Andrew, AL.

Jones, John C.: 28, enlisted 7/03/61, single, jeweler. Mortally wounded through arm and body Manassas 8/29/62, died 9/05/62. Born in England. Hometown: Enon, AL.

Jones, P.O.: Died 9/07/62.

Jones, Watt P.: 22, enlisted 7/03/61, single, teacher. Elected 1LT. Severely wounded arm amputated 8/28/62. Died smallpox 2/05/63. "A gallant officer." Hometown: Midway, AL.

Jordan, William Christopher: 26, enlisted 3/

15/62, married, farmer. Severely wounded Fort Gilmore 9/29/64. Hometown: Midway, AL.

Kelly, Henry H.: 21, enlisted 7/03/61, single, farmer. Killed Hazel River 8/22/62. Hometown: Pine Grove, AL.

Kendrick, Benjamin E.: 23, enlisted 7/03/61, married, farmer. Mortally wounded and captured Gettysburg 7/03/63, died 7/04/63. Hometown: Spring Hill, AL.

Kendrick, Daniel Lingey: 21, enlisted 8/18/62, single, farmer. Detailed as teamster (ambulance driver). Discharged 12/11/61 for disability, reenlisted and served to surrender. Light complexion, blue eyes, light hair. Hometown: Spring Hill, AL.

Kendrick, Henry Jefferson: 26, enlisted 8/15/62, married, farmer. Died 11/01/62. Hometown: Midway, AL.

Kendrick, Robert S.: 23, enlisted 8/18/62, single, student. Discharged 5/15/62 and reenlisted. Wounded left foot and captured Gettysburg 7/03/63, exchanged 2/18/65. Hometown: in AL.

Kendrick, W.B.: 21, single, teacher. Elected 3LT in 37th Al 7/??/62, promoted CPT Company E, 42nd Al. Hometown: in AL.

Kennedy, Alsa: 21, enlisted 7/03/61, single, farmer. Killed Gettysburg 7/02/63. Hometown: Midway, AL.

King, Harmon LaFayette: 20, enlisted 8/15/62, single, farmer. Died 3/31/63 smallpox. NOK: Wiley King, father. Hometown: Haw Ridge, AL.

King, James M.: 23, enlisted 7/03/61, single, farmer. Died 3/25/63. NOK: Wiley King, father. Hometown: Indian Creek, AL.

King, Wiley Washington: 21, enlisted 8/15/62, married, farmer. Died 6/08/63 typhoid. NOK: Elizabeth King, wife. Hometown: Haw Ridge, AL.

Lane, Andrew John: 25, enlisted 3/15/62, married, farmer. Wounded Fredericksburg left leg amputated 12/19/62. Hometown: Enon, AL.

Lane, Elish: 21, enlisted 7/03/61, single, farmer. Severely wounded grapeshot through right thigh Gettysburg 7/02/63. Died 3/05/64 smallpox. Hometown: Enon, AL.

Lane, Emery A.: 19, enlisted 4/27/61, single, clerk. Transferred from a MS regiment. Severely wounded right shoulder Manassas 8/28/62 and Wilderness 5/06/64. Served to Lee's surrender. Hometown: Corinth, MS.

Lane, Eugene Polk: 19, enlisted 3/15/62, single, farmer. Promoted 3CPL 1/01/64. Served to surrender. Hometown: Enon, AL.

Lary, Samuel D.: 28, enlisted 7/03/61, married,

editor. Discharged 4/04/62. Hometown: Union Springs, AL.

Lawson, J.H.: Hospital 9/13/63.

Lee, James P.: 24, enlisted 3/15/62, single, farmer. Mortally wounded Sharpsburg 9/17/62, died 12/01/62. Hometown: Midway, AL.

Little, John: 35, enlisted 7/03/61, single, ditcher. Discharged 9/15/62. Hometown: Indian Creek, AL.

McCaskill, Neal A.: 21, enlisted 7/03/61, single, farmer. Mortally wounded Suffolk 5/03/63. Hometown: Pine Grove, AL.

McDonald, Jackson "Jack": 46, enlisted 7/03/61, married, farmer. Wounded Manassas 8/28/62, Sharpsburg 12/19/62, and Gettysburg 7/02/63. Discharged 7/13/64. Hometown: Indian Creek, AL.

McDonald, John: 20, enlisted 8/15/62, single, farmer. Died 1/13/63 tuberculosis. Hometown: Haw Ridge, AL.

McJunkins, Samuel B.: 19, enlisted 7/03/61, single, minster/teacher. Wounded Manassas shoulder and arm 8/28/62. Discharged 8/08/63. Hometown: Indian Creek, AL.

McMillan, A.P.: 23, enlisted 3/08/62, single, farmer. Wounded Fredericksburg 12/19/62. Killed Gettysburg 7/02/63. Hometown: Midway, AL.

McMillan, Edward: 21, enlisted 7/03/61, single, student. Killed Manassas 8/28/63. Hometown: Midway, AL.

McMillan, John: 24, enlisted 3/08/62, married, farmer. Killed Cold Harbor 6/27/62. Hometown: Midway, AL.

McWhorter, H.J.: Died 1/19/62. NOK: Samantha McWhorter, mother. Hometown: Indian Creek, AL.

McWhorter, John C.: 20, enlisted 7/03/61, single, farmer. Died 12/12/62 typhoid. NOK: Samantha McWhorter, mother. Hometown: Indian Creek, AL.

McWhorter, William A.: 25, enlisted 7/03/61, single, farmer. Discharged 2/01/62, "shot hand, amputation of fingers." 5'10", fair complexion, blue eyes, auburn hair. Hometown: Indian Creek, AL.

Manning, J.B.: Hospital 9/26/62.

Melze, Thomas: Hospital 9/27/62, fingers amputated. Hometown: in AL.

Milligan, Danie: 26, enlisted 3/15/62, single, ditcher. Deserted Winchester 5/25/62. Wounded Manassas 8/28/62 "through right shoulder and left arm." Born in Ireland. Hometown: Pine Grove, AL.

Mills, Thomas J.: 24, enlisted 7/03/61, single, farmer. Detailed as teamster. Wounded Sharpsburg 9/17/62. Hometown: Pine Grove, AL.

Ming, George: 20, enlisted 7/03/61, single, farmer. Died 10/24/61 measles. Hometown: in AL.

Ming, Samuel Jackson: 30, enlisted 7/03/61, single, farmer. Served to Lee's surrender. Hometown: Indian Creek, AL.

Ming, William Jackson: 24, enlisted 7/03/61, single, farmer. Wounded leg Hazel River 8/22/62 and head Chickamauga 9/20/63. Served to Lee's surrender. Hometown: Indian Creek, AL.

Mosley, William D.: 20, enlisted 7/03/61, single, farmer. Mortally wounded side Cold Harbor 6/08/62, died 6/16/62. NOK: Francis M. Mosley, father. "Good and brave soldier." Hometown: Midway, AL.

Neffman, A.J.: Hospital 1/17/62 rheumatism.

Newman, Charles O.: 21, enlisted 7/03/61, single, clerk. Captured Gettysburg 7/02/63, sent to Fort Delaware, DE. Took oath and released 6/14/65. 6'0", sallow complexion, gray eyes, dark hair. Hometown: Midway, AL.

Norris, Hardy K.: 21, enlisted 7/03/61, single, farmer. Wounded Cold Harbor 6/27/62. Mortally wounded and captured right lung, breast and abdomen Gettysburg 7/02/63. Hometown: Indian Creek, AL.

Owens, Elijah W.: 25, enlisted 7/03/61, single, farmer. Transferred from Company C 07/??/62. Killed Manassas 8/28/62. NOK: Sarah Hawkins, mother. Hometown: Midway, AL.

Owens, George J.: 20, enlisted 7/03/61, single, student. Captured Gettysburg 7/02/63, sent to Fort Delaware, DE. Took oath and released 6/14/65. 5'4", sallow complexion, brown eyes, brown hair. Hometown: Midway, AL.

Owens, Isaac C.: 23, enlisted 7/03/61, single, carpenter. Killed Sharpsburg 9/17/62. Hometown: Midway, AL.

Parker, Cadee A.: 20, enlisted 7/03/61, single, student. Mortally wounded lungs Gettysburg 7/03/63, died pneumonia 7/21/63. Hometown: Mt. Andrew, AL.

Payne, John Martin: 19, enlisted 7/03/61, single, farmer. Severely wounded Manassas 8/28/62, Lookout Valley 10/28/63, slightly wounded hand Spotsylvania 5/08/64, and severely wounded thigh Darbytown Road 10/07/64. Promoted 2CPL, 5SGT 4/01/62, and 2SGT 6/01/63. Hometown: Midway, AL.

Phillips, James P.: 21, enlisted 3/18/62, married, farmer. Wounded Manassas 8/28/62. Captured 1/22/64, sent to Camp Chase, OH. Hometown: Spring Hill, AL.

Phillips, Robert: 20, enlisted 3/18/62, married, farmer. Died 5/09/62 typhoid. Hometown: Spring Hill, AL.

Pope, George W.: 20, enlisted 3/18/62, married, farmer. Wounded Fredericksburg 12/19/62. Transferred from Company L 1/01/63. Captured Gettysburg 7/02/63, sent to Point Lookout, MD. Exchanged 2/18/65. Captured Macon, GA, 4/20–21/65. Hometown: Indian Creek, AL.

Posey, John W.: 19, enlisted 7/03/61, single, farmer. Court-martialed. Severely wounded left hip Chester Station 6/08/64. Hometown: Pine Grove, AL.

Pruett, Jacob: 40, enlisted 7/03/61, single, merchant. Killed Chickamauga 9/19/63. Hometown: Midway, AL.

Pugh, Whitson: 24, enlisted 3/08/62, single, farmer. Wounded Fredericksburg 12/19/62. Killed Gettysburg 7/02/63. Hometown: Midway, AL.

Seay, Van: 24, enlisted 7/03/61, single, farmer. Died 9/26/61 measles. Hometown: Spring Hill, AL.

Stone, Charles T.: 18, enlisted 7/03/61, single, farmer. Died 9/25/61 measles. Hometown: Midway, AL.

Stone, Henry D.: 25, enlisted 7/03/61, married, brick mason. Killed Gettysburg 7/02/63. Hometown: Midway, AL.

Sweeney, D.H.: 17, enlisted 12/15/63, single, farmer. Captured Wilderness 5/06/64, sent to Point Lookout, MD. Paroled 3/14/65. Hometown: Spring Hill, AL.

Sweeney, E.B.: 20, enlisted 7/03/61, single, farmer. Captured Gettysburg 7/02/63, sent to Fort Delaware, DE. Died 1/14/64 pneumonia. Hometown: Spring Hill, AL.

Sweeney, James P.: 48, enlisted 7/03/61, married, farmer. Discharged 1/08/64. 5'9", florid complexion, blue eyes, black hair. Hometown: Spring Hill, AL.

Tarver, John A.: 19, enlisted 7/03/61, single, farmer. Severely wounded hip Manassas 8/29/62. Discharged 8/23/64 to Invalid Corps with duty at Troy, AL. Paroled Montgomery, AL, 5/31/65. 6'0", fair complexion, blue eyes, light hair. Hometown: Indian Creek, AL.

Tarver, William L.: 20, enlisted 7/03/61, single, farmer. Died 11/30/61 typhoid. Hometown: Indian Creek, AL.

Thompson, Thomas P.: 38, enlisted 7/03/61, married, farmer. Wounded Sharpsburg 9/17/62. Killed Knoxville 11/27/63. Hometown: Indian Creek, AL.

Waldrop, Larkin: 22, enlisted 7/03/61, single, merchant. Discharged 12/17/61 hip joint. 5'10", dark complexion, blue eyes, sandy hair. Hometown: Midway, AL.

Watley, William L.: Died 3/10/62.

Wesley, W.S.: 30, enlisted 7/03/61, married, farmer. Promoted 3SGT and 2SGT 9/01/63.

Killed Deep Bottom 8/14/63. Hometown: Indian Creek, AL.

Westbrook, J.D.: Captured Gettysburg 7/02/63, sent to Fort Delaware, DE.

Wheeler, James H.: 25, enlisted 7/03/61, single, farmer. Wounded Manassas 8/30/62. Killed Williamsburg Road head 10/27/64. Hometown: Indian Creek, AL.

White, Robert Q.: 23, enlisted 7/01/61, single, farmer. Died 10/06/61 typhoid. Hometown: Midway, AL.

White, Thomas L.: 18, enlisted 3/04/64, single, student. Mortally wounded leg amputated Wilderness 5/06/64, died 5/29/64. Hometown: Midway, AL.

Willis, James R.: 42, enlisted 8/15/62, married, farmer. Killed Suffolk 5/03/63. Hometown: Haw Ridge, AL.

Willis, John "Jack": 17, enlisted 8/10/63, single, farmer. Deserted 12/18/63. Appointed as drummer when recruited, never returned from furlough. Hometown: Pine Grove, AL.

Wright, Henry C.: 19, enlisted 3/15/62, single, student. Discharged 12/30/62 aneurism aorta. 6'0", dark complexion, gray eyes, light hair. Hometown: Spring Hill, AL.

Wright, John L.: 24, enlisted 7/03/61, single, farmer. Severely wounded left thigh Hazel River 8/22/62, left thigh amputated 11/21/62. Discharged 9/26/64 and assigned to Invalid Corps with duty at Columbus, GA. Hometown: Spring Hill, AL.

Wright, Richard E.: 22, enlisted 7/03/61, single, teacher. Elected 3LT, promoted 2LT 9/22/62, 1LT 3/27/63, and CPT 4/28/63. Severely wounded arm and both lungs Manassas 8/28/62. Resigned 8/15/63. Hometown: Spring Hill, AL.

Wright, Thomas D.: 27, enlisted 3/18/62, single, student. Mortally wounded Chickamauga 9/19–20/63, died 9/22/63. Hometown: Spring Hill, AL.

Wright, W.B.: 26, enlisted 7/03/61, single, farmer. Died 9/22/61 measles. Hometown: Spring Hill, AL.

Company C

Acre, William T.: 20, enlisted 7/03/61, single, shoemaker. Promoted 4CPL 9/01/63. Killed head Chickamauga 9/20/63. NOK: W.M. Acre, father. Hometown: Creek Stand, AL.

Atkinson, Morgan L.: 16, enlisted 3/25/62, single, student. Reported dead and dropped from the rolls 4/??/64. Hometown: Creek Stand, AL.

Avery, Samuel T.: 21. Died 6/07/62. Hometown: Creek Stand, AL.

Baker, Francis "Frank" M.: 19, enlisted 4/03/61, single, farmer. Discharged 1/17/62. 5'9", dark complexion, dark eyes, dark hair. Hometown: Creek Stand, AL.

Baker, Joseph W.: 24, enlisted 7/03/61, married, farmer. Wounded Cross Keys 6/08/64. Killed 2nd Cold Harbor by an artillery shell 6/04/64. Hometown: Creek Stand, AL.

Baker, William A.: 27, enlisted 3/05/62, married, farmer. Wounded hand Lookout Valley 10/27/63. "Ball entered left palm fracturing middle finger, disabling use of hand." Hometown: Creek Stand, AL.

Berry, John M.: 30, single. Deserted 9/03/61. Hometown: Columbus, GA.

Bibby, Bailey: 33, enlisted 7/03/61, married, tanner. Promoted 4SGT 2/01/62, 3SGT 4/??/62, and 2SGT 9/01/62. Killed head Gettysburg 7/02/63. Hometown: Creek Stand, AL.

Bradshaw, Ephram: 34, enlisted 8/15/62, married, farmer. Died measles 1/04/63. Hometown: Newton, AL.

Bradshaw, James J.: 32, enlisted 8/15/62, married, farmer. Died. Hometown: Newton, AL.

Braswell, James: 23, enlisted 3/18/62, married, farmer. Died typhoid 5/24/62. Hometown: Creek Stand, AL.

Burdett, Alfred M.: Captured Spotsylvania 5/12/64, sent to Elmira, NY. Died chronic diarrhea 9/05/64. Hometown: in AL.

Burks, Benjamin J.: 22, enlisted 7/03/61, single, farmer. Severely wounded Cold Harbor 6/27/62. Hometown: Creek Stand, AL.

Burt, John A.: 21, enlisted 7/03/61, married, farmer. Severely wounded thigh Wilderness 5/06/64 and Darbytown arm 10/13/64. Served to Lee's surrender. Hometown: Creek Stand, AL.

Burt, William H.: 23, enlisted 3/03/62, married, farmer. Discharged 5/31/62. Hometown: Creek Stand, AL.

Cargill, Thomas A.: 23, enlisted 7/03/61, single, farmer. Captured 6/10/62 and paroled 6/??/62. Wounded Chickamauga 9/19–20/63. AWOL late '63-64. "A dead expense to the government." Hometown: Creek Stand, AL.

Chandler, N.G.: Captured Knoxville 11/25/63, sent to Rock Island, IL. Hometown: in AL.

Chatham, Joshua Lewis: 18, enlisted 7/03/61, single, farmer. Wounded Chickamauga 9/19/63 and severely wounded Fussell's Mill 8/16/64. Paroled Montgomery, AL. Hometown: Creek Stand, AL.

Coghill, Thomas A.: Deserted/captured 8/03/64. 5'11", light complexion, blue eyes, light hair. Hometown: in AL.

Coleman, Thomas J.: 42, enlisted 2/28/62, married, farmer. Captured Gettysburg 7/02/63. Hometown: Huntsville, AL.

Cooper, David S.: 21, enlisted 7/03/61, single, farmer. Sick pneumonia, left in hands of the enemy Knoxville 12/09/63. Died 1/24/64. Hometown: Creek Stand, AL.

Cooper, James A.: 23, enlisted 7/03/61, single, farmer. Died 11/18/61 chronic diarrhea. NOK: Wiley L. Cooper, father. Hometown: Creek Stand, AL.

Cooper, William H.: 20, enlisted 2/27/62, single, farmer. Wounded Chickamauga 9/20/63 and slightly wounded thigh Darbytown Road 10/13/64. Awarded Southern Cross of Honor 12/10/64. 5'7", light complexion, gray eyes, light hair. Hometown: Creek Stand, AL.

Crawley, Jesse W.: Discharged 8/17/63. 5'6", fair complexion, yellow eyes, light hair. Hometown: in AL.

Crawley, William: 45, enlisted 9/20/61, married, farmer. Substitute for J.E. Ellison. Discharged 12/04/61. 5'9", fair complexion, gray eyes, sandy hair. Hometown: in AL.

Crowley, Alfred: 40, enlisted 7/03/61, married, farmer. Killed bowels Chickamauga 9/20/63. NOK: Mary Crowley. Hometown: Creek Stand, AL.

Crowley, Allen: 23, enlisted 7/03/61, married, farmer. Promoted 4CPL, 3CPL 12/01/61, 2 CPL 2/01/62, 5SGT 9/01/62, 4SGT 7/01/63, and 3SGT. Wounded Cross Keys 6/08/62, Shepherdstown 9/19/62, and severely wounded Chickamauga 9/20/63. Hometown: Creek Stand, AL.

Daniel, Stephen H.: 18, enlisted 10/01/61, single, clerk. Detailed as nurse. Ordered arrested and sent to prison. Hometown: Hardaway, AL.

Davis, Frank A.: 24, enlisted 7/03/61, single, farmer. Died pneumonia 4/28/62. Hometown: Creek Stand, AL.

Dozier, Tilman H.: 21, enlisted 7/03/61, single, farmer. Died typhoid 11/29/61. NOK: Ezekial A. Dozier, father. Hometown: Warrior Stand, AL.

Draughn, Hardy C.: 23, enlisted 8/15/62, single, farmer. Died 12/14/63. NOK: John W. Draughn, father. Hometown: Newton, AL.

Draughn, John R.: 20, enlisted 8/15/62, single, farmer. Severely wounded breast Fort Harrison 9/30/64. Hometown: Newton, AL.

Ellison, Abraham P.: 40, enlisted 8/15/62, married, farmer. Discharged 8/31/61. 5'8", dark complexion, blue eyes, dark hair. Hometown: Creek Stand, AL.

Ellison, James H.: 24, enlisted 7/03/61, single, farmer. Elected 1SGT 10/??/61, 2LT 2/01/62, and CPT 8/01/62. Killed Gettysburg head 7/02/63. "One of the finest specimens of young manhood I ever beheld." Hometown: Enon, AL.

Ellison, James Matthew: 27, elected 2LT 7/03/61, married, farmer. Promoted 1LT 2/01/62. Resigned 12/20/62. Hometown: Creek Stand, AL.

Ellison, J.J.: Died pneumonia 4/16/62. 5'8", dark complexion, blue eyes, dark hair.

Etheridge, James T.: 16, enlisted 7/03/61. Severely wounded Cold Harbor 6/27/62. Died typhoid 5/03/64.

Floyd, Henry: 21, enlisted 9/09/61, married, farmer. Discharged 5/12/62, "Imbecillitas and chronic inflammation of knee joints." 5'6", fair complexion, gray eyes, dark hair. Hometown: Troy, AL.

Fowler, Benjamin: 30, enlisted 8/15/61, married, farmer. Died at home 8/01/63. NOK: Elizabeth, Fowler. Hometown: Troy, AL.

Funderburg, Jacob C.D.: 26, enlisted 8/18/61, married, farmer. Hometown: Orangeburg, SC.

Grantham, Blaney S.: 24, enlisted 7/03/61, married, stage driver. Died pneumonia 11/01/61. Hometown: Creek Stand, AL.

Guerry, Douglas D.: 19, enlisted 4/28/61, single, mechanic. Transferred from 4th AL. Promoted 5SGT 6/01/63, 4SGT 9/01/63, and 3SGT 9/01/64. Served to Lee's surrender. Hometown: Enon, AL.

Guerry, John E.: 16, enlisted 7/03/61, single, student. Promoted 4CPL 2/01/63, 3CPL 9/11/63, and 1CPL 9/01/64. Wounded Manassas 8/29/62. Died at home 12/04/64. Hometown: Creek Stand, AL.

Guerry, Legrand Lafayette: 23, enlisted 4/28/61, married, mechanic. Promoted 1SGT 2/01/62, 2LT 8/01/62, 1LT 12/22/62, and CPT 7/02/63. Hometown: Midway, AL.

Guerry, Nehemire "General" D.: 37, enlisted 7/03/61, married, farmer. BG before the war of state troops. Resigned 12/11/62 "bad health." Hometown: Oswitchee, AL.

Guerry, Peter V.: 45, enlisted 7/03/61, married, farmer. Elected CPT. Killed Cold Harbor 6/26/62. Hometown: Creek Stand, AL.

Guerry, Thomas J.: 21, enlisted 3/10/62, single, farmer. Captured Knoxville 12/05/63. Died pneumonia 1/15/64. Hometown: Creek Stand, AL.

Guy, Joseph: 28, enlisted 7/03/61, single, farmer. Died typhoid 11/27/62. Hometown: Warrior Stand, AL.

Halton, H.: Captured Spotsylvania 5/12/64, sent to Elmira, NY. Released 5/15/65.

Head, John M.: 18, enlisted 7/03/61, single,

farmer. Wounded Chickamauga 9/20/63, slightly wounded Wilderness 5/06/64, and Petersburg 7/03/64. Hometown: Creek Stand, AL.

Hunt, Elijah M.: 40, enlisted 7/03/61, married farmer. Discharged hernia 10/08/61. Hometown: Creek Stand, AL.

Hunt, Thomas C.: 19, enlisted 7/03/61, single, farmer. Died 12/08/61 diarrhea. Hometown: Creek Stand, AL.

Hurn, Miles: 35, enlisted 2/28/62, married, farmer. Died. Hometown: Creek Stand, AL.

Hurt, William "Billy" H.: 16, enlisted 7/03/61, single, student. Wounded Sharpsburg 9/17/62. Captured Gettysburg 7/02/63, sent to Fort Delaware, DE. Took oath and released 6/14/65. 5'6", ruddy complexion, dark eyes, dark hair. Creek Stand, AL.

Hydrick, Luther W.: 14, enlisted 10/17/64, single, farmer. Hometown: Blackville, SC.

Jackson, David J.: 21, enlisted 7/03/61, single, farmer. Mortally wounded Cold Harbor 6/27/62. NOK: A.D. Jackson, father.

Jackson, Finny F.: 27, enlisted 7/03/61, married, farmer. Died chronic diarrhea 11/12/61. Hometown: Creek Stand, AL.

Johnson, Luther D.: 22, enlisted 2/27/62, married, farmer. Severely wounded Cross Keys hand amputated 6/08/62. Discharged 7/10/62. 5'6", fair complexion, gray eyes, dark hair. Hometown: Creek Stand, AL.

Kennedy, C.H.: Paroled Montgomery, AL. 5/15/65.

Key, John G.: 35, enlisted 7/03/61, married, farmer. Severely wounded Manassas 8/28/62. Captured Dandridge, TN, 1/29/64, left behind "very sick and unable to march." Died Rock Island, IL. Measles 3/24/64. Hometown: Creek Stand, AL.

Lloyd, Benjamin F.: 27, enlisted 7/03/61, single, merchant. Died typhoid 12/03/61. Hometown: Creek Stand, AL.

Lloyd, William Bailey: 18, enlisted 7/03/61, single, student. Elected 3CPL, promoted 5SGT 5/06/62, 4SGT 9/01/62, 3LT 2/16/63, 2LT 2/16/63, and 1LT 7/16/63. Wounded Hazel River 8/22/62, slightly wounded thigh Petersburg 6/19/64, and shell fragment Deep Bottom 8/14/64. Hometown: Creek Stand, AL.

McDonald, Richard M.: 16, enlisted 7/03/61, single, farmer. Wounded Gettysburg 7/02/63. Captured with ambulance train 7/04/63, sent to Fort Delaware, DE. Took oath and released 5/10/65. 5'7", dark complexion, gray eyes, dark hair. Hometown: Warrior Stand, AL.

McGrady, Ivy: 16, enlisted 7/03/61, single, farmer. Killed Cold Harbor 6/27/62. NOK:

Martha C. McGrady, mother. Hometown: Creek Stand, AL.

McGrady, James E.: 21, enlisted 7/03/61, single. Died typhoid 10/05/61. NOK: Martha C. McGrady, mother. Hometown: Creek Stand, AL.

Mansel, Amos P.: 18, enlisted 8/15/61, single, farmer. Wounded Cold Harbor 6/27/62. Killed head Gettysburg 7/02/63. "An excellent soldier." Hometown: Troy, AL.

Mansel, John E.: 19, enlisted 8/15/61, single, farmer. Died measles 12/06/61. NOK: Elizabeth Mansel, mother. Hometown: Troy, AL.

Mansel, Samuel J.: 28, enlisted 9/20/61, single, farmer. Died 11/20/61. Hometown: Troy, AL.

Mansel, William H.: 20, enlisted 8/15/61, single, farmer. Severely wounded Cold Harbor knee 6/27/62. Severely wounded Gettysburg left side, arm, and thigh 7/02/63 and captured 7/04/63. Paroled 8/??/63. "Fine, patriotic soldier." Hometown: Troy, AL.

Mims, R.H.: 30, enlisted 7/03/61, married, farmer. Died measles 10/05/61. NOK: Mary W. Mims, wife. Hometown: Creek Stand, AL.

Minor, L.M.: Discharged 1/18/62 disease kidney and spine. Hometown: in AL.

Murdock, Samuel J.: 23, enlisted 7/03/61, married, farmer. Mortally wounded Fredericksburg 12/13/62, died 12/15/62. Hometown: Creek Stand, AL.

Murdock, William J.: 24, enlisted 7/03/61, single, farmer. Elected 2SGT. Died typhoid 2/05/62. Hometown: Creek Stand, AL.

Nelson, Thomas L.: 27, enlisted 7/03/61, married, mechanic. Elected 4SGT. Died chronic diarrhea Macon, GA, while on his way home 2/05/62. NOK: Charlotte Nelson, wife. Hometown: Enon, AL.

Powell, Henry: Died 12/05/61.

Pugh, James T.: 44, enlisted 7/03/61, married, farmer. Died pneumonia 11/03/61. NOK: Jane Pugh, wife. Hometown: Creek Stand, AL.

Pugh, Zachariah C.: 39, enlisted 7/03/61, married, farmer. Wounded Lookout Valley 10/27/63. Died dysentery 9/07/64. Hometown: Creek Stand, AL.

Reeves, James M.: 35, enlisted 10/27/62, married, farmer. Died 4/17/64. Hometown: Creek Stand, AL.

Russell, John S.: 38, enlisted 3/17/62, single, farmer. Died typhoid 6/01/62. Hometown: Creek Stand, AL.

Russell, Richard M.: 30, enlisted 3/17/62, married, farmer. 5'8", dark complexion, black eyes, black hair. Hometown: Creek Stand, AL.

Seegar, J.E.: 2CPL, promoted 5SGT 2/??/62, 4SGT 5/??/62, 3SGT 9/??/62, and 2SGT

9/??/63. Wounded and captured Gettysburg 7/02/63, sent to Fort Delaware. Took oath and released 6/14/65. 5'4", dark complexion, gray eyes, dark hair. NOK: Nancy Seegar, wife. Hometown: in AL.

Shelton, Andrew J.: 42, enlisted 7/03/61, single, farmer. Captured Lookout Valley 10/29/63, sent to Camp Morton, IN. Exchanged. Hometown: Creek Stand, AL.

Singleton, J.M.: 42, enlisted 7/03/61, married, farmer. Killed Cross Keys grapeshot below throat 6/08/62. NOK: Adeline H. Singleton, wife. Hometown: Creek Stand, AL.

Singleton, Thomas: 20, enlisted 7/03/61, single, farmer. Mortally wounded Cross Keys 6/27/62, died 8/27/62. Fair complexion, gray eyes, dark hair. NOK: B.H. Singleton, father. Hometown: Wetumpka, AL.

Singleton, William Stephen P.: 23, enlisted 7/03/61, single, farmer. Promoted 4CPL 9/01/62, 3CPL 2/01/63, and 5SGT 9/01/64. Wounded Knoxville 11/29/63 and slightly wounded ear Wilderness 5/06/64. Served to Lee's surrender. Hometown: Wetumpka, AL.

Skinner, James M.: 23, enlisted 7/03/61, married, farmer. Killed Cold Harbor 6/27/62. NOK: Martha L. Skinner, wife. Hometown: Creek Stand, AL.

Skinner, John T.: 20, enlisted 7/03/61, single, farmer. Recruited as drummer. Captured 6/02/62, exchanged. Severely wounded Cold Harbor 6/27/62. Hometown: Columbus, GA.

Slaton, James A.: 18, enlisted 7/03/61, single, student. Wounded and captured Sharpsburg right side 9/17/62, paroled 9/27/62. Captured Gettysburg 7/02/63, Fort Delaware. Took oath and released 6/14/65. 5'10", dark complexion, gray eyes, light hair. Hometown: Creek Stand, AL.

Slaton, William J.: 20, enlisted 7/03/61, single, farmer. Died typhoid/pneumonia 4/06/62. NOK: Elisha Slaton, father. Hometown: Creek Stand, AL.

Snipes, John F.: 30, enlisted 3/??/62, married, farmer. Mortally wounded thigh and captured Sharpsburg 9/17/62, died 10/15/62. NOK: M.B. Snipes, wife. Hometown: Creek Stand, AL.

Sorrell, John: 20, enlisted 8/15/62, single, farmer. Died typhoid 4/07/63. NOK: August L. Sorrell, wife. Hometown: Newton, AL.

Springs, Lewis: Enlisted 7/03/61. Deserted and captured Knoxville 12/11/63.

Streetman, Thornton J.: 21, enlisted 7/03/61, single, farmer. Died cholera 6/20/63. Hometown: Creek Stand, AL.

Strickland, Benson: 22, enlisted 7/03/61, single, farmer. Promoted 1CPL 12/01/61. Mortally

wounded Cold Harbor 6/27/62, died 7/07/62. Hometown: Creek Stand, AL.

Strickland, Simeon: 18, enlisted 7/03/61, single, farmer. Wounded Manassas 8/29/62 and Lookout Valley 10/27/63. Hometown: Creek Stand, AL.

Talbot, E.C. 16, enlisted 7/03/61, single, farmer. Killed (shot in head) Chickamauga 9/19/63. Hometown: Creek Stand, AL.

Thompson, William: 49, enlisted 7/03/61, single, farmer. Detailed as nurse. Discharged 3/15/64, hemorrhoids. Hometown: Sandfort, AL.

Tinnery, John: 48, enlisted 8/05/61, married, farmer. Deserted 8/08/61 Wilmington, SC. Hometown: Columbus, GA.

Turner, John B.: 16, enlisted 7/03/61, single, farmer. Wounded Cold Harbor 6/27/62, Chantilly 9/01/62, and severely wounded in the neck by sharpshooter Deep Bottom 7/11/64. Hometown: Creek Stand, AL.

Turner, William: 20, enlisted 7/03/61, single, farmer. Died measles 10/25/61. NOK: Sarah Turner, mother. Hometown: Creek Stand, AL.

Vinson, Elisha P.: 27, enlisted 7/03/61, married, miller. Promoted 1CPL 2/11/62. Mortally wounded Manassas 8/28/62, died 8/29/62. Hometown: Huntsville, AL.

Vinson, Green B.: 30, enlisted 3/09/62, married, farmer. Wounded Manassas 8/28/62, Fredericksburg 12/19/62, and severely wounded Knoxville 11/29/63. Served to Lee's surrender. Hometown: Creek Stand, AL.

Walker, Silas: 41, enlisted 3/25/62, married, farmer. Wounded Sharpsburg 9/17/62. Served to Lee's surrender. Hometown: Creek Stand, AL.

Ward, Samuel: Enlisted 8/18/62. Discharged 2/22/63 fluid in lungs. 5'10", dark complexion, hazel eyes, black hair. Hometown: in AL.

Watts, Thomas R.: 25, enlisted 3/01/62, married, farmer. Captured 4/06/65, sent to Libby Prison, VA. Released 6/21/65. 5'8¾", light complexion, gray eyes, brown hair. Hometown: Creek Stand, AL.

Wheeler, Thomas: 50, enlisted 7/03/61, single, farmer. Discharged 6/10/62. 5'10", dark complexion, blue eyes, dark hair. Hometown: Creek Stand, AL.

Wicker, Joel: 17, enlisted 7/03/61, single, farmer. Mortally wounded Cold Harbor 6/27/62. NOK: Wiley Wicker, father. Hometown: Creek Stand, AL.

Wicker, Julius A.: 18, enlisted 7/03/61, single, farmer. Captured Gettysburg 7/02/63, sent to Fort Delaware, DE. Took oath and released 6/14/65. 5'6", sallow complexion, blue eyes, light hair. Hometown: Creek Stand, AL.

Wilkerson, Bascom K.: 16, enlisted 7/03/61, single, farmer. Deserted and captured 12/16/64 Hometown: Creek Stand, AL.

Woodham, Eugene B.: 18, enlisted 7/03/61, single, farmer. Wounded Cold Harbor 6/27/62 and Manassas 8/29/62. Killed Suffolk, shell burst under him, 5/03/63. Hometown: Creek Stand, AL.

Company D

Adams, Thomas A.: 22, enlisted 7/03/61, single, farmer. AWOL most of the time, deserted 1/01/63. Hometown: New Topia, AL.

Albritton, W.H.: 20, enlisted 3/08/62, single, farmer. Deserted from hospital 5/01/63. Hometown: Clayton, AL.

Bailey, George W.: 30, enlisted 7/03/61. Wounded Cold Harbor 6/27/62 (thumb), Fredericksburg 12/19/62, and Chickamauga 9/19–20/63. Discharged to Invalid Corps 7/05/64. Hometown: Clayton, AL.

Bailey, Robert: Died 7/05/62. NOK: Henry Bailey. Hometown: Louisville, AL.

Beathy, Robert.: 21, enlisted 7/03/61, single, farmer. Killed Cross Keys 6/08/62. Hometown: Clayton, AL.

Bell, J.P.: 24, enlisted 3/08/62, married, farmer. Promoted 3CPL 11/01/62. Wounded Manassas 8/30/62. Died typhoid 1/03/63. Hometown: Fort Browder, AL.

Benefield, Arnold: 44, enlisted 3/08/62, married, farmer. Discharged "chronic rheumatism-wasting of muscles" 11/13/62. 5'11", fair complexion, blue eyes, light hair. Hometown: Clayton, AL.

Biddy, Robert: 44, enlisted 7/03/61, single, farmer. Mortally wounded Cross Keys 6/08/62, died 7/05/62. Hometown: in AL.

Blount, Andrew J.: 19, enlisted 3/08/62, farmer. Wounded Manassas 8/28/62 and Fredericksburg 12/19/62. Tree fell on him and fractured thigh Bull Gap, TN. Hometown: in AL.

Bonds, R. Lafayette: 25, enlisted 3/08/62, married, farmer. Deserted Wilderness 5/06/64 while detailed as "tanner." Hometown: Clayton, AL.

Brook, John J.: Wounded Manassas 8/30/62. Died.

Brown, C.W.: 25, enlisted 3/20/62. Died 10/11/62. Hometown: Newton, AL.

Brown, William L.: 35, enlisted 7/03/61, married, farmer. Died 2/05/62. Hometown: Clayton, AL.

Burkhalter, D.D.: 22, enlisted 7/03/61, married, farmer. Promoted 3CPL, 1CPL 6/01/63, and 4SGT 3/01/64. Severely wounded Wilderness (left arm) 5/06/64. Served to Lee's surrender. Dark complexion, hazel eyes, dark hair. Hometown: Ft. Browder, AL.

Campbell, John S.: 47, enlisted 9/13/61, married, farmer. Discharged 11/20/61 "physical debility." Hometown: New Topia, AL.

Caraker, John "Jack" V.: 16, enlisted 3/08/62, single, farmer. Wounded Cold Harbor 6/27/62, Sharpsburg 9/17/62, and mortally wounded Darbytown Road 10/13/64, died 10/29/64. Hometown: Ft. Browder, AL.

Caraker, William H.: 20, enlisted 3/08/62. Died of typhoid 12/08/62. Hometown: Ft. Browder, AL.

Carroll, Rufus: 18, enlisted 8/20/61. Died of pneumonia 11/18/61. 5'5", dark complexion, black eyes, black hair. Hometown: Clayton, AL.

Carter, William R.: 23, enlisted 7/03/61, single, farmer. Died of measles 11/22/61. Hometown: Clayton, AL.

Coats, A.J.: Wounded and captured Sharpsburg 9/19/62.

Cody, M.B.: 22, enlisted 9/01/62, single, farmer. Died of disease 10/28/62. Hometown: Cowikee, AL.

Condry, John D.: 23, enlisted 7/03/61, single, farmer. Died of disease 11/08/61. 5'8", dark complexion, black eyes, black hair. Hometown: Clayton, AL.

Cook, J.C.: 25, enlisted 8/24/62. single, farmer. Wounded left leg, discharged 4/23/63. Fair complexion, gray eyes, ? hair. Hometown: in AL.

Cooper, J.W.: 18, enlisted 7/03/61, single, farmer. Killed Manassas 8/28/62. Hometown: Clayton, AL.

Creel, Duncan S.: 18, enlisted 7/03/61, single, farmer. Discharged 12/26/61. 5'2", fair complexion, blue eyes, sandy hair. Hometown: Clayton, AL.

Cumby, H.D.: Elected 1CPL. Discharged 6/15/62. Hometown: in AL.

Davis, Wright E.L.: 25, enlisted 3/08/62, single, farmer. Discharged 5/24/62. Hometown: Clayton, AL.

Day, Henry J.: 20, enlisted 3/01/64, single, farmer. Served to Lee's surrender. Hometown: Andalusia, AL.

Day, J.W.: Enlisted 7/03/61. Served to Lee's surrender. Hometown: Andalusia, AL.

Douglas, A.W.: 24, enlisted 7/03/61, single, farmer. Wounded Cold Harbor 6/27/62. Promoted CPL 8/01/62. Killed Manassas 8/28/62. Hometown: Troy, AL.

Eidson, J.W.: 23, enlisted 7/03/61, single, farmer. Captured Gettysburg 7/02/63, sent Ft. Delaware, DE. Died of disease 10/03/63. Hometown: Pine Level, AL.

Eidson, James J.: 24, enlisted 7/03/61, single, farmer. Died of measles 9/26/61. Hometown: in AL.

Eidson, James R.: 21, enlisted 7/03/61, married, farmer. Wounded Cross Keys 6/08/62. Promoted 4CPL. Captured Gettysburg 7/02/63, sent Ft. Delaware, DE. Took oath and released 6/07/65. 6'2", ruddy complexion, gray eyes, brown hair. Hometown: Ft. Browder, AL.

Eidson, Milledge: 22, enlisted 8/17/61, single, farmer. Deserted 10/01/63. Hometown: in SC.

Eidson, William: 24, enlisted 8/17/61, married, farmer. Detailed as teamster. Captured Lookout Mountain 10/29/63. Enlisted in U.S. service 3/24/65. Hometown: in SC.

Garland, William: 17, enlisted 3/08/62, single, farmer. Mortally wounded Cross Keys 6/08/62, died 7/01/62. Hometown: Ft. Browder, AL.

Gillis, R.L.: 26, enlisted 10/19/61, single, farmer. Wounded right hand Cold Harbor 6/27/61. Discharged 10/24/62. 5'11", dark complexion, hazel eyes, dark hair. Hometown: Troy, AL.

Gilver, A.B.: Captured Gettysburg 7/02/63, sent to Ft. Delaware.

Gregory, F.L.: 24, enlisted 7/03/63, single, farmer. Severely wounded Chickamauga 9/20/63. Served to Lee's surrender. Hometown: Cowikee, AL.

Hall, Brook Duncan: 22, enlisted 9/20/61, single, farmer. Discharged (disease of heart) 4/04/62. 6'0", fair complexion, blue eyes, light hair. Hometown: Ft. Browder, AL.

Hall, David: 42, enlisted 7/03/63, married, farmer. Discharged hypertrophy of heart 10/02/62. Hometown: Eufaula, AL.

Hall, J.C.: Died measles 9/22/61. Hometown: Ft. Browder, AL.

Hall, William W.: 23, enlisted 7/03/61, single, farmer. Died 7/04/62. NOK: John W. Hall. Hometown: Ft. Browder, AL.

Harrod, William A.: Wounded Manassas 8/28/62. Killed Sharpsburg 9/17/62. NOK: Sarah Harrod. Hometown: Ft. Browder, AL.

Hartzog, Francis "Frank": 35, enlisted 7/03/61, married farmer. Wounded Darbytown Road 10/??/64. Hometown: in AL.

Hartzog, L. Daniel: 27, enlisted 7/03/61, single, farmer. Killed Gettysburg 7/02/63. 5'10", dark complexion, hazel eyes, black hair. Hometown: Clayton, AL.

Herrod, W.C.: 30, enlisted 8/19/62, married, farmer. Died 10/15/62. NOK: Nancy Herrod, wife. Hometown: Clayton, AL.

Hatcher, James J.: 31, enlisted 7/03/61, married, merchant. Elected 1SGT. Promoted 3LT 10/21/61, 2LT 12/05/61, 1LT 7/24/63, and CPT 2/15/65. Transferred to Company L 6/02/63. Severely wounded arm Chester Station 6/17/64. Served to Lee's surrender. Hometown: Ft. Browder, AL.

Head, Edmond P.: 31, enlisted 7/03/61, single, farmer. Elected 3LT. Promoted 2LT 10/21/61, and 1LT 12/05/61. Killed Battle Mountain 7/24/63 Hometown: Cowikee, AL.

Helms, Jesse: 20, enlisted 3/08/62, married, farmer. Died 9/04/62, stroke. NOK: Mary Ann Helms, wife. Hometown: Clayton, AL.

Helms, William T.: enlisted 7/03/61, single, farmer. Wounded Sharpsburg 9/17/62. Captured Deep Bottom 8/14/64, released 5/13/65. Hometown: in AL.

Hill, Blanton "Blant" A.: 24, enlisted 7/03/61, single, farmer. Elected 1LT, promoted CPT 9/04/61. Slightly wounded Cold Harbor 6/27/62. Mortally wounded hip Deep Bottom 8/16/64. "His company, the regiment, and the Confederate Army lost in him a valuable officer." Hometown: Ft. Browder, AL.

Hill, George G.: 45, enlisted 7/03/61, married, wagoneer. Elected 2CPL. Died 1/02/62. NOK: A.S. Hill, wife. Hometown: Ft. Browder, AL.

Hill, R.W.: Died 9/02/64, mortally wounded. Hometown: Ft. Browder, AL.

Hudgins, John W.: 19, enlisted 7/03/61, single, farmer. Wounded Fredericksburg 12/19/62. Deserted and captured 2/24/64 Washington, D.C. 5'11¾", dark complexion, black eyes, brown hair. Hometown: Ft. Browder, AL.

Jackson, Charles J.: 27, enlisted 7/03/61, single, farmer. Captured Gettysburg 7/02/63, sent to Ft. Delaware. Exchanged 1/16/64. Captured Deep Bottom 8/14/64. Hometown: New Topia, AL.

Jackson, S. Robert: 20, enlisted 9/20/61, single, farmer. Died pneumonia 11/19/61. Hometown: Louisville, AL.

Jeffcoat, A.J.: 21, enlisted 7/03/61, married, farmer when. Wounded right hand Sharpsburg 9/17/62. AWOL and jailed Blakely, GA. Hometown: Ft. Browder, AL.

Jeffcoat, Franklin: 20, enlisted 7/03/61, single, farmer. Detailed nurse Ft. Gaines, GA. Hometown: Ft. Browder, AL.

Johnson, Felder: 20, enlisted 7/03/61, single, farmer. Promoted CPL 7/01/62, 4SGT 10/01/62, and 3SGT. Captured Gettysburg 7/

02/63, sent to Ft. Delaware, DE. Took oath and released 6/14/65. 5'8", fair complexion, blue eyes, dark hair. Hometown: in AL.

Johnson, James T.: 27, enlisted 3/08/62, single, farmer. Died typhoid 5/06/62. Hometown: Enon, AL.

Johnson, William Washington: 19, enlisted 7/03/61, single, farmer. Promoted CPL 7/01/62, 3SGT 10/01/62, and 2SGT. Wounded Malvern Hill 7/02/62. Awarded Southern Cross of Honor 12/10/64. Served to Lee's surrender. Hometown: Ft. Browder, AL.

Jones, Robert Samuel "Sam": 21, enlisted 7/03/61, single, farmer. Wounded Cold Harbor 6/27/62. Awarded Southern Cross of Honor 12/10/64. Served to Lee's surrender. Hometown: Ft. Browder, AL.

Lewis, William R.: 20, enlisted 7/03/61, single, farmer. Killed Cold Harbor 6/27/62. 5'4", dark complexion, dark eyes, dark hair. Hometown: Eufaula, AL.

Long, James Harvey: 21, enlisted 7/03/61, single, farmer. Promoted 1SGT 8/01/63. Wounded Lookout Valley 10/27/63. Served to Lee's surrender. Hometown: Ft. Browder, AL.

McBride, T.W.: 27, enlisted 2/01/62, single, farmer. Died chronic diarrhea 9/04/62. Hometown: in AL.

McGilvary, Angus: 23, enlisted 7/03/61, single, farmer. Wounded Malvern Hill 7/02/62. Captured Gettysburg 7/02/63, sent to Ft. Delaware, DE. Exchanged 9/17/63. Killed by sharpshooter Petersburg 6/21/64. Hometown: in AL.

McGilvary, W.A.: 21, enlisted 7/03/61, farmer. Died typhoid/diarrhea 11/29/61. Hometown: Clayton, AL.

McGrady, Robert: Married. Died. NOK: Rachel C. McGrady, wife. Hometown: in AL.

Maddux, James R.: 25, enlisted 3/01/62, single, farmer. Wounded Cold Harbor 6/27/62. Discharged 7/01/63 due to wounds. 6'0", fair complexion, brown eyes, brown hair. Hometown: Cowikee, AL.

Matthews, J.B.: 27, enlisted 7/03/61, single, farmer. Severely wounded Chickamauga 9/20/63. Detailed to Columbus, GA, to Quartermaster. Hometown: Reynolds, GA.

McIntosh, Angus A.: 28, enlisted 7/03/61, single, farmer. Promoted 2LT 5/25/62. Wounded Cross Keys 6/08/62. Killed Cold Harbor 6/27/62. NOK: Archibald McIntosh, father. Hometown: in AL.

Moffette, Thomas S.: 21, enlisted 7/03/61, married, farmer. Captured Cross Keys 6/08/62, paroled Winchester 6/??/62. Wounded Sharpsburg 9/17/62. Mortally wounded Dan-

dridge, TN, 1/16/64, died 5/01/64. Hometown: Clayton, AL.

Newton, Douglass: 24, enlisted 7/03/61, single, farmer. Discharged 12/16/61 disability.

Newton, James D.: 24, enlisted 7/03/61, single, farmer. Discharged deformity of the hand 12/14/61. 5'8", dark complexion, black eyes, black hair. Hometown: Ft. Browder, AL.

Newton, John H.: 18, enlisted 7/03/61, single, farmer. Detailed ambulance driver. Wounded knee Chickamauga 9/20/63. Discharged 9/06/64, assigned to Invalid Corps with duty at Eufaula, AL. Hometown: Ft. Browder, AL.

Newton, William C.: 21, enlisted 7/03/61, single, farmer. Promoted SGT 12/01/61. Detailed ambulance driver. Killed Sharpsburg 9/17/62. "Splendid soldier." NOK: John K. Newton, father. Hometown: Ft. Browder, AL.

Pate, Thomas: 28, enlisted 3/08/62, married, farmer. Wounded Manassas 8/30/62. Killed 9/30/64 Ft. Harrison. Hometown: Ft. Browder, AL.

Patterson, Newton: 26, enlisted 7/03/61. Died 12/15/61. Hometown: Ft. Browder, AL.

Patterson, Soloman: 18, enlisted 7/03/61, single, farmer. Mortally wounded Manassas 8/28/62, died 9/08/62. Hometown: Ft. Browder, AL.

Quattlebaum, W.H. 18, enlisted 3/10/62, single, farmer. Wounded Cold Harbor 6/27/62 and Chickamauga 9/19–20/63. Awarded Southern Cross of Honor 12/10/64. Served to Lee's surrender. Hometown: Ft. Browder, AL.

Reaves, Thomas Jefferson: 18, enlisted 7/03/61, single, farmer. Wounded Manassas 8/28/62 and severely wounded foot 8/16/64. Hometown: Ft. Browder, AL.

Robertson, W.J.: 18, enlisted 7/03/61, single, farmer. Wounded Sharpsburg 9/17/62, Fredericksburg 12/19/62, and slightly thigh 10/07/64. Hometown: Troy, AL.

Russell, G.W.: 25, enlisted 7/03/61. Died 5/20/64. Hometown: Clayton, AL.

Spence, S. Lewis: 24, enlisted 7/03/61, single, teacher. Wounded Sharpsburg 9/17/62. Promoted 1SGT 10/05/62. Captured 10/29/63 Lookout Valley, sent to Camp Morton. Died chronic diarrhea 7/30/64. Hometown: Ft. Browder, AL.

Stevens, Benjamin F.: 24, enlisted 11/10/61, single, farmer. Hired as substitute for brother (Stevens, J.A.). Captured Gettysburg 7/02/63, sent to Ft. Delaware. Died inflammation of brain 9/23/63. Hometown: Cowikee, AL.

Stevens, J.A.: 30, enlisted 8/20/61, single, farmer. Discharged 11/16/61 by substitute (brother Stevens, Benjamin F.) Hometown: Cowikee, AL.

Streeter, Benjamin F.: 30, enlisted 3/08/62, single, farmer. Wounded Cold Harbor 6/27/62. Discharged 3/23/63 by substitute (brother Godwin Streeter). Hometown: Cowikee, AL.

Streeter, Godwin 26, enlisted 3/23/63, single, farmer. Substituted for brother Benjamin F. Streeter. Captured Deep Bottom 8/14/64, sent to Point Lookout, MD. Exchanged 2/10/65. Hometown: Cowikee, AL.

Thornton, Dozier: 21, enlisted 7/03/61, single, clerk. Wounded Cold Harbor 6/27/62. Promoted 1SGT 11/16/61, 3LT 7/01/62, 2LT 1/??63, and 1LT 7/24/63. "An excellent soldier and a faithful officer." Severely wounded "right heel, right buttock, and left leg" Fussell's Mill. Hometown: Ft. Browder, AL.

Thurman, J. 33, enlisted 12/16/61, single, farmer. Discharged chronic pneumonia 1/03/62. 5'9", sallow complexion, blue eyes, black hair. Substitute for J.T. Hall. Hometown: Ft. Browder, AL.

Trawick, J.: Died pneumonia and meningitis 1/19/62. Hometown: in AL.

Tucker, Daniel: 24, enlisted 7/03/61, single, farmer. Died 11/21/61. Hometown: in AL.

Turner, Edwin A.: 22, enlisted 7/03/61, single, farmer. Died 11/01/61. NOK: Charlotte Turner, wife. Hometown: Cowikee, AL.

Varnadore, Thomas: 32, enlisted 7/03/61, married, farmer. Severely wounded shoulder by sharpshooter 2nd Cold Harbor 6/04/64. Hometown: Clayton, AL.

Ward, R.: Died 11/21/61.

Williamson, H.J.: 24, enlisted 7/03/61, single, farmer. Wounded Hazel River 8/23/62 and slightly wounded leg Darbytown Road 8/14/64. Hometown: in AL.

Williford, J.H.: 21, enlisted 7/03/61, single, clerk. Elected 3SGT. Died measles 9/26/61. NOK: M.C. Williford, father. Hometown: Ft. Browder, AL.

Willingham, E.T.: Died 4/09/62.

Wilson, James S.: 28, enlisted 7/03/61, single, farmer.
Elected 2LT, promoted 1LT 10/21/61. Resigned 1/08/62. Hometown: Cowikee, AL.

Wilson, James: 23, enlisted 7/03/61, single, farmer. Wounded Manassas 8/28/62. Killed Chickamauga 9/20/63. Hometown: Cowikee, AL.

Wright, Franklin: enlisted 4/23/61, married. Killed Cold Harbor 6/27/62. NOK: Phebe Wright, wife. Hometown: Ft. Browder, AL.

Zorn, David H.: 20, enlisted 7/03/61, single, farmer when. Severely wounded arm (amputated) Cold Harbor 6/27/62. Hometown: Clayton, AL.

Company E

Abbott, Guilford L.: 23, enlisted 7/03/61, married, farmer. Died typhoid 6/07/62. NOK: J.A. Abbott, wife. Hometown: Daleville, AL.

Alexander, John: 17, enlisted 3/03/62, single, farmer. Mortally wounded Chickamauga 9/20/63, died 9/22/63. Hometown: Newton, AL.

Ammons, Stephen: 16, enlisted 9/26/64, single, farmer. Hometown: Sarah Gordo, FL.

Andrews, James: 28, enlisted 11/15/64, married, blacksmith. Served to Lee's surrender. Hometown: Ozark, AL.

Aplin, John: 21. Died pneumonia 2/02/62. Hometown: in AL.

Armor, Junius A.: 18, enlisted 7/03/61, single, farmer. Died pneumonia 6/19/62. Hometown: Clintonville, AL.

Athon, Rufus A.: 27, enlisted 7/03/61, single, farmer. Killed Cold Harbor 6/27/62. Hometown: Westville, AL.

Atkinson, Cornelius V.: 16, enlisted 3/03/62, single, farmer. Captured Gettysburg 7/02/63, sent to Ft. Delaware. 5'4", fair complexion, blue eyes, dark hair. Took oath and released 6/14/65. Hometown: Newton, AL.

Austin, Albert W.: 21, enlisted 7/03/61, single, farmer. Captured Gettysburg 7/02/63, sent to Ft. Delaware. 5'10", light complexion, gray eyes, dark hair. Took oath and released 6/14/65. Hometown: Daleville, AL.

Bailey, Micajah C.: Died 5/28/62. NOK: Mary Bailey, wife. Hometown: Clopton, AL.

Barker, Samuel: 28, enlisted 7/03/61, single, farmer. Died pneumonia 12/11/61. Hometown: Daleville, AL.

Barnes, Coleman F.: 18, enlisted 8/15/62, single, farmer. Wounded Chickamauga 9/20/63. Discharged for wounds 9/13/64. Hometown: Barnes Cross Roads, AL.

Barnes, William J.: 20, enlisted 8/10/61, single, farmer. Died 6/12/62. NOK: Absolom Barnes, father. Hometown: Barnes Cross Roads, AL.

Bell, Joseph H.: 21, enlisted 7/03/61, single, farmer. Mortally wounded leg (amputated) Fussell's Mill 8/16/64, died 11/16/64. Hometown: Daleville, AL.

Bigbie, Benjamin F.: 24, enlisted 7/03/61, farmer. Detailed as teamster. Wounded Sharpsburg 9/17/62. Captured Gettysburg 7/02/63, sent to Ft. Delaware, DE. Died 1/11/64. Hometown: in AL.

Blackwell, James: Wounded in both thighs (per Union records), 11/??/62. Hometown: in AL.

Bracewell, Thomas R.: 28, enlisted 10/27/63, married, farmer. Wounded arm (amputated) and captured Deep Bottom 8/14/64, sent to

Point Lookout, MD. 5'5", swathy complexion, blue eyes, brown hair. Hometown: Daleville, AL.

Bradwell, R.T.: Discharged 11/12/61.

Breare, Joseph R.: 29, enlisted 7/03/61, married, lawyer. Born in England. Promoted 3LT 2/05/62 and 2LT 6/05/62. Captured Gettysburg 7/02/63, sent to Ft. Delaware, DE. Exchanged 3/17/64 and spent the rest of the war AWOL. Arrest warrant issued 4/16/64. Hometown: Newton, AL.

Briley, Micajah "Cage": 26, enlisted 3/08/62, married, farmer. Died typhoid 5/28/62. Hometown: Clayton, AL.

Briley, William H.: 23, enlisted 3/01/62, married, farmer. Detailed as shoemaker. Wounded Cold Harbor 6/27/62. Deserted east TN. 4/21/64. Hometown: Barnes Cross Roads, AL.

Brooks, Alpheus W.: 27, enlisted 7/03/61, single, farmer. Deserted east TN, rejoined regiment. Deserted 8/16/64, court-martialed and shot. Hometown: Daleville, AL.

Brooks, Andrew J.: Enlisted 7/03/61, single, farmer. Elected 3CPL. Died 10/07/62 while at home. Hometown: Daleville, AL.

Brooks, Esau: 53, enlisted 7/03/61, married, farmer. Elected CPT. Resigned 2/08/62. Hometown: Daleville, AL.

Brooks, Lawrence D.: 22, enlisted 7/03/61, single, farmer. Severely wounded left leg Cold Harbor 6/27/62. Discharged 8/15/64, assigned to Invalid Corps, worked as a clerk Ft. Gaines, GA. Hometown: Daleville, AL.

Brown, Green: 42, enlisted 3/03/62, single, farmer. Discharged 8/18/62 "phthisis of the lungs with great emaciation." 6'2", dark complexion, dark eyes, dark hair. Hometown: Westville, AL.

Bryan, Daniel F.: 26, enlisted 7/03/61, married, merchant. Elected 2LT, resigned 11/15/61. Hometown: Daleville, AL.

Bryan, Thomas Allen: 28, enlisted 7/03/61, married, farmer. Elected 1SGT, furnished substitute 11/12/61. Hometown: Daleville, AL.

Bryant, John F.: Died pneumonia 2/01/62. NOK: Nancy Bryant, wife. Hometown: in AL.

Butts, William E.: 20, enlisted 3/27/62, single, farmer. Died 8/20/62. Hometown: Barnes Cross Roads, AL.

Byrd, Richard D.: 21, enlisted 10/22/61, single, farmer. Detailed as teamster. Wounded Cold Harbor 6/27/62. Captured Mossy Creek, TN, 1/02/64, sent to Rock Island, IL. Took oath and released 2/22/65. 5'11", dark complexion, blue eyes, light hair Hometown: Westville, AL.

Cameron, Henry A.: 26, enlisted 11/06/61. Substitute for Allen Bryan. Promoted 2CPL 12/28/62. Killed Suffolk 5/03/63. Hometown: Westville, AL.

Carmichael, Jesse Malcolm: 26, enlisted 3/03/62, married, farmer. Wounded right hand (amputated) Sharpsburg 9/19/62. Discharged. Hometown: Sylvan Grove, AL.

Chalker, John W.: 21, enlisted 7/03/61, single, farmer. Died pneumonia 11/22/61. NOK: William Chalker, father. Hometown: Westville, AL.

Clark, Henry: 21, enlisted 7/03/61, single, farmer. Died typhoid 8/06/62. Hometown: Haw Ridge, AL.

Collins, Uriah: 20, enlisted 10/07/61, single, farmer. Died pneumonia 11/16/61. NOK: Sarah Collins, wife. Hometown: Westville, AL.

Collins, Wiley W.: 29, enlisted 3/03/62, married, lawyer. Died typhoid 6/13/63. Hometown: Newton, AL.

Conner, J.B.: Enlisted 10/01/62. Killed Chickamauga 9/19/63. Hometown: in AL.

Conway, S.R.: Died 11/08/61.

Cotton, Elbert A.: 39, enlisted 3/03/62, married, farmer. Wounded Knoxville 11/20/63 and slightly wounded shoulder Williamsburg Road 10/27/64. 5'4", fair complexion, blue eyes, dark hair. Hometown: Daleville, AL.

Cotton, Henry Carney: 27, enlisted 3/08/62, single, farmer. Died 5/20/62. NOK: Seth Cotton, father. Hometown: Daleville, AL.

Cotton, John J.: 22, enlisted 7/03/61, single, farmer. Died 11/20/61 pneumonia. NOK: Seth Cotton, father. Hometown: Daleville, AL.

Cotton, Joseph William: 20, enlisted 10/07/61, single, farmer. Wounded Sharpsburg 9/17/62, Chickamauga 9/19–20/63, and severely wounded arm Fussell's Mill. Hometown: Daleville, AL.

Cowen, James P.: 20, enlisted 7/03/61, single, farmer. Wounded Chantilly 9/01/62. Captured Deep Bottom 8/14/64, sent to Point Lookout, MD, and exchanged 3/17/65. Hometown: Clintonville, AL.

Crim, John: 21, enlisted 3/03/62, single, farmer. Died chronic diarrhea 8/26/64. Hometown: Sylvan Grove, AL.

Cudrey, J.: Died diarrhea 2/26/62.

Curenton, B. Newton: 20, enlisted 10/07/61, married, farmer. Severely wounded chest Deep Bottom 6/14/64. Served to Lee's surrender. Hometown: Westville, AL.

Curenton, Elbert W.: 23, enlisted 8/18/62, married, farmer. Wounded Chickamauga 9/20/63. Discharged 7/18/64. Hometown: Westville, AL.

Curenton, Jasper: 18, enlisted 8/18/62, single, farmer. Killed Gettysburg 7/02/63. NOK: Mary Curenton, mother. Hometown: Westville, AL.

Daughtry, Benjamin A.: 22, enlisted 3/03/62, single, farmer. Severely wounded Lookout Valley 10/28/63. Deserted and captured 2/24/65, given oath and transported to Pensacola, FL. Hometown: Newton, AL.

Daughtry, James H.: 22, enlisted 3/03/62, single, farmer. Died 6/29/62, typhoid. Hometown: Newton, AL.

Davis, George W. Lafayette: 16, enlisted 7/02/61, single, farmer. Died 6/17/62. NOK: Absalom Davis, father. Hometown: Daleville, AL.

Davis, William B.: 18, enlisted 7/02/61, single, farmer. Detailed hospital. Served to Lee's surrender. Hometown: Daleville, AL.

Dean, Benjamin F.: 30, enlisted 7/03/61, single, farmer. Mortally wounded Chickamauga 9/19–20/63, died 11/20/63. Hometown: Barnes Cross Roads, AL.

Dean, James D.: 30, enlisted 8/05/62, single, farmer. Died capillary bronchitis 5/19/63. NOK: Jesse Dean, father. Hometown: Barnes Cross Roads, AL.

Dean, Joseph J.: 20, enlisted 8/14/61, single, farmer. Wounded Manassas 8/30/62, Fredericksburg 12/19/62, severely wounded head Fussell's Mill 8/16/64. Hometown: Barnes Cross Roads, AL.

Deloach, Archibald: 28, enlisted 5/03/62, married, farmer. Died chronic diarrhea 5/20/62. NOK: Nancy Deloach, wife. Hometown: Newton, AL.

Dillard, Crawford George: 29, enlisted 8/01/62, married, farmer. Wounded Sharpsburg 9/17/62. 5'7", fair complexion, auburn hair. Hometown: Barnes Cross Roads, AL.

Dillard, James E.: 17, enlisted 8/13/64, single, farmer. Served to Lee's surrender. Hometown: Barnes Cross Roads, AL.

Dillard, Thomas G.: 24, enlisted 8/05/62, married, farmer. Wounded Fussell's Mill 8/16/64. Served to Lee's surrender. Hometown: Barnes Cross Roads, AL.

Dillard, William T.: 20, enlisted 8/05/62, married, farmer. Served to Lee's surrender. Hometown: Barnes Cross Roads, AL.

Dooling, William: 26, enlisted 8/03/62, married, farmer. Wounded Sharpsburg 9/17/62. Captured Gettysburg 7/02/63, died chronic diarrhea 11/27/63. NOK: Catherine Dooling, wife. Hometown: High Bluff, AL.

Duke, Daniel: Enlisted 3/04/62. Died measles 5/22/62.

Eason, William: 24, enlisted 3/03/62, married, farmer. Died 12/24/62. NOK: Emily Eason, wife. Hometown: Newton, AL.

Edwards, Ambrose Newton: 21, enlisted 7/03/61, single, farmer. Promoted 2SGT 5/16/62 and 1SGT 7/25/62. Wounded Sharpsburg 9/17/62 and Fredericksburg 12/19/62. Captured Gettysburg 7/02/63. Took oath and released 6/11/65. 5'10", light complexion, blue eyes, light hair. Hometown: Westville, AL.

Edwards, James "Jim" Russell: 21, enlisted 7/03/61, single, farmer. Wounded Manassas 8/30/62. Promoted 5SGT 9/16/63, 2SGT 6/10/64, and 2LT 10/30/64. Awarded Southern Cross of Honor 12/10/64. Served to Lee's surrender. Hometown: Ariton, AL.

Edwards, William A.: 26, enlisted 7/03/61, married, farmer. Elected 1LT, promoted CPT 3/06/63. Resigned 9/02/63. Hometown: Westville, AL.

Edwards, Young: 19, enlisted 7/03/61, single, farmer. Wounded Manassas 8/28/62, Sharpsburg 9/17/62, and Fredericksburg 12/19/62. Captured Knoxville 12/10/63, sent to Ft. Delaware, DE. Hometown: Westville, AL.

Faust, Henry: 22, enlisted 3/03/62, married, farmer. Wounded hand Chickamauga 9/20/63. Deserted 10/20/63. Hometown: Daleville, AL.

Faust, William L.: 16, enlisted 7/03/61, single, farmer. Captured Gettysburg 7/02/63, sent to Ft. Delaware, DE. 5'10", fair complexion, gray eyes, black hair. Took oath and released 6/14/65. Hometown: Daleville, AL.

Fleming, Benjamin "Barry" W.: 19, enlisted 7/03/61, single, farmer. Promoted 5SGT 8/01/64. Wounded Sharpsburg 12/19/62 and severely wounded left forearm 12/10/64. 5'8", fair complexion, hazel eyes, light hair. Hometown: Clintonville, AL.

Fleming, George W.: 20, enlisted 7/03/61, single, farmer. Died pneumonia 11/02/61. Hometown: Clintonville, AL.

Fleming, William C.D. "Doss": 19, enlisted 8/14/61, single, farmer. Captured Gettysburg 7/02/63, sent Ft. Delaware, DE. Took oath and released 6/14/65. 5'9", light complexion, hazel eyes, light hair. Hometown: Clintonville, AL.

Flowers, Eason: 19, enlisted 1/01/63, single, farmer. Killed Lookout Valley 10/27/63. Hometown: in AL.

Flowers, Jesse: 25, enlisted 8/15/62, married, farmer. Mortally wounded right shoulder Fussell's Mill 8/16/64, died hemorrhage 9/22/64. Hometown: Westville, AL.

Garner, Josiah: 32, enlisted 8/14/61, married, farmer. Transferred to Company F 8/31/63.

Died 10/11/63. Hometown: Barnes Cross Roads, AL.

Gergan, William: Died typhoid 6/17/62. Hometown: in AL.

Griffin, John W.: 20, enlisted 3/03/62, single, farmer. Died 6/12/62. NOK: Elizabeth Griffin, mother. Hometown: Daleville, AL.

Grimes, Daniel G.: 20, enlisted 7/03/61, single, farmer. Died typhoid 11/13/61. NOK: Edy R. Evans, mother. Hometown: Daleville, AL.

Grimes, Joseph W.: 20, enlisted 7/03/61, single, farmer. Died typhoid/pneumonia 12/23/61. NOK: Edy R. Evans, mother. Hometown: Daleville, AL.

Hardy, John: Died 4/14/64 typhoid.

Harris, Charles "Charlie" J.: 19, enlisted 3/08/62, single, farmer. Died dysentery 6/03/62. NOK: John Harris, father. Hometown: Daleville, AL.

Harris, William Y.: 21, enlisted 7/03/61, single, farmer. Killed Chickamauga 9/19/63. NOK: John Harris, father. Hometown: Daleville, AL.

Hayden, Augustus C.: 30, enlisted 7/03/61, married, painter. Captured 11/30/63. Took oath. Hometown: Daleville, AL.

Henderson, Michael E.: 24, enlisted 7/03/61, married, farmer. Died 2/24/63. Hometown: Daleville, AL.

Hogg, George F.: 27, enlisted 10/27/63, married, farmer. Served to Lee's surrender. Hometown: Westville, AL.

Hogg, Samuel: 23, enlisted 7/03/61, married, farmer. Elected 2SGT. Severely wounded cheek Wilderness 5/06/64. Served to Lee's surrender. Hometown: Westville, AL.

Holmes, W.H.: Died 5/06/62.

Howell, William Franklin: 26, enlisted 3/04/62, single, farmer. Died 5/02/62. NOK: James H. Howell, father. Hometown: Newton, AL.

Hughs, A.M.: 40, enlisted 7/03/61, married, lawyer. Discharged 11/25/61. 6'2", dark complexion, dark eyes, dark hair. Hometown: Newton, AL.

Jackson, A.F.: 30, enlisted 7/27/61, married, farmer. Discharged rheumatism 10/10/62. Hometown: Barnes Cross Roads, AL.

Jackson, J.E.: Died typhoid 10/16/61.

Jackson, John A.: 28, enlisted 7/03/61, married, farmer. Died 10/06/61. Hometown: Barnes Cross Roads, AL.

Jernigan, Jackson "Jack": 20, enlisted 10/07/61, single, farmer. Severely wounded Suffolk 5/03/63. Captured Morristown, TN, 4/16/64, sent to Camp Morton, IN. NOK: Elizabeth Jernigan, wife.

Jernigan, William T.: 26, enlisted 7/03/61, single, farmer. Died 1/12/62. NOK: Nancy Jernigan, wife. Hometown: Barnes Cross Roads.

Johnson, J. Randel: 36, enlisted 7/03/61, married, farmer. Promoted 4SGT and 3SGT 12/01/61. Discharged neuralgia 3/17/62. 5'9", dark complexion, light eyes, dark hair. Hometown: Newton, AL.

Johnson, James Earvin: 40, married, farmer. Discharged 2/26/62. 5'6", fair complexion, dark eyes, light hair. Hometown: Barnes Cross Roads, AL.

Johnson, W. Marion: enlisted 8/15/62, married, farmer. 6'0", fair complexion, black eyes, dark hair. Hometown: Newton, AL.

Johnson, William F.: enlisted 3/03/62, single, farmer. Mortally wounded and captured Gettysburg 7/02/63, died 7/16/63. Hometown: Newton, AL.

Johnston, L.: Died smallpox 12/21/62.

Jolly, William H.: 18, enlisted 8/12/61, single, farmer. Served to Lee's surrender. "First class soldier." Hometown: Barnes Cross Roads, AL.

Jones, Charley C.: 26, enlisted 7/03/61, married, carpenter. Severely wounded Hazel River 8/22/62. Served to Lee's surrender. Hometown: Westville, AL.

Jones, Elvin: 23, enlisted 8/15/62, married, farmer. Wounded Chickamauga 9/19/62. Served to Lee's surrender. Hometown: Westville, AL.

Jones, John E.: 21, enlisted 7/03/61, single, teacher. Elected 3LT. Promoted 2LT 7/26/61 and CPT 2/08/62. Wounded Manassas 8/29/62 and Chickamauga 9/19/62. Discharged 7/08/64 to Invalid Corps. Served to Lee's surrender. Hometown: Westville, AL.

Jones, John H.: 19, enlisted 8/01/61, single, farmer. Died measles 6/17/62. Hometown: in AL.

Jones, Joseph G.: 18, enlisted 8/01/61, single, farmer. Slightly wounded thigh Fussell's Mill. Served to Lee's surrender. Hometown: Westville, AL.

Jones, Oliver Marcellus: 30, farmer. Discharged amputated forearm 10/07/61. 6'0", light complexion, hazel eyes, dark hair. Hometown: in AL.

Jones, Simpson: 28, enlisted 8/11/62, married. Died tuberculosis 12/17/62. NOK: Martha Jane Jones, wife. Hometown: Elba, AL.

Jones, William W.: 25, enlisted 7/03/61, single, teacher. Wounded Sharpsburg 9/17/62. Killed Lookout Valley 10/27/63. Hometown: Westville, AL.

Jones, Wyatt R.: 18, enlisted 7/03/61, single, farmer. Died pneumonia 5/01/62. Hometown: Westville, AL.

Keahey, Green: 22, enlisted 3/03/62, single,

farmer. Killed 2nd Cold Harbor 6/03/64. "A splendid soldier." Hometown: Skipperville, AL.

Keahey, Jackson E.: 18, enlisted 8/15/62, single, farmer. Killed Lookout Valley 10/27/63. Hometown: in AL.

Keahey, Miles L: 28, enlisted 3/08/62, single, farmer. Captured Wilderness 5/06/64, sent to Elmira, NY, exchanged 3/??/65. Hometown: Skipperville, AL.

Keath, John A.: 26, enlisted 7/03/61, married, farmer. Discharged hernia 8/20/63. Hometown: Daleville, AL.

Kennan, Robert L.: 19, enlisted 7/03/61, single, clerk. Killed Chickamauga 9/19/63. Hometown: Westville, AL.

Kennedy, Coleman: enlisted 3/03/62, married, farmer. Died 5/26/62. Hometown: Newton, AL.

Knight, Matthew: 19, enlisted 10/07/61, single, farmer. Deserted 4/28/64 Bristol, TN. Hometown: Haw Ridge, AL.

Lammons, D.: Died pneumonia 3/19/62.

Lammons, James: 19, enlisted 8/15/61, single, farmer. Wounded Knoxville 11/20/63 and severely wounded head Darbytown Road 10/07/64. Served to Lee's surrender. Hometown: Barnes Cross Roads, AL.

Landingham, John H.: 22, enlisted 3/03/61, single, farmer. Captured Gettysburg 7/02/63, sent to Ft. Delaware, DE, and died chronic diarrhea 8/11/63. Hometown: in AL.

Lanier, Benjamin A.: 28, enlisted 8/07/61, married, farmer. Promoted 3SGT. Wounded Lookout Valley 10/27/63 and severely wounded side Fussell's Mill. Captured Amelia Courthouse 4/06/65, sent to Point Lookout, MD. Took oath and released 6/14/65. 5'8¾", dark complexion, gray eyes, black hair. "A splendid soldier." Hometown: Daleville, AL.

Latimer, James: 31, enlisted 8/15/62, married, farmer. Wounded Fredericksburg 12/19/62 and severely wounded Gettysburg 7/02/63. Killed Fussell's Mill 8/16/64. Hometown: Barnes Cross Roads, AL.

McGee, S.F.: 18, enlisted 10/07/61. Died chronic diarrhea 11/12/61. Hometown: Westville, AL.

McMurphy, Richard: Died. NOK: Clementine McMurphy, wife.

McSwain, Daniel: 40, enlisted 11/05/64, miller. Served to Lee's surrender. Hometown: Ozark, AL.

McSwain, John: 18, enlisted 3/26/62, single. Died double pneumonia 5/29/62. NOK: Angus McSwain. Hometown: Newton, AL.

Martin, Aaron: 23, enlisted 7/03/61, married, farmer. Died Hometown: Daleville, AL.

Martin, Benjamin J.: 19, enlisted 7/03/61, single,

farmer. 12/10/64 awarded Southern Cross of Honor. Served to Lee's surrender. "Excellent soldier." Hometown: Westville, AL.

Martin, James P.: 18, enlisted 7/03/61, single, farmer. Severely wounded left foot and hip and captured Shepherdstown 9/18/62 and exchanged. Captured Knoxville 12/03/63, sent to Rock Island, IL. Hometown: Westville, AL.

Martin, Jesse R.: 23, enlisted 1/02/62, farmer. Killed Lookout Valley 10/27/63. Hometown: Westville, AL.

Meeks, Thomas J.: 24, enlisted 8/03/62, farmer. Died chronic diarrhea 10/10/62. Hometown: Barnes Cross Roads, AL.

Messer, James: 18, enlisted 8/03/62, single, farmer. Died 10/01/62. NOK: Dempsey Messer, father. Hometown: Ozark, AL.

Mills, Thomas Sidney: 19, enlisted 7/03/61, single, farmer. Elected 2CPL, promoted 1CPL 7/13/64, and 4SGT 8/01/64. Wounded Cold Harbor 6/27/62, Sharpsburg head 9/17/62, severely wounded Gettysburg 7/02/63, and severely wounded shoulder Fussell's Mill 8/16/64. Served to Lee's surrender. Hometown: Daleville, AL.

Mills, Wesley B.: 25, enlisted 7/03/61, married, farmer. Elected 1CPL, promoted 1SGT 12/12/61, and 2LT 4/23/62. Killed Cross Keys 6/08/62. Hometown: Daleville, AL.

Mizell, Charles L.: 19, enlisted 7/03/61, single, farmer. Promoted 2SGT. Captured Gettysburg 7/02/63, sent to Ft. Delaware, DE. Took oath and released. 6'0", sallow complexion, blue eyes, light hair. Hometown: Westville, AL.

Mizell, John W.: enlisted 7/03/61, single, farmer. Elected 3SGT. Died pneumonia 12/19/61. Hometown: Westville, AL.

Mizell, William "Billy" Capers: 17, enlisted 7/03/61, single, farmer. Severely wounded leg Cold Harbor 6/27/64. Chickamauga 9/20/63, and slightly wounded Spotsylvania 5/08/64. "No better soldier in the regiment." Hometown: Ozark, AL.

Mobley, William W.: 17, enlisted 7/03/61, single, farmer. Captured Sharpsburg 9/17/62 and paroled. Severely wounded Chickamauga 9/19/63 and slightly wounded foot Wilderness 5/06/64. Served to surrender. Hometown: Westville, AL.

Moore, William B.: 25, enlisted 3/03/62, married. Died typhoid 5/24/62. NOK: Martha E. Moore, wife. Hometown: Westville, AL.

Morrell, John Loftin: 20, enlisted 3/03/62, single, farmer. Wounded Fredericksburg 12/19/62. Captured Gettysburg, sent Ft. Delaware, DE. Took oath and released 6/14/65. 5'9", fair complexion, brown eyes, dark hair. Hometown: Newton, AL.

Morrell, Jordan B.: 30, enlisted 3/03/62, married, farmer. Captured Knoxville 12/03/63, sent to Rock Island, IL. Hometown: in AL.

Morrell, Thomas M.: 27, enlisted 3/03/62, married, farmer. Wounded Manassas 8/30/62. Deserted and captured 4/28/64. Took oath and sent to Jeffersonville, IN, 7/16/64. 5'7", light complexion, blue eyes, dark hair. Hometown: Newton, AL.

Morrow, J.B.: Captured Knoxville 12/13/63, sent to Camp Chase, OH.

Mullins, Samuel Q.: 23, enlisted 3/03/62. Served to Lee's surrender. "A splendid soldier." Hometown: Newton, AL.

Munn, John: 25, enlisted 8/15/62, married, farmer. Severely wounded Chickamauga 9/19–20/63 and severely wounded right leg (amputated) Darbytown Road 10/13/64. Captured Richmond after surrender, sent to Point Lookout, MD, died chronic diarrhea 7/09/65. Hometown: Skipperville, AL.

Murphy, Andrew: Detailed to hospital, deserted 12/31/64.

Murphy, John: 22, enlisted 3/03/62, single, farmer. Severely wounded Chickamauga 9/20/63. Discharged 11/30/64 to Invalid Corps. Deserted 1/04/65. Hometown: High Bluff, AL.

Murphy, Richard: Single. Died typhoid 12/12/62. NOK: Clementine Murphy, mother. Hometown: High Bluff, AL.

Murphy, Thomas: 19, enlisted 3/03/62,single. Killed Cold Harbor 6/27/62. NOK: Clementine Murphy, mother. Hometown: Newton, AL.

Neal, Richard A.: 20, enlisted 7/03/61, single, farmer. Died measles 9/25/61. Hometown: Westville, AL.

Nevels, Hartwell B.: 40, enlisted 8/07/61, married, brick mason. Mortally wounded Cold Harbor 6/27/62, died 6/29/62. NOK: Permelia Nevels, wife. Hometown: Daleville, AL.

Newman, Robert E.: 27, enlisted 3/04/62, married, farmer. Died 8/10/62 NOK: Mary E. Newman, wife. Hometown: Newton, AL.

Nobles, John M.: 19, enlisted 3/04/62, married, farmer. Died typhoid 5/19/62. NOK: Savannah Noblin, wife. Hometown: Newton, AL.

Painter, William Rufus: 20, enlisted 10/01/61, single, farmer. Captured Gettysburg 7/02/63, sent to Ft. Delaware, DE. Took oath and released 6/14/65. 5'10", fair complexion, brown eyes, dark hair. Hometown: Haw Ridge, AL.

Parish, Marcellus: 19, enlisted 8/07/61, single, farmer. Died typhoid 10/23/61. NOK: James Parish, father. Hometown: Daleville, AL.

Pate, Jerimiah: 30, enlisted 3/03/62, married, farmer. Died typhoid 4/07/62. NOK: Harriet Pate, wife. Hometown: High Bluff, AL.

Pate, Thomas: 28, enlisted 3/03/62, single, merchant. Hometown: High Bluff, AL.

Patterson, Alan D.: 28, enlisted 8/02/61, single, merchant. Promoted 2LT 11/16/61. Died 2/28/62. Hometown: Barnes Cross Roads, AL.

Patterson, John W.: 16, enlisted 3/03/62, single, farmer. Died typhoid. 6/12/62. NOK: James J. Patterson, father. Hometown: Barnes Cross Roads, AL.

Patterson, Robert E.: 21, enlisted 8/14/61, single, farmer. Promoted 2CPL and 1CPL 8/12/63. Killed Spotsylvania 5/09/64. NOK: James J. Patterson, father. Hometown: Barnes Cross Roads, AL.

Peek, Anderson: 20, enlisted 8/15/62, single, farmer. Served to Lee's surrender.

Peek, John: 18, enlisted 8/15/62, single, farmer. Died at home 4/16/63. Hometown: Elba, AL.

Peters, Bedred: 18, enlisted 3/03/62, single, farmer. Discharged "youth and want of development" 11/10/62. 4'10", dark complexion, gray eyes, dark hair. Hometown: High Bluff, AL.

Peters, James: 23, enlisted 3/03/62, single, farmer. Died 1/08/63. Hometown: High Bluff, AL.

Peters, James R.: 45, enlisted 3/04/62, married, farmer. Died measles 6/14/62. NOK: Rachel Ann Peters, wife. Hometown: High Bluff, AL.

Peters, John C.: 27, enlisted 3/03/62, married, farmer. Died pneumonia 5/21/62. NOK: Mistie Peters, wife. Hometown: High Bluff, AL.

Peters, Silas B.: 21, enlisted 3/03/62, single, farmer. Severely wounded arm Wilderness 5/06/64. Hometown: High Bluff, AL.

Pouncey, Abel John: 21, enlisted 3/03/62, single, farmer. Died typhoid 9/19/61. 6'0", fair complexion, blue eyes, light hair. NOK: Jesse Pouncey, father. Hometown: Daleville, AL.

Pouncey, R.L.: Died chronic diarrhea 11/08/61. Hometown: in AL.

Pouncey, Samuel R.: 18, enlisted 7/03/61, single, farmer. Died 11/08/61. NOK: Jesse Pouncey, father. Hometown: Daleville, AL.

Pouncey, William T.: Enlisted 7/03/61. Captured Gettysburg 7/02/63, sent to Ft. Delaware, DE. Took oath and released 6/14/65. Sallow complexion, gray eyes, light hair. Hometown: Daleville, AL.

Powell, Abraham "Abram": 21, enlisted 3/03/62, married, farmer. Wounded Sharpsburg 9/17/62. Served to Lee's surrender. 12/10/64 awarded Southern Cross of Honor. 5'8", fair complexion, blue eyes, light hair. Hometown: High Bluff, AL.

Powell, James J.: 18, enlisted 3/04/62, single, farmer. NOK: John Powell, father. Hometown: High Bluff, AL.

Powell, John H.: Died 5/24/62.

Preston, Samuel J.: 18, enlisted 7/03/61, single, farmer. Detached engineer. Severely wounded Chickamauga 9/19/63. Deserted and captured 2/20/65. Hometown: Haw Ridge, AL.

Price, John W.: 18, enlisted 7/03/61, single, farmer. Severely wounded 10/17/63 Raccoon Mountain and slightly wounded leg 8/16/64 Fussell's Mill. Hometown: Daleville, AL.

Roundtree, Arthur R.: 28, enlisted 4/09/62, married, teacher. Captured Gettysburg 7/02/63, sent to Ft. Delaware, DE. Took oath and released 6/14/65. 5'10", sallow complexion, blue eyes, dark hair. Hometown: Newton, AL.

Saunders, Frank J.: 28, enlisted 7/03/61, single, artist. Wounded finger Fredericksburg 12/19/62. Hometown: Westville, AL.

Saunders, George Wilson: 20, enlisted 7/03/61, single, farmer. Promoted 2CPL 6/01/64, and 1CPL 8/01/64. 5'2", fair complexion, blue eyes, dark hair. Hometown: Daleville, AL.

Saunders, Julius J.: 23, enlisted 7/03/61, single, farmer. Discharged "ankylosis of knee." 6'1", light complexion, blue eyes, dark hair. Hometown: Westville, AL.

Saunders, Thomas M.: 22, enlisted 8/07/61, married, farmer. Killed Sharpsburg 9/17/62. NOK: Susan Saunders, wife. Hometown: Daleville, AL.

Scogin, Green B.: 18, enlisted 7/03/61, single, farmer. Severely wounded Cold Harbor 6/27/62. Hometown: Daleville, AL.

Scogin, J.M.: 56, enlisted 7/03/61, married, farmer. Discharged "infirmity from age." 6'0", dark complexion, dark eyes, dark hair. Hometown: Daleville, AL.

Scogin, William H.: 21, enlisted 7/03/61, single, carpenter. Elected 4SGT, promoted 1SGT 4/23/62, 3LT 7/02/62, and 2LT 10/??/62. Captured Falling Waters 7/14/63, sent to Point Lookout, MD, died 9/11/63. Hometown: Daleville, AL.

Sellers, William N.: 20, enlisted 3/03/62, married, farmer. Wounded Manassas 8/30/62. Killed Sharpsburg 9/17/62. NOK: Eliza J. Sellers. Hometown: High Bluff, AL.

Simmons, James H.: 5'7", fair complexion, blue eyes, light hair. Paroled Montgomery 6/24/65.

Skinner, John L.: 23, enlisted 3/03/62, single, farmer. Wounded Cold Harbor 6/27/62. Discharged deafness 5/01/63. Hometown: Newton, AL.

Smith, Columbus B.: Killed Gettysburg 7/02/63.

Smith, Jordan T. Died "disease of heart" 3/06/63/ NOK: Mary Smith, wife. Hometown: Newton, AL.

Snell, David: 25, enlisted 4/09/62, married, farmer. Killed Lookout Valley 10/29/63. NOK: C.L. Snell, wife.

Stephens, Wiley J.: Enlisted 3/03/62, single. Killed Cold Harbor 6/27/62. NOK: Wiley Stephens, father. Hometown: Geneva, AL.

Thomas, William H.: 20, enlisted 7/03/61, single, farmer. Died typhoid 10/23/61. NOK: Philip Thomas, father. Hometown: Daleville, AL.

Tomlin, John L.: 25, enlisted 8/10/61, married, farmer. Died measles 9/26/61. NOK: Nancy R. Tomlin, wife. Hometown: Daleville, AL.

Tommie, Augustus B.: 40, enlisted 11/05/64, married, mechanic. Served to Lee's surrender. Hometown: Bryerville, AL.

Trawick, William R.: 40, enlisted 11/05/64, married, mechanic. Served to Lee's surrender. Hometown: in AL.

Vance, Warren W.: 26, enlisted 8/15/62, married, farmer. Severely wounded Fredericksburg 12/13/62. Deserted and captured 2/20/65. Hometown: in AL.

Vance, Wayne: 23, enlisted 7/03/61, single, farmer. Died measles 10/13/61. NOK: Sarah Vance, mother. Hometown: Westville, AL.

Wade, Samuel: 24, enlisted 8/15/62, single, farmer. Mortally wounded leg Fussell's Mill, died 8/25/64. Hometown: High Bluff, AL.

Walding, Benjamin V. 23, enlisted 3/03/62, single, farmer. Severely wounded Sharpsburg 9/17/62. Transferred to Co. I, 57th AL, promoted 1LT. Hometown: Newton, AL.

Walding, James J.: 20, enlisted 7/03/61, married, farmer. Died typhoid 4/09/63. 5'8", dark complexion, dark eyes, dark hair. NOK: Sarah Walding, wife. Hometown: Newton, AL.

Welch, James Martin: 18, enlisted 7/03/61, single, farmer. Captured Gettysburg 7/02/61, sent to Ft. Delaware, DE. Joined U.S. 3rd Maryland Cavalry. Hometown: Westville, AL.

West, Joseph J.: 20, enlisted 10/04/61, married, farmer. Died typhoid/pneumonia 11/01/61. NOK: Cornelia West, wife. Hometown: Westville, AL.

Williams, James Matthews: enlisted 7/03/61, single, farmer. Promoted 3SGT 8/01/64. Wounded Sharpsburg 9/17/62, severely wounded Fredericksburg 12/19/62, and severely wounded shoulder 8/14/64 Deep Bottom. Served to Lee's surrender. Hometown: Ariton, AL.

Windham, Harmon H.: 22, enlisted 3/28/61, single, farmer. Severely wounded Sharpsburg 9/17/62. Discharged 4/13/63. 5'10", fair complexion, gray eyes, dark hair. Hometown: Barnes Cross Roads, AL.

Windham, James K.: 29, enlisted 3/03/63, single, farmer. Discharged "Anasarca" (accumulation of fluid) 3/05/63. 5'8", dark complexion, dark eyes, black hair. Hometown: Newton, AL.

Windham, William H.: 26, enlisted 3/03/63, married, farmer. Deserted and captured 2/15/64 Bristol, TN. 5'7", fair complexion, dark eyes, dark hair. Hometown: Newton, AL.

Woodham, Steven M.: 28, enlisted 3/03/63, married, farmer. Severely wounded left foot Sharpsburg 9/17/62. Captured 5/22/64, sent to Point Lookout, MD, exchanged 9/18/64. Hometown: Newton, AL.

Yelverton, John B.: 28, enlisted 3/03/63, single, mechanic. Severely wounded thigh (shell fragment) Fussell's Mill 8/16/64. Captured, sent to Point Lookout, MD. Took oath and released 6/26/65. 5'6", florid complexion, blue eyes, black hair. Hometown: Newton, AL.

Company F

Adams, Andrew Q.: 20, enlisted 3/04/62, single, farmer. Died measles 5/06/62. Hometown: Brundidge, AL.

Adams, John W. 22, enlisted 3/04/62, farmer. Discharged 3/12/64. Hometown: in AL.

Adkins, J. Calvin: 28, enlisted 3/01/62, married, farmer. Died 7/26/62. NOK: Mary Ann Adkins, wife. Hometown: in AL.

Agerton, A.N.: Enlisted 8/19/62, single. Served to Lee's surrender. Hometown: in AL.

Amos, William D.: 21, enlisted 3/01/62, single, farmer. Discharged chronic bronchitis 2/11/64. Dark complexion, black eyes, black hair. Hometown: Troy, AL.

Anderson, Bartley C.: 21, enlisted 7/03/61, single, farmer. Killed Manassas 8/30/62. NOK: J.W. Anderson. Hometown: Brundidge, AL.

Andrews, Stephen E.: 22, enlisted 7/03/61, single, dentist. Mortally wounded, died 7/18/62. Hometown: in AL.

Baker, Nicholas: 36, enlisted 3/01/62, married, farmer. Transferred to Company L 3/??/63. Hometown: in AL.

Baker, George W.: 33, enlisted 3/01/62, married, farmer. Severely wounded Cross Keys 6/08/62. Discharged wounds 8/15/63. Hometown: in AL.

Barefoot, David: 29, enlisted 3/01/62, married, farmer. Died 6/03/62. NOK: David Barefoot, father. Hometown: in AL.

Baxley, Redin: 30, enlisted 3/01/62, married, farmer. Wounded Manassas 8/26/62 and left arm and lung Lookout Valley 10/28/63. Discharged loss use of arm, collapsed lung 9/20/64. 5'8", light complexion, gray eyes, black hair. Hometown: in AL.

Beasley, William R.: 22, enlisted 8/19/62, married, farmer. Killed Spotsylvania 5/12/64. Hometown: in AL.

Bell, Daniel: Enlisted 7/03/61, farmer. 4'0", light complexion, black eyes, light hair. Hometown: in AL.

Bowman, D.W.: 35, enlisted 3/01/62, married, farmer. Died pneumonia 5/30/62. NOK: Lucinda Bowman, wife. Hometown: in AL.

Bray, Green C.: 18, enlisted 8/03/63, single, farmer. Wounded Chickamauga 9/20/63 and Campbell's Station, TN. 11/15/63. Discharged. Hometown: in AL.

Bray, John N.: 20, enlisted 7/03/61, single, farmer. Promoted 2CPL 12/29/62, 5SGT 12/??/63, and 3SGT 12/20/63. Wounded Cold Harbor 6/27/62, Manassas 8/30/62, and slightly wounded neck Wilderness 5/06/64. Served to Lee's surrender. Hometown: in AL.

Brazil, George, W.: 27, enlisted 7/03/61, single, carpenter. Promoted 1CPL 8/09/62 and 4SGT 10/01/64. Wounded Cross Keys 6/08/62, Sharpsburg 9/17/62, and slightly wounded thigh Spotsylvania 5/08/64. Served to Lee's surrender. Hometown: in AL.

Bridges, James W.: Enlisted 8/19/62, single, farmer. Died typhoid 12/09/62. NOK: James M. Bridges, father. Hometown: in AL.

Brown, Daniel C.: Enlisted 3/01/62, married, farmer. Discharged 5/22/62. Hometown: Brundidge, AL.

Browning, Sampson: 26, enlisted 7/03/61, married, farmer. Discharged 5/22/62. Hometown: Brundidge, AL.

Bussey, James: 18, enlisted 12/19/61, single, farmer. Died 10/15/62. Hometown: Troy, AL.

Bussey, Zacharia: 47, enlisted 3/01/62, married, farmer. Wounded Cold Harbor 6/08/62. Discharged 10/27/62. Hometown: Troy, AL.

Calhoun, J.M.: 34, enlisted 7/03/61, married, mechanic. Died pneumonia 2/20/62. Hometown: Brundidge, AL.

Carlisle, Green F.: 22, enlisted 7/03/61, single, clerk. Killed Cold Harbor 6/27/62. Hometown: in AL.

Carter, William Wilburn: 18, enlisted 3/01/62, single, farmer. Mortally wounded right foot Fredericksburg 12/19/62, died 12/29/62.

NOK: Seaborn Carter, father. Hometown: in AL.

Chancellor, William Jackson: 30, enlisted 7/03/61, single. Died pneumonia 5/14/62. NOK: Rebecca Chancellor, mother. Hometown: in AL.

Childs, Green L.: 30, enlisted 7/03/61, married, mechanic. Slightly wounded Cross Keys 6/08/62. Killed Cold Harbor 6/27/62. Hometown: in AL.

Cody, Robert C.: 19, enlisted 7/03/61, farmer. Discharged paralysis 4/12/62. 5'5", dark complexion, blue eyes, dark hair. Hometown: in AL.

Collier, Thomas A.: 30, enlisted 7/03/61, single, merchant. Captured Sharpsburg 9/19/62. Wounded and captured Wilderness while serving as litter bearer 5/06/64, sent to Elmira, NY. Took oath and released 6/14/65. 5'9½", florid complexion, hazel eyes, gray hair. Hometown: in AL.

Cox, Eli: 30, enlisted 7/03/61, single, farmer. Wounded and captured Lookout Valley 10/28/63, sent to Rock Island, IL. Took oath and released 6/17/65. 6'½", florid complexion, hazel eyes, gray hair. Hometown: in AL.

Crane, William: 25, enlisted 3/01/62, married, farmer. Wounded Cold Harbor 6/27/62, Battle Mountain 7/24/63, and Chickamauga 9/19/63. AWOL much of '64. Hometown: in AL.

Crenshaw, James M.: 20, enlisted 7/03/61, single, farmer. Died typhoid/pneumonia 11/12/63. NOK: Rebecca Crenshaw, mother. Hometown: in AL.

Crenshaw, Joseph "Joe": Wounded Sharpsburg 9/17/62 and Knoxville right shoulder 11/??/63. Discharged to Invalid Corps 9/10/64. Hometown: in AL.

Crocker, Bethel D.: 18, enlisted 3/01/62, married, farmer. Died fever 7/02/62. Hometown: in AL.

Crocker, John W.: Enlisted 3/03/62, married, farmer. Died 5/15/62. NOK: Francis Crocker, wife. Hometown: Troy, AL.

Daughtry, James: 21, enlisted 3/03/62, single, farmer. Discharged 6/13/62. Hometown: in AL.

David, Logan: 21, enlisted 7/03/61, single, farmer. Died 4/05/62. Hometown: in AL.

Davis, Miles H.: 21, enlisted 7/03/61, single, farmer. Died typhoid 11/21/61. NOK: Rebecca Crenshaw, mother. Hometown: in AL.

Dixon, Shadrack F.: 24, enlisted 7/03/61. Deserted 9/26/61. Hometown: in AL.

Downing, Acy M.: 34, enlisted 7/03/61, married, farmer. Wounded hand (amputated) Cold Harbor 6/27/62. Discharged 10/03/62.

5'9", dark complexion, blue eyes, black hair. Hometown: in AL.

Downing, William: 30, enlisted 7/03/61, married, farmer. Died typhoid 11/09/61. NOK: Lurency Downing, wife. Hometown: in AL.

Driggers, Christopher Columbus: 23, enlisted 3/01/62, single, farmer. Died 7/04/62. Hometown: in AL.

Edwards, William A.: 25, enlisted 8/19/62, single, farmer. Died acute diarrhea 4/03/63. Hometown: in AL.

Elliott, Isaiah: 21, enlisted 7/03/61, single, farmer. Promoted 2CPL 6/01/64 and 5SGT 10/01/64. Wounded Cold Harbor 6/27/62. Hometown: in AL.

Etheridge, William T.: 18, enlisted 9/01/62, single, farmer. Died pneumonia 3/28/63. NOK: Harris Etheridge, father. Hometown: Newton, AL.

Faircloth, William R.: enlisted 7/03/61, single, farmer. Died typhoid 12/07/61. Hometown: in AL.

Farmer, Agerton, Sr.: 44, enlisted 11/01/63, married, farmer. Hometown: in AL.

Farmer, Agerton, Jr.: 17, enlisted 11/01/63, single, farmer. Killed Knoxville 11/25/63. Hometown: in AL.

Farmer, David: 18, enlisted 3/01/62, single, farmer. Wounded Cold Harbor 6/27/62. Killed Knoxville 11/25/63. Hometown: in AL.

Ferror, James J.: 17, enlisted 3/25/64, single, farmer. Slightly wounded foot Spotsylvania 5/10/64. Hometown: in AL.

Flowers, Isham L.: 18, enlisted 7/03/61. Died pneumonia 11/26/61. Hometown: Brundidge, AL.

Flowers, William H.: 25, enlisted 3/01/62, married, farmer. Deserted and captured Knoxville 12/05/64, sent to Camp Chase, OH. Hometown: in AL.

Folks, Francis A.: 18, enlisted 7/03/61, single, farmer. Died typhoid 12/13/61. NOK: Rebecca Black, mother. Hometown: in AL.

Frazier, David: 26, enlisted 3/01/62, married, farmer. Transferred to Company L 3/01/63. Hometown: in AL.

Fuquay, Stanton: 18, enlisted 11/01/63, single, farmer. Hometown: in AL.

Galloway, Benjamin H.: 18, enlisted 7/03/61, single, farmer. Detailed as teamster. Served to Lee's surrender. Hometown: in AL.

Galloway, James I.: 24, enlisted 7/03/61, married, farmer. Killed Sharpsburg 9/17/62. NOK Mary A. Galloway, wife. Hometown: Troy, AL.

Garner, Joseph: 30, enlisted 8/07/61, married, farmer. Mortally wounded Chickamauga 10/19/63, died 10/20/63. Hometown: in AL.

Gibson, John Wilson: 16, enlisted 7/03/61, single, student. Wounded Knoxville 11/25/63. Promoted 3CPL 10/01/64. Served to Lee's surrender. Hometown: in AL.

Glenn, G.D.: 21, enlisted 7/03/61, single, farmer. Killed Manassas 8/30/62. Hometown: in AL.

Glenn, Hershall V.: 16, enlisted 3/04/62, single, farmer. Captured Sharpsburg 9/17/62, sent to Ft. Delaware, exchanged. 12/10/64 awarded Southern Cross of Honor. Served to Lee's surrender. Hometown: Brundidge, AL.

Glenn, Walter S.: 25, enlisted 3/01/62, married, farmer. Killed Cold Harbor 6/27/62. NOK: Lucretia A. Glenn, wife. Hometown: in AL.

Graham, Owens Walker: Captured 12/16/64, sent to Camp Douglas, IL.

Graves, Andrew J.: 19, enlisted 7/03/61, single, farmer. Died 4/15/62. NOK: Eli P. Graves, father. Hometown: in AL.

Greenway, J. Wilson: 20, enlisted 7/03/61, single, student. Severely wounded Lookout Valley 10/28/63. Transferred to Company E, 59th Alabama 9/25/64. Hometown: in AL.

Gregors, Columbus: Died typhoid 7/03/62.

Grice, George W.: 23, enlisted 7/03/61, single, farmer. Severely wounded Manassas 8/28/62 and Chickamauga 9/20/63. Discharged 7/02/64 to the Invalid Corps with duty at Columbus, GA. Hometown: in AL.

Grice, James E.: 18, enlisted 7/03/61, single, farmer. Killed Cedar Run by artillery 8/09/62. NOK: Samuel Grice, father. Hometown: in AL.

Harden, John R.: 21, enlisted 7/03/61, single, farmer. Died pneumonia 1/09/62. Hometown: in AL.

Harden, Willis R.: 25, enlisted 7/03/61, single, mechanic. Killed Cold Harbor 6/27/62. Hometown in AL.

Hearn, James S.: 47, enlisted 7/03/61, single, farmer. Discharged physical disability, nephritis 12/04/61. Hometown: in AL.

Hewitt, John A.: Paroled Montgomery, AL. 5'7", dark complexion, dark eyes, black hair. Hometown: in AL.

Hicks, Georgia N.: 25, enlisted 7/03/61, single, farmer. Discharged tuberculosis 1/09/63. 5'11", dark complexion, blue eyes, dark hair. Hometown: in AL.

Hill, William: 28, enlisted 3/01/62, single, farmer. Died 5/24/62. Hometown: in AL.

Hilliard, W.: 28, enlisted 7/03/61, single, farmer. Discharged chronic rheumatism 4/07/63. 6'0", dark complexion, blue eyes, dark hair. Hometown: in AL.

Hollaway, Thomas H.: 34, enlisted 8/19/62, married, farmer. Wounded Chickamauga 9/19/63. Served to Lee's surrender. NOK: Elizabeth Hollaway, wife. Hometown: in AL.

Holmes, William: 22, enlisted 3/01/62, single, farmer. Died measles 5/06/62. Hometown: in AL.

Hough, John B.: 20, enlisted 8/19/62, single, farmer. Served to Lee's surrender. NOK: M.J. Hough, wife. Hometown: in AL.

Hough, Peter James: 21, enlisted 3/04/62, single, farmer. Wounded Cold Harbor 6/27/62 and slightly wounded leg Fussell's Mill 8/16/64. Hometown: Union Springs, AL.

Hough, William D.: 24, enlisted 7/03/61, single, mechanic. Elected 3SGT and promoted 2SGT. Killed Manassas 8/28/62. Hometown: in AL.

Howell, Samuel: 46, enlisted 9/24/61, married, mechanic. Discharged 7/22/64 to Invalid Corps, assigned as shoemaker with duty in Columbus, GA. Hometown: in AL.

Hughes, W.W.: 18, enlisted 7/03/61, single, farmer. Discharged hernia 8/20/61. Hometown: in AL.

Hussey, Jefferson "Jeff" E.: 22, enlisted 3/19/62, married, farmer. Wounded Chickamauga 9/20/63. Deserted 10/??/64. Paroled Montgomery, AL, 5/12/65. 5'10", dark complexion, hazel eyes, dark hair. Hometown: Victoria, AL.

Hutchinson, Edward A.: 22, enlisted 7/03/61, single, farmer. Wounded Cold Harbor 6/27/62, Manassas 8/28/62, and severely wounded Lookout Valley 10/28/63. Hometown: in AL.

Hutchinson, J.: 20, enlisted 7/03/61, single, farmer. Wounded 9/13/62 Harpers Ferry. Captured Gettysburg 7/02/63. Hometown: in AL.

Hutchinson, James B.: 20, enlisted 7/03/61, married, farmer. Wounded Sharpsburg 9/17/62. Captured Gettysburg 7/02/63, sent to Ft. Delaware, DE. Took oath and released 6/14/65. 6'0", fair complexion, gray eyes, dark hair. Hometown: in AL.

Jackson, A.N.: 22, enlisted 3/01/62, married, farmer. Killed Manassas 8/28/62. NOK: Eliza F. Jackson, wife. Hometown: in AL.

Jackson, Archibald: Enlisted 7/03/61, married, farmer. Wounded Knoxville 11/25/63. 12/10/64 awarded Southern Cross of Honor. Killed 12/1/64. Hometown: in AL.

Jackson, John: 39, enlisted 3/04/62, married, farmer. Detailed as a shoemaker. Slightly wounded thigh 10/10/64. Awarded Southern Cross of Honor 12/10/64. Hometown: in AL.

Jackson, Levi: 23, enlisted 7/03/61, single, farmer. Died measles 9/26/61. NOK: James R. Jackson, father. Hometown: in AL.

Johnston, John D.: 23, enlisted 7/03/61, single. Died diarrhea 5/16/62. NOK: Thomas Johnston, father. Hometown: in AL.

Ketcham, Bartley W.: 36, enlisted 1/01/63, married, farmer. Severely wounded leg Spotsylvania 5/08/64. Hometown: in AL.

Ketcham, James K.: 17, enlisted 5/13/64, farmer. AWOL. Hometown: in AL.

Ketcham, William Washington: 18, enlisted 8/19/62, single, farmer. Severely wounded head 2nd Cold Harbor 6/05/64. Hometown: in AL.

Kidd, Leander: 34, enlisted 8/19/62, married, farmer. Died 11/15/62 NOK: Mary Ann Kidd, wife. Hometown: Barnes Cross Roads, AL.

King, Rufus: 44, enlisted 7/03/61, single, mechanic. Captured Wilderness 5/06/64, sent to Elmira, NY. Died pneumonia 2/01/65. Hometown: in AL.

Knowles, L. Scott: 25, enlisted 3/27/62, married, farmer. Captured Cross Keys, paroled Winchester. Promoted 2SGT and 1SGT 12/01/63. Captured Richmond 4/03/65. 5'9", dark complexion, dark eyes, dark hair. Hometown: in AL.

Knowles, S.P.: Enlisted 7/18/61. Discharged "diseased arm" 10/18/61. Hometown: in AL.

Lacroy, G.B. 33, enlisted 3/01/62, married, farmer. Captured Gettysburg, sent to Ft. Delaware, DE, died pneumonia 8/15/63. Hometown: in AL.

Lane, Wyatt: 30, enlisted 7/03/61, farmer. Discharged 4/23/62 disability. 5'8", dark complexion, black eyes, black hair. Hometown: in AL.

Langford, James A.: 30, enlisted 8/19/62, single, farmer. Promoted 2CPL 12/20/63. Wounded Chickamauga 9/19–20/63. Captured Wilderness 5/06/64, sent to Elmira, NY, died measles 2/06/65. Hometown: in AL.

Langford, James W.: 36, enlisted 8/19/62, farmer. Severely wounded right forearm Wilderness. Discharged "lost use of right hand." 5'10", dark complexion, brown eyes, black hair. Hometown: in AL.

Langford, William A.J.: Married. Died 10/12/62. NOK: Martha W. Langford, wife. Hometown: in AL.

LaPeter, H.M. Died typhoid 11/07/61.

Lassiter, Henry M. 24, enlisted 7/03/61, single, farmer. Died 11/09/61. Hometown: in AL.

Lassiter, James L.: 22, enlisted 3/01/62, married, farmer. Died fever 5/15/62. NOK: Louisa Lassiter, wife. Hometown: in AL.

Lewis, Ben H.: 34, enlisted 7/03/61, married, mechanic. Resigned "protracted sickness" 2/02/62. Hometown: Brundidge, AL.

Lewis, James E.: 18, enlisted 3/04/62, single, farmer. Wounded foot Hazel River 8/22/62. Hometown: in AL.

Lewis, William: 22, enlisted 3/04/62, single, farmer. Died pneumonia 5/12/62. NOK: Sarah E. Lewis, wife. Hometown: in AL.

Lindsey, Joseph P.: 24, enlisted 3/01/62, single, farmer. Died pneumonia 7/07/62. NOK: Dennis Lindsey, father. Hometown: in AL.

Lindsey, Thomas J.: 17, enlisted 7/03/61, single, farmer. Discharged "too young" 5/10/62. Hometown: in AL.

Lindsey, William: 18, enlisted 7/03/61, single, farmer. Severely wounded Cold Harbor 6/27/62. Killed Gettysburg 7/02/63. Hometown: in AL.

Logan, David S.: Enlisted 7/03/61. Died anasarca 3/27/62. Hometown: in AL.

Logan, Frank M.: 24, enlisted 8/08/62, single, farmer. Served to Lee's surrender. Hometown: in AL.

McDowell, Alexander "Alex": 23, enlisted 7/03/61, single, farmer. Discharged 5/21/62. 5'10", light complexion, blue eyes, light hair. Hometown: in AL.

McDowell, John S.: 19, enlisted 7/03/61, single, farmer. Discharged 3/15/62. Hometown: in AL.

McDowell, William D.: 24, enlisted 7/03/61, married, farmer. Mortally wounded and captured Sharpsburg 9/17/62, died 10/06/62. NOK: Elizabeth J. McDowell, wife. Hometown: in AL.

Malone, George Y.: 35, enlisted 7/03/61, married, merchant. Elected 1LT. Promoted CPT 2/02/62. Wounded Cold Harbor 6/27/62. Resigned 3/18/63. Hometown: Brundidge, AL.

Meredith, Matthew E.: 28, enlisted 3/01/62. Detailed as nurse. Wounded right hand (lost 3 fingers) Cross Keys 6/08/62, left side Gettysburg 7/02/63, and left hip Chester Station 6/16/64. Hometown: in AL.

Metts, Frank M.: 26, enlisted 8/19/62, married, saddler. Captured Gettysburg 7/02/63. Hometown: Barnes Cross Roads, AL.

Miles, Dennis W.: 27, enlisted 7/03/61, single, mechanic. Wounded forearm Gettysburg. Killed Knoxville 11/25/63. Hometown: Brundidge, AL.

Minshew, C.O.: 32, enlisted 7/03/61, married, farmer. Wounded Cold Harbor 6/27/62 and Battle Mountain groin 7/17/63. Discharged 3/21/64. Hometown: White Water, AL.

Minshew, Daniel L.: Enlisted 7/03/61, married, farmer. Died typhoid 11/06/61. NOK: Joseph S. Minshew, father. Hometown: in AL.

Minshew, Philip L.: 22, enlisted 7/03/61, single, teacher. Wounded Lookout Valley 10/28/63.

Served to Lee's surrender. Hometown: Far-
land, AL.

Mobley, Anderson: 22, enlisted 3/01/62, married, farmer. Wounded and captured Lookout Valley 10/27/63, sent to Rock Island Barracks, IL. Paroled Montgomery 6/05/65. 6'0",
dark complexion, black eyes, dark hair.
Hometown: White Water, AL.

Mobley, Simon G.: 32, enlisted 7/03/61, mar-
ried, farmer. Wounded left leg (amputated)
Chickamauga. Discharged 9/29/64 Invalid
Corps. Hometown: White Water, AL.

Moore, James Pitts: 19, enlisted 7/03/61, single,
student. Served as orderly to BG Trimble.
Captured Gettysburg, sent Ft. Delaware, DE.
Took oath and released 6/14/65. Sallow complexion, brown eyes, dark hair. Hometown:
in AL.

Myhand, Jesse W.: 35, enlisted 3/04/62, married, farmer. Severely wounded legs 2nd Cold
Harbor. Hometown: White Water, AL.

Nicholson, Pleasant W.: 24, enlisted 7/03/61,
single, merchant. Elected 1SGT, promoted
3LT 4/26/62, and 2LT 3/18/63. Wounded
Manassas 8/30/62. Captured French Broad
River, TN 1/20/64, sent to Ft. Delaware, DE.
Took oath and released 6/16/65. 5'9", dark
complexion, blue eyes, dark hair. Hometown:
in AL.

Norris, James Reece: 30, enlisted 7/03/61,
single, teacher. Captured Sharpsburg 9/18/
62, paroled 10/25/62. Promoted 3SGT 8/
01/62 and 2SGT 12/20/63. "An excellent soldier." Hometown: in AL.

Norris, Robert C.: 23, enlisted 7/03/61, single,
student. Detailed as SGT MAJ. Discharged
9/27/64, elected officer in 60th Alabama.
"One of the best soldiers in the regiment."
Hometown: in AL.

Paul, J.A.: 27, enlisted 3/01/62, married, farmer.
Wounded Manassas 8/30/62 and Chicka-
mauga 9/20/63. Served to Lee's surrender.
Hometown: White Water, AL.

Paulk, William Thomas: 17, enlisted 8/??/63.
Served to Lee's surrender. Hometown: in AL.

Peacock, Noah D.: 23, enlisted 8/19/62, married, farmer. Wounded and captured Knoxville 12/05/63, sent to Camp Chase, OH.
Hometown: Barnes Cross Roads, AL.

Perry, James T.: 24, enlisted 7/03/61, single,
farmer. Killed Cold Harbor 6/27/62. NOK:
John Perry, father. Hometown: Abbeville, AL.

Pippin, Edward T.: 28, enlisted 7/03/61, married, farmer. Died 1/10/62. NOK: Sarah A.
Perry, wife. Hometown: Perote, AL.

Powell, Abraham "Abe": 20, enlisted 8/19/62,
single, farmer. Died 12/12/62. Hometown:
Barnes Cross Roads, AL.

Prior, John T.: 20, enlisted 3/01/62, single, student. Wounded Chickamauga 9/20/63. Served
to Lee's surrender. Hometown: Brundidge,
AL.

Prior, Thomas J.: Elected 3LT, promoted 2LT
2/02/62, and 1LT 3/18/63. Slightly wounded
shoulder Spotsylvania 5/08/64. Served to
Lee's surrender. Hometown: in AL.

Ramage, J.F.: 21, enlisted 7/03/61, single, farmer.
Discharged 4/26/62 "deteriorating ulna."
5'11", light complexion, blue eyes. Hometown: Abbeville, AL.

Ray, David G.: 20, enlisted 3/01/62, single,
farmer. Wounded Fredericksburg 12/19/
62 and Chickamauga 9/19–20/63. Killed
(chest) Ft. Harrison 9/30/64. Hometown: in
AL.

Reeves, George B.: 17, enlisted 7/03/61, single,
painter. Captured Gettysburg 7/02/63, sent
to Ft. Delaware. Took oath and released. 5'3",
fair complexion, brown eyes, black hair.
Hometown: Brundidge, AL.

Reeves, William N.: 24, enlisted 7/03/61, single,
painter. Detailed ward master at hospital.
Wounded Cold Harbor 6/27/62. Promoted
2CPL 10/01/64. Served to Lee's surrender.
Hometown: in AL.

Reynolds, James M.: 25, enlisted 7/03/61, single,
farmer. Discharged necrosis (deterioration)
tibia 1/29/62. 5'9", dark complexion, dark
eyes, dark hair. Hometown: Troy, AL.

Rodgers, J.: Wounded Sharpsburg 9/17/62.

Rodgers, Stephen J.: 26, enlisted 3/01/62, married, farmer. AWOL. Slightly wounded thigh
10/30/64. Hometown: in AL.

Roundtree, Francis "Frank" Marion: 21, enlisted
7/03/61, single, farmer. Detailed as teamster.
Served to Lee's surrender. Hometown: in
AL.

Rudd, F.M.: 24, enlisted 7/03/61, married,
farmer. Killed Cold Harbor 6/27/62. NOK:
Nancy Rudd, wife. Hometown: Victoria, AL.

Rudd, James E.: 27, enlisted 7/03/61, married,
farmer. Served to Lee's surrender. Hometown: Rocky Head, AL.

Rudd, M.V.: 19, enlisted 3/01/62, single, farmer.
Slightly wounded face Wilderness 5/06/64.
Served to Lee's surrender. Hometown: Rocky
Head, AL.

Rudd, William E.: 21, enlisted 7/03/61, single,
farmer. Captured Gettysburg 7/02/63, sent
to Ft. Delaware, DE. Took oath and released
6/14/65. 5'6", sallow complexion, brown eyes,
dark hair. Hometown: Rocky Head, AL.

Seay, Thomas J.: Enlisted 7/03/61. Elected
2CPL. Captured Knoxville 11/??/63. Hometown: in AL.

Seay, William James: 24, enlisted 3/27/62, married, farmer. Wounded Manassas 8/30/62 and severely wounded leg Wilderness 5/06/64. Served to Lee's surrender. Hometown: in AL.

Sellers, Matthew S.: 30, enlisted 3/01/62, married, farmer. Died measles/pneumonia. NOK: Emily G. Sellers, wife. Hometown: Troy, AL.

Sheffield, John W.: 18, enlisted 8/19/62, single, farmer. Severely wounded and captured Knoxville 11/25/63, sent to Camp Chase, OH. Hometown: Barnes Cross Roads, AL.

Sheffield, Joseph "Joe" Franklin: 28, enlisted 8/19/62, single, farmer. 5'11", fair complexion, hazel eyes, dark hair. Hometown: Barnes Cross Roads, AL.

Sheffield, T.B.: 25, enlisted 8/19/62, married, farmer. Died 11/21/63. Hometown: Barnes Cross Roads, AL.

Smith, Andrew J.: 26, enlisted 7/03/61, married, farmer. Hired substitute 12/19/61 (James Bussey). Hometown: Brundidge, AL.

Smith, Francis M.: 32, enlisted 7/03/61, married, farmer. Served to Lee's surrender. "Never was made a better soldier." Hometown: Brundidge, AL.

Smith, Jordan D.: 21, enlisted 7/03/61, married, farmer. Died typhoid 11/08/61. NOK: Mary M. Smith, wife. Hometown: in AL.

Smith, W.J.: 20, enlisted 7/03/61, single, carpenter. Deserted 8/25/64. Hometown: Barnes Cross Roads, AL.

Sneed, S. Morton: 33, enlisted 3/01/62, married, farmer. Severely wounded Cold Harbor 6/27/62. Detached as hospital guard. Discharged 12/20/64. Hometown: Brundidge, AL.

Stafford, L.E.: 33, enlisted 3/01/62, married, merchant. Captured Falling Waters 7/20/63, sent to Ft. Delaware. Died 10/11/63. Hometown: Louisville, AL.

Stallings, Silas J.: 43, enlisted 7/03/61, married, carpenter. Discharged 6/22/62. 5'9", light complexion, blue eyes, light hair. Hometown: Brundidge, AL.

Stamford, Robert C.: Enlisted 7/03/61, married. Died pneumonia 12/12/61. NOK: Martha M. Stanford, wife. Hometown: in AL.

Stephens, Daniel J.: 29, enlisted 3/01/62, married, farmer. Wounded Manassas 8/28/62 and severely wounded Battle Mountain 7/24/63. Hometown: in AL.

Tatum, Alfie M.: Enlisted 7/03/61. Discharged physical disability 1/06/62. Hometown: Banks, AL.

Tillery, William J.: 30, enlisted 3/01/62, married, farmer. Wounded Cold Harbor 6/27/62 Detailed Pioneer Corps. Died acute dysentery 6/20/64. Hometown: Rocky Head, AL.

Tillman, S.P.: 26, enlisted 7/03/61, single, shoemaker. Died hemoptitis (coughing up blood) 7/05/64. Hometown: Brundidge, AL.

Trent, William: Enlisted 8/19/62, single, farmer. Died 10/29/62. Hometown: Rocky Head, AL.

Wadsworth, John N.: 19, enlisted 7/03/61, married, farmer. Promoted 4SGT 4/26/62, 1SGT 10/01/62, 3LT 3/25/63, and 2LT 2/02/63. Slightly wounded head Spotsylvania 5/12/64. Hometown: in AL.

Warren, J.J.B.: 23, enlisted 7/03/61, single, farmer. Died 4/26/62. NOK: George B. Warren, father. Hometown: Cambleton, FL.

Warrick, Dempsey R.: Enlisted 3/01/62, married, farmer. Died 5/15/62. NOK: Nancy Warrick, wife. Hometown: in AL.

Watson, Joseph: 17, enlisted 8/19/62, single, farmer. Discharged 8/07/63. Hometown: Rocky Head, AL.

Weaver, William H.: 20, enlisted 7/03/61, single, farmer. Died chronic diarrhea 1/29/62. Hometown: Rocky Head, AL.

Wigham, F.G.: Deserted 1/??/62. Hometown: in AL.

Williams, DeKalb: 28, enlisted 7/03/61, single, farmer. Elected 2LT. Promoted 1LT 2/07/62 and CPT 2/02/63. Wounded Sharpsburg 9/17/62 and Chickamauga 9/19–20/63. Hometown: Brundidge, AL.

Williams, Francis M.: 27, enlisted 10/01/62, married, farmer. Died typhoid 3/24/63. Hometown: Brundidge, AL.

Wilson, James D.: 21, enlisted 7/03/61, married, farmer. Discharged chronic rheumatism 12/04/61. Hometown: Brundidge, AL.

Wilson, Joseph: 17, enlisted 11/01/63, single, farmer. Severely wounded shoulder Darbytown Road 10/07/64. Hometown: Brundidge, AL.

Wilson, Reuben Anderson: 24, enlisted 7/03/61, single, farmer. Killed Cold Harbor 6/27/62. NOK: Reuben Wilson, father. Hometown: Brundidge, AL.

Wilson, S.D.: 24, enlisted 7/03/61, single, physician. Detailed hospital steward. Severely wounded wrist (accidental) Darbytown Road 10/13/64. Discharged 1/24/65 to Invalid Corps. Hometown: Troy, AL.

Wood, C.K.: 22, enlisted 12/14/61, single, loafer. Deserted 12/26/61. Hometown: Charleston, SC.

Wynick, Samuel W.: Enlisted 9/30/64. Served to Lee's surrender.

Young, Eliga: 26, enlisted 3/04/62, married, farmer. Mortally wounded Sharpsburg 9/17/62, died 11/11/62. Hometown: in AL.

Company G

Abbott, Charles M.: 17, enlisted 7/03/61, single, loafer. Discharged tuberculosis 1/26/62. 5'3", light complexion, blue eyes, dark hair. Hometown: Abbeville, AL.

Abbott, James S.A.: 24, enlisted 7/03/61, single, clerk. Wounded Malvern Hill 7/02/62. Discharged constriction of muscles in left arm 9/16/62. 5'8", dark complexion, gray eyes, dark hair. Hometown: Abbeville, AL.

Acree, Thomas H.: 30, enlisted 7/03/61, married, teacher. Served to Lee's surrender. 5'8", fair complexion, blue eyes, dark hair. Hometown: Sylvan Grove, AL.

Adkins, Oliver M.: 21, enlisted 8/15/62, married, farmer. Died typhoid/pneumonia 11/29/61. Hometown: Clopton, AL.

Alexander, William C.: 27, enlisted 7/03/61, single, farmer. Captured Gettysburg 7/02/63, sent to Ft. Delaware, DE. Died pleurisy 2/08/64. Hometown: Echo, AL.

Askew, Carter: 27, enlisted 7/03/61, married, teacher. Mortally wounded Fredericksburg 12/13/62, died 12/15/62. Hometown: Lawrenceville, AL.

Bagwell, James H.A.: 20, enlisted 8/15/62, single, farmer. Killed Gettysburg 7/02/63. Hometown: Echo, AL.

Bagwell, John N.: 21, enlisted 3/10/62, single, farmer. Died typhoid 5/21/62. NOK: R.R. Bagwell, father. Hometown: Echo, AL.

Bagwell, Larkin R.: 21, enlisted 7/03/61, single, merchant. Severely wounded leg (amputated) Chickamauga 9/19/63. Hometown: Ozark, AL.

Bagwell, William R.: 22, enlisted 3/01/62, single, farmer. Died catarrh and bronchitis 6/19/62. NOK: R.R. Bagwell, father. Hometown: Echo, AL.

Balkom, John M.: 21, enlisted 2/28/62, single, farmer. Died typhoid 5/04/62. Hometown: Goline, AL.

Balkom, Josiah: Enlisted 7/03/61, teacher. Elected 1SGT. Killed (head) Sharpsburg 9/17/62. 5'11", dark complexion, black eyes, dark hair. Hometown: Dale County, AL.

Balkom, Madson Larkin: 18, enlisted 8/15/62, single, farmer. Captured Gettysburg 7/03/63, sent to Ft. Delaware, DE. Took oath and released 6/14/65. 5'8", fair complexion, blue eyes, light hair. Hometown: Goline, AL.

Barnes, J.M.: 32, enlisted 7/03/61, single, farmer. Discharged hernia 9/12/61. Hometown: Echo, AL.

Blalock, Charles S.: 43, enlisted 7/03/61, married, farmer. Died chronic diarrhea 6/11/62. 6'1", light complexion, blue eyes, sandy hair.

NOK: Elizabeth Blalock, wife. Hometown: Newton, AL.

Bowen, William E.: 22, enlisted 7/03/61, married, carpenter. Killed Manassas 8/28/62. Hometown: Abbeville, AL.

Box, Martin Van Buren: 20, enlisted 7/03/61, single, farmer. Died heat exhaustion after Cold Harbor 6/27/62. NOK: Lemons Box, father. Hometown: Abbeville, AL.

Box, William S.: 22, enlisted 7/03/61, single, farmer. Captured 6/21/64 Elk Creek, TN, sent to Camp Douglas, IL. Died pneumonia 1/31/65. Hometown: Abbeville, AL.

Brainard, Henry C.: 21, enlisted 7/03/61, single, student. Elected 3LT, promoted 2LT 2/26/62 and CPT 4/28/63. Killed Gettysburg 7/02/63. "A fine officer—patriotic, faithful and brave as any in the regiment." Hometown: Lawrenceville, AL.

Brantley, Edward R.: 40, enlisted 3/08/62. Captured Front Royal 6/06/62, exchanged 8/06/62. Captured Lookout Valley 10/29/63, sent to Camp Morton, IN, died 2/09/65. Hometown: Clopton, AL.

Brantley, Willliam R.: 16, enlisted 2/16/64, single, farmer. Mortally wounded Chester Station 6/11/64, died 6/23/64. Hometown: Clopton, AL.

Bullard, William N.: 16, enlisted 7/03/61, single, farmer. Severely wounded Cross Keys 6/08/62. Promoted 4CPL 6/01/64. Deserted and captured 1/21/65. Took oath and transferred to Jacksonville, FL. Hometown: Abbeville, AL.

Byrd, George: 19, enlisted 7/03/61, single, farmer. Mortally wounded Cold Harbor 6/27/62, died 8/12/62. Hometown: in AL.

Byrd, Major Ed: 20, enlisted 7/03/61, single, farmer. Killed Gettysburg 7/02/63. Hometown: Franklin, AL.

Byrd, Richard L.: 19, enlisted 3/04/62, single, farmer. Died measles 6/30/62. Hometown: Franklin, AL.

Campbell, R.M.: Captured Petersburg 4/25/65.

Cannon, David Crockett: 15, enlisted 7/03/61, married, farmer. Detailed as orderly for regimental commander. Severely wounded Chickamauga 9/20/63 and Darbytown Road 10/07/64. Awarded Southern Cross of Honor 12/10/64. Deserted and captured 1/20/65. Took oath and sent to Jacksonville, FL. Hometown: Franklin, AL.

Cannon, Thomas Benton: 17, enlisted 7/03/61, single, farmer. Discharged physical disability 1/14/62. 5'5", sallow complexion, gray eyes, dark hair. Hometown: Franklin, AL.

Carr, Joseph J.: 22, enlisted 7/03/61, single, farmer. Mortally wounded Sharpsburg 9/

17/62, died 10/10/62. 5'10", light complexion, blue eyes, black hair. Hometown: Lawrenceville, AL.

Carr, William Young: 20. Served most of the war as a teamster. Served to Lee's surrender. Hometown: Lawrenceville, AL.

Cawdry, James: 23, enlisted 7/03/61, single, farmer. Died 3/04/62. Hometown: Otho, AL.

Cling, W.M.: Died 11/16/61. Hometown: in AL.

Cockcroft, Alexander: 21, enlisted 7/03/61, single, farmer. Wounded Manassas 8/29/62. Captured Chickamauga 9/20/63, sent to Camp Douglas, died pneumonia 2/24/64. Hometown: Lawrenceville, AL.

Cody, Barnett Hardeman: 17, enlisted 7/03/61, single, clerk. Elected 4CPL. Promoted 3LT 1/16/63 and 2LT 5/12/63. Mortally wounded groin and captured Gettysburg 7/02/63, died infection 7/23/63. Hometown: Franklin, AL.

Cook, Willliam M.: 16, enlisted 7/03/61, single, farmer. Died typhoid 11/06/61. Hometown: Clopton, AL.

Creech, Joshua C.: 25, enlisted 8/15/62, single. Killed Fort Harrison 9/30/64. Hometown: Sylvan Grove, AL.

Culver, Isaac F.: 19, enlisted 7/03/61, single, farmer. Elected 1LT. Resigned 2/26/62. Hometown: Lawrenceville, AL.

Deffnall, William J.: 23, enlisted 3/02/62, single, mechanic. Mortally wounded left arm Deep Bottom 8/14/64, died 9/17/64. "He was one of the most gallant soldiers—mortally wounded carrying the colors of the 15th Alabama." Hometown: in AL.

Deel, James O.: 28, enlisted 8/15/62. Wounded groin and captured Knoxville 12/05/63, died 12/12/63. Hometown: in AL.

Dickinson, Samuel: 24, enlisted 7/03/61, married, farmer. Killed Cold Harbor 6/27/62. 5'8", dark complexion, black eyes, black hair. NOK: Henrietta Dickinson, wife. Hometown: Clopton, AL.

Dozier, Augustus H.: 16, enlisted 7/03/61, single, farmer. Wounded Sharpsburg 9/17/62 and Spotsylvania 5/??/64. Served to Lee's surrender. Hometown: Abbeville, AL.

Dukes, George L.: 19, enlisted 7/03/61, single, farmer. Severely wounded Manassas 8/28/62. Captured Gettysburg 7/02/63, died Fort Delaware, DE, 9/??/64. Hometown: Abbeville, AL.

Enfinger, Cornelius: 22, enlisted 8/15/62, married, farmer. Wounded Chickamauga 9/20/63. Went home on furlough and didn't return. AWOL, then declared deserted 10/27/64. NOK: Sarah Enfinger, wife. Hometown: Echo, AL.

Enfinger, William: 17, enlisted 8/15/62, single,

farmer. Captured Gettysburg 7/02/63, sent to Ft. Delaware, DE. Took oath and released 6/14/65. 5'5", sallow complexion, hazel eyes, dark hair. Hometown: Echo, AL.

Fears, James S.: 20, enlisted 7/03/61, single, farmer. Died chronic diarrhea 11/12/61. 6'0", light complexion, blue eyes, brown hair. Hometown: Franklin, AL.

Fears, William: 30, enlisted 7/03/61, single, farmer. Severely wounded (lost eye) Cross Keys 6/08/62. Slightly wounded chest Fussell's Mill 8/16/64. Hometown: Franklin, AL.

Galloway, Francis M.: 18, enlisted 7/03/61, farmer. Discharged physical disability 1/09/62. 5'8", light complexion, blue eyes, yellow hair. Hometown: Clopton, AL.

Galloway, James W.: 19, enlisted 7/03/61, single, farmer. Deserted Cashtown, PA. 7/02/63. Hometown: Clopton, AL.

Galloway, Ransom J.: 18, enlisted 3/25/63, single, farmer. Captured Gettysburg 7/02/63, sent to Ft. Delaware, died 8/31/63 typhoid. Hometown: Abbeville, AL.

Galloway, William M.: 24, enlisted 7/03/61. Mortally wounded Lookout Valley 10/28/63, died 11/14/63. Hometown: Abbeville, AL.

Gamble, Alexander "Alex": 20, enlisted 2/28/62, single, farmer. Died at home 8/05/64. Hometown: Abbeville, AL.

Gamble, John L.: 18, enlisted 3/04/62, single, farmer. Died diarrhea 3/04/62. NOK: H.F. Gamble, father. Hometown: Clopton, AL.

Gamble, William A.: 24, enlisted 2/28/62, married, farmer. Died at home typhoid 6/02/63. Hometown: Abbeville, AL.

Gentry, John T.: Enlisted 7/03/61. Died typhoid 6/19/62. Hometown: Otho, AL.

Goodman, Henry G.: 25, enlisted 7/03/61, married, farmer. Died typhoid 1/25/62. NOK: Henry Goodman, Sr., father. Hometown: Clopton, AL.

Griffin, Alexander A.: 20, enlisted 3/01/62, married, farmer. Died 5/11/62. 5'6", dark complexion, black eyes, dark hair. Hometown: Lawrenceville, AL.

Griffin, Daniel: 22, enlisted 7/03/61, single, farmer. Discharged 2/06/62. 5'5", dark complexion, black eyes, dark hair. Hometown: Lawrenceville, AL.

Griffin, James: 27, enlisted 7/03/61, single, farmer. Mortally wounded Fredericksburg 12/19/62, died at home 3/23/63: NOK: Alsey A. Griffin, father. Hometown: Lawrenceville, AL.

Harrell, Joseph E.: 24, enlisted 7/03/61, married, farmer. Discharged acute diarrhea 5/24/62. Hometown: Lawrenceville, AL.

Harris, Charles H.F.: 18, enlisted 7/03/61, single, farmer. Wounded Darbytown Road 10/07/64. Discharged 4/13/65. Served to Lee's surrender. Hometown: in AL.

Harvey, Augustus B.: 20, enlisted 3/09/62, single, farmer. Killed Manassas 8/28/62. Hometown: Franklin, AL.

Hickman, Frederick: 20, enlisted 7/03/61, single, farmer. Died 12/28/61. NOK: Sarah Hickman, mother. Hometown: Franklin, AL.

Hickman, Jones: 18, enlisted 7/03/61, single, farmer. Mortally wounded Manassas 8/28/62, died 9/24/62. Hometown: in AL.

Hicks, Irvin: 20, enlisted 7/03/61, single, farmer. Severely wounded thigh Spotsylvania 5/08/64. Deserted and captured 10/10/64, took oath. Hometown: in AL.

Hicks, Lewis: 24, enlisted 7/03/61, single, farmer. Promoted 1CPL 1/10/62. Mortally wounded face (jaws broken) Sharpsburg 9/17/62, died 10/11/62. "There was no better soldier ... cool and calculating under fire." Hometown: in AL.

Holloway, William R.: 37, enlisted 8/15/62, married, farmer. Detailed as teamster. Killed head Gettysburg 7/02/63. NOK: Elizabeth Holloway, wife. Hometown: Westville, AL.

Holly, William R.: 42, enlisted 7/03/61, married, farmer. Transferred from Company K. "Splendid soldier, brave, with fine judgment in battle." Hometown: Lawrenceville, AL.

Holmes, Morris: 49, enlisted 7/03/61, married, farmer. Died measles 9/29/61. Hometown: Hillardsville, AL.

Holmes, Pulaski: 22, enlisted 3/01/62, single, farmer. Died 5/12/63. Hometown: Hillardsville, AL.

Holmes, William: 18, enlisted 7/03/61, single, farmer. Severely wounded Fussell's Mill 8/16/64. Hometown: Hillardsville, AL.

Huggins, Andrew J.: 25, enlisted 7/03/61, single, farmer. Wounded Manassas 8/28/62 and slightly wounded side Darbytown Road 9/30/64. Deserted and captured 1/26/65, took oath and transferred to Jacksonville, FL. Hometown: Cureton Bridge, AL.

Hughes, Seaborn "Bebe" S.: 18, enlisted 7/03/61, single, farmer. Served to Lee's surrender. "A fine soldier." Hometown: Abbeville, AL.

Hutto, Ephraim: 22, enlisted 7/03/61, single, farmer. Died 1/01/62. Hometown: Lawrenceville, AL.

Hutto, George Washington: 22, enlisted 3/02/62, married, farmer. Discharged urinary tract infection 11/11/62, died 12/07/62. 5'6", fair complexion, hazel eyes, light hair. Hometown: Lawrenceville, AL.

Jenkins, George: 20, enlisted 7/03/61, married, farmer. Wounded Hazel River 8/22/62. Captured Gettysburg 7/02/63, sent to Ft. Delaware, DE. Took oath and released 6/14/65. Fair complexion, blue eyes, dark hair. NOK: Margaret Jenkins, wife. Hometown: Millgrove, AL.

Johnson, Henry B.: 20, enlisted 7/03/61, single, farmer. Wounded Cold Harbor 6/27/62. Mortally wounded Fredericksburg 12/19/62, died 1/04/63. Hometown: in AL.

Johnson, James W.: 19, enlisted 7/03/61. Discharged 4/15/62. Hometown: Lawrenceville, AL.

Jones, Seaborn: 40, enlisted 7/03/61, married, farmer. Discharged tuberculosis 4/04/62. 5'10", dark complexion, black eyes, dark hair. Hometown: in AL.

Jordan, John C.: 24, enlisted 7/03/61, single, farmer. Severely wounded Cold Harbor 6/27/62. Killed right leg Gettysburg 7/02/63. Hometown: Abbeville, AL.

Kelley, Samuel O.: 21, enlisted 7/03/61, single, farmer. Captured Gettysburg, sent to Ft. Delaware, DE, exchanged 10/31/64. Served to Lee's surrender. Hometown: in AL.

Kincey, Charles S.: 18, enlisted 7/03/61, single, farmer. Wounded Sharpsburg 9/19/62. Paroled Montgomery, AL 5/14/65. 5'7", light complexion, blue eyes, light hair. Hometown: Abbeville, AL.

King, James: Paroled 5/1–11/65. 5'6", light complexion, hazel eyes, brown hair. Hometown: in AL.

King, William T.: 19, enlisted 7/03/61, single, farmer. Died pneumonia 1/01/62. NOK: John L. King, father. Hometown: Abbeville, AL.

Kinnon, D.C.: Slightly wounded chest 10/07/64 Darbytown Road.

Kirkland, Aaron S.: 35, enlisted 8/15/62, married, farmer. Wounded right leg and captured Gettysburg 7/04/63. Exchanged 9/??/64. Hometown: Flag Pond, AL.

Kirkland, Allen A.: Enlisted 7/03/61. Drummer. Served to Lee's surrender. Hometown: Abbeville, AL.

Kirkland, Calvin J.: 22, enlisted 7/03/61, single, farmer. Killed Manassas 8/28/62. NOK: James Kirkland, father. Hometown: Abbeville, AL.

Kirkland, Pulaski "Pugh": 16, enlisted 7/03/61, single, farmer. Slightly wounded back 10/07/64 Darbytown Road. Served to Lee's surrender. NOK: William T. Kirkland, father. Hometown: Abbeville, AL.

Lane, J.T.: 40, enlisted 7/03/61, married, farmer. Mortally wounded Chickamauga 9/20/63, died 9/22/63. NOK: Elender Lane, wife. Hometown: Abbeville, AL.

Lester, J.H.: Captured Wilderness 5/05/64, sent to Elmira, NY. Hometown: in AL.

Lingo, Elijah W. 25, enlisted 7/03/61, single, farmer. Promoted 4CPL 1/??/62, 3CPL, 2CPL, 5SGT 1/??/64, and 3SGT 4/15/64. Severely wounded right ankle Darbytown Road. Served to Lee's surrender. Hometown: Abbeville, AL.

Long, Nathaniel A.: 31, enlisted 3/08/62, married, farmer. Detailed as nurse. Discharged 5/29/63. Hometown: Echo, AL.

Lowell, John D.: Discharged 6/30/64. 6'0", fair complexion, black eyes, dark hair. Hometown: in AL.

Mabin, Moses G.: 20, enlisted 7/03/61, married, farmer. Promoted 5SGT 8/31/62. Mortally wounded Sharpsburg 9/17/62, died 9/20/62. Hometown: Abbeville, AL.

Mabin, Thomas M.: 19, enlisted 3/01/62, married, farmer. Died measles and pneumonia 5/12/62. Hometown: Abbeville, AL.

McArdle, Bernard "Barney": 34, enlisted 3/04/62, married, farmer. Captured Macon, GA, 4/20–21/65. Hometown: Abbeville, AL.

McClellan, Daniel: 33, enlisted 7/03/61, married, farmer. Elected 1CPL. Wounded Fredericksburg 12/19/62. Discharged disease of the heart to Invalid Corps, assigned to cartridge factory in Columbus, GA. Captured Macon, GA, 5/30/65. Hometown: Abbeville, AL.

McClendon, Augustus: 17, enlisted 7/03/61, single, farmer. Promoted 5SGT, 4SGT 5/12/63, 1SGT 7/12/63, 3LT 11/24/63, and 2LT 8/31/64. Served to Lee's surrender. Hometown: in AL.

McCoy, John J.: 17, enlisted 3/20/62, married, farmer. Wounded Knoxville 11/29/63, severely wounded head 2nd Cold Harbor 6/03/64, and severely wounded leg Fussell's Mill 8/16/64. Hometown: Abbeville, AL.

McKnight, Robert S.: 20, enlisted 7/03/61, single, farmer. Severely wounded head Cold Harbor 6/27/62 (minie ball flattened out on forehead). Served to Lee's surrender. Hometown: Abbeville, AL.

McKnight, William J.: 21, enlisted 7/03/61, single, farmer. Wounded left ring finger Manassas 8/28/62. Served to Lee's surrender. Hometown: Abbeville, AL.

McLeod, Christopher Columbus: 20, enlisted 7/03/61, single, farmer. Discharged 7/27/62. Hometown: Hillardsville, AL.

McLeod, Covington B.: 18, enlisted 5/09/62, single, farmer. Discharged 8/21/64. 5'10", fair complexion, blue eyes, light hair. Hometown: Hillardsville, AL.

McLeod, Henry W.: 16, enlisted 7/03/61, single, farmer. Slightly wounded heel Darbytown Road 10/07/64. Served to Lee's surrender. Hometown: Hillardsville, AL.

McLeod, John T.: 25, enlisted 7/03/61, single, farmer. Promoted 4SGT 7/12/63 and 2SGT. Killed Knoxville 11/25/63. NOK: Donald McLeod, father. Hometown: Hillardsville, AL.

McMath, Lott W.: Enlisted 7/03/61, single, farmer. Elected 2CPL. Killed Manassas 8/28/62. NOK: Hachahiah McMath, father. Hometown: Hillardsville, AL.

Medlock Robert L.: 23, enlisted 8/15/62, married, farmer. Severely wounded Chickamauga 9/20/63. Deserted 1/16/64. Hometown: Newton, AL.

Melton, Bryant: 27, enlisted 11/07/63, married, farmer. Severely wounded leg Fussell's Mill 8/16/64. Hometown: Franklin, AL.

Melvin, James M.: 18, enlisted 5/08/62, single, farmer. Wounded in foot. Served to Lee's surrender. Hometown: in AL.

Melvin, John: 22, enlisted 7/03/61, single, farmer. Detailed as a teamster. Wounded foot Cross Keys 6/08/62. Discharged Invalid Corps 7/16/64. Hometown: in AL.

Melvin, John T.: 20, enlisted 5/08/62, single, farmer. Court-martialed 2/18/63. Wounded left arm Gettysburg 7/02/63. Captured Knoxville 11/27/63, sent to Rock Island, IL. Took oath and released 6/19/65. 5'7", fresh complexion, gray eyes, fair hair. Hometown: in AL.

Merrit, David W.: 31, enlisted 3/20/63, married, farmer. Wounded. Deserted and captured 1/20/65. Took oath and sent to Savannah, GA. Hometown: Abbeville, AL.

Merrit, Francis "Frank" M.: 22, enlisted 7/03/61, single, clerk. Elected 3CPL. Discharged 11/24/61. 5'8", light complexion, blue eyes, light hair. Hometown: Abbeville, AL.

Merrit, G.: Discharged asthma 11/26/61. Hometown: Abbeville, AL.

Merrit, Stewart: Enlisted 7/03/61. Deserted 6/27/62. Hometown: Abbeville, AL.

Miller, James H.: 22, enlisted 7/03/61, single, farmer. Wounded Manassas 8/29/62 and severely wounded right thigh Darbytown Road 10/07/64. Captured Richmond hospital 4/03/65, held in Libby Prison. Took oath and released. 5'8", light complexion, blue eyes, dark hair. Hometown: Franklin, AL.

Miller, Thomas J.: 17, enlisted 7/15/63, single, farmer. Wounded Chickamauga. Mortally wounded thigh Darbytown Road 10/07/64. Hometown: in AL.

Mitchell, William B.: 18, enlisted 7/03/61, single, farmer. Died typhoid 1/03/62. NOK:

John Mitchell, father. Hometown: Hillardsville, AL.

Momon, George M.: 20, enlisted 3/04/62, married, farmer. Died pneumonia 4/29/62.
Hometown: in AL.

Moore, William G.: Enlisted 7/03/61, married,
farmer. Mortally wounded Chickamauga
9/20/63, died 9/22/63. Hometown: Abbeville, AL.

Morris, Benjamin D.: 18, enlisted 3/18/62,
single, farmer. Wounded Cold Harbor 6/27/
62. Died typhoid 11/20/62. Born in NY.
Hometown: Franklin, AL.

Morris, Cornelius V.: 44, enlisted 7/03/61, married, merchant. Promoted 2LT 2/26/62 and
CPT 1/01/63. Appointed Regimental Commissary. Resigned 1/21/63. Hometown:
Franklin, AL.

Morris, James R.: 41, enlisted 7/03/61, married,
farmer. Detailed as hospital steward. Served
to Lee's surrender. 5'6", light complexion,
brown eyes, black hair. Born in New York.
Hometown: Franklin, AL.

Murphy, Andrew: 20, enlisted 7/03/61, single,
farmer. Died battle fatigue Cold Harbor
6/27/62. Hometown: Abbeville, AL.

Murphy, William G.: 25, enlisted 7/03/61,
single, farmer. Died 4/01/62. Hometown:
Abbeville, AL.

Nobles, James M.: 20, enlisted 7/03/61, married, farmer. Died typhoid 10/13/61. 5'11",
light complexion, blue eyes, auburn hair.
NOK: Lewis Nobles, wife. Hometown: Franklin, AL.

Oates, John A.: 25, enlisted 5/11/61, single,
lawyer. Transferred from Company A, 6th
Alabama. Promoted 3LT 4/13/62, 2LT, and
1LT 4/25/63. Mortally wounded hips and
legs (7 times) Gettysburg 7/02/63, died pyre-
mia (blood poisoning) 7/25/63. Hometown:
Abbeville, AL.

Oates, William Calvin: Enlisted 7/03/61, married, lawyer. Elected CPT, promoted MAJ 4/
28/63 and LTC 12/07/64. Severely wounded
arm (amputated) Fussell's Mill 8/16/64.
NOK: Sarah Toney Oates, wife. Hometown:
Abbeville, AL.

O'Dell, James: 28, enlisted 8/18/62, married,
farmer. Killed Knoxville 11/25/63. Hometown: Sylvan Grove, AL.

Oliver, William W.: 25, enlisted 3/04/62, single,
farmer. Died 5/12/62. Hometown: Abbeville,
AL.

Ott, Henry: 35, enlisted 8/15/62, married,
farmer. Severely wounded arm (amputated)
Chickamauga 9/20/63. Hometown: Newton,
AL.

Parker, Robert: 24, enlisted 7/03/61, single,

farmer. Captured Sharpsburg 9/17/62, paroled 9/20/62. Wounded left lung and left
thigh and captured Gettysburg 7/02/63, exchanged 9/29/63. Severely wounded by
sharpshooter right arm (amputated) 2nd
Cold Harbor. Discharged Invalid Corps
12/24/64 with duty at Eufaula. Hometown:
Mill Grove, AL.

Parrish, John S.: 22, enlisted 2/22/62, married,
farmer. AWOL, deserted 1/16/64 Dandridge,
TN. Hometown: in AL.

Parrish, William J.: 19, enlisted 7/03/61, single,
farmer. Wounded Cross Keys hand (lost 2
fingers) 6/08/62 and severely wounded right
leg (broke) Moccasin Point 9/30/63. Hometown: Abbeville, AL.

Phillips, William: 21, enlisted 7/03/61, single,
farmer. Wounded hand Fredericksburg
12/19/62 and severely wounded Chickamauga 9/20/63. Hometown: in AL.

Pound, James W.: 21, enlisted 7/03/61, single,
clerk. Elected 4SGT, promoted 3SGT 5/
12/63 and 1SGT. Detailed as ambulance
driver. Wounded Sharpsburg 9/17/62 and
captured Gettysburg 7/02/63, sent to Ft.
Delaware. Took oath and released 6/14/65.
5'10", sallow complexion, brown eyes, light
hair. Hometown: Clopton, AL.

Raleigh, Charles W.: 17, enlisted 7/03/61, single,
farmer. Captured Gettysburg 7/02/63, sent
to Ft. Delaware, DE, and exchanged. Deserted 3/19/65. Hometown: Abbeville, AL.

Renfroe, Charlton L.: 19, enlisted 7/03/61, single, farmer. Wounded Manassas 8/30/62 and
severely wounded left elbow Chickamauga
9/19/63. Discharged 11/15/64 to Invalid
Corps. Paroled Montgomery, AL, 5/22/65.
5'11", light complexion, gray eyes, light hair.
Hometown: Franklin, AL.

Renfroe, Charlton L.: 21, enlisted 7/03/61, single, farmer. Detached to Ordnance, Columbus, GA (harness maker). Thrombosis in left
leg following typhoid. Hometown: Franklin,
AL.

Renfroe, Green C. 23, enlisted 5/15/61, single,
teacher. Detached as corps sharpshooter.
Promoted SGT MAJ at time of Lee's surrender. Hometown: Franklin, AL.

Riley, Daniel: 28, enlisted 8/15/62, married,
farmer. Severely wounded Gettysburg 7/02/
63. AWOL and deserted. Hometown: Echo,
AL.

Riley, Edward, Jr.: 19, enlisted 8/15/62, single,
farmer. Died 11/20/62. 6'0", light complexion,
blue eyes, light hair. NOK: Edward Riley, Sr.
Hometown: Echo, AL.

Riley, G.: Died 1/01/62 pneumonia. Hometown:
in AL.

Riley, George: 20, enlisted 8/15/62, married, farmer. Died 6/18/63 typhoid. NOK: Nancy H. Riley, wife. Hometown: Echo, AL.

Riley, Gillum: 34, enlisted 8/15/62, married, farmer. Severely wounded chest Fussell's Mill 8/16/64. Deserted. Hometown: Echo, AL.

Riley, John: 22, enlisted 8/15/62, married, farmer. Deserted and captured 1/26/65. Hometown: Echo, AL.

Riley, Samuel: 30, enlisted 8/15/62, married, farmer. NOK: Mary M. Riley, wife. Hometown: Echo, AL.

Roney, Alfred A.: 19, enlisted 3/03/62, single, farmer. Wounded left thigh and captured Gettysburg 7/05/63, exchanged immediately. Served to surrender. Hometown: Abbeville, AL.

Roney, James: 19, enlisted 3/01/62, married, farmer. Died 4/03/62. 5'10" light complexion, gray eyes, dark hair. NOK: Carolina Roney, wife. Hometown: Abbeville, AL.

Roney, James A.: 21, enlisted 7/03/61, single, farmer. Wounded head Manassas 8/28/62. Detailed as nurse. Deserted and captured 1/20/65. Hometown: Abbeville, AL.

Roney, John W.: 24, enlisted 7/03/61, single, farmer. Died 5/09/62. Hometown: Abbeville, AL.

Roney, Maurice L.: 23, enlisted 3/08/62, married, farmer. Died 5/09/62. 5'8", light complexion, black eyes, dark hair. NOK: Elender Roney, wife. Hometown: Abbeville, AL.

Sasser, Lewis M.: 22, enlisted 8/15/62, married, farmer. Deserted and captured 2/09/65. Took oath 2/12/65. 5'8", dark complexion, blue eyes, dark hair. Hometown: Columbia, AL.

Satcher, Herrin F.: 23, enlisted 7/03/61, single, farmer. Deserted. Killed 4/02/65. May have received Southern Cross of Honor 12/10/64. Hometown: Mill Grove, AL.

Sauls, John Henry: 23, enlisted 7/03/61, single, farmer. Wounded Manassas 8/28/62. Disabled and sent home, no discharge papers found. Hometown: Otho, AL.

Shepard, James N.: 32, enlisted 7/03/61, single, farmer. Severely wounded Cold Harbor 6/27/62. Mortally wounded left thigh and captured Gettysburg 7/02/63, died 8/26/63. Hometown: Curenton's Bridge, AL.

Shepard, John D.: 15, enlisted 3/20/63, single, farmer. Slightly wounded thigh Spotsylvania 5/08/64. Served to Lee's surrender. Hometown: Abbeville, AL.

Shepard, John D.: 24, enlisted 7/03/61, single, farmer. Promoted 1CPL and 4SGT 12/01/63. Slightly wounded hand Darbytown Road 10/07/64. Deserted and captured 2/09/65. 6'0", dark complexion, brown eyes, light hair. "One

of the best soldiers I ever saw." Hometown: Otho, AL.

Shepard, Tolison N.: 20, enlisted 2/28/62, married, farmer. Wounded Sharpsburg 9/17/62 and severely wounded Knoxville 11/25/63. Hometown: Louisville, AL.

Sholar, Allen W.: 20, enlisted 7/03/61, single, clerk. Detailed as nurse. Wounded Chantilly 9/01/62. 7/02/63 Gettysburg, went to fill canteens, never returned. Hometown: in AL.

Short, Richard: 30, enlisted 7/03/61, single, farmer. Captured Gettysburg 7/02/63, sent to Ft. Delaware, DE, died scurvy 11/07/63. Hometown: Otho, AL.

Smith, Aaron: 19, enlisted 3/04/62, single, farmer. Discharged pneumonia 4/20/62. 5'4", light complexion, blue eyes, sandy hair. Hometown: Abbeville, AL.

Smith, John Needham: 19, enlisted 7/03/61, single, farmer. Wounded shoulder Malvern Hill 7/02/62. Killed Chickamauga 9/20/63. Hometown: Franklin, AL.

Smith, William: 21, enlisted 7/03/61, single, farmer. Deserted 2/09/64. Hometown: Echo, AL.

Sowell, John D.: Enlisted 3/08/62, single, farmer. Served to Lee's surrender. Hometown: Newton, AL.

Steeley, John R.: 48, enlisted 7/03/61, married, man. Discharged tuberculosis 12/15/61. 5'6", light complexion, blue eyes, dark hair. Hometown: Clopton, AL.

Stone, Alexander "Alex": 16, enlisted 3/01/62, single, farmer. Paroled. Hometown: Otho, AL.

Stone, Christopher C.: 21, enlisted 7/03/61, single, farmer. Severely wounded Cold Harbor 6/27/62. Captured Gettysburg 7/02/63, sent to Ft. Delaware. Took oath and released 6/14/65. 5'6", ruddy complexion, gray eyes, brown hair. Hometown: Otho, AL.

Stone, John M.: 20, enlisted 7/03/61, single, farmer. Wounded Manassas 8/29/62. Promoted 4CPL 12/??/63. Killed Wilderness 5/06/64. Hometown: Otho, AL.

Sumner, George W.: 20, enlisted 7/03/61, single, farmer. Died 12/02/61. NOK: James Sumner, father. Hometown: in AL.

Trawick, James A.: 19, enlisted 7/03/61. Promoted 2CPL and 5SGT 5/12/63. Wounded lost eye and captured Knoxville 12/05/63, sent to Rock Island, IL. Hometown: in AL.

Trawick, Rathbone: 21, enlisted 7/03/61, single, farmer. Died 1/20/62. 5'11", light complexion, blue eyes, sandy hair. NOK: M.R. Trawick, mother. Hometown: in AL.

Trimmer, William: Enlisted 7/03/61, single, farmer. Wounded Fredericksburg 12/19/62.

Killed Gettysburg 7/02/63. Hometown: Clopton, AL.

Vickers, Young J.: 18, enlisted 3/10/62, single, farmer. Severely wounded legs Wilderness 5/06/64, "disabled through both legs." Hometown: Lawrenceville, AL.

Waddell, D.B.: 27, enlisted 7/03/61, married, clerk. Served as regimental adjutant 10/13/62. Promoted 2LT 9/19/63 and CPT 8/31/64. Hometown: Seale Station, AL.

Wadsworth, Benjamin R.: 20, enlisted 7/03/61, single, farmer. Died 12/22/62. NOK: Willis Wadsworth, father. Hometown: Abbeville, AL.

Ward, Edward J.J.: 19, enlisted 7/03/61, single, farmer. Wounded Cold Harbor 6/27/62. Mortally wounded abdomen Darbytown Road 10/07/64, died 10/08/64 Hometown: Abbeville, AL.

Watson, James Thomas: 24, enlisted 7/03/61, married, farmer. Died typhoid 11/25/61. 5'11", dark complexion, black eyes, black hair. NOK: Sarah Ann D. Watson, wife. Hometown: Lawrenceville, AL.

Watson, John S.: 29, enlisted 7/03/61, single, farmer. Died typhoid 10/25/61. Hometown: Lawrenceville, AL.

Watson, William A.: 23, enlisted 7/03/61, married, farmer. Killed Manassas 8/28/62. Hometown: Lawrenceville, AL.

Whatley, John C.: 25, enlisted 7/03/61, single, farmer. Promoted 5SGT 8/08/63 and 1SGT 11/25/63. Severely wounded Chickamauga 9/20/63 and mortally wounded Wilderness 5/06/64, died 5/09/64. Hometown: Otho, AL.

Whatley, John H.: 19, enlisted 7/03/61, single, farmer. Promoted 5SGT 12/05/63. Severely wounded Cold Harbor 6/27/62 and severely wounded thigh Fussell's Mill 8/16/64. Hometown: Otho, AL.

Whitehead, Jacob: 24, enlisted 3/01/62, married, farmer. Severely wounded right arm Sharpsburg 9/17/62. Discharged for wounds 6/15/63. Hometown: Abbeville, AL.

Wiggins, George M.: 18, enlisted 7/03/61, single, farmer. Severely wounded Manassas 8/30/62. Discharged 10/02/63. Hometown: in AL.

Wofford, Josiah J.: 44, enlisted 7/03/61, married, farmer. Discharged 7/17/64 for "overage." Hometown: Abbeville, AL.

Woodham, Edward C.: 40, enlisted 10/11/63, married, farmer. Hometown: Goline, AL.

Woodham, J.E.: 26, enlisted 7/03/61, married, farmer. Captured Gettysburg 7/02/63. Hometown: in AL.

Woodham, James R.: 19, enlisted 7/03/61, single, farmer. Severely wounded Gettysburg 7/02/63. Deserted 2/11/64. Joined U.S. Company F, 1st Florida Cavalry. Hometown: Sylvan Grove, AL.

Woodham, John: 16, enlisted 8/15/64, single, farmer. Wounded Darbytown Road 10/27/64. Deserted and captured 1/26/65. Hometown: Goline, AL.

Woodham, John A.: 26, enlisted 8/15/62, married, farmer. Captured Wilderness 5/06/64, sent to Elmira, NY. Died 6/04/65 chronic diarrhea. Hometown: Goline, AL.

Woodham, Robert N.: Enlisted 7/03/61. Discharged amputation of fingers 1/06/62. 5'6", dark complexion, gray eyes, black hair. Hometown: in AL.

Woodham, Samuel E.: 22, enlisted 7/03/61, single, farmer. Wounded Sharpsburg 9/17/62 and Fredericksburg 12/19/62. Captured Gettysburg 7/02/63, sent to Ft. Delaware, DE. Took oath and released 6/14/65. 5'5", dark complexion, blue eyes, light hair. Hometown: Newton, AL.

Woodham, Uriah: 20, enlisted 8/15/62, single, farmer. Severely wounded leg (amputated) Chickamauga 9/20/63. Hometown: Goline, AL.

Company H

Acree, Thomas H.: 30, enlisted 8/15/62, married, teacher. Served to Lee's surrender. Hometown: Echo, AL.

Addeway, William.: 24, enlisted 7/03/61, married, farmer. Died pneumonia 12/16/61. Hometown: Glenville, AL.

Andrews, Henry: 20, enlisted 2/15/62, single, farmer. Killed Knoxville 11/27/63. Hometown: Newton, AL.

Archibald, John G.: Enlisted 7/03/61, married, painter. Promoted 5CPL and 5SGT. Severely wounded Sharpsburg 8/17/62 and Wilderness 5/06/64. Appointed ensign 6/14/64. Hometown: Eutaw, AL.

Bailey, William L.: 19, enlisted 7/03/61, single, farmer. Wounded Manassas 8/30/62. Discharged 2/19/64. Hometown: Newton, AL.

Bard, A.J.: Died typhoid 1/23/62.

Barentine, James: 26, enlisted 7/03/61, married, farmer. Died 1/??/62. Hometown: Lawrenceville, AL.

Barentine, Joseph: 24, enlisted 7/03/61, single, farmer. Died 12/??/61. Hometown: Lawrenceville, AL.

Barker, Robert: 30, enlisted 7/03/61, married, mechanic. Died 1/??/62. Hometown: in AL.

Bartlett, John E.H.: 22. Discharged 8/22/61. Hometown: in AL.

Benson, James F.: 18, enlisted 7/03/61, single, farmer. Died 12/25/61. Hometown: Newton, AL.

Benton, Necy: 24, enlisted 7/03/61, single, mechanic. Killed Fredericksburg 12/19/62. Hometown: in AL.

Berry, John T.: 18, enlisted 7/03/61, single, farmer. Captured Wilderness 5/06/64, sent to Elmira, NY. Took oath and released 6/14/65. 6'½", dark complexion, blue eyes, light hair. Hometown: Kings, AL.

Blackshear, Ira: 21, enlisted 7/03/61, single, farmer. Discharged epilepsy 8/18/61. Hometown: Newton, AL.

Boothby, Frank L.: 23, enlisted 7/03/61, single, bookkeeper. Wounded severely head Chickamauga 9/20/63 and slightly wounded shoulder Spotsylvania 5/08/64. Died acute dysentery 12/15/64. Hometown: Norfolk, VA.

Brooks, Thomas J.: 22, enlisted 7/03/61, single, farmer. Severely wounded Suffolk 5/03/63 and leg Ft. Harrison 9/30/64. Served to Lee's surrender. Hometown: Elba, AL.

Brown, James: 22, enlisted 7/03/61. Wounded Williamsburg Road 10/27/64. Hometown: Glenville, AL.

Brown, John: 30, enlisted 7/03/61, single, shoemaker. Discharged 4/09/62. 5'9", fair complexion, gray eyes, dark hair. Hometown: Kings, AL.

Brown, William Samford: 27, enlisted 8/15/62, married, farmer. Mortally wounded Chickamauga 9/20/63, died 9/23/63. Hometown: Skipperville, AL.

Byrd, Ira: 24, enlisted 8/15/62, single, farmer. Died chronic diarrhea 11/16/62. NOK: Isham Byrd, father. Hometown: Sylvan Grove, AL.

Byrd, Robert L.: 26, enlisted 8/15/62, married, farmer. Died 1/23/63. NOK: Margaret Byrd, wife. Hometown: Sylvan Grove, AL.

Carmichael, Arch: 18, enlisted 7/03/61, single, farmer. Elected 3CPL. Mortally wounded Sharpsburg 9/17/62, died 11/04/62. Hometown: Newton, AL.

Carroll, John, Jr. 19, enlisted 7/03/61. Died meningitis 11/04/62. Hometown: in AL.

Carroll, William M.: 24, enlisted 7/03/61, married, farmer. Died 12/10/61. Hometown: Clopton, AL.

Carter, J.F.: Died typhoid 10/01/61. Hometown: in AL.

Carter, Thomas J.: 26, enlisted 8/10/61, married, carpenter. Died measles 9/30/62. Hometown: in AL.

Coleman, Richard: 24, enlisted 3/14/61, single, farmer. Transferred from 1st Alabama. Mor-

tally wounded Cold Harbor 6/27/62, died 7/01/62. Hometown: in AL.

Cowart, John W.: 21, enlisted 7/03/61, single, farmer. Promoted 4SGT and 2SGT. Captured Gettysburg 7/02/63, paroled 7/31/63. Slightly wounded hand Darbytown 10/07/64. Served to Lee's surrender. Hometown: Newton, AL.

Crawford, James W.: 19, enlisted 10/18/62, single, farmer. Captured Gettysburg (on water detail) 7/02/63, sent to Ft. Delaware, DE. Took oath and released 6/14/65. 5'8", sallow complexion, hazel eyes, gray hair. Hometown: Abbeville, AL.

Crews, James M.: 17, enlisted 6/29/64, single, student. Hometown: Glenville, AL.

Crews, William: 18, enlisted 7/03/61, single, student. Promoted Ordnance SGT 10/07/63. Wounded Sharpsburg 9/17/62. Served to Lee's surrender. Hometown: Glenville, AL.

Cunningham, James: 14, enlisted 9/15/63, single, farmer. Drummer. Hometown: Augusta, GA.

Curry, Martin L.: 30, enlisted 8/15/62, single, farmer. Died at home 10/20/64. Hometown: Newton, AL.

Dean, Abb: 36, enlisted 7/03/61, married, farmer. Discharged 5/??/62. Hometown: Barnes Cross Roads, AL.

Eason, Green S.: 33, enlisted 7/03/61, married, carpenter. Mortally wounded and captured Sharpsburg 9/17/62, died 10/21/62. NOK: Elizabeth Eason, mother. Hometown: Newton, AL.

Etheridge, Shadrack H.: 28, enlisted 7/03/61, married farmer. Detailed as nurse. Died typhoid 11/09/61. NOK: Lydia Ann Etheridge, wife. Hometown: Kings, AL.

Evans, G.G.: 5'4", light complexion, black eyes, dark hair. Paroled Montgomery, AL, 5/13/65. Hometown: in AL.

Gafford, William H.: 22, enlisted 7/03/61, married, carpenter. Died 11/09/61 measles. NOK: Georgia Ann Gafford, wife. Hometown: Newton, AL.

Gary, Harlem James: 33, enlisted 7/03/61, married, carpenter. Promoted 2CPL. Captured Woodstock 6/03/62, sent to Ft. Delaware, DE, exchanged 9/??/62. Transferred to 35th Georgia 3/??/63. Hometown: Clopton, AL.

Gill, George W.: 20, enlisted 7/03/61, single, farmer. Wounded Gettysburg 7/02/63 and severely wounded Ft. Harrison 9/30/64. Hometown: Glenville, AL.

Gill, T.A.: 19, enlisted 7/03/61, single, farmer. Died typhoid 12/08/61. Hometown: Glenville, AL.

Gill, William, Jr.: 24, enlisted 3/14/62, married,

shoemaker. Died 5/17/62. Hometown: Glenville, AL.

Gill, William, Sr.: 50, enlisted 7/03/61, married, shoemaker. Died measles and pneumonia 5/12/62. Hometown: Glenville, AL.

Gillenwater, William: 24, enlisted 3/23/62, married, blacksmith. Killed 2nd Cold Harbor 6/03/64. Hometown: Glenville, AL.

Gilmore, James: 21, enlisted 7/03/61, married, farmer. Died 11/30/61. Hometown: Lawrenceville, AL.

Graves, H.A.: Died apoplexy (stroke) 5/08/62 Hometown: in AL.

Gray, Thomas B.: 26, enlisted 3/14/62, single, clerk. Promoted to 1SGT. Detailed as Quartermaster SGT 4/18/64. Wounded Gettysburg 7/02/63 and Darbytown 10/07/64. Transferred to 13th Virginia 10/12/64. Hometown: in AL.

Hammack, William H.: 20, enlisted 7/03/61, single, farmer. Slightly wounded left foot Knoxville 11/25/63. Captured 12/05/63, sent to Ft. Delaware, DE. Took oath and released 6/14/65. 5'5", light complexion, blue eyes, light hair. Hometown: Kings, AL.

Henderson, William: 23, enlisted 7/03/61, single, farmer. Died cirrhosis 12/23/61. Hometown: Glenville, AL.

Hendley, J.D.L.: 20, enlisted 7/03/61, single, farmer. Captured 7/04/63, sent to Ft. Delaware, DE, and exchanged 2/25/65. Hometown: Hings Springs, AL.

Hendley, Jeff B.: 20, enlisted 7/03/61, single, farmer. Mortally wounded Cold Harbor 6/27/62, died 7/04/62. Hometown: Lawrenceville, AL.

Hendley, William R.: 19, enlisted 8/15/62, single, brick mason. Promoted CPL 5/01/63. Deserted 7/17/63, captured 7/23/63, escaped from hospital 2/23/64. Hometown: Lawrenceville, AL.

Herrin, J.T.: Died pneumonia 12/13/62. NOK: William Herrin. Hometown: in AL.

Herring, T.J.: 18, enlisted 8/15/62, single, farmer. Captured Spotsylvania 7/05/64, sent to Elmira, NY. Died chronic diarrhea 6/04/65. Hometown: Sylvan Grove, AL.

Holly, Welcome L.: 20, enlisted 7/03/61, single, farmer. Killed Chickamauga 9/20/63. Hometown: Kings, AL.

Holmes, Abner: 21, enlisted 7/03/61, single, farmer. Wounded Manassas 8/30/62. Captured Gettysburg 7/02/63, sent to Ft. Delaware, DE, & Point Lookout, MD. Died chronic diarrhea 11/08/63. Hometown: Lawrenceville, AL.

Holmes, Alvin: 23, enlisted 7/03/61, single, farmer. Wounded Fredericksburg 12/13/62.

5'5", fair complexion, gray eyes, light hair. Hometown: Lawrenceville, AL.

Holmes, Augustus: 19, enlisted 3/16/63, single, farmer. Captured Gettysburg 7/02/63, sent to Ft. Delaware, DE. Died smallpox 4/11/64. Hometown: Lawrenceville, AL.

Holsey, Mark M.: 30, enlisted 2/01/62, single, druggist. Wounded Cold Harbor 6/27/62. Detached as druggist to hospital. Hometown: Glenville, AL.

Houghton, Mitchell Bennett: 18, enlisted 7/03/61, single. printer. Severely wounded Chantilly by shell over right temple 9/01/62. Captured Lookout Valley 10/29/63, sent to Camp Morton, OH. Paroled Montgomery, AL. 5/24/65. 5'10", dark complexion, dark eyes, light hair. Hometown: Newton, AL.

Johnson, L.D.: Discharged 7/14/62. Hometown: in AL.

Jones, Alfred M.: 21, enlisted 7/03/61, single, farmer. Detailed to stay with wounded in Knoxville, captured 1/05/64, sent to Rock Island, IL. Exchanged or paroled and served to Lee's surrender. Hometown: Newton, AL.

Jones, George W.: 19, enlisted 7/03/61, single, farmer. Discharged but died 5/06/62 before receiving papers. Hometown: Newton, AL.

Jones, John J.: 30, enlisted 7/03/61, single, merchant. Severely wounded Cold Harbor 6/27/62 and severely wounded wrist 2nd Cold Harbor 6/03/64. Served to Lee's surrender. Hometown: Clopton, AL.

Josey, Ransom J.: 24, enlisted 7/03/61, single, farmer. Died pneumonia 2/27/62. NOK: John Josey, father. Hometown: Newton, AL.

Keels, John: 32, enlisted 7/03/61, married, farmer. Severely wounded Manassas 8/28/62. Mortally wounded Gettysburg 7/02/63, died 7/04/63 "bullet cut his throat, and he ran across the mountain breathing at his neck." Hometown: Kings, AL.

Lee, Cader A.: 20, enlisted 8/10/62, single, farmer. Promoted 2CPL and 1CPL. Transferred to Company E 1/01/65. Served to Lee's surrender. Hometown: Newton, AL.

Lee, Timothy C.: 18, enlisted 7/02/61, single, farmer. Discharged 12/25/62, loss of hearing by shell explosion Cold Harbor 6/27/62. 5'9", fair complexion, blue eyes, light hair. Hometown: Newton, AL.

Loflin, Thomas: 34, enlisted 7/03/61, married, farmer. Died measles 10/05/61. Hometown: in AL.

Loveless, Judge D.: 19, enlisted 7/03/61, single, farmer. Wounded Manassas 8/28/62. Captured Gettysburg, 7/03/63, sent to Ft. Delaware, DE. Took oath and released 6/14/65.

5'10", sallow complexion, blue eyes, black hair. Hometown: Kings, AL.

Lunsford, David J.: 30, enlisted 7/03/61, single, farmer. Took oath Point Lookout, MD. 7/25/65. 5'11", florid complexion, hazel eyes, dark hair. Hometown: Monroe, GA.

Lynn, Alexander "Alex": 19, enlisted 10/12/63, single, farmer. Captured (left sick) Knoxville 12/09/63. Died typhoid/pneumonia Knoxville 12/17/63. Hometown: Lawrenceville, AL.

Lynn, Marshall N.: 17, enlisted 7/19/63, single, farmer. Died 2/11/64. Hometown: Lawrenceville, AL.

Lynn, Matthew W.: 19, single, farmer. Wounded Darbytown 10/07/64. Hometown: Lawrenceville, AL.

McClaren, N.: Died typhoid 11/08/62. Hometown: in AL.

McGuire, Micheal: 19, enlisted 7/03/61, single, clerk. Promoted 4CPL. Captured Gettysburg 7/02/61, sent to Ft. Delaware, DE. Took oath and released 6/14/65. 5'7", fair complexion, blue eyes, dark hair. "A splendid soldier." Hometown: Glenville, AL.

McIntire, James A.: 23, enlisted 5/05/62, single, farmer. Wounded Cedar Mountain 8/09/62. Captured Gettysburg 7/02/63, sent to Ft. Delaware, DE. Took oath and released 6/14/65. 5'10", sallow complexion, blue eyes, dark hair. Hometown: Newton, AL.

McIntire, John Cunningham: 25, enlisted 8/10/61, single, teacher. Severely wounded Cold Harbor 6/27/62, wounded Chickamauga 9/20/63, and severely wounded forearm Fussell's Mill. Paroled Montgomery, AL, 6/12/65. 5'10", fair complexion, blue eyes, light hair. Hometown: Newton, AL.

McIntire, Thomas Jefferson: 19, enlisted 7/03/61, single, farmer. Wounded Fredericksburg 12/19/62 and wounded thumb (amputated) Chickamauga 9/19/63. Detailed as a nurse in Macon, GA. Served to Lee's surrender. Hometown: Newton, AL.

McLendon, Newton: 21, enlisted 8/15/62, married, farmer. Died 11/08/62. Hometown: Sylvan Grove, AL.

McLeod, John F.: 21, enlisted 7/03/61, single, farmer. Captured Gettysburg 7/02/63, sent to Ft. Delaware, DE. Took oath and released 6/14/65. 5'8", fair complexion, brown eyes, dark hair. Hometown: Newton, AL.

McLeod, William A.: 19, enlisted 7/03/61, single, farmer. Killed Cold Harbor 6/27/62. NOK: Neal McLeod, father. Hometown: Newton, AL.

McNeill, Neely E.: 30, enlisted 8/15/62, married, farmer. Captured Gettysburg 7/02/63.

Died 12/02/63 chronic diarrhea. NOK: Sarah McNeill, wife. Hometown: Newton, AL.

Manning, Henry: 19, enlisted 7/03/61, single, brick mason. Killed Manassas 8/30/62. Hometown: Union Springs, AL.

Melvin, John: 20, enlisted 7/03/61, single, farmer. Killed Cold Harbor 6/27/62. Hometown: in AL.

Melvin, McKinney A.: 22, enlisted 7/03/61, single, farmer. Detached as teamster. Wounded left hip and thigh Gettysburg 7/02/63. AWOL (joined a Mississippi regiment?). Hometown: Sylvan Grove, AL.

Metcalf, James H.: 35, enlisted 7/03/61, married, minister. Elected 2LT. Resigned 5/19/62. Hometown: Florence, GA.

Milligan, A.L.: 34, enlisted 7/03/61, married, lawyer. Promoted 1LT and transferred to 54th Alabama 3/28/63. Discharged 9/28/64. "First-class soldier." Hometown: Newton, AL.

Moody, Charles A.: 18, enlisted 7/03/61, single, student. Promoted 3SGT. Severely wounded Manassas 8/28/62. Mortally wounded Petersburg 6/25/64. Hometown: Glenville, AL.

Murphy, Henry J.: 20, enlisted 7/03/61, single, farmer. Wounded Fredericksburg 12/19/62. Promoted 4CPL 8/30/63. Wounded Chickamauga 9/19/63. Severely wounded arm 2nd Cold Harbor 5/27/64. Discharged to Invalid Corps 10/13/64. Hometown: Abbeville, AL.

Oliver, Joseph: 55, enlisted 7/03/61. Died typhoid 10/28/61. NOK: Mahala Oliver, wife. Hometown: in AL.

Paine, G. Thomas: 20, enlisted 7/03/61, single, farmer. Died asthma 12/28/61. Hometown: Louisville, AL.

Palmer, Levi Madison: 18, enlisted 7/03/61, single, farmer. Discharged 4/10/62. Hometown: Midland City, AL.

Pape, Alexander: Served to Lee's surrender. Hometown: in AL.

Parish, John: 28, enlisted 7/03/61, married, blacksmith. Discharged chronic diarrhea 2/21/62. 5'10", dark complexion, dark eyes, black hair. Hometown: Skipperville, AL.

Parish, Thomas Jefferson "Jeff": 18, enlisted 7/03/61, single, farmer. Deserted 8/05/63, supposedly joined a cavalry command. Hometown: in AL.

Peacock, Samuel H.: 21, enlisted 7/03/61, single, farmer. Wounded Hazel River 8/22/62 and Sharpsburg 9/17/62. Detailed as nurse. Captured Wilderness 5/06/64, sent to Elmira, NY. Paroled 3/14/65. Hometown: Skipperville, AL.

Pierce, John W.: 19, enlisted 7/03/61, single, farmer. Died 5/28/62. NOK: Jonathan M. Pierce, father. Hometown: Newton, AL.

Pope, Alex: 18, enlisted 19/29/63, single, farmer. Hometown: Sylvan Grove, AL.

Pope, Archibald: 22, enlisted 8/15/62, married, farmer. Severely wounded leg Williamsburg Road 10/27/64. Hometown: Sylvan Grove, AL.

Pope, Calvin: 25, enlisted 8/15/62, married, farmer. Wounded right thigh and captured Gettysburg 7/02/63. Severely wounded body Darbytown Road 10/07/64. Hometown: Midland City, AL.

Ray, Alex: 18, enlisted 7/03/61, single, farmer. Died 2/26/62 "Congestion Brain." NOK: Manning Ray, father. Hometown: Kings, AL.

Ray, Thomas L.: 19, enlisted 3/10/62, single, farmer. Died 6/15/62 "Parotitis and Bronchitis." NOK: Elijah Ray, father. Hometown: Kings, AL.

Reneau, Barton S.: 30, enlisted 8/10/61, married, buggy maker. Wounded left thigh Cold Harbor 6/27/62. Detailed as nurse. Served to Lee's surrender. Hometown: Newton, AL.

Reynolds, William P.: 17, enlisted 7/03/61, single, farmer. Killed Manassas 8/28/62. NOK: Elizabeth Blackshire, mother. Hometown: Lawrenceville, AL.

Reynolds, William W.: Enlisted 8/11/61. Killed Cold Harbor 6/27/62. NOK: Margaret C. Reynolds, wife. Hometown: Newton, AL.

Rice, Frank M.: 24, enlisted 8/10/61, single, farmer. Wounded Fredericksburg 12/19/62 and Gettysburg 7/02/63. Hometown: Newton, AL.

Richardson, William N.: 33, enlisted 7/03/61, single, man. Elected CPT. Captured Lookout Valley 10/29/63, sent to Point Lookout, MD, and Ft. Delaware, DE. Took oath and released 6/10/65. 5'8", ruddy complexion, brown eyes, light hair. Hometown: Glenville, AL.

Russ, John W.: Enlisted 8/10/61, married, farmer. Severely wounded right thigh (amputated). Discharged to Invalid Corps 12/16/64. Hometown: Lawrenceville, AL.

Shearly, Abner P.: 34, enlisted 7/03/61, married, farmer. Died at home 10/30/62. Hometown: Lawrenceville, AL.

Sheppard, John Thomas: 18, enlisted 7/03/61, single, farmer. Died 3/15/62. NOK: Charles Sheppard, father. Hometown: Adkinson, AL.

Sims, James M.: 17, enlisted 7/03/61, married, farmer. Promoted 3CPL 6/20/63, 1CPL 1/01/64, and 3SGT 8/01/64. Wounded Chickamauga 9/19–20/63, slightly wounded wrist Wilderness 5/06/64, and severely wounded arm Darbytown Road 9/30/64. Served to Lee's surrender. Hometown: Newton, AL.

Smith, Isaiah "Isa": 18, enlisted 7/03/61, single,

farmer. Wounded leg (amputated) Chickamauga 9/20/63. Hometown: in AL.

Smith, John D.L.: 29, enlisted 8/15/62, married, farmer. Wounded left foot and captured Gettysburg, paroled 8/??/63. Served to Lee's surrender. Hometown: Sylvan Grove, AL.

Smith, Jonathan "John" N.: Enlisted 7/03/61, married, farmer. Captured Knoxville 10/29/63, sent to Camp Morton, OH. Hometown: Kings, AL.

Smith, Joshua Lawrence: 19, enlisted 7/03/61, single, farmer. Served to Lee's surrender. Hometown: Kings, AL.

Smith, Lenuel C.N.: 27, enlisted 8/15/62, married, farmer. Slightly wounded arm 10/07/64. Served to Lee's surrender. Hometown: Sylvan Grove, AL.

Smothers, Michael C.: 25, enlisted 8/15/62, married, farmer. 5'11", fair complexion, dark eyes, dark hair. Hometown: Sylvan Grove, AL.

Spivey, Benjamin J.: 19, enlisted 7/03/61, single, farmer. Killed Cold Harbor 6/27/62. NOK: Josiah Spivey, father. Hometown: Adkinson, AL.

Spivey, Benjamin J.: 22, enlisted 7/03/61, single, farmer. Died 3/??/62. Hometown: Lawrenceville, AL.

Spurlock, Daniel A.: 27, enlisted 3/10/62, married, farmer. Mortally wounded Cold Harbor 6/27/62, died 7/04/62. NOK: Mary E. Spurlock, wife. Hometown: Kings, AL.

Spurlock, George W.: Enlisted 3/10/62, married, farmer. Died typhoid 5/27/62. NOK: Solomon Spurlock, father. Hometown: Kings, AL.

Stanton, F.D.: Physician. Elected 3LT, promoted 2LT 5/19/62. Hometown: Old Columbia, AL.

Tew, Alexander "Alex": 23, enlisted 7/03/61, single, farmer. Died pneumonia 3/03/62. Hometown: Adkinson, AL.

Tew, Joel: 19, enlisted 7/03/61, single, farmer. Wounded Manassas 8/28/62. Served to Lee's surrender. Hometown: Adkinson, AL.

Tew, John: 21, enlisted 7/03/61, single, farmer. Left sick Knoxville and captured 12/09/63, died pneumonia Knoxville. Hometown: in AL.

Thomas, David H.: 24, enlisted 7/03/61, single, merchant. Elected 4SGT, promoted 2SGT, 1SGT, and 2LT. wounded Fredericksburg 12/13/62, Chickamauga 9/20/63, Knoxville 11/25/63, and severely wounded hip and back Wilderness 5/06/64. Hometown: Old Town, AL.

Thomas, Elisha J.: 22, enlisted 7/03/61, single, farmer. Died typhoid 12/27/61. Hometown: Lawrenceville, AL.

Thomas, William H.H.: 19, enlisted 7/03/61, single, farmer. Discharged 3/??/62. Hometown: Lawrenceville, AL.

Walden, Thomas H.: 18, enlisted 7/03/61, single, farmer. Died typhoid 1/18/62. Hometown: Lawrenceville, AL.

Walker, Daniel S.: 20, enlisted 7/03/61, married, farmer. Killed Cold Harbor 6/27/62. 6'0", dark complexion, blue eyes, dark hair. NOK: Sarah Jane Walker, wife. Hometown: Buford, AL.

Weston, William W.B.: 26, enlisted 3/27/62, single, shoemaker. Transferred from 1st Alabama. Severely wounded Cold Harbor 6/27/62. Captured Gettysburg, sent to Ft. Delaware, died fever 3/12/64. Hometown: in AL.

Whitehead, James M.: 22, enlisted 7/03/61, married, lawyer. Severely wounded left thigh (amputated) Cold Harbor 6/27/62. Hometown: Newton, AL.

Wiggins, Stephen M.: 20, enlisted 8/15/62, single, farmer. Died typhoid 10/27/62. NOK: Rachel Wiggins, wife. Hometown: Sylvan Grove, AL.

Williams, Abb B.: 24, enlisted 3/14/62, single, farmer. Died typhoid 6/??/62. Hometown: Glennville, AL.

Wilson, William L.: 35, enlisted 7/03/61, married, farmer. Elected 1SGT, promoted 3LT and 2LT 5/19/62 Wounded left leg (amputated) and captured Knoxville 12/04/63, sent to Johnson's Island. Exchanged 11/26/64. .Hometown: Columbia, SC.

Windham, James Russell: 53, enlisted 7/03/61, married, farmer. Died typhoid 11/10/61. NOK: Anetta Windham, wife. Hometown: Newton, AL.

Windham, John N.: 24, enlisted 7/03/61, married, teacher. Promoted CPL 5/10/62. Mortally wounded Malvern Hill 7/01/62, died 7/04/62. NOK: Samuel Windham, father. Hometown: Newton, AL.

Wood, William D.: 25, enlisted 7/03/61, single, lawyer. Elected 1LT. Wounded Hazel River 8/22/62 and Sharpsburg 9/17/62. Resigned 8/01/63. Hometown: in AL.

Yelverton, Harrison "Harris" Crawford: 18, enlisted 7/03/61, single, farmer. Wounded Hazel River 8/22/62 and severely wounded Chickamauga 9/20/63. Served to Lee's surrender. Hometown: Newton, AL.

Company I

Andress, Isaac Newton: 19, enlisted 7/03/61, single, farmer. Severely wounded Cold Harbor 6/27/62. Served to Lee's surrender. Hometown: Troy, AL.

Arnold, W.R.: 29, enlisted 7/03/61, single, clerk. Elected 1SGT. Discharged cystitis 1/24/62. 5'4", dark complexion, hazel eyes, dark hair. Hometown: Troy, AL.

Ballard, James P.: 20, enlisted 7/03/61, single, farmer. Served to Lee's surrender. Hometown: in AL.

Barnett, Brantley G.: 20, enlisted 7/03/61, single, farmer. Promoted 3CPL 8/03/62 and 4SGT 6/01/64. Served to Lee's surrender. Received Southern Cross of Honor 12/10/64. Hometown: Orion, AL.

Beecher, Jefferson F.: 61, enlisted 7/03/61, blacksmith. Discharged hernia 11/26/61. 6'2", dark complexion, hazel eyes, brown hair. Born in New Haven, CT. Hometown: in AL.

Bell, Joseph: 23, enlisted 7/03/61, single, mechanic. Severely wounded Manassas 8/30/62. Captured and paroled 11/??/62. Served to Lee's surrender. Hometown: Troy, AL.

Bennett, George: Served to Lee's surrender.

Bennett, John 16, enlisted 3/28/64, single, farmer. Paroled Montgomery, AL. 5/30/65. 4'10", fair complexion, blue eyes, dark hair. Hometown: Troy, AL.

Blair, Leroy: 28, single. Died typhoid 1/02/62. NOK: John Blair, father. Hometown: in AL.

Bolton: Died pneumonia and typhoid 11/14/61.

Bond, Julian D.: 25, single. Discharged 12/20/61. Hometown: in AL.

Boyd, Casper W.: 29, enlisted 7/03/61, single, farmer. Mortally wounded Cross Keys 6/08/62, died 6/26/62. Hometown: Orion, AL.

Brantley, William S.: 27, enlisted 7/03/61, single, farmer. Died measles 10/13/61. NOK: S.L. Brantley, father. Hometown: Orion, AL.

Brown, Pulaski H.: 26, enlisted 7/03/61, married, doctor. Detailed as assistant surgeon. Promoted 2LT 6/28/63 and 1LT 12/01/64. Transferred to Company K 6/27/63. Wounded both hands 2nd Cold Harbor 6/04/64. Assigned to Bemiss Hospital Opelika 02/??/65. Took oath Montgomery, AL, 6/07/65. 6'1", fair complexion, black eyes, dark hair. Hometown: Troy, AL.

Brown, William J.: 21, enlisted 7/03/61, single, farmer. Died typhoid 11/18/61. Hometown: Oluster, AL.

Burgess, Squire H.: 19, enlisted 7/03/61, single, farmer. Served to Lee's surrender. Hometown: Oluster, AL.

Burgess, V.B.: Enlisted 7/03/61, single, farmer. Died pneumonia 1/20/62 Hometown: Oluster, AL.

Cargile, James T.: Died typhoid 10/16/61. Hometown: Orion, AL.

Carpenter, Coleman N.: 20, enlisted 7/03/61, single, farmer. Captured Gettysburg 7/02/63. Took oath and released 6/14/65. 5'10", ruddy complexion, gray eyes, light hair. Hometown: Troy, AL.

Carpenter, William A.: 28, enlisted 7/03/61, single, farmer. Hit in the head with a pole and assigned light duty (teamster). Assigned to Invalid Corps 3/08/64. 5'10", fair complexion, gray eyes, light hair. Hometown: Troy, AL.

Carter, John E.: 24, enlisted 7/03/61. Promoted 3LT 3/25/62 and 2LT 6/01'62. Wounded Sharpsburg 9/17/62. Resigned 8/14/63 due to disability from gunshot wound. Hometown: Troy, AL.

Cartwright, W.J.: Discharged epilepsy 1/23/62. Hometown: in AL.

Catrett, Israel: 40, enlisted 9/15/61. Discharged 10/31/61. 5'10", dark complexion, dark eyes, dark hair. Hometown: in AL.

Catrett, John M.: 21, enlisted. Wounded Knoxville 11/25/63 and severely wounded side Spotsylvania 5/08/64. Hometown: Stockton, AL.

Catrett, William M.: 35. Discharged hernia 2/06/62. 5'9½", dark complexion, blue eyes, dark hair. Hometown: in AL.

Champion, Frank D.: 19, enlisted 7/03/61, single, clerk. Detailed as orderly to BG Trimble. Promoted SGT. Captured Stoneman's Raid 5/14/63 but paroled for "want of means of transportation." Captured 7/06/63 (after Gettysburg), sent to Point Lookout, MD, escaped 5/20/64. Served to Lee's surrender. Hometown: Troy, AL.

Champion, Jackson A.: 25, enlisted 2/28/62, married, farmer. Mortally wounded Fredericksburg 12/13/62, died 12/23/62. NOK: Rebecca Champion, wife. Hometown: Troy, AL.

Coleman, C.: Died Erysipelas (skin infection). Hometown: Troy, AL.

Coombs, William P.: 17, enlisted 7/03/61. Wounded Sharpsburg 9/17/62 and Chickamauga 9/20/63. Killed Hanover Junction 5/25/64 by sharpshooter. NOK: Mary Habbie, mother. Hometown: Troy, AL.

Craig, Jackson V.: 28, enlisted 7/03/61, single, farmer. Died 1/01/62. NOK: Mary Houston, mother. Hometown: Orion, AL.

Craig, W. Thomas: 28, enlisted 7/03/61, single. Killed Cold Harbor 6/27/62. NOK: David Craig, father. Hometown: Troy, AL.

Davenport, Green W.: 20, enlisted 7/03/61, single, farmer. Wounded Hazel River 8/23/62. Killed Wilderness 5/06/64. Hometown: Troy, AL.

Dean, Frederick A.: 18, enlisted 7/03/61, single, farmer. Discharged 1/20/62. Hometown: Orion, AL.

Deese, John Quills: 16, enlisted 7/03/61. Wounded Fredericksburg 12/19/62 and severely wounded foot Ft. Harrison 9/30/64. Hometown: in AL.

Devane, Jasper: 25, enlisted 7/03/61. Killed Sharpsburg 9/17/62. Hometown: in AL.

Dorris, Henry: 16, enlisted 7/03/61, single, farmer. Killed Fussell's Mill 8/16/64. Hometown: Orion, AL.

Duck, William R.: 21, enlisted 7/03/61, single, farmer. Killed Fussell's Mill 8/16/64. Hometown: Dublin, Ireland.

Dukes, Nathan T.: 26. Died typhoid 1/01/62. Hometown: Orion, AL.

Dukes, William M.: 21, enlisted 3/03/61, single, farmer. Died pneumonia 3/13/62. NOK: O.A. Dukes, father. Hometown: Orion, AL.

Edwards, Lorenzo J.: 24, enlisted 7/03/61, single. Died 6/17/62. NOK: William Edwards, father. Hometown: Troy, AL.

Evans, John C.: 18, enlisted 7/03/61, single, farmer. Severely wounded eye Cold Harbor 6/2/7/62. Discharged 10/24/62. 5'7", fair complexion, yellow eyes, dark hair. Hometown: Orion, AL.

Farmer, Alexander "Alex" T.: 27, enlisted 7/03/61, married, farmer. Mortally wounded Cold Harbor 6/27/62, died 7/08/62. NOK: Martha Jane Farmer, wife. Hometown: Troy, AL.

Faulk, Philip J.: 23, enlisted 7/03/61, married. Died pneumonia 12/15/61. NOK: Timothy S. Faulk, father. Hometown: in AL.

Florden, James C.: 20, enlisted 7/03/61. Died pneumonia 11/19/61. NOK: Mary Flowers, mother. Hometown: in AL.

Folmar, Isaac Parson: 23, enlisted 3/01/62. Served to Lee's surrender. Hometown: in AL.

Foster, Columbus W.: 21, enlisted 7/03/61, single, farmer. Wounded Chickamauga 9/19–20/63. Transferred to Navy 9/28/63. 6'0", dark complexion, dark eyes, black hair. Hometown: Union Springs, AL.

Freeman, Bailey T.: 17, enlisted 7/03/61, single, farmer. Promoted 4CPL. Served to Lee's surrender. 5'9", light complexion, gray eyes, dark hair. Hometown: Farriorville, AL.

Fullmore, Ashberry J.: 18, enlisted 7/03/61, single. Died measles 9/23/61. NOK: Mary Fullmore, mother. Hometown: in AL.

Gardner, Benjamin.: 52, enlisted 7/03/61, married, lawyer. Elected CPT. Resigned 12/15/61. Hometown: in AL.

Gardner, Samuel "Sam" Harwell: 16, enlisted 7/03/61, single, student. Promoted 4CPL 10/01/61 and 2 CPL. Wounded Sharpsburg

9/17/62. Killed Gettysburg 7/02/63. Hometown: Troy, AL.

Gardner, Stephen D.: 24, enlisted 3/01/62, married, farmer. Died typhoid 7/02/62. NOK: Permina Gardner, wife. Hometown: Oluster, AL.

Gillis, Augus: 22, enlisted 7/03/61. Promoted 3CPL 10/03/61. Died pneumonia 5/11/62. Hometown: in AL.

Gilmer, William H. 26, enlisted 3/01/62, married, farmer. Transferred to Company L 8/08/62. Hometown: Troy, AL.

Goles, C.N.: Died pneumonia 12/12/61.

Graham, Alfred B.: 19, enlisted 7/03/61, single, farmer. Detached Provost Guard and Division Quartermaster. Wounded Chickamauga 9/19/63. Served to Lee's surrender. Hometown: Orion, AL.

Grey, Thomas A.: 18, enlisted 7/03/61, single, farmer. Slightly wounded chest Ft. Harrison 9/30/64. Served to Lee's surrender. Hometown: Troy, AL.

Hale, Richard Alfred: 40, enlisted 7/03/61, married, farmer. Deserted 4/11/62–9/25/63. Captured 11/02/63, sent to Camp Morton, IN. Paroled from Libby Prison 4/24/65. Hometown: Troy, AL.

Hamill, George W.: 17, enlisted 7/03/61, single, farmer. Died measles 10/05/61. 5'10", light complexion, blue eyes, dark hair. NOK: Jonathan L. Hamill, father. Hometown: Troy, AL.

Hanchy, J.: 17, enlisted 7/03/61, single, clerk. Promoted 1SGT 9/23/63. Captured Sharpsburg 9/27/62. Killed Dandridge, TN, 1/17/64. Hometown: Troy, AL.

Harris, Joshua Warren: 16, enlisted 9/01/64, single, farmer. Served to Lee's surrender. Hometown: in AL.

Harris, Richard Andrew Jackson: 15, enlisted 3/17/64, single, painter. Detailed as musician and colonel's orderly. Served to Lee's surrender. Hometown: Greenville, AL.

Harris, Seaborn N.: 19, enlisted 7/03/61, single, student. Wounded Manassas 8/30/62. Mortally wounded Chickamauga 9/20/63, died 12/04/63. Hometown: Farriorville, AL.

Hartsfield, James F.: 21, enlisted 7/03/61, single, clerk. Detailed as teamster. Wounded left thigh. Paroled Montgomery 5/24/65. 6'0", dark complexion, gray eyes, dark hair. Hometown: Troy, AL.

Hazellwood, Jefferson "Jeff": Captured Knoxville 11/25/63, sent to Rock Island Barracks, IL. Hometown: in AL.

Helms, John: Enlisted 9/01/62, married, farmer. Slightly wounded chest Darbytown Road 10/07/64. 5'9", light complexion, blue eyes, dark hair. Hometown: Newton, AL.

Hightower, James T.: 19, enlisted 7/03/61, single, farmer. Detailed as teamster. Served to Lee's surrender. Hometown: Troy, AL.

Hill, James: 18, enlisted 1/01/63, single, farmer. Detailed as courier. Served to Lee's surrender. Hometown: Troy, AL.

Hill, Jeptha: 19, enlisted 7/03/61, single, clerk. Hometown: Orion, AL.

Hoffman, M.: Paroled Montgomery, AL. 6/10/65. 5'10", dark complexion, dark eyes, dark hair. Hometown: in AL.

Holland, Thomas J.: 39, enlisted 8/03/61, single, saddler. Mortally wounded Chickamauga 9/20/63, died 9/22/63. "Made a fine soldier." Hometown: Troy, AL.

Hotten, Richard D.: 19, enlisted 7/03/61. Discharged mental infirmity 11/06/61 6'0", dark complexion, hazel eyes, dark hair. Hometown: in AL.

Jeter, George W.: 23, enlisted 3/01/62, married, farmer. AWOL. Shot self in hand. Paroled Montgomery, AL, 6/03/65. 5'6", dark complexion, blue eyes, dark hair. Hometown: Troy, AL.

Jeter, Marion J.: Enlisted 3/01/62, married, farmer. AWOL. Died measles 6/12/62. NOK: Lucy P. Jeter, wife. Hometown: Troy, AL.

Jones, Bird H.: 18, enlisted 7/03/61, single, farmer. Discharged disability 1/25/62. Hometown: Troy, AL.

Jones, James David: 17, enlisted 7/03/61, single, farmer. Wounded Dandridge, TN, 1/16/64. Slightly wounded leg Darbytown Road 10/07/64. Served to surrender. Hometown: Troy, AL.

King, William C.: 31, enlisted 8/19/61, married, grocer. Died at home 2/09/62. Melanie King, wife. Hometown: Troy, AL.

Linton, George Washington: 18, enlisted 7/03/61, single, farmer. Severely wounded Cold Harbor 6/27/62. Served to Lee's surrender. Hometown: Farriorville, AL.

Linton, William Thomas: 28, enlisted 7/03/61, single, farmer. Severely wounded Cross Keys 6/08/62. Detailed as nurse at hospital. Captured Knoxville 12/05/63, sent to Rock Island, IL. Took oath and released 6/18/65. 5'11", fresh complexion, blue eyes, brown hair. Hometown: in AL.

Little, John N.: 22, enlisted 7/03/61. Died typhoid 10/07/61. Hometown: Troy, AL.

Logan, George W.: 21, enlisted 7/03/61, single, painter. Elected 3SGT. Killed by cannon Fredericksburg 12/19/62. Hometown: Orion, AL.

Long, James B.: 32, enlisted 5/14/62, married, farmer. Detailed as teamster. Died 8/06/64. Hometown: Troy, AL.

Lynch, Patrick: 31, enlisted 7/03/61, single, ditcher. Born in Ireland. Transferred to Company K 10/19/62. Hometown: Orion, AL.

McAllister, William James: 16, enlisted 7/03/61, single, farmer. Promoted 4CPL and 2CPL 6/01/64. Served to Lee's surrender. "Very fine soldier." Hometown: Troy, AL.

McCarra, Williamson: 17, enlisted 3/01/64, single, student. Served to Lee's surrender. Hometown: Troy, AL.

McClendon, A. Green: 20, enlisted 9/23/63, single, farmer. Wounded Knoxville 11/25/63. Paroled Montgomery. 5'9", light complexion, gray eyes, red hair. Hometown: Troy, AL.

McClendon, John: 22, enlisted 3/01/62, married, farmer. Served to Lee's surrender. Hometown: Troy, AL.

McCleod, William: 18, enlisted 7/03/61, single, farmer. Wounded left ear Sharpsburg 9/17/62. Served to Lee's surrender. Hometown: Troy, AL.

McCormick, George W.: 34, enlisted 7/03/61, single, farmer. Wounded Manassas 8/28/62. Killed Mechanicsville 6/01/64 by sharpshooter. Hometown: Hallsville, AL.

McCormick, John C.: 26, enlisted 3/04/62, married, farmer. Wounded right shoulder (amputated) and captured Gettysburg 7/02/63. Discharged Invalid Corps 9/09/64. Hometown: Hallsville, AL.

McLeod, Hugh: 27, enlisted 3/01/62, married, farmer. Wounded Manassas 8/30/62 and slightly wounded hand Ft. Harrison 9/30/64. Paroled Montgomery, AL. 6/16/65. 5'10" fair complexion, blue eyes, dark hair. Hometown: Hallsville, AL.

McLeod, Neal: 21, enlisted 3/01/62, single, farmer. Severely wounded right shoulder Gettysburg 7/02/63, captured 7/20/63. Paroled Montgomery, AL. 6/16/65. 5'8" red complexion, gray eyes, black hair. Hometown: Hallsville, AL.

McMoy, Robert "Bob" Edward: 25, enlisted 3/01/62, married, farmer. Wounded (loss of left thumb and index finger) Cold Harbor 6/27/62. Hometown: Farriorville, AL.

Mallet, Charles N.: 19, enlisted 7/03/61, single, farmer. Elected 3CPL, reduced in rank for missing Fredericksburg. Seriously wounded left thigh Gettysburg 7/02/63. AWOL. Paroled Montgomery, AL, 6/08/65. 5'9", light complexion, blue eyes, light hair. Hometown: Orion, AL.

Martin, Thomas: 32, enlisted 3/01/62, married, farmer. Wounded right shoulder and captured Gettysburg 7/04/63. Exchanged 11/12/63. Hometown: New Providence, AL.

Matthews, George A.C.: 23, enlisted 7/03/61,

single, farmer. Elected 2SGT, promoted 3LT 10/01/62, 2LT 9/01/63, 1LT 3/01/64 and CPT. Severely wounded shoulder Chester Station 6/16/64. Paroled Montgomery, AL, 6/07/65. 5'7", fair complexion, blue eyes, dark hair. Hometown: Brundidge, AL.

Moates, O.J.: 22, enlisted 3/01/62, married, farmer. Captured and paroled Winchester 6/??/62. Severely wounded Knoxville 11/25/63. Deserted and captured 1/19/65. Took oath and transported to Jacksonville, FL. Hometown: Greenville, AL.

Morrison, James M.: 18, enlisted 3/01/62. Died 7/02/62. Hometown: Hallsville, AL.

Morrison, Roderick: Enlisted 7/03/61. Captured Knoxville 12/04/63, sent to Rock Island, IL. Died smallpox 1/24/65. Hometown: Hallsville, AL.

Mosley, B. Wright: 31, enlisted 9/01/62, married, farmer. Killed Ft. Harrison 9/30/64. Hometown: Hallsville, AL.

Murphy, Daniel Buford: 26, enlisted 7/03/61, single, clerk. Detached as Enrolling Officer Pike County. Paroled Montgomery, AL, 5/24/65. 5'9", dark complexion, dark eyes, black hair. Hometown: Troy, AL.

Newman, Isaac N.: 17, enlisted 7/23/64, single, farmer. Paroled Montgomery 6/02/65. Hometown: Troy, AL.

Nordan, Thomas J.: 19, enlisted 7/03/61, single, farmer. Severely wounded Fredericksburg 12/19/62. Transferred to 60th Alabama 3/18/64. Hometown: Troy, AL.

Norris, James Larkin: 24, enlisted 7/03/61, single, farmer. Killed Petersburg 5/06/64. NOK: Leta Norris, mother. Hometown: Troy, AL.

Ogletree, Absalom J.: 26, enlisted 3/01/61, married, clerk. Detailed as teamster. Captured Gettysburg, sent to Ft. Delaware. Took oath and released 6/14/65. Sallow complexion, dark eyes, dark hair. Hometown: Troy, AL.

Oliver, William H.: 23, enlisted 7/03/61, single, farmer. Died 11/24/64. NOK: Mary L. Wingard, mother. Hometown: Orion, AL.

Osburn, J. Henry: 31, enlisted 7/03/61, married, farmer. Detailed as teamster. Served to surrender. Hometown: in AL.

Owens, Clem: 18, enlisted 3/01/63, single, farmer. Died measles 6/22/64. Hometown: Olustee, AL.

Owens, Isaac Marion: 42, enlisted 7/03/61, married, mechanic. Wounded 9/17/64. Paroled Montgomery, AL, 5/23/65. 5'8", fair complexion, blue eyes, sandy hair. Hometown: Orion, AL.

Owens, Joseph James: 17, enlisted 1/23/64, single, farmer. Died measles 6/21/64. Hometown: Orion, AL.

Ozburne, Henry Jasper: 31, enlisted 7/03/61, married, farmer. Detailed as teamster. Hometown: Orion, AL.

Page, James E.: 17, enlisted 7/03/61, single, farmer. AWOL. Deserted and captured 3/13/64. Hometown: in AL.

Park, Frank: 33, enlisted 7/03/61, single, physician. Elected 1LT and promoted CPT 12/15/61. Mortally wounded lungs 11/25/63. Captured 12/05/63, died 12/25/63. "Fine officer, splendid disciplinarian, and commanded the respect and confidence of his men." Hometown: Orion, AL.

Park, John W.: 18, enlisted 7/03/61, single, student. Killed Cold Harbor 6/27/62. 5'11", light complexion, blue eyes, light hair. NOK: J.T.S. Park, father. Hometown: Orion, AL.

Parks, Isaac H.: Enlisted 7/03/61. Served to Lee's surrender. Hometown: in AL.

Peters, Benton W.: 19, enlisted 7/03/61, single, farmer. Wounded Chickamauga 9/19/63. Severely wounded leg Darbytown Road 10/07/64. Hometown: Troy, AL.

Peters, N.J.: Enlisted 3/01/63. Captured Gettysburg, sent to Ft. Delaware, DE, and exchanged 10/31/64. Paroled Montgomery, AL. 5'6", light complexion, gray eyes, dark hair. Hometown: in AL.

Pitts, S. Perry: 27, enlisted 7/03/61. Captured Cross Keys 6/08/62, paroled 6/26/62. Killed Manassas 8/29/62. NOK: Rebecca Ellen Pitts, daughter Hometown: in AL.

Powell, George E.: 19, enlisted 7/03/61, single, clerk. Wounded right arm Fredericksburg 12/19/62. Killed 5/11/64 Spotsylvania. Hometown: Troy, AL.

Powell, H.C.: 18, enlisted 9/01/62, single, farmer. Severely wounded shoulder Darbytown Road 10/13/64. Paroled Montgomery, AL. 5'4", fair complexion, gray eyes, light hair. Hometown: Troy, AL.

Powell, Kinion Pierce: 24, enlisted 7/03/61, single, farmer. Wounded Chickamauga 9/19/63. Severely wounded face Ft. Gilmer 10/07/64. Paroled Montgomery 6/17/64 5'8", fair complexion, blue eyes, light hair. Hometown: Troy, AL.

Powell, William P.: 21, enlisted 3/01/62, single, farmer. Killed Wilderness 5/06/64. NOK: Charlotte Powell, wife. Hometown: Troy, AL.

Powell, Wilson: Enlisted 9/18/62. Captured Wilderness 5/06/64, sent to Elmira, NY. Released 6/23/65. 6'1½", florid complexion, blue eyes, auburn hair. Hometown: in AL.

Pugh, N.D.: Enlisted 3/20/64. Slightly wounded leg Wilderness 5/06/64. Died chronic diarrhea 6/26/64. Hometown: Troy, AL.

Raddock, James D.: 20, enlisted 7/03/61, single, farmer. Discharged 12/17/61. Hometown: Troy, AL.

Railey, Thomas B.: 22, enlisted 3/01/62, married, farmer. Served to Lee's surrender. Hometown: in AL.

Redman, John: 16, enlisted 7/03/61, single, farmer. Wounded Chickamauga 9/20/63. Killed Darbytown Road 10/07/64. Hometown: Orion, AL.

Rotton, Daniel L.: 23, enlisted 7/03/61. Died pneumonia 11/14/61. Hometown: Orion, AL.

Rushing, Solomon James: 19, enlisted 7/03/61, single, farmer. Severely wounded Cold Harbor 6/27/62 and wounded Darbytown Road 10/07/64. Awarded Southern Cross of Honor 12/10/64. Hometown: Troy, AL.

Sanders, Alsey F.: 25, enlisted 7/03/61, single, farmer. Elected 2 CPL, promoted 4SGT, and 3SGT 2/01/64. Slightly wounded left arm Wilderness 5/06/64. Hometown: Troy, AL.

Satcher, James W.: 16, enlisted 7/03/61, single, farmer. Wounded Fredericksburg 12/19/62. Severely wounded right thigh and captured Knoxville 12/03/63, sent to Camp Morton, IN. Hometown: Orion, AL.

Scarbrough, James W.: 23, enlisted 7/03/61. Wounded Cold Harbor 6/27/62. Transferred to 37th Alabama, elected 2LT. NOK: M.E. Scarbrough, wife. Hometown: in AL.

Segars, M.J.: 16, enlisted 3/28/64, single, farmer. Wounded Wilderness 5/06/64. Served to Lee's surrender. Hometown: Troy, AL.

Simmons, James B.: 19, enlisted 7/03/61, single, farmer. Died typhoid 10/21/61. NOK: John Simmons, father. 5'3", dark complexion, gray eyes, dark hair. Hometown: Troy, AL.

Smedley, Capel S.: 18, enlisted 3/01/63, single, farmer. Captured Gettysburg, sent to Ft. Delaware. Exchanged 7/31/63 and served to surrender. Hometown: Troy, AL.

Smedley, Randolph C.: 22, enlisted 7/03/61, single, farmer. Elected 4CPL, promoted 5SGT 7/01/63 and 1SGT 6/01/64. Acting Quartermaster SGT. Served to Lee's surrender. Hometown: Troy, AL.

Smith, William N.: 17, enlisted 3/01/62, single, farmer. Killed Hazel River 8/22/62 NOK: Samuel M. Smith, father. Hometown: Troy, AL.

Smyth, S.B.: 17, enlisted 3/01/62, single, farmer. Severely wounded leg (amputated) Darbytown Road 10/07/64. Discharged to Invalid Corps 2/13/65 with duty at Montgomery. 5'9", fair complexion, blue eyes, light hair. Hometown: in AL.

Starke, A.W.: 22, enlisted 7/03/61, married, lawyer. Elected 3LT and promoted 2LT. Resigned 5/12/62. Hometown: Troy, AL.

Stewart, Sidney A.: Enlisted 7/03/61. Captured Gettysburg, sent to Ft. Delaware. Died smallpox 11/10/63. Hometown: in AL.

Strickland, Blackman: 18, enlisted 9/29/63, single, farmer when. Served to Lee's surrender. Hometown: Troy, AL.

Strickland, John: 18, enlisted 7/03/61, single, farmer. Severely wounded Cold Harbor 6/27/62. Captured Gettysburg, sent to Ft. Delaware. Took oath and released 6/14/65. 5'9", sallow complexion, blue eyes, light hair. Hometown: in AL.

Strickland, William H.: 25, enlisted 7/03/61, single, clerk. Elected 2LT, promoted 1LT 12/15/61 and CPT 12/25/63. Severely wounded left hand Fussell's Mill 8/16/64. Hometown: Troy, AL.

Stroud, David: 22, enlisted 7/03/61, single, farmer. Detached as provost guard. Served to Lee's surrender. Hometown: Troy, AL.

Thigpen, T.H.: 26, enlisted 5/01/62, married, farmer. Discharged 7/15/62. Hometown: Oluster, AL.

Thomas, Elenda R.: 18, enlisted 7/03/61, single, student. Detailed as baggage guard. Wounded thigh, right arm and shoulder (partial paralysis) Cross Keys 6/08/62. Discharged 8/06/63. 5'6", dark complexion, blue eyes, dark hair. Hometown: Troy, AL.

Thompson, Hiram A.: 19, enlisted 7/03/61, single, clerk. Elected 1CPL, promoted 3SGT, and 2SGT 2/01/64. Slightly wounded Wilderness 5/06/64. Served to Lee's surrender. Hometown: Troy, AL.

Tilman, A.: 26, enlisted 5/01/62, married, farmer. Discharged 7/15/62. Hometown: Oluster, AL.

Tucker, Asberry: Died measles 9/23/61 Hometown: in AL.

Underwood, John J.: Enlisted 7/03/61, single, farmer. Killed Sharpsburg 9/17/62. Hometown: Troy, AL.

Walker, Richard: 18, enlisted 3/01/62, single, farmer. Killed Cold Harbor 6/27/63. NOK: Felix Walker, father. Hometown: Hallsville, AL.

Walters, Thomas A.: 27, enlisted 7/03/61, married, farmer. Severely wounded leg Cross Keys 6/08/62 and wounded Sharpsburg 9/17/62. Discharged heart disease 7/14/63. 5'7½", florid complexion, blue eyes, light hair. Hometown: Troy, AL.

Walters, William E.: 24, enlisted 7/03/61, single, farmer. Died typhoid 2/06/62. Hometown: Orion, AL.

Weaver, William J.: 27, enlisted 7/03/61, married, farmer. Died 12/02/61. Hometown: Troy, AL.

Whatley, Alfred A.: Enlisted 3/01/62, married. Died pneumonia 5/31/62. NOK: Adeline Whatley, wife. Hometown: in AL.

Whatley, James: 20, enlisted 7/03/61, single, farmer. Killed Cold Harbor 6/27/62. NOK: Labin Whatley, father. Hometown: Troy, AL.

White, George Jefferson: 27, enlisted 3/11/62, married, farmer. Killed Hazel River 8/22/62. Hometown: Troy, AL.

White, John J.: 20, enlisted 7/03/61, single, clerk. Promoted 2SGT and 1SGT. Killed Spotsylvania 5/11/64. Hometown: in AL.

Willia, James B.: 21, enlisted 7/03/61, single, farmer. Died pneumonia 3/20/62. Hometown: Orion, AL.

Wilson, Bradberry: 21, enlisted 7/03/61, single, farmer. Captured Cross Keys 6/08/62, exchanged 8/01/62. Killed Petersburg 6/21/64. NOK: M Henderson, mother. Hometown: Troy, AL.

Wilson, Bryant: 41, enlisted 7/03/61, married, farmer. Exchanged 8/05/62. Promoted 2CPL 8/11/63, 1CPL, and 5SGT 6/01/64. Paroled Montgomery, AL, 6/08/65. 5'8", dark complexion, blue eyes, dark hair. Hometown: Troy, AL.

Wilson, Simon D.: 24, enlisted 7/03/61, married, stage driver. Detailed as teamster. Severely wounded right arm (amputated) 6/01/64. Discharged anchylosis (stiffness of joint) to Invalid Corps with duty at Montgomery, AL. Paroled Montgomery, AL, 6/07/65. 6'3", fair complexion, dark eyes, dark hair. Hometown: Troy, AL.

Wilson, Thomas: 17, enlisted 10/28/64, single, farmer. Served to Lee's surrender. Hometown: Troy, AL.

Wolfe, Hayne L.: 21, enlisted 7/03/61, single, farmer. Served to Lee's surrender. Hometown: Orion, AL.

Wolfe, Jacob H.M.: 31, enlisted 7/03/61, single, farmer. Served to Lee's surrender. Hometown: Orion, AL.

Youngblood, William 22, enlisted 7/03/61, single, farmer. Detached as courier for Longstreet. Hometown: Troy, AL.

Company K

Albritton, Thomas J.: 25, enlisted 8/15/62, married, farmer. Wounded and captured Gettysburg 7/02/63, sent to Ft. Delaware, DE, and Point Lookout, MD. Died smallpox 11/14/63. Hometown: Ozark, AL.

Alexander, Asa: 25, enlisted 7/03/61, single,

farmer. Died typhoid 11/02/61. 5'8", light complexion. Hometown: Eufaula, AL.

Allen, Henry M:. 18, enlisted 7/03/61, single, farmer. Killed Manassas 9/30/62. 5'10", light complexion, gray eyes. Hometown: Eufaula, AL.

Anderson, Barbour William: 23, enlisted 8/15/62, married, farmer. Died 10/23/62. NOK: Nancy Anderson, wife Hometown: Ozark, AL.

Anderson, Carnes Patillo: Enlisted 8/15/62, married, farmer. 5'8", fair complexion, hazel eyes, light hair. Hometown: Newton, AL.

Anderson, Scott Manly: 18, enlisted 8/15/62, single, farmer. Captured Gettysburg 7/02/63, sent to Ft. Delaware. Died chronic diarrhea 4/06/64. Hometown: Ozark, AL.

Bailey, James J.: 22, enlisted 7/03/61, married, farmer. Died typhoid 10/27/61. Hometown: Eufaula, AL.

Bailey, William F.: 32, enlisted 7/03/61, married, farmer. Died home on furlough 5/05/63. Hometown: Eufaula, AL.

Batchelor, Edmond: Enlisted 11/??/64. Deserted and captured 2/19/65. Sent to Pensacola. Hometown: Montgomery, AL.

Baugh, Alexander R.: 22, enlisted 7/03/61, single, clerk. Elected 2LT and promoted 1LT 1/11/62. Shot self in hand and resigned 9/13/62. Hometown: Eufaula, AL.

Beasley, Daniel: 25, enlisted 8/15/62, married, farmer. Severely wounded body Fussell's Mill 10/07/64. Hometown: Newton, AL.

Beasley, John C.: 29, enlisted 8/15/62, married, farmer. Died pneumonia Ft. Delaware, DE, 3/04/64. Hometown: Ozark, AL.

Beemans, Isaac: Enlisted 8/15/61. Died typhoid/pneumonia 11/11/61. Hometown: in AL.

Bell, Columbus C.: 18, enlisted 7/03/61. Wounded Cold Harbor 6/27/62 and right thigh 4/??/65. Hometown: in AL.

Bell, Joseph: 23, enlisted 7/03/61, single, mechanic. Severely wounded Manassas 8/30/62. Hometown: in AL.

Bell, William L.A.: 30, enlisted 7/03/61. Died measles 11/04/61. Hometown: Eufaula, AL.

Bennett, Arthur: 16, enlisted 7/23/64. Served to Lee's surrender. Hometown: Eufaula, AL.

Benton, James H.: 40, enlisted 7/03/61, married, mechanic. Discharged 11/25/61. 5'8", dark complexion, blue eyes, black hair. Hometown: Eufaula, AL.

Bethune, William J.: Elected 3LT, promoted 1LT 1/11/62 and CPT 9/12/62. Severely wounded face Gettysburg 7/02/63. Detached as enrolling officer for Conscript Department 1/16/64. Served to Lee's surrender. Hometown: in AL.

Blackshear, Jesse W.: 18, enlisted 7/03/61, single, farmer. Discharged epilepsy 11/25/61. Hometown: Eufaula, AL.

Boone, John R.: 18, enlisted 7/03/61, single, student. Severely wounded forearm 2nd Cold Harbor 6/03/64. 5'5", fair complexion, blue eyes, light hair. Hometown: Eufaula, AL.

Brannon, James Thomas: 30, enlisted 4/16/61, married, merchant. Wounded 4/23/62. Killed Manassas 8/30/62. Hometown: Eufaula, AL.

Brannon, Pat: 14, enlisted 7/03/61, single, student. Drummer. Served to Lee's surrender. Hometown: Columbus, GA.

Brannon, Robert "Bob" W.: 21, enlisted 7/03/61, single, bookkeeper. Elected 1CPL and promoted 5SGT. Mortally wounded Chickamauga 9/19/63, died 9/25/63. Hometown: Eufaula, AL.

Bray, John C.: 38, enlisted 11/16/64, married, merchant. Hometown: Eufaula, AL.

Brazell, W.: Married, farmer. Died 3/30/62. Hometown: Eufaula, AL.

Brown, James M.: 21, enlisted 7/03/61, single, farmer. Wounded left hand Fredericksburg 12/19/62. Killed Gettysburg 7/02/63. Hometown: Eufaula, AL.

Bryan, William A.: 16, enlisted 4/21/64. Hometown: in AL.

Bush, Amos: Killed Cold Harbor 6/27/62. Hometown: in AL.

Bynum, William Turner: 18, enlisted 4/01/63, single, famer. Wounded Gettysburg 7/02/63. Discharged 5/10/65, paroled Albany, GA. Hometown: Eufaula, AL.

Cade, James L.: 25, enlisted 7/03/61. Severely wounded right leg Hazel River 8/22/62. Served to Lee's surrender. Hometown: Midway, AL.

Caison, James H.: 21, enlisted 11/01/61, single, farmer. Wounded thigh Sharpsburg 9/17/62. Captured Lookout Valley 10/27/63, sent to Camp Morton, IN. Died pneumonia 1/09/64. Hometown: Eufaula, AL.

Canady, Daniel: 19, enlisted 7/03/61. Died "Congestion of Brain" 3/14/62. Hometown: Eufaula, AL.

Carter, John J.: 17, enlisted 7/03/61, single, farmer. Promoted CPL 5/19/63. Deserted 7/02/63, recaptured 7/19/63 and reduced in rank. Deserted again 8/05/63. Rejoined 5/01/64. Held prisoner in Richmond (Castle Thunder). Deserted and captured by Union 10/24/64. Hometown: Eufaula, AL.

Cherry, Owen: 24, enlisted 7/03/61, single, laborer. Born in Ireland. AWOL. Deserted 5/01/63. Captured 4/24/64. Took oath 6/24/64. Hometown: Eufaula, AL.

Clark, Pat: 28, enlisted 7/03/61, single, laborer. Born in Ireland. Deserted 8/09/62. Hometown: Eufaula, AL.

Craft, Reuben J.: 22, enlisted 7/03/61, single, mason. Wounded and captured Gettysburg 7/02/63. Hometown: Eufaula, AL.

Culpeper, Benjamin Franklin: 27, enlisted 11/01/61, single, clerk. Slightly wounded hand Wilderness 5/06/64 and wounded 2nd Cold Harbor 6/03/64. Served to Lee's surrender. Hometown: Eufaula, AL.

Cummings, Nelson: 34, enlisted 4/11/62, married, farmer. Wounded Cross Keys 6/08/62 and right thigh Chickamauga 9/19/63. Served to Lee's surrender. Hometown: Eufaula, AL.

Dudley, G.W.: 30, enlisted 7/03/61, married, farmer. Captured Gettysburg 7/02/63. Signed oath and released 6/11/65. 5'10", dark complexion, hazel eyes, gray hair. Hometown: Eufaula, AL.

Espy, Robert "Rob" Marion: 23, enlisted 7/28/61, single, farmer. Captured Lookout Valley 10/29/63, sent to Camp Morton, IN. Took oath and released 6/12/65. 5'8¾", florid complexion, gray eyes, dark hair. Hometown: Abbeville, AL.

Evans, William W.: 19, enlisted 7/03/61. Killed Cold Harbor 6/27/62. NOK: Evaline Evans, mother. Hometown: Eufaula, AL.

Faulk, Clark J.: 35, enlisted 7/03/61, married, mechanic. Wounded foot Darbytown Road 10/07/64. Awarded Southern Cross of Honor 12/10/64. Hometown: Eufaula, AL.

Frederick, George W.: 40, enlisted 7/03/61, single, farmer. Discharged physical disability 12/14/61. 5'8", dark complexion, blue eyes. Hometown: Otho, AL.

Garner, Zennimon: 18, enlisted 8/15/62, single, farmer. Wounded Fredericksburg 12/19/62. AWOL. Hometown: Ozark, AL.

Ginwright, William C.: 25, enlisted 7/03/61, married, farmer. Died measles 11/11/61. NOK: Nancy E. Ginwright, wife. Hometown: Eufaula, AL.

Godwin, Robert G.: 27, enlisted 11/10/62, single, farmer. Captured Falling Waters 7/14/63, exchanged 11/01/63. Captured Richmond and placed in Libby Prison 4/06/65. Hometown: Ozark, AL.

Gray, James H.: 26, enlisted 7/03/61, single, mechanic. Wounded Cedar Mountain 8/09/62. Mortally wounded right chest Lookout Valley 10/28/63, died 10/30/63. Hometown: in AL.

Green, Marion W.: 21, enlisted 7/03/61, single, farmer. Severely wounded head Spotsylvania 5/11/64. Hometown: Clopton, AL.

Grice, Evans G.: 18, enlisted 7/03/61, single, farmer. Wounded left knee Fredericksburg 12/13/62. Slightly wounded head Darbytown Road 10/13/63. Awarded Southern Cross of Honor 12/10/64. Served to Lee's surrender. Hometown: Eufaula, AL.

Grice, John H.: 20, enlisted 7/03/61, single, farmer. Killed Cold Harbor 6/27/62. Hometown: Eufaula, AL.

Grice, Stephen R. 24, enlisted 3/31/62, married, farmer. Mortally wounded Sharpsburg 9/17/62, died 10/10/62. Hometown: Eufaula, AL.

Grice, William O.: 22, enlisted 4/04/62, single, farmer. Died 4/11/63. Hometown: Eufaula, AL.

Ham, Andrew Jackson: 20, enlisted 7/03/61, single, farmer. Died 9/29/61. 5'8", fair complexion, blue eyes. NOK: Smith Ham, father. Hometown: Eufaula, AL.

Harper, John: Enlisted 7/03/61. Died 7/28/61 "fell overboard boat in Chattahoochee and drowned." NOK: Mary Harper, wife. Hometown: Eufaula, AL.

Harrell, Joshua C.: 24, enlisted 7/03/61, married, farmer. Detailed as regimental fifer 9/01/62. Hometown: in AL.

Harrell, William Hall: 27, enlisted 7/03/61, married, farmer. Wounded and captured Gettysburg 7/02/63, sent to Ft. Delaware, DE. Hometown: Eufaula, AL.

Hart, Henry C.: 31, enlisted 7/03/61, married, merchant. Elected CPT, resigned 9/12/62. Hometown: Eufaula, AL.

Hill, Jeptha: 19, enlisted 7/03/61, single, clerk. Commissary SGT. Served to Lee's surrender. 5'7", dark complexion, gray eyes, dark hair. Hometown: in AL.

Hill, Woodruff F.: 18, enlisted 7/03/61, single, farmer. Promoted 3CPL 4/01/62 and 1CPL. Severely wounded left leg Darbytown Road 10/07/64. Sent to Point Lookout, MD, took oath and released 6/26/65. 5'6", dark complexion, hazel eyes, black hair. Awarded Southern Cross of Honor 12/10/64. Hometown: Eufaula, AL.

Hobbs, Daniel C.: 22, enlisted 7/03/61, single, farmer. Died measles 9/22/61. Hometown: Eufaula, AL.

Holly, William R.: 42, enlisted 7/03/61, married, farmer. Transferred to Company G 8/01/62. Hometown: Abbeville, AL.

Hooper, Arch B.: 21, enlisted 7/03/61, single, farmer. Discharged 3/23/64. Hometown: in AL.

Ingram, John I.: Enlisted 4/12/62. Wounded thigh and left arm (amputated) and captured Gettysburg 7/02/63. Died 8/13/63. Hometown: Eufaula, AL.

Jennings, Pat: 18, enlisted 7/03/61, single,

farmer. Transferred to a SC regiment. 9/??/61. Hometown: Eufaula, AL.

Johnson, Josiah: 20, enlisted 7/03/61, single, farmer. Died measles 10/16/61. Hometown: Eufaula, AL.

Johnson, Samuel: 25, enlisted 8/15/62, married, farmer. Deserted. Hometown: Ozark, AL.

Kenny, Dennis P.: 25, enlisted 7/03/61, single, mason. Born Ireland. Killed Cross Keys 6/06/62. 5'9½", light complexion, gray eyes. Hometown: Eufaula, AL.

Langford, Robert A.: 26, enlisted 4/04/62, married, farmer. Died diarrhea 8/25/62. Hometown: Eufaula, AL.

Langston, Jesse: 23, enlisted 7/03/61, single, farmer. Died 6/21/62. Hometown: Eufaula, AL.

Lloyd, John: 24, enlisted 8/15/62, married, farmer. "Wounded himself in right hand." "Utterly no account." Hometown: Ozark, AL.

Lloyd, William M.: 19, enlisted 8/15/62, married, miller. Wounded left leg (amputated) Knoxville 11/23/63. Captured 12/05/63, sent to Camp Chase, IL, and Ft. Delaware, DE. Hometown: Ozark, AL.

Loflin, James Morgan: 16, enlisted 8/05/64, single, farmer. Served to surrender. Hometown: Glennville, AL.

Lynch, Patrick "Pat": 20, enlisted 7/03/61, single, ditcher. Born in Ireland. Captured Gettysburg 7/02/63, sent to Ft. Delaware, DE. Joined 3rd Maryland Cavalry (Union). Hometown: Troy, AL.

McGee, Seaborn F.: 18, enlisted 7/03/61, single, farmer. Mortally wounded Manassas 8/30/62, died 9/15/62. 5'9", light complexion. NOK: Alfred McGee, father. Hometown: in AL.

McGee, William A.: 20, enlisted 7/03/61, single, farmer. Died pneumonia 5/18/62. 5'9", light complexion, blue eyes, auburn hair. Hometown: in AL.

McIntyre, Patrick "Pat": 26, enlisted 7/03/61, married, laborer. Captured Chickamauga 9/19/63, sent to Camp Douglas, IL. Hometown: Eufaula, AL.

McKilcane, Burrel V.: 18, enlisted 7/03/61, single, farmer. Wounded Sharpsburg 9/17/62. Captured Gettysburg 7/02/63, sent to Ft. Delaware, DE, died 8/30/63. Hometown: Eufaula, AL.

McKinney, William A.: 19, enlisted 7/03/61, single, farmer. Died pneumonia 11/09/61. Hometown: in AL.

McMurray, Oliver: 39, enlisted 7/03/61, single, laborer. Born Ireland. Discharged 1/18/62. Hometown: in AL.

Madden, Cicero: 23, enlisted 7/03/61, married,

farmer. Promoted CPL 12/04/62 and 3SGT 1/01/63. Captured Gettysburg 7/02/63, sent to Ft. Delaware, died typhoid 1/29/64. Hometown: Eufaula, AL.

Mims, Elijah E.: 25, enlisted 8/15/62. Died typhoid 5/26/63. Hometown: Ozark, AL.

Moore, John Cassels: 31, enlisted 11/25/64, married, farmer. Served to Lee's surrender. Hometown: Eufaula, AL.

Morris, Richard: 40, enlisted 7/03/61, married, clerk. Promoted 3SGT, 1SGT, and 2LT 9/13/62. Resigned 6/14/63. Hometown: Eufaula, AL.

Murdock, James L.: 23, enlisted 7/03/61, single, laborer. Wounded and captured Gettysburg, sent to Ft. Delaware. Took oath and released 6/14/65. 6'0", ruddy complexion, blue eyes, dark hair. Hometown: Eufaula, AL.

Murphy, A.: Died measles 11/11/62.

Nelson, John: 23, enlisted 7/03/61, single, laborer. Born in Ireland. Wounded Fredericksburg 12/19/62. Killed Gettysburg 7/02/63 "while trying to drift to the rear 1SGT O'Conner held him by the collar, he was killed." Hometown: Eufaula, AL.

O'Connor, Patrick "Pat": 23, enlisted 7/03/61, single, tanner. Born in Ireland. Promoted 3SGT 10/08/62, 1SGT 5/19/63, and 3LT 12/13/63. Killed 2nd Cold Harbor 6/01/64. "One of the finest soldiers in the company." Hometown: Columbus, GA.

O'Hara, William T.: 22, enlisted 7/03/61, single, farmer. Died pneumonia 11/10/61. NOK: Allen M. O'Hara, father. Hometown: Eufaula, AL.

O'Herren, Pat: 31, enlisted 7/03/61, single, laborer. Born in Ireland. Deserted Malvern Hill 7/02/62. Hometown: Eufaula, AL.

Patterson, James T.: 20, enlisted 4/11/62, married, mechanic. 5'10", fair complexion, hazel eyes, black hair. Hometown: Eufaula, AL.

Perryman, H.: Died 4/05/63. Hometown: in AL.

Porter, Fred M.: 24, enlisted 7/03/61, single, clerk. Elected 1SGT. Promoted 2LT 1/11/62 and 1LT 9/12/62. Wounded Hazel River 8/22/62. Mortally wounded Chickamauga 9/19/63, died 10/27/63. Hometown: Eufaula, AL.

Quick, John: 34, enlisted 4/04/62, married, shoemaker. Died in Winchester. Hometown: Eufaula, AL.

Redmon, Mack: 24, enlisted 7/03/61, single, farmer. Died 6/01/62. Hometown: in AL.

Redmon, Marion: 24, enlisted 7/03/61, married, farmer. Died 1/15/62. NOK: John Redmon, brother. Hometown: in AL.

Rhodes, James M.: 37, enlisted 7/03/61, married, farmer. Slightly wounded hand Wilderness 5/06/64. Fractured left arm 4/05/65. Hometown: in AL.

Roberts, Andrew J.: 21, enlisted 7/03/61, single. Wounded Fredericksburg 12/19/62. Served to Lee's surrender. Hometown: Eufaula, AL.

Roberts, George A.: 35, enlisted 7/03/61, married, merchant. Elected 1LT. Resigned 1/11/62. Hometown: in AL.

Rogers, Sidney Lawrence: 18, enlisted 7/03/61, single, farmer. Discharged measles and youth 12/11/61. 5'8", light complexion, blue eyes, sandy hair. Hometown: Eufaula, AL.

Rutledge, James: 34, enlisted 7/03/61, married, laborer. Wounded Gettysburg 7/02/63. Captured Wilderness 5/06/64, sent to Elmira, NY. Refused exchange. Took oath and released 6/24/65. 5'8", dark complexion, dark eyes, dark brown hair. Hometown: Eufaula, AL.

Seegars, John A.: Enlisted 7/03/61. Captured Knoxville 12/05/63, sent to Ft. Delaware, DE, and exchanged 9/14/64. Served to Lee's surrender. Hometown: in AL.

Sellars, E.A.: Enlisted 3/11/62. Captured Gettysburg, sent to Ft. Delaware, DE. Died chronic diarrhea 4/29/65.

Shepherd, Robert Edmund: 70, enlisted 7/03/61, married, physician. Born in New Jersey. Detailed as a hospital steward and promoted to surgeon. Hometown: Eufaula, AL.

Skinner, William E.: 29, enlisted 7/03/61, married, farmer. Captured Sharpsburg 9/17/62 and exchanged 11/10/62. Died 10/06/64 at home in Eufaula, AL. Hometown: Eufaula, AL.

Smith, James D.: 40, enlisted 4/04/62, married, mechanic. Discharged 6/30/64. Hometown: Clayton, AL.

Snow, L.M.: 22, enlisted 7/03/61, single, farmer. Died 10/01/61. Hometown: Eufaula, AL.

Spencer, G.E.: 23, enlisted 7/03/61, single, farmer. Wounded head and captured Gettysburg 7/02/63. Discharged to Invalid Corps with duty in Greenville, AL. 8/23/64. Paroled 6/07/65. 5'11", light complexion, blue eyes, auburn hair. Hometown: Henderson Store, AL.

Spurlock, James A.: Enlisted 7/03/61. Wounded Fredericksburg 12/19/62. Killed Knoxville 11/25/63. Hometown: in AL.

Spurlock, M.R.: Farmer. Discharged 4/18/63. 5'4" fair complexion, blue eyes, dark hair. Hometown: in AL.

Spurlock, Ras S.: 18, enlisted 7/03/61, single, farmer. Discharged 12 01/61. Hometown: Eufaula, AL.

Stephens, James: 22, enlisted 8/15/62, married, farmer. Promoted to CPL. Discharged tuber-

culosis 12/02/62. Died 12/04/62. NOK: Ludia Stephens, wife. Hometown: Ozark, AL.

Stephens, Levi, Jr.: 18, enlisted 8/15/62, single, farmer. Died typhoid 4/05/63. NOK: Levi Stephens, Sr., father. Hometown: Ozark, AL.

Strickland, Evin: 28, enlisted 7/03/61, married, farmer. Discharged 11/13/61. Hometown: Eufaula, AL.

Sylvester, James E.: 18, enlisted 7/03/61, single, clerk. Promoted 3SGT. Killed Manassas 8/28/62. NOK: Thomas K. Sylvester, father. Hometown: Eufaula, AL.

Tate, James F.: 23, enlisted 7/03/61, married, farmer. Wounded Sharpsburg 9/17/62. Captured Gettysburg, sent to Ft. Delaware, DE. Died smallpox 11/29/63. Hometown: Eufaula, AL.

Thornton, Joseph B.: 24, enlisted 7/03/61, single, physician. Died cystitis (inflammation of bladder) 9/20/61. Hometown: Eufaula, AL.

Thweatt, Pink: 18, enlisted 7/03/61, single, clerk. Discharged 12/11/61. Hometown: Eufaula, AL.

Toney, William: 20, enlisted 7/03/61, single, student. Elected 2SGT. Mortally wounded Cross Keys 6/08/62, died 7/15/62. NOK: William Toney, Sr., father. Hometown: Eufaula, AL.

Towler, James R.: 28, enlisted 4/04/62, married, farmer. Captured Cross Keys 6/08/62, paroled 6/08/62, exchanged 8/05/62. Captured Bethal Church, sent to Elmira, NY. Died smallpox 1/25/65. 5'5½". Hometown: Eufaula, AL.

Watts, James R.: 24, enlisted 7/03/61, single. Promoted 2CPL 1/01/63. Wounded Chickamauga 9/19/63. Served to Lee's surrender. Hometown: Eufaula, AL.

Wellborne, Randolph W.: 18, enlisted 7/03/61, single, student. Promoted CPL, 4SGT, and 2SGT 11/19/62. Wounded hand Cross Keys 6/08/62. Mortally wounded Chickamauga 9/20/63, died 9/23/63. NOK: Solon A. Wellborne, father. Hometown: Eufaula, AL.

White, F.L.: Mortally wounded, died 5/31/64.

Wicker, Henry W.: 40, enlisted 7/03/61, married, engineer. Detached as teamster. Discharged 10/05/64 "time as conscript up." Hometown: Bushville, AL.

Wicker, Julius C.: 18, enlisted 2/13/62, single, farmer. Served to Lee's surrender. Hometown: Bushville, AL.

Wilkins, John W.: 23, enlisted 7/03/61, married, engineer. Died typhoid 10/24/64. Hometown: Eufaula, AL.

Woodall, James H.: 30, enlisted 8/15/62, married, farmer. Born CT. Wounded Chickamauga 9/19–20/63. Discharged loss of vision 1/23/64. Hometown: Newton, AL.

Woodward, Elijah: 28, enlisted 8/15/62, married, farmer. Born CT. Deserted and captured Frederick, MD. 7/04/63, sent to Ft. Delaware, DE. Took oath and released 5/10/65. 5'8", dark complexion, black eyes, black hair. Hometown: in AL.

Worthington, Charles M.: 22, enlisted 7/03/61, married, farmer. Wounded Cross Keys 6/08/62. Detached as tax collector, Barbour County. Hometown: in AL.

Company L

Abercrombie, Alfred S.: 20, enlisted 3/15/62. Died of pneumonia 5/15/62. NOK: Mary D. Abercrombie, mother. Hometown: Perote, AL.

Allen, John W.: 22, enlisted 3/11/62, single, farmer. Detailed as ambulance driver and hospital guard. Served to Lee's surrender. Hometown: Pine Grove, AL.

Allen, R.W.: 18, enlisted 12/03/63, single, farmer. Mortally wounded shoulder at Fussell's Mill 8/16/64. Hometown: Perote, AL.

Anderson, Joseph: Enlisted 8/21/62. Captured at Gettysburg 7/01/63. Hometown: Newton, AL.

Baker, Nicholas: 30, enlisted 3/11/62, married, farmer. Transferred from Company F 3/01/63. Wounded right thigh at Chickamauga (caused paralysis). Detached to Columbus, GA. Quartermaster. Hometown: Monticella, AL.

Banks, G.W.: 20, enlisted 3/11/62, married, farmer. NOK: Mary Banks, wife. Hometown: Perote, AL.

Bass, Benagay: 30, enlisted 3/11/62, married, farmer. Went AWOL, captured and held at Camp Cooper, Macon, GA. Wounded 12/08/64. Served to Lee's surrender. Hometown: Perote, AL.

Bassett, James N.: 18, enlisted 3/11/62, single, farmer. Died of chronic diarrhea 6/27/62. Hometown: Perote, AL.

Bates, David: 20, enlisted 3/11/62, married, farmer. Died of acute diarrhea following measles 5/12/62. Hometown: Perote, AL.

Bates, William: 18, enlisted 3/11/62, single, farmer. Died of typhoid 5/02/62. Hometown: Perote, AL.

Bean, James F.: 18, enlisted 3/11/62, single, farmer. Wounded Knoxville 11/25/63 and slightly in side Fussell's Mill 8/16/64. Promoted 3SGT 3/01/64 and 2SGT 12/xx/64. Awarded Southern Cross of Honor 12/10/64.

Reduced in rank due to disobedience of orders. Hometown: Farriorville, AL.

Blair, Levi:: 28, enlisted 7/03/61, single, farmer. Deserted/captured 1/22/65.

Bonner, Charles H.: Enlisted 3/11/62, farmer. Elected 2CPL Promoted 4SGT 12/31/62. Killed 9/20/63 Chickamauga.

Bonner, Dixon D.: 24, enlisted. Promoted 1SGT 10/31/62. Wounded Gettysburg 6/02/63, severely thigh Spotsylvania 5/06/64, and seriously in arms and side Fussell's Mill 10/07/64.

Bonner, Robert A.: 18, enlisted 3/11/61, single, farmer. Died 5/06/62. NOK: Wyatt Bonner, father.

Bonner, William A.: 30, enlisted 3/11/62, married, farmer. Died 5/06/62.

Boswell, J.F.: 25, enlisted 3/11/62, single, farmer. AWOL at time of Lee's surrender. Hometown: Farriorville, AL.

Boswell, J.W.: Enlisted 3/11/62. AWOL for the last two years. Hometown: in AL.

Brooke, Marcus L.: 22, married, farmer. Severely wounded Cold Harbor 6/27/62. Discharged 10/25/62. 5'10", dark complexion, hazel eyes, dark hair. Hometown: Perote, AL.

Brown, William A.: 23, enlisted 3/11/62, married, farmer. Mortally wounded Cedar Run 8/09/62. NOK: Adaline Brown, wife. Hometown: in AL.

Bryan, Lee M.: 19, enlisted 3/11/62, student. Elected 1LT. Severely wounded Cold Harbor 7/06/62. Resigned 3/28/63. 6'0", fair complexion, blue eyes, light hair. Took oath in Montgomery, AL, 5/23/65.

Coffield, J.C.: Enlisted 3/11/62. Died Erysipelas (skin infection) 8/05/62.

Cole, J.J.: 24, enlisted 3/11/62, single, farmer. Died typhoid 5/15/62.

Collins, Thomas R.: 16, enlisted 3/11/62. Wounded Fredericksburg 12/19/62. Promoted 2CPL 1/01/63 and 4SGT 12/01/64. Awarded Southern Cross of Honor 12/10/64. Served to Lee's surrender.

Cope, James: 23, enlisted 3/11/62, single, farmer. Died fever 7/09/62. NOK: John Cope, father.

Cope, Thomas: 20, enlisted 3/11/62, single, farmer. Detached as a guard at Augusta, GA, powder works 1863–64.

Dean, Charles K.: 19, enlisted 3/11/62, single, farmer. Wounded slightly in leg Darbytown Road 10/07/64.

Dorn, William: 20, enlisted 3/11/62, married, farmer. Died camp fever 5/07/62. NOK: Martha T. Dorn, wife.

Eddins, P.R.: 29, enlisted 5/05/62, married, farmer. Wounded slightly chest at Darbytown

Road 10/07/64. Served to Lee's surrender. NOK: A.A. Eddins, wife.

Emerson, Francis M.: 30, enlisted 7/03/61, married, farmer. Promoted 2LT 7/30/62. Mortally wounded Manassas 8/30/62, died 9/12/62. NOK: Martha F. Emerson, wife.

Foster, J.F.: 30, enlisted 3/11/62, married, farmer. AWOL much of the time.

Frazier, David M.: 26, enlisted 3/11/62. Transferred from Company F. Wounded Darbytown 10/07/64.

Garrett, George W.: 30, enlisted 3/11/62, married, farmer. Sick and captured Gettysburg 6/02/63, escaped 10/01/63. Severely wounded shoulder Ft. Harrison 9/30/64. Served to Lee's surrender. Hometown: Pine Grove, AL.

Garrett, H. Turner: 21, single, farmer. Died 5/25/62. NOK: Elizabeth Garrett, mother.

Gause, Jesse L.: 30, enlisted 3/11/62, married, farmer. Killed Hazel River 8/22/62. NOK: Martha Gause, wife. Hometown: Perote, AL.

Gay, Gilbert M.: 25, enlisted 3/11/62, married, farmer. Died typhoid 7/30/62. NOK: Mary A. Gay, wife. Hometown: Perote, AL.

Gilmore, Angus M.: 30, enlisted 3/11/62, married, blacksmith. Died pneumonia 4/30/62.

Gilmore, W.H.: 28, enlisted 3/11/62, married, teacher. Transferred from Company I 8/19/62. Severely wounded Manassas 8/28/62. Killed by artillery at Lookout Valley 10/30/63.

Green, John: 27, enlisted 3/11/62, single, farmer. Died 4/30/62. NOK: William A. Green, father. Hometown: Perote, AL.

Green, Lovett: 20, enlisted 3/11/62, single, farmer. Died 4/15/62. NOK: William A. Green, father. Hometown: Perote, AL.

Hardy, S.T.: 25, enlisted 3/11/62, married, shoemaker. Wounded at Cedar Run 8/09/62. Detailed at Columbus, GA, as a shoemaker and Montgomery, AL, Quartermaster. Hometown: Perote, AL.

Hart, Allen F.: 49, enlisted 3/11/62, married, farmer. Detailed as a litter bearer and medical attendant. Served to Lee's surrender. Hometown: in AL.

Hart, Reuben: 21, enlisted 3/11/62, married, farmer. Died 5/14/62. NOK: Mary A. Hart, wife. Hometown: Mount Hilliard, AL.

Haynes, W.A.: 25, enlisted 3/11/62, married, coachsmith. Detached as ambulance driver and gunsmith. Served to Lee's surrender. Hometown: Pine Level, AL.

Henderson, George R.: 18, enlisted 5/20/62, single, farmer. Wounded in knee and right shoulder and captured at Gettysburg 7/02/63, exchanged 5/01/64. Served to Lee's surrender. Hometown: Perote, AL.

Henderson, Joseph: 24, enlisted 3/11/62, single, farmer. Captured at Gettysburg 7/02/63 and sent to Ft. Delaware, DE. Died of chronic diarrhea 6/04/64. Hometown: Perote, AL.

Henderson, Matthew: 26, enlisted 5/20/62, married, farmer. Served as litter bearer. Detached as nurse in Columbus, GA. Hometown: in AL.

Hicks, G.W.: 19, enlisted 3/11/62, single, farmer. Severely wounded Chickamauga 9/20/63. Transferred to Company D 1/31/65. Hometown: Farriorville, AL.

Hicks, James W.: 40, enlisted 3/11/62, single, farmer. Discharged 1/02/64. Hometown: in AL.

Hill, Robert H.: 26, enlisted 3/11/62, married, physician. Elected CPT. Killed at Cross Keys 6/08/62. Oates wrote, "A good officer and all the time at his post." NOK: Lizzie Lee Hill, wife. Hometown: in AL.

Hooks, Daniel L.: 26, enlisted 3/11/62. Elected 2LT 3/15/62. Died 5/28/62. Hometown: Indian Creek, AL.

Hooks, Thomas J.: 36, enlisted 3/11/62, married, farmer. Died 5/15/62. NOK: Francis C. Hooks, wife. Hometown: in AL.

Hough, Joseph E.: 47, enlisted 3/11/62, married, farmer. Detached as hospital banker in Montgomery, AL. Paroled Montgomery, AL, 5/10/65. 5'8", light complexion, gray eyes, gray hair. Hometown: in AL.

Johnson, Charles C.: 22, enlisted 5/30/62, married, farmer. Died 1/15/62. NOK: Matilda Johnson, wife. Hometown: Coffeeville, AL.

Kelley, David A.: 26, elected 4CPL 3/11/62, married, farmer. Reduced in rank for disobedience 12/13/62. Captured at Gettysburg 7/02/63 and sent to Ft. Delaware, DE. Took oath and released 6/14/65. 6'0", dark complexion, gray eyes, dark hair. Hometown: in AL.

Kelley, James T.: 26, enlisted 3/11/62, married, farmer. Hometown: Perote, AL.

Lain, W.L.: 27, enlisted 3/11/62, married, farmer. Wounded at Cedar Run 8/09/62 and Chickamauga 9/20/63. Promoted CPL 3/??/64 and 2SGT 6/30/64. Served to Lee's surrender. Oates writes that he was "a splendid soldier." Hometown: in AL.

Lloyd, J.: 27, enlisted 10/25/64, single, farmer. Transferred from Company E, 25th Battalion 10/25/64. Served to Lee's surrender. Hometown: in AL.

Lloyd, Leroy: 19, enlisted 3/11/62, single, farmer. Awarded Southern Cross of Honor 12/10/64. Served to Lee's surrender. Hometown: Perote, AL.

Long, Benjamin Franklin: Enlisted 5/09/62. Fair

complexion, black eyes, light hair. Transferred to Company L 1/01/65. Served to Lee's surrender. Hometown: Comer, AL.

McClaney, James: 28, enlisted 3/11/62, married, farmer. Severely wounded Cold Harbor 6/27/62. Elected tax collector for Pike County and discharged 10/08/63. Hometown: Farriorville, AL.

McClendon, Howell: 28, enlisted 3/11/62, married, painter. Mortally wounded Cold Harbor 6/27/62, died 7/01/62. NOK: Sarah McClendon, wife. Hometown: Mt. Hillis, AL.

McMorris, Philip "Phil": 25, enlisted 3/11/62, single, farmer. Captured Gettysburg 7/02/63 and sent to Ft. Delaware, DE. Died typhoid 8/12/63. Hometown: in AL.

Matthews, E.T.: 25, enlisted 5/05/62, married, farmer. Mortally wounded Spotsylvania 5/13/64. Hometown: in AL.

Matthews, J.L : 27, enlisted 3/11/62, single, farmer. Died typhoid 8/29/62. Hometown: in AL.

May, J.D.: 20, single, student. Discharged 6/19/62. 5'9", dark complexion, black eyes, black hair. Hometown: Helican, AL.

Meredith, Eli: 28, enlisted 3/05/62, married, farmer. Wounded Cross Keys 6/08/62. Detailed as a nurse in Columbus, GA, and Charlotte, NC. Paroled in Charlotte, NC, 5/02/65. Hometown: Monticella, AL.

Mims, David J.: Died pneumonia 4/21/62. NOK: Sarah Mims, wife.

Moore, Joseph F.: 26, enlisted 3/11/62, single, farmer. Died diarrhea 5/16/62. Hometown: Mt. Hilliard, AL.

Morgan, W.G.: 38, enlisted 8/20/62, married, farmer. Wounded Fredericksburg 12/19/62. Captured Gettysburg 7/02/63 and sent to Ft. Delaware, DE, and Point Lookout, MD. Exchanged 11/01/64. Served to Lee's surrender. Hometown: Newton, AL.

Nelms, H.: 38, enlisted 3/11/62, married, farmer. Discharged 1/02/64 rheumatism and atrophy of muscle in right thigh. Hometown: Farriorville, AL.

Newton, John L.: 30, enlisted 3/11/62, married, farmer. Wounded Fredericksburg 12/19/62. Wounded left leg and captured Gettysburg 7/02/63. Paroled 7/31/63. Severely wounded foot Darbytown 10/07/64. Hometown: Clayton, AL.

Norris, Hugh: 38, enlisted 3/11/62, married, farmer. Detailed as hospital cook and guard. Served to Lee's surrender. Hometown: Farriorville, AL.

Norris, W.: 21, enlisted 3/11/62, single, farmer. Died of disease 5/08/62. Hometown: Indian Creek, AL.

Osburne, J.L.: 17, enlisted 5/11/62, single, farmer. Wounded Chickamauga 9/20/63. Promoted to 5SGT. Served to Lee's surrender. Hometown: Abbeville, AL.

Osburne, M.A.: 21, enlisted 5/11/62, single, farmer. Died 6/10/64. Hometown: Abbeville, AL.

Outlaw, W.Z.: 28, enlisted 3/11/62, married, farmer. Died chronic diarrhea 5/12/63. Hometown: Perote, AL.

Owens, William: 23, enlisted 3/11/62, married, farmer. Wounded Manassas 8/28/62. Served to Lee's surrender. Hometown: Indian Creek, AL.

Paul, Robert: 32, enlisted 3/11/62, married, farmer. Elected 3LT. Died 5/24/62. NOK: Susanna Paul, wife. Hometown: Perote, AL.

Peach, George W.: 22, enlisted 3/11/62, single, farmer. Elected 1SGT. Mortally wounded Cold Harbor 6/27/62, died 7/21/62. NOK: George Peach, father. Hometown: Perote, AL.

Perkins, Henry L.: 17, enlisted 3/11/62, single, farmer. Wounded right shoulder Sharpsburg 9/17/62. Hometown: Perote, AL.

Posey, H.H.: 27, enlisted 3/15/62, married, farmer. Discharged 7/11/63 anchylosis (stiffness of joint). 5'8", fair complexion, blue eyes, light hair. Hometown: Mt. Hilliard, AL.

Post, Noah: 25, enlisted 3/11/62, married, farmer. Detailed as teamster. Promoted 1CPL. Served to Lee's surrender. Hometown: Friar's Bridge, AL.

Post, Simon: 38, enlisted 3/11/62, married, farmer. Detailed as teamster. Captured Salisburg, NC, 4/12/65. 5'5½", dark complexion, blue eyes, dark hair. Hometown: Friar's Bridge, AL.

Raford, Philip: Enlisted 3/11/62, married, blacksmith. Died 10/04/62. Hometown: Perote, AL.

Renfrew, Neal: 20, enlisted 3/11/62, married, farmer. Died pneumonia 6/17/62. NOK: Sarah E. Renfrew. Hometown: in AL.

Renfrew, Thomas: 22, enlisted 3/11/62, married, farmer. Died smallpox 10/04/62. Hometown: in AL.

Renfroe, Enoch: 24, enlisted 3/11/62, married, farmer. Wounded right leg amputated Cold Harbor 6/27/62. AWOL. Hometown: in AL.

Riley, John N.: 26, enlisted 3/11/62, married, farmer. NOK: Amanda Riley. Hometown: in AL.

Rich, Ewen A.: 24, enlisted 3/11/62, married, farmer. Elected 5SGT. Promoted 3SGT. Reduced in rank for disobeying orders. Captured "while foraging the dead" Mossy Creek 1/22/64 and sent to Rock Island, IL, and

Camp Chase, OH. Died smallpox 4/18/64. Hometown: Arbenter, AL.

Robertson, William Elias: 25, enlisted 3/11/62, married, farmer. Severely wounded Cross Keys 6/08/62. Captured Chickamauga 9/19/63. Exchanged and discharged 7/20/64. Hometown: Pine Grove, AL.

Rogers, G.W.: 30, enlisted 3/11/62, married, farmer. Died measles 5/11/62. Hometown: Perote, AL.

Rowell, Rich W.: 27, enlisted 3/11/62, married, farmer. Discharged 2/25/63 general debility. Wounded Chickamauga 9/20/63. Captured 4/06/65 and sent to Libby Prison, Richmond, VA. Took oath and released 6/30/65. 5'7", light complexion, gray eyes, dark brown hair. Hometown: Mt. Hilliard, AL.

Sellers, Evander D.: 20, enlisted 3/11/62, single, farmer. Died pneumonia 5/28/62. NOK: Elisha H. Sellers. Hometown: in AL.

Sellers, William Preston: 20, enlisted 3/11/62, single, farmer. Captured Gettysburg 7/02/63. Died chronic diarrhea 3/11/64. Hometown: in AL.

Simmons, J.S.: 27, enlisted 3/11/62, married, physician. Promoted to surgeon 10/11/63. Hometown: Farriorville, AL.

Smith, Elijah: 20, enlisted 3/11/62, single, farmer. Killed Sharpsburg 9/17/62. NOK: Mary Smith, mother. Hometown: Perote, AL.

Smith, Wesley: 25, enlisted 3/11/62, married, carpenter. Killed Knoxville 11/25/63. Hometown: China Grove, AL.

Snider, G.M.: Died chronic diarrhea 6/11/62.

Stewart, J.F.: 18, enlisted 3/11/62, married, farmer. Captured Gettysburg 7/02/63, sent to Ft. Delaware, DE. Took oath and released 6/14/65. 5'5", sallow complexion, hazel eyes, dark hair. Hometown: Perote, AL.

Stough, David J.: 25, enlisted 3/11/62, married, farmer. Killed Cold Harbor 6/27/62. Hometown: Friar's Bridge, AL.

Stough, J.H.: 39, enlisted 3/11/62, married, farmer. Captured Gettysburg 7/02/63, sent to Ft. Delaware, DE. Took oath and released 6/14/65. 5'8", sallow complexion, brown eyes, dark hair. Hometown: Friar's Bridge, AL.

Strom, Joseph: Enlisted 3/11/62. Died typhoid 9/04/62. NOK: Lucy Strom, mother. Hometown: in AL.

Trawick, John T.: 25, enlisted 3/11/62, married. Died pneumonia 6/27/62. NOK: Mary E. Trawick, wife. Hometown: Friar's Bridge, AL.

Vinson, Levin: 35, enlisted 3/11/62, married, blacksmith. Elected 4SGT. Killed Gettysburg 7/02/63. NOK: Mary A. Vinson, wife. Hometown: Blue Port, AL.

Wicker, Robert H.: 21, enlisted 3/11/62, single, farmer. Wounded Cold Harbor 6/27/62. Promoted 2LT 10/02/62. Captured Gettysburg 7/02/63, sent to Ft. Delaware, DE, and Point Lookout, MD. Took oath and released 6/12/65. 5'7", light complexion, blue eyes, dark hair. Hometown: Perote, AL.

Williamson, John: 20, enlisted 3/11/62, single, farmer. Died pneumonia 6/25/62. Hometown: Perote, AL.

Willis, W.T.: 25, enlisted 3/11/62, married, farmer. Died pneumonia 7/01/63. Hometown: Pine Grove, AL.

Appendix B: 15th Alabama Infantry Regiment Battle Flag

According to tradition, this flag was presented to the regiment (Col. James Cantey accepting) at Ft. Mitchell in the summer of 1861, by Miss Mary Chambers of Russell County. While the regiment probably did receive a flag at that time, this flag could not have been issued any earlier than November 1861. This flag was among those manufactured by three sewing circles in Richmond, Virginia, at the request of Confederate Quartermaster Colin Selph. According to former Colonel A.A. Lowther, 15th Alabama Infantry, this flag was carried by the regiment during Stonewall Jackson's Valley campaign and fought under at the battles of Winchester, Cross Keys and Port Republic of that campaign. It was again fought under at Cold Harbor, in the campaign against McClellan below Richmond, and at Cedar Run. When the regiment was issued a new flag, Lowther retained possession of this flag. The flag was presented to the Alabama Department of Archives and History by Lowther's daughter Miss Virginia Lowther of Macon, Georgia. It was received on March 18, 1927.

Alabama Department of Archives and History

The 15th Alabama Battle Flag (courtesy Alabama Department of Archives and History, Montgomery, Alabama).

Appendix C: Reunion of the 15th Alabama Infantry

Reunion of the 15th Alabama Infantry Regiment at Montgomery, Alabama, November 12 and 13, 1902 (courtesy Alabama Department of Archives and History, Montgomery, Alabama).

Appendix D:
Regimental Statistics

Enrollment

Enrolled				Surrendered		
Officers	**Men**	**Aggregate**		**Officers**	**Men**	**Aggregate**
78	1555	1633		15	204	219

Casualties

Killed				Died of Wounds		
Officers	**Men**	**Aggregate**		**Officers**	**Men**	**Aggregate**
17	168	185		8	72	80

Other Deaths and Prisoners of War

Died of Disease				Absent/Captured		
Officers	**Men**	**Aggregate**		**Officers**	**Men**	**Aggregate**
8	430	438		5	131	136

Other Separations

Resigned	Retired	Discharged	Transferred	Deserted
29	21	183	46	51

J. Gary Laines and Morris M. Penny, *Law's Alabama Brigade in the War Between the Union and the Confederacy,* pp. 365–366.

Chapter Notes

Chapter One

1. Val L. McGee, *Claybank Memories: A History of Dale County, Alabama* (Dale County Historical Society), p. 29.

2. We know the Faust family was in Sumter County, Georgia, in December 1860 because Henry got married there. We know William joined Company E, 15th Alabama at Westville, Alabama, in July 1961.

3. Ages were taken from the 1860 Census.

4. Death certificates obtained from Ancestry.com and their gravestones.

5. Marriage certificate obtained from Sumter County, Georgia, probate.

6. For a description of prewar Ozark, Alabama, read McGee, pp. 19–29.

7. William did join the Confederate Army on July 2, 1861, at the age of 16, although his enlistment records reflect that he joined at 18. He served through all the battles in the east until captured at Gettysburg exactly two years after enlisting and spent the rest of the war confined at Fort Delaware. After the war he married Missouri Ellen Stubbs and they had seven children before he died on May 15, 1884. He is buried at Pleasant Ridge Cemetery in Arguta, Alabama. He is my great-grandfather and the inspiration for this book.

8. McGee, pp. 39–40.

9. "Uncle Billy," as he was affectionately called by the citizens of Ozark, did build and run the Mixon Hotel in Ozark. The Mixon Hotel became the social hub of the community in postwar Dale County.

10. William's description came from his Oath of Allegiance signed on June 14, 1865.

11. Mary Love Fleming, "Dale County and its People During the Civil War," *Alabama Historical Quarterly* (Spring 1957): p. 67.

12. For a description of Westville, Alabama, read Fleming, pp. 61–109.

13. Obtained from the 1860 Census and Fleming (see above).

14. McGee, pp. 35–36.

15. Roll of Daleville, Alabama, militia, signed October 3, 1860, found in Ancestry.com.

16. All of this information was obtained from their enlistment records from the Alabama Civil War Database from the Alabama Department of Archives and History.

17. This information was gathered by an examination of the 1860 Census.

18. Daniel and Thomas were twins.

19. Obtained from Soldier Service Enlistment Records and 1860 Census.

20. Glenn W. LaFantasie, *Gettysburg Requiem: The Life and Lost Causes of Confederate Colonel William C. Oates*, p. 29.

21. Fleming, p. 67.

22. William married Eliza Jones White on January 5, 1858. In the 1860 Census William is 24 and Eliza is 22. As stated, William is working as a mechanic. William commanded Company E after the resignation of Essau Brooks and was later promoted to captain on February 8, 1862. William was wounded at the Battle of Fredericksburg on December 19, 1862. He resigned on August 28, 1863, returned home and became a minister. William and his brothers moved to Texas after the war. William and Eliza had eight children. William died on December 12, 1926, in Dallas, Texas.

23. William A. Edwards, "A Most Interesting Letter," dated November 11, 1915, addressed to William E. Painter; published in the *Southern Star* on Jan. 5, 1916.

24. Ibid.

25. Ambrose Edwards, *A History of Company E, 15th Alabama Infantry Regiment.* http://www.flemingmultimedia.com/15thAlaCoE/15thALhistory.html.

26. William Robert Houghton and Mitchell B. Houghton, *Two Boys in the Civil War and After* (Montgomery, AL: Paragon Press, 1912), p. 17.

27. Ibid., p. 17.

28. Prewar information on Private Houghton was gathered from Houghton, pp. 16–17, and the 1860 Census. In 1860, Mitchell was living with his parents and two younger sisters in Newton. In 1870, Mitchell is living in Union Springs, Alabama, working as a clerk and living with his sister, whose husband was killed at Gettysburg. In the 1880 Census, Mitchell is

still in Union Springs living with his mother and sister and working as a merchant. In 1910, Mitchell is living in Montgomery with his nephew and niece, working as a farmer. Apparently, Mitchell never married. Civil War records describe him as 5'10", light hair, dark eyes, and dark complexion.

29. John Fletcher Treutlen married Carolina (Carrie) in 1855. In the 1860 Census he is a merchant in Eufaula with three children. Captain Treutlen never officially commanded the company, as he was elected to lieutenant colonel, or second in command of the 15th Infantry. He resigned his commission on April 28, 1863, citing "feeble health"; Surgeon Shepherd cited specifically: "Pulmonary hemorrhage on several occasions." In 1870, he is still living in Eufaula working as an insurance agent with six children. In 1880, John and Carrie are living in Washington, D.C., with two children; he is working as a "clerk in Capitol." In 1890, he is still living in Washington running a boarding house. John died February 28, 1908, in Eufaula.

30. Houghton, p. 18.

31. William C. Oates, *The War Between the Union and Confederacy and Its Lost Opportunities*, pp. 709–711.

32. W.A. McClendon, *Recollections of War Times, by an Old Veteran While Under Stonewall Jackson and Lieutenant General James Longstreet, How I Got In, and How I Got Out*, p. 16.

33. See McClendon's book below for a brief biography but specific information about his service in the war from his service records. Gus worked his way up through the ranks from second corporal to first lieutenant. He was wounded once at Fussell's Mill on August 16, 1864, when a spent round struck him in the lip and loosened two teeth. He was in command of Company G at the time of surrender. After the war Gus married Lake Erie Perry on November 24, 1865, and they had six children. Gus spent the remainder of his life in Abbeville as a farmer. He died on April 19, 1921, and is buried at Pleasant Grove Baptist Church in Henry County, Alabama.

34. McClendon, p. 11.

35. Ibid., p. 11.

36. Ibid., p. 14.

37. Enlistment records show that William signed up on July 3, 1861, but this is not in line with his recollection that the Battle of Manassas (July 21, 1861) happened before he signed up. The reason for this is that the enlistees "signed up" in their militia assembly areas but were asked to sign up again for "three years or the duration of the war" once in the regimental assembly areas. This was a requirement to join the Confederate Army.

38. LaFantasie, *Gettysburg Requiem*, p. 30.

39. McClendon, p. 15.

40. Ibid., p. 15.

41. Ibid., p. 15. This would be the last time William saw his father, who would die two years later on June 23, 1863.

42. Ibid., p. 16.

43. Ibid., p. 16.

44. These men were probably late arrivals or new recruits, as Oates states that his company was the last to arrive at Fort Mitchell.

45. McClendon, p. 20.

46. Oates, pp. 673–679.

47. Archibald would be wounded at Knoxville, Tennessee, on November 26, 1863, and killed on December 10, 1864—the same day he would receive the Southern Cross of Honor.

48. Obtained from the 1860 Census.

49. McClendon, p. 29.

50. Oates, p. 69.

51. McClendon, p. 19.

52. Houghton, p. 19.

53. Oates, pp. 70–71.

54. Ibid., p. 69.

55. Oates, pp. 69–70. Oates remained extremely bitter about what he felt was this manipulation by Colonel Cantey, as he wrote about the incident forty-five years later. Note there is no "J" company in Civil War regiments because of the 19th-century similarity of the written "I" and "J." Company L from Perote (then in Pike, now Bullock County, Alabama) would be added in the spring of 1862.

56. http://en.wikipedia.org/wiki/15th_Regiment_Alabama_Infantry.

57. McClendon, pp. 22–23.

58. Ibid., p. 19.

59. Oates, p. 74.

60. Houghton, p. 19.

61. McClendon, p. 20.

62. Barnett Hardeman Cody, "Letters of Barnett Hardeman Cody and others, 1861–1864," *Georgia Historical Quarterly* 23 (1939): p. 283.

63. *The War of the Rebellion: A Compilation of the Official Records of the Union and Confederate Armies*, 70 vols. (Washington, D.C.: U.S. War Department, 1880–1901). Hereinafter referred to as OR.

64. From Wikipedia.

65. Houghton, p. 22 and pp. 57–58.

66. Cody, p. 287 and p. 363. Of this last mess, by the way, Balkom was killed at Sharpsburg, Oates and Cody at Gettysburg, while Woodham alone survived the war.

67. Fleming.

Chapter Two

1. Houghton, p. 20.

2. Samuel D. Lary, "Sam Lary's Scraps from my Knapsack," *Alabama Historical Quarterly* 18, no. 4 (Winter 1956): p. 508.

3. Oates, p. 75.

4. Cody, p. 284.

5. McClendon, p. 28.

6. *Atlanta Constitution*, "Career of Father Brannan, Confederacy's Youngest Enlisted Soldier," p. 5. The article highlighted a very interesting life, in which "danger had a charm to him and he really enjoyed the thrill of battle." After the war, Patrick became a lawyer and practiced in Kentucky and Texas, even becoming a Texas district attorney. Giving that up, he entered the ministry and was a priest at the Church of the Holy Family in Columbus.

7. 1860 Census.

8. Oates, p. 748.

9. Ibid., p. 75.

10. Lary, p. 509.

11. McClendon, p. 26.

12. Oates, p. 75.

13. Lary, p. 509.

14. McClendon, p. 35.

15. Ibid., pp. 76–77; Henry Gray, *Anatomy, Descriptive and Applied*, 18th ed. (Philadelphia: Lea & Febiger, 1910).

16. Oates, p. 76.

17. Lary, p. 514.

18. LaFantasie, p. 33.

19. McClendon, p. 37.

20. Ibid, p. 39.

21. Lary, pp. 511–12.

22. OR, p. 81.

23. Houghton, pp. 20–21.

24. *AHQ.*

25. Glen LaFantasie, *Alabama Historical Quarterly* 18, no. 3–4 (Fall-Winter 1961): pp. 291–299.

26. LaFantasie, p. 34.

27. Glenn W. LaFantasie, "Civil War Soldiers: Decimated by Disease," *Articles Featuring Civil War Soldiers from History Net Magazines*, p. 8. This article was first published in *Military Historical Quarterly* (Spring 2004).

28. Ibid.

29. Contained in a letter written to his wife, Marcena, just prior to the Battle of Cross Keys, in which Martin was killed. The letter was found on his body and mailed to the family 30 years later. This letter was found in Ancestry.com and will henceforth be called "Stough Letter."

30. Oates, p. 85.

31. Houghton, p. 21.

32. Ibid., p. 21.

33. Ibid., p. 20.

34. Ibid., p. 22.

35. Oates, p. 85.

36. Ibid., p. 632.

37. McClendon, pp. 48–49.

38. Ibid., p. 49.

39. Casper W. Boyd, "His Last Letters Written Home," *Alabama Historical Quarterly* 23 (1961): pp. 291–292. Private Boyd is still living with his parents, Alfred and Caroline, in the 1860 Census. A series of letters written to them is published in the *Alabama Historical Quarterly* 23, pages 291–298. He was wounded at Cross Keys on June 8, 1862, and died from his wounds on June 29, 1862. The last letter to his parents was written by his nurse, Kate V. Brand; with it she encloses a ring and a lock of his hair.

40. Ibid., pp. 291–292.

41. Stough Letter.

42. Houghton, pp. 58–59.

43. Ibid., p. 59.

44. Cody, p. 288.

45. *AHQ* 23 (Fall-Winter 1961): pp. 294.

46. Stough Letter.

47. Ibid., p. 288.

48. Boyd, 296.

49. Houghton, p. 179.

Chapter Three

1. http://www.goodreads.com/author/quotes/546888.Stonewall_Jackson.

2. This strategic situation was taken from Shelby Foote's superb *The Civil War: A Narrative*, vol. 1, pp. 417, 419, and 440.

3. Foote, vol. 1, p. 435.

4. Cody, p. 365.

5. J.M. Ellison married Camilla Searcy Key in 1857. She was a relative of Francis Scott Key. The young couple lived on a plantation in Creek Stand, Alabama. Joseph was elected second lieutenant on July 26, 1861. However, he submitted his resignation on November 13, 1862, because J.H. Ellison was promoted over him. Regimental commander A.A. Lowther endorsed the resignation with, "The officer resigning is not fit to be an officer of any grade for reasons too numerous to mention." First Lieutenant Ellison joined the 3rd Georgia Cavalry and reached the rank of captain. Several wartime letters to his wife were published in *Georgia Historical Quarterly* 48, no. 2 (June 1964): pp. 229–238.

6. Peter Videau Guerry married Mary A. Harris in South Carolina in 1854. Peter had already been married to Frances and they had two sons and a daughter. In 1850 the couple are living in Columbus, Georgia. In 1860 Peter and Mary are farming at Creek Stand, Alabama. Peter was elected Captain by the Macon County Commissioners, which later became Company C, 15th Alabama Infantry Regiment. Oates describes Captain Guerry as "a gentleman of irreproachable morals, kind-hearted, good-natured and a very efficient officer." Captain Guerry led his company through the Valley Campaign but was shot through the head and killed instantly at the Battle of Cold Harbor on June 27, 1862.

7. Letter from Private Casper W. Boyd, Company I, to his parents in Troy, written on May 3, 1862. *Alabama Historical Quarterly* 23 (1961): p. 292. Private Boyd would receive a gunshot wound during the Valley Campaign and would die in the Confederate Hospital in Charlottesville, Virginia, on June 26, 1862.

8. This requisition was found in Captain Hill's service records.

9. Oates, p. 93.

10. Boyd, pp. 293–294.

11. Houghton, p. 28.

12. McClendon, p. 60.

13. Letter from William A. Edwards written to W.E. Painter on November 11, 1915. "A Most Interesting Letter," *Southern Star*, January 5, 1916.

14. James M. Ellison, "War Letters (1862)," *Georgia Historical Quarterly* 48 (June 1964): pp. 230–231.

15. Ibid., p. 233.

16. Houghton, p. 29.

17. Ellison, p. 231.

18. Oates, pp. 632–633.

19. Oates describes Henry Brainard as a "fine officer—patriotic, faithful and brave as any in the regiment" in his book, pp. 674–675. He would eventually be promoted to captain and command Company G at Gettysburg, where he was killed. His last words were, "O God, that I could see my mother!"

20. McClendon, p. 61.

21. Oates writes that William Richardson "was a bachelor and wealthy farmer residing near Glennville [Alabama]. He was very eccentric; was an officer of great courage, but very little disciplinary power," p. 709.

22. LaFantasie, p. 43.

23. Oates describes Moses Maybin on pp. 692–693 as "a splendid soldier." He had an old black man to take care of him so there was no need for him to mess with the other soldiers, which caused him to be ostracized. He was accepted by the officers, for his slave would often cook for them. His military records are mixed up with those of Thomas M. Maybin. A letter from Captain Oates was found describing him as 5'9", light complexion, blue eyes, brown hair, and a farmer.

24. Oates, p. 693.

25. Dekalb Williams later commanded the company and was promoted to captain. Oates describes him as a gentleman of good morals and fine deportment on page 654 of his book. He served until Lee's surrender, and after the war went into the mercantile business in Brundidge, then Troy, Alabama.

26. Susie K. Senn, a compilation of Civil War letters gathered from *The Southern Advertiser* and published in a book titled *Pike County, Alabama's Civil War News*, p. 76.

27. LaFantasie, p. 44.

28. Casualty list was created based on individual histories from service records.

29. Oates, pp. 105–106.

30. Ibid., p. 101.

31. Senn, p. 73.

32. Foote, vol. 1, p. 464.

33. Ewell's After Action Report from OR, Vol. XI, Part 2.

34. Alabama Archives, *Fifteenth Alabama Infantry Regiment* (hereinafter referred to as A.A.).

35. McClendon, p. 78.

36. Ibid., p. 96.

37. Ibid., p. 96.

38. McClendon, p. 79.

39. Ibid., p. 81.

40. 1860 Census.

41. McClendon, p. 81.

42. Oates, p. 117; also McClendon, pp. 81–82.

43. OR, Vol. XI, Part 2, pp. 614–616, Colonel Trimble's Report.

44. LaFantasie, *Gettysburg Requiem*, p. 45; McClendon, p. 82.

45. Captain Peter Guerry was probably the wealthiest man in the regiment. A farmer in Macon County, Alabama, he was the owner of 46 slaves. Oates describes him on page 607 of his book as "a gentleman of irreproachable morals, kind-hearted, good-natured and a very efficient officer."

46. Oates, p. 607.

47. OR, Vol. XI, Part 2, pp. 614–616, Colonel Trimble's Report.

48. OR, Vol. XI, Part 2, pp. 605–606. This incident was mentioned in General Ewell's Report. This is one of the few instances I have seen a private mentioned for his actions in a division commander's after action report. Frank Champion was the "Audie Murphy" of the regiment. After this battle, he worked directly on Colonel Trimble's staff as an orderly and often scouted behind enemy lines. He was captured on May 14, 1863, during Stoneman's Raid into Virginia but paroled due to "want of transportation." He was again captured after the Battle of Gettysburg on July 6, 1863, and imprisoned at Point Lookout, Maryland. He is the only member of the regiment that I am aware of who escaped from any prison, which he did on May 20, 1864. He continued to serve faithfully until the end of the war. After the war Oates wrote that he became "one of Pike County's best citizens." Frank married Delilah Ann Enzor in 1867 and they had the following children: Virginia (1868), Ira (1869), Delilah (1873), and Crissie (1876). Oates writes that Frank "became a prominent newspaperman" in Montgomery, Alabama. The 1870 Census states that Frank couldn't read or write, which would explain why he was never promoted to an officer's rank. This census also says that he was farming at Pike Cross Roads. The 1880 Census says he *could* read and write and was still farming. The 1900 Census has him working as a "collector," and also says he could read and write.

49. Oates, p. 693. Robert would not only survive his wound but would serve the rest of the war until the surrender on April 9, 1865. After the war, he returned to Henry County, Alabama, and served as justice of the peace.

50. Private Morris would be hospitalized and recover from his wound, but would die of typhoid fever at Hospital #21 in Richmond on November 27, 1862.

51. McClendon, p. 87.

52. OR, p. 88.

53. OR.

54. Locke Weems was adjutant of the regiment, but after the promotion of A.A. Lowther, Colonel Canty appointed him commander of Company A. Oates writes in his book on pp. 588–589, "He was a splendid officer ... admired for his soldierly and gentlemanly conduct." Military records tell us that he died on July 10, 1862, thirteen days after the battle at Cold Harbor.

55. Oates, on page 653–654 of his book, describes George Malone as "very impulsive ... yet no man had a heart more overflowing with human sympathy and kindness." After discharge he lived in Brundidge, Alabama, and was engaged in the mercantile business.

56. Statistics were compiled from the individual soldier's service records.

57. OR, Vol. XI, part 2, pp. 605–606.

58. Foote, p. 516.

59. McClendon, p. 90.

60. Ibid., pp. 92–93.

61. William A. Edwards, Letter from Pate, Texas, 1897.

62. William A. Edwards moved to Dale County from Russell County in order to join his two brothers in the Dale County Beauregards. He was elected first lieutenant and assumed command upon the resignation of Esau Brooks. He remained the company commander of the Beauregards for the next two years but resigned on August 28, 1863, stating that "he did not

feel himself capable of commanding his company." Oates writes on page 631 of his book that he "was a very good man, but became so excited in battle that he scarcely knew what he was doing." After the war William claimed his resignation was due to the fact that he refused to work under Lowther, the regimental commander. He became a Methodist minister. After the war, he and his brothers all moved to Texas, where he died in Dallas on December 12, 1926. He was married to Eliza Jones White on January 5, 1858, and had two sons and six daughters.

63. Oates, p. 128; LaFantasie, p. 49.
64. McClendon, p. 105.
65. Compiled from soldiers' service records.
66. Compiled from soldiers' service records.
67. Houghton, p. 23.
68. Oates, p. 134.
69. Foote, pp. 618–619.
70. Houghton, p. 23.
71. Foote, vol. 1, p. 619.
72. Ibid., vol. 1, p. 623.
73. Oates, pp. 136–137.
74. Houghton, p. 24.
75. Oates, p. 137.
76. Ibid., p. 138.
77. McClendon, p. 119.
78. Ibid., p. 123.
79. Houghton, p. 25.
80. Oates, p. 145.
81. Captain Francis Key Shaaf is one of the most interesting characters in the Fighting Fifteenth. Originally from Columbus, Georgia, he was the only member of the regiment that I know of who was a sergeant in the regular army prior to the Civil War. When the war broke out he quit the regular army and enlisted into the 1st Kentucky Infantry on November 1, 1861. Since Captain Lowther was his brother-in-law, he transferred to Company A, 15th Alabama Infantry on August 14, 1862. Oates describes him on page 585 of his book as a "very remarkable man ... slender, muscular, with a quick, nervous manner, and one of the best officers in the regiment ... always conspicuously doing his duty." After the war he rejoined the regular cavalry.
82. Isaac Ball Feagin was born in Jones County, Georgia, on July 17, 1833. Oates describes Captain Feagin as "courageous and faithful" on page 589 of his book. Captain Feagin commanded Company B up to Second Manassas, after which he commanded the regiment until Sharpsburg, where he was wounded by a shell fragment. While he was home on furlough for the wound he married Sarah "Sally" J. Hall on December 17, 1862. He was promoted to lieutenant colonel on April 28, 1863, was wounded and captured at Gettysburg, and had his right leg amputated at the thigh. He was succeeded by Oates to lieutenant colonel. He was exchanged on March 10, 1864, and assigned to the Invalid Corps on December 7, 1864. After the war, he was elected sheriff of Barbour County, 1866–1876, and became the probate judge in 1880. Isaac died on May 2, 1900, in Midway, Alabama.
83. Oates, p. 144.
84. Houghton, p. 26.

85. Ibid., p. 26.
86. Oates, p. 143.
87. McClendon, p. 128.
88. Ibid., p. 128.
89. Ibid., p. 129.
90. Ibid., p. 132.
91. Ibid., p. 133.
92. Oates, p. 146.
93. Houghton, p. 26.
94. Foote, vol. 1, p. 640.
95. Compiled from soldiers' service records.
96. Compiled from soldiers' service records.
97. Compiled from soldiers' service records.
98. Houghton, p. 70.
99. Oates, p. 756.

Chapter Four

1. Joseph M. Ellison, "War letters (1862)," *Georgia Historical Quarterly* 48 (June 1964): p. 235. Letter to his wife in September 1862.
2. Foote, p. 662.
3. Ibid., p. 662.
4. Ibid., p. 663.
5. Ibid., p. 663.
6. McClendon, p. 142.
7. Ibid., p. 142.
8. Foote, vol. 1, p. 680.
9. McClendon, p. 158.
10. Ibid., p. 160. Captain Feagin's court-martial was held on February 18, 1863; as stated in the text, he was exonerated. In fact, in the acting brigade commander's report, Colonel Walker wrote that Captain Feagin "behaved with a gallantry consistent with his high reputation for courage and that of the regiment he commanded."
11. Edwards autobiography.
12. OR, Vol. XIX, Part 1, p. 977.
13. A.A.
14. Compiled from soldiers' service records.
15. McClendon, p. 172.
16. Senn, excerpted from *Southern Advertiser*, pp. 123–124. Randolph Smedley letter to his father, December 17, 1862, in *Southern Advertiser* (Troy, Alabama). Randolph was 22 years of age when he enlisted into the Quitman Guards. He was a single farmer living with his father, David B. (60), mother, Maria (61), and brother Capel S. (15). David was a Methodist minister. Randolph was elected fourth corporal when the company initially mustered on July 3, 1861. He was promoted fifth sergeant on July 1, 1863. He would be captured at Gettysburg the next day and exchanged on July 31, 1863. He was promoted to first sergeant on June 1, 1864, and surrendered with General Lee on April 9, 1865. Oates states that he died of fever in the fall of '65.
17. Foote, vol. 2, pp. 21–22.
18. Ibid., p. 22.
19. McClendon, p. 176.
20. http://www.brainyquote.com/quotes/authors/r/robert_e_lee.html.
21. Foote, vol. 2, pp. 38–39.

22. LaFantasie, p. 60.
23. Oates, p. 167.
24. Senn, p. 124.
25. Ibid., p. 124.
26. Foote, vol. 1, p. 43.
27. Ibid., vol. 1, p. 43.
28. Ibid., p. 44.
29. OR, Vol. XXI, pp. 543 and 561.
30. Compiled from soldiers' service records.
31. OR, Vol. XXXIII, pp. 672–673.
32. I counted these figures up from the campaigns based upon Foote's *The Civil War*.
33. Found in a letter written by William Edwards to Rufus Painter, dated November 11, 1863, published in the *Southern Star*, Jan. 5, 1915. Jesse Flowers already had a family in 1860 so he must have moved with his family to Newton, Alabama. Jesse (28) is farming with his wife, Piney (26), and Robert (6). Jesse was enlisted by Lieutenant Breare into the Dale County Beauregards on August 15, 1862. During the Battle of Suffolk, his company commander, Captain Edwards, describes an incident in which, after losing one of his best soldiers in battle, Private Flowers "carried him back to a camp" and rushed back to the front line "with his sleeves rolled up to his elbows and said, 'Captain, they have killed my old mess mate and best friend and I am now ready to fight until they kill me or I kill some of them.'" Private Flowers was severely wounded in the right shoulder at the Battle of Fussell's Mill on August 16, 1864. On November 30 he died from the wound. His death certificate states that he had a "fracture of the right humerus" and that he was a farmer. It further states that he had $28 on him. Long after the war, his company commander said of him and another soldier that "two braver soldiers never shouldered a musket or wore the Confederate gray."
34. J. Gary Laine and Morris M. Penny, *Law's Alabama Brigade in the War Between the Union and the Confederacy*, p. 45.
35. Oates, p. 175.
36. Laine and Penny, p. 47.
37. LaFantasie, p. 72.
38. McClendon, p. 192.
39. Oates, p. 619.
40. Laine and Penny, p. 64. James Willis was from Creek Stand.
41. Edwards in his letter previously mentioned. Jesse would be mortally wounded in the right shoulder at Fussell's Mill on August 16, 1864. Their company commander said of them that "two braver soldiers never shouldered a musket or wore Confederate gray." Jesse lived in Westville and Henry lived in Daleville before the war.
42. Laine and Penny, p. 63.
43. A.A.
44. Laine and Penny, p. 65. Noah Feagin enlisted at the age of 17 as a private but rose to the rank of captain and was commanding Company B at the time of surrender. After General Lee became president of Washington College in Lexington, Virginia, Noah attended that university and graduated. He then became a lawyer and practiced law in Union Springs, Anniston, and Birmingham, Alabama. Governor Oates appointed him as a judge in 1895.

45. Foote, vol. 2, p. 255.
46. Compiled from soldiers' service records.
47. Laine and Penny, p. 65.
48. Ibid., p. 66.
49. Houghton, p. 38.
50. Edwards in his letter previously mentioned.
51. Houghton, p. 38.
52. Ibid., pp. 164–165.
53. Edwards letter.
54. Oates, p. 688.
55. Oates, p. 763. This couldn't be confirmed with military records; however, it is noted in the Alabama database for Civil War soldiers.
56. Ibid., p. 175.
57. Houghton, p. 166.
58. W.C. Woodall, *Atlanta Constitution*, "Eventful Career of Father Brannan, Confederacy's Youngest Enlisted Soldier," p. 5.

Chapter Five

1. Oates, p. 220.
2. Cody, p. 362.
3. Oates, p. 189.
4. Houghton, p. 32.
5. Oates, p. 190.
6. Ibid., p. 193.
7. Ibid., p. 198.
8. LaFantasie, p. 76.
9. Laine and Penny, p. 67.
10. Ibid., p. 195.
11. According to Oates, after surviving the war William was elected sheriff of Pike County. He moved to Birmingham and Montgomery. For several years after the war he was national committeeman of the Republican Party and Third Auditor of the Treasury at Washington.
12. William Youngblood, "Unwritten History of the Gettysburg Campaign," *Southern Historical Society Papers* 38, pp. 312–318.
13. Jeffrey Stocker, ed., *From Huntsville to Appomattox*, p. 101.
14. Houghton, p. 32.
15. John Bell Hood, *Advance and Retreat*, p. 54.
16. Arthur J.L. Fremantle, *Three Months in the Southern States, April–June 1863*, p. 293.
17. LaFantasie, p. 81.
18. James Longstreet, *From Manassas to Appomattox*, p. 365; Laine and Penny, p. 77.
19. Ward, "Incidents and Personal Experiences," p. 347.
20. Laine and Penny, p. 87. After the war Isaac became a merchant and resided in Clayton.
21. Oates, p. 212.
22. Foote, vol. 2, p. 501.
23. Foote, vol. 2, p. 502.
24. Ibid., p. 504.
25. Oates, p. 219.
26. Oates, pp. 673–674. Accounts of this are also contained in Cody, p. 270. The note on "eight" bullets was taken from his profile on Ancestry.com.

27. See LaFantasie, pp. 119–120, for an excellent account of the care given to Oates and Cody in the Union V Corps, II Division Hospital after the battle.

28. Ibid., pp. 612–613.

29. Ibid., p. 688.

30. Edwards letter.

31. Oates, p. 744.

32. Ibid., p. 103.

33. Laine and Penny, p. 104.

34. Oates, p. 220.

35. Ibid., p. 220.

36. Laine and Penny, p. 107.

37. Oates, pp. 771–772. Second Lieutenant Wicker would remain a prisoner of war for the rest of the war. He was released on June 12, 1865. His Oath describes him as "light complexion, dark hair, blue eyes, 5'7". Robert married a Clara and became a schoolteacher after the war.

38. Ibid., p. 108.

39. Oates, p. 107.

40. Laine and Penny, p. 108.

41. Jordan, p. 45.

42. Laine and Penny, p. 111.

43. Oates, pp. 597–598. William was a nineteen-year-old mechanic living at home in Hatchechubbee, Russell County, Alabama, in the 1860 Census. Twenty-two-year-old Fifth Sergeant Johns would be exchanged in late September 1863. On January 29, 1864, he was at Walker Hospital in Columbus, Georgia, and his wound was described as a "G.S. [gunshot] wound fracturing the femur middle ⅓. Permanent disability without operation…. Dr. wanted to reset … to cause uniting of bone. Patient refuses on the ground that his life will be further jeopardized."

44. OR, Vol. XLIV, pp. 392–393.

45. First Sergeant James Gibbs Hitchcock is mentioned in Oates's book on p. 596. This wound would be the first of three that he received during the war. Military records show this was a flesh wound to the left shoulder. He would again be wounded at the Wilderness and at Fussell's Mill. He was severely wounded at the Wilderness in the arm and given a 50-day furlough. The nature of his wound from Fussell's Mill is undetermined. He surrendered with the Army of Northern Virginia on April 9, 1865. After the war he married Sarah Evlyn Hall. Oates writes that he lost a hand in a cotton gin. First Sergeant Hitchcock died on December 4, 1919.

46. Private William Crosby "Doss" Fleming was wounded and captured at Gettysburg. He was held at Ft. Delaware for the duration of the war. His niece wrote that he contracted smallpox while in prison but recovered and was released on June 14, 1865. He was described as having "light complexion, light hair, hazel eyes, and 5'9"." Doss would die in Geneva County, Alabama, on September 16, 1928.

47. Private William Preston Sellers would be sent to Fort Delaware, where he died of chronic diarrhea on March 12, 1864. He was buried on the Jersey Shore opposite the fort.

48. Senn, pp. 199–202.

49. 15th Regiment Alabama Infantry, Wikipedia, p. 5.

50. First Lieutenant Head was acting assistant quartermaster during the muster call of May–June 1863, per his service records.

51. LaFantasie, p. 123.

52. Quote from General Albin Schoepf in *Unlikely Allies: Fort Delaware's Prison Community in the Civil War*, by Dale Fetzer and Bruce Mowday, p. 120.

53. Ibid., p. 108.

54. Compiled from soldiers' service records.

55. W. Hoffman to E.M. Stanton, June 15, 1862, OR, Series II, IV. 23: Report of A.M. Clark, Surgeon and Acting.

56. wikipedia.org/wiki/Albin_Francisco_Schoepf

57. *Prisons, Paroles and POWs*, "Fort Delaware: Starvation in a Land of Plenty."

58. Fetzer and Mowday, p. 113.

59. John S. Swann, "Prison Life at Fort Delaware," *West Virginia History*. hppt://www.wvculture.org/history/journal.

60. Randolph A. Shotwell, *The Papers of Randolph Abbott Shotwell*.

61. Brian Temple, *The Union Prison at Fort Delaware: A Perfect Hell on Earth*, p. 43.

62. William H. Morgan, *Personal Reminiscences of the War 1861–5*, p. 226.

63. Henry C. Dickenson, *Diary of Capt. Henry C. Dickinson, C.S.A.* Copy at Fort Delaware Society Library, p. 41.

64. Fetzer and Mowday, p. 114.

65. Shotwell Diary.

66. Swann, p. 5.

67. Fetzer and Mowday, p. 113.

68. Ibid., p. 121.

69. Temple, p. 61.

Chapter Six

1. 1860 Census.

2. Obtained from soldiers' service record.

3. Oates, p. 253.

4. Laine and Penny, p. 142.

5. Ibid., p. 142.

6. Ibid., p. 257.

7. Ibid., p. 262.

8. Ibid., p. 606.

9. Ibid., p. 264.

10. Senn, pp. 219–223.

11. Oates, pp. 264–265.

12. Ibid., p. 271.

13. McClendon, p. 213.

14. Houghton, p. 38.

15. Jordan, p. 56.

16. Ibid., pp. 57–58.

17. Oates, p. 276.

18. Houghton, pp. 40–41.

19. Oates, p. 278.

20. Billie survived the war and became a merchant in Milledgeville, Georgia.

21. Oates, p. 280.

22. Ibid., p. 289.

23. Wikipedia, p. 5.

24. McClendon, p. 194.

25. Laine and Penny, p. 190.

26. Ibid., p. 191.
27. Jordan, pp. 65–66.
28. Houghton, p. 40.
29. Oates, pp. 283–284.
30. Compiled from soldiers' service records.
31. McClendon, p. 223.
32. Laine and Penny, p. 201.
33. McClendon, p. 66.
34. Foote, vol. 2, p. 839.
35. Ibid., pp. 864–865.
36. Ibid., p. 865.
37. Wikipedia, p. 5.
38. Compiled from soldiers' service records.
39. Laine and Penny, p. 214.
40. Houghton, p. 69.
41. Compiled from soldiers' service records.
42. Houghton, 38.
43. Ibid., pp. 60–61.
44. Ibid., pp. 62–63.
45. Ibid., pp. 81–82.
46. Ibid., pp. 82–83.

Chapter Seven

1. Senn, p. 272. Contained in a letter dated May 3, 1864, to "Dear Uncle" from James Wilson Greenway. James worked his way up through the ranks and was third sergeant when he wrote this letter. He passed a Brigade Examining Board and was promoted to second lieutenant and elected to that rank in Company E, 59th Alabama Infantry Regiment on September 6, 1864.
2. Laine and Penny, p. 231.
3. Ibid., p. 231.
4. Ibid., p. 232.
5. Oates, pp. 343–344.
6. Ibid., p. 344. Oates extracted this quote from the "February 1879 of the *Southern Historical Society papers*," but failed to give a page number.
7. Ibid., p. 344; Laine and Penny, p. 237.
8. Ibid., p. 344.
9. Ibid., p. 345.
10. Ibid., p. 346.
11. Ibid., p. 347.
12. Laine and Penny, p. 240.
13. Jordan, p. 74.
14. Foote, vol. 3, p. 214.
15. http://en.wikipedia.org/wiki/15th_Regiment_Alabama_Infantry, p. 5.
16. Compiled from soldiers' service records.
17. Foote, vol. 3, p. 189.
18. Senn, p. 276.
19. Oates, p. 354.
20. Ibid., p. 353.

21. Ibid., p. 355.
22. Laine and Penny, p. 258–260.
23. Oates, p. 757.
24. Foote, vol. 3, p. 223.
25. Compiled from soldiers' service records.
26. McClendon, p. 235.
27. Ibid., p. 235.
28. Ibid., p. 235.
29. Ibid., p. 235.
30. Oates, p. 366.
31. Ibid., p. 367.
32. http://www.history.com/this-day-in-history/union-disaster-at-cold-harbor.
33. http://en.wikipedia.org/wiki/15th_Regiment_Alabama_Infantry, p. 5.
34. Foote, vol. 3, p. 310.
35. Compiled from soldiers' service records.
36. *Columbus* (Georgia) *Daily Sun*, September 1, 1864; Laine and Penny, p. 296.
37. Laine and Penny, p. 287.
38. Ibid., p. 288.
39. Ibid., pp. 289–290.
40. Ibid., pp. 293–295.
41. Oates, p. 725; Laine and Penny, p. 295.
42. Oates, p. 380; McClendon, pp. 215–216; Jordan, p. 92; Laine and Penny, p. 297.
43. Soldier's service record.
44. Laine and Penny, p. 295; Jordan, p. 100.
45. Soldier's service record.
46. Laine and Penny, p. 296.
47. http://en.wikipedia.org/wiki/15th_Regiment_Alabama_Infantry, p. 5.
48. Compiled from soldiers' service records.
49. Houghton, p. 83.
50. Foote, vol. 3, p. 629.
51. Ibid., p. 629.
52. Ibid., p. 629.
53. Ibid., p. 630.
54. Laine and Penny, p. 299.
55. OR, Vol. VII, pt. 2, p. 1303.
56. McClendon, pp. 237–238.
57. Compiled from soldiers' service records.
58. McClendon, pp. 243–244.
59. Laine and Penny, pp. 307–308.
60. Ibid., p. 309.
61. Ibid., p. 309.
62. McClendon, p. 247.
63. OR, Vol. XII, pt. 1, pp. 146–147, 690.
64. Ibid., p. 741.
65. McClendon, p. 248.
66. Compiled from soldiers' service records.
67. McClendon, pp. 248–249.
68. Compiled from soldiers' service records.
69. Laine and Penny, p. 333.
70. Compiled from soldiers' service records.

Bibliography

Alabama Civil War Service Database. Alabama Department of Archives and History, Montgomery, AL. www.archives.alabama.gov/civilwar/search.cfm.

Ancestry.com.

Boyd, Casper W. "His Last Letters Written Home." *Alabama Historical Quarterly* 23 (Fall/Winter 1961): pp. 291–298.

Cody, Barnett H. "Letters of Barnett Hardeman Cody and others, 1861–1864." *Georgia Historical Quarterly* 23 (1939).

Edwards, William A. "A Most Interesting Letter." *Southern Star* (Ozark, AL), November 11, 1915.

Ellison, J.M. *Georgia Historical Quarterly* 48, no. 2 (June 1964): pp. 229–238.

Fetzer, Dale, and Bruce Mowday. *Unlikely Allies: Fort Delaware's Prison Community in the Civil War.* Mechanicsburg, PA: Stackpole, 2000.

Fleming, Mary L. "Dale County and Its People During the Civil War." *Alabama Historical Quarterly* (Spring 1957): pp. 61–109.

Foote, Shelby. *The Civil War.* 3 vols. New York: Random House, 1974.

Footnote.com. Confederate Service Records. www.fold3.com/.

Freeman, Douglas Southall. *Lee's Lieutenants: A Study in Command.* 3 vols. New York: Scribner's, 1944.

Fremantle, Arthur J.L. *Three Months in the Southern States, April–June 1863.* Lincoln: University of Nebraska Press, 1991.

Gray, Henry. *Anatomy, Descriptive and Applied.* 18th ed. Philadelphia: Lea & Febiger, 1910.

History.com/this-day-in-history/union-disaster-at-cold-harbor.

Hood, John Bell. *Advance and Retreat.* Bloomington: Indiana University Press, 1959.

Houghton, William Robert, and Mitchell B. Houghton. *Two Boys in the Civil War and After.* Montgomery, AL: Paragon, 1912; reprinted, Narrative Press, 2004.

Jordan, William C. *Some Events and Incidents During the Civil War.* Montgomery, AL: Paragon Press, 1909.

LaFantasie, Glenn W. "Decimated by Disease." *Military History Quarterly* 16 (Spring 2004): pp. 86–92.

_____. *Gettysburg Requiem: The Life and Lost Causes of Confederate Colonel William C. Oates.* New York: Oxford University Press, 2006.

Laine, J. Gary, and Morris Penny. *Law's Alabama Brigade in the War Between the Union and the Confederacy.* Shippensburg, PA: White Mane, 1996.

Lary, Samuel D. "Sam Lary's Scraps from My Knapsack." *Alabama Historical Quarterly* 18, no. 4 (Winter 1956): p. 508.

Longstreet, James. *From Manassas to Appomattox.* Philadelphia: Nabu, 2010.

McClendon, William A. *Recollections of War Times, by an Old Veteran While Under Stonewall Jackson and Lieutenant General James Longstreet.* Tuscaloosa: University of Alabama Press, 2010.

McGee, Val L. *Claybank Memories: A History of Dale County, Alabama.* Ozark, AL: Dale County Historical Society, 1989.

Oates, William C. *The War Between the Union and Confederacy and Its Lost Opportunities.* Dayton, OH: Morningside Bookshop, 1974.

Official Records of the Union and Confederate Armies in the War of the Rebellion. Washington, D.C.: U.S. Government Printing Office, 1894–1922.

Senn, Susie K. *Pike County Alabama's Civil War News.* A compilation of Civil War letters from *The Southern Advertiser.*

Shotwell, Randolph A. *The Papers of Randolph Abbott Shotwell.* Raleigh: North Carolina Historical Commission, 1931.

Stocker, Jeffrey, ed., *From Huntsville to Appomattox.* Knoxville: University of Tennessee Press, 1996.

Swann, John S. *West Virginia History.* West Virginia Archives and History.

Tanner, Robert G. *Stonewall in the Valley: Thomas J. "Stonewall" Jackson's Shenandoah Valley Campaign, Spring 1862.* Garden City, NY: Doubleday, 1976.

Temple, Brian. *The Union Prison at Fort Delaware: A Perfect Hell on Earth.* Jefferson, NC: McFarland, 2003.

Tucker, Phillip Thomas. *Storming Little Round Top: The 15th Alabama and Their Fight for the High Ground, July 2, 1863.* Cambridge, MA: Da Capo Press, 2002.

Wikipedia. *15th Alabama Infantry Regiment* (Online). en.wikipedia.org/wiki/15th_Regiment_Alabama_Infantry, pp. 1–5.

Woodall, W.C. "Career of Father Brannan, Confederacy's Youngest Soldier." *Atlanta Constitution,* Atlanta, GA (5/31/1902). The Sunny South, p. 5.

Youngblood, William. "Unwritten History of the Gettysburg Campaign." *Southern Historical Society Papers* 38, pp. 312–318.

Index

Numbers in *bold italics* indicate pages with photographs.